grower's market

Leanne Kitchen

grower's market
cooking with seasonal produce
over 200 recipes for every occasion

MURDOCH BOOKS

contents

introduction

In developed countries, the weekly expedition to the supermarket to stock up on necessary supplies has become routine. Everything you need to run a household can be procured there; from detergents to deli items, greeting cards to green vegetables and frozen sweet treats to fresh fruits, meats and fish. Convenient and one-stop, those wide aisles, piercing fluoroscent lights and commodious trolleys make food shopping a no-brainer—in fact, we've almost forgotten that there was once an entirely different way to hunt and gather. Almost, that is, but not quite.

Over the past decade, there has been a quiet, significant shift in food shopping options with the rise in popularity of grower's and farmer's markets. Ironically, this represents a return to more traditional food retail, and a time when every town had its own market—farmers would typically bring their produce, freshly dug, picked or gathered and sell direct to buyers. There were no middle-men, no transportation issues, no drawn-out storage, no gas-induced ripening, no specially-developed varieties bred to withstand the rigours of long-distance distribution and supply. In fact, nothing fancy at all—just good, simple, honest food, delivered at its seasonal peak.

While it is a sad fact that many of our seasonal foods have been reduced to mere commodity items (think of tomatoes, apples or strawberries, for example), thankfully not everyone is prepared to settle for the attendant loss of both flavour and varietal quirks that go with it. While it is handy to have salad vegetables in the dead of winter, or out-of-season produce shipped in from far-flung hemispheres, there is no doubt that a rising number of cooks, rather than embracing bland convenience, are instead returning to such under-threat values as 'flavour', 'seasonal usage', 'heirloom varieties' and 'boutique-scale production'.

To an extent, this interest is driven by a modern breed of restaurant chef, who increasingly favours 'top quality seasonal produce cooked simply'. Another contributing factor is fatigue with our complex, rat-race lifestyle and a nostalgic yearning for the values of a slower time when one ate what the earth offered up when it saw fit, and each season's bounty was a refreshing change from the previous one. International travel and exposure to true food cultures, where seasonal availability dictates what is put on the table, and where taste and quality of even the humblest of ingredients are extolled above all else, has done much to alert us to the emptiness of a wholly supermarket-dependent existence.

The fact is, we've become increasingly separated from the source of our food—grower's markets, and the spirit that motivates them, are bridging this gap. Urbanites can't hope to turn back clocks and exist in rural idylls, but they can, through patronage of a local market, move closer to that place and that person that is the source of their food—and be enriched in the process.

Shopping at grower's markets requires thought, planning and effort but the results are not just superior-flavoured food. Ambling, basket-in-arm, through stalls bursting with fragrantly ripe fruits, just-dug potatoes splotched with rich, damp earth, and bright, perky leaves, shoots and herbs, is as much nourishment for the soul as it is for the body. Stall-holders offer tastings, insights, advice and information that often can't be found elsewhere. Buying in-season represents better monetary value too, and gluts provide opportunities to make jams, preserves, or to freeze in bulk, such fleeting delights as cherries, apricots or figs, for out-of-season use. There's no wasteful packaging or exposure to blinding display lights (which can diminish nutrient content and shorten produce life) at the market, not to mention the refreshing absence of congested check-outs and harried shoppers.

Not everyone though has access to a grower's market, and in such instances, sleuthing to find a reputable greengrocer becomes necessary. Find a purveyor who is passionate about their suppliers and produce, who can give you information about fruit and vegetable varieties and details about how, when and where they were grown. Settle for nothing less than perfectly in-season, full-flavoured produce, cook them beautifully and reconnect with the seasonal rhythms that give such a meaningful pace to each and every year.

fruit

grapefruit
kumquat
lemon
lime
mandarin and tangerine
orange
blackberries
blackcurrants
blueberries
boysenberries
fig
gooseberries
grapes
raspberries
strawberries
apricot
cherries
date
peach and nectarine
plum
banana
coconut
kiwi fruit
mango
papaya
passionfruit
pineapple
apple
pear
quince
melons
pomegranate
tamarillo

grapefruit

fruit ▪ **citrus**
season ▪ **peak season winter–early spring**

A relatively modern fruit, the grapefruit is the result of cross-pollination between the pomelo and sweet orange; it was discovered in Barbados around 300 years ago. The fruit is named for the way it grows—in heavy bunches on an attractive tree with thick, glossy leaves.

The original grapefruit were white-fleshed, had many seeds and were smaller than the fruit we know today. Modern grapefruit varieties have been bred for appearance and size and their flavour is less intense than that of older varieties—if you happen to find smaller, not-so-perfect looking fruits which will most likely be full of seeds, do buy them and savour their sharp-sweet, juicy difference.

culinary uses

A halved grapefruit, hot and bubbling with melted sugar and garnished with a maraschino cherry, is a breakfast cliché, but delicious nonetheless. Often relegated to the marmalade pot, the grapefruit can be a most elegant fruit—its slightly bitter edge is a wonderful complement to seafood, salad greens, avocado and even Campari.

Pink grapefruit tossed through a Thai-style prawn or crab salad, or a mixture of yellow and pink grapefruit doused in a cinnamon and mint-infused syrup, are memorable combinations. Grapefruit makes a refreshing granita, while sweetened, frozen juice (perhaps fortified with quantities of vodka) is a tasty, popsicle-style treat.

selection and storage

Grapefruit are classified as white, pink or ruby; these describe the flesh, not the skin colour. Choose fruit that feels heavy for its size, with tight skin and no soft spots. Grapefruit has optimum flavour when not chilled so, if refrigerated, bring to room temperature before eating.

Grapefruit will keep for 3–4 weeks, stored in the crisper section of the refrigerator—or for about 1 week at room temperature. The membranes and pith are rather bitter and are best removed—to do this, use a small, sharp knife to slice off all the peel and pith and then cut between membranes to remove each segment.

ginger and grapefruit pudding with mascarpone cream

Preheat the oven to 170°C (325°F/Gas 3). Grease six 170 ml (5½ fl oz/⅔ cup) ramekins or pudding moulds (basins).

Finely grate 2 teaspoons of zest from the ruby grapefruit and set aside. Cut the grapefruit widthways, about one-third of the way down, to give two uneven size pieces. Peel the larger piece of grapefruit, removing any white pith, and cut the flesh into six 1 cm (½ inch) slices. Squeeze 3 teaspoons of juice from the remaining grapefruit. Finely chop the stem ginger.

Combine the grapefruit juice, ginger syrup and golden syrup in a small bowl. Divide the mixture among the ramekins and top with a slice of grapefruit, trimming to fit.

Put the butter and sugar in a bowl and beat with electric beaters until pale and smooth. Beat in the eggs, one at a time. Sift in the flour and ground ginger, add the grapefruit zest, chopped ginger and milk and mix well. Divide the mixture among the ramekins.

Cover each ramekin with foil and put them in a deep roasting tin. Pour in enough boiling water to come halfway up the side of the ramekins. Cover the roasting tin with foil, sealing the edges well. Bake the puddings for 30–35 minutes, or until set.

To make the mascarpone cream, mix the mascarpone cheese, cream and icing sugar in a small bowl until smooth. To serve, gently invert the puddings onto serving plates and serve with the mascarpone cream.

1 large ruby grapefruit
40 g (1½ oz/⅓ cup) drained, stem ginger in syrup plus 3 teaspoons syrup, extra
1½ tablespoons golden syrup (dark corn syrup)
125 g (4½ oz) unsalted butter, softened
115 g (4 oz/½ cup) caster (superfine) sugar
2 eggs, at room temperature
185 g (6½ oz/1½ cups) self-raising flour
1 teaspoon ground ginger
80 ml (2½ fl oz/⅓ cup) milk

mascarpone cream

125 g (4½ oz/heaped ½ cup) mascarpone cheese
125 ml (4 fl oz/½ cup) pouring (whipping) cream
1 tablespoon icing (confectioners') sugar, sifted

citrus ▪ grapefruit

kumquat

fruit ▪ **citrus**
season ▪ **winter**

selection and storage

Choose kumquats that have firm, shiny, unblemished skin—check carefully for any signs of mould or fruit that has been squashed, and avoid these. Store kumquats in the refrigerator for up to 2 weeks, or at cool room temperature for several days.

The kumquat, despite its resemblance to a dwarfed orange and its bittersweet tangy, citric taste, is technically not a citrus fruit at all; it has a genus, *Fortunella*, all its own. To qualify as citrus, fruit needs to have 8–15 segments, where kumquats have just 3–6. Generally though, it is classified with citrus fruits because in many respects it truly is a citrus-like fruit.

With its small oblong to round fruit, the kumquat has attractive golden-red, sweetish skin that does not need to be peeled before eating, and somewhat biting flesh. Although it can be eaten raw, most find the kumquat too tart and intensely-flavoured for this purpose. Kumquats are most commonly pickled to make a delicious accompaniment to smoked or gamey meats, made into a particularly delicious marmalade (either on its own or in combination with oranges or grapefruit), preserved in a brandied syrup or candied whole for use as a flavouring in ice creams, fruit compotes and other desserts.

varieties

The nagami *(Fortunella margarita)* is the most commonly grown kumquat and has slightly ovoid fruits with tart flesh and quite pungent, sweet skin. Marumi *(F. japonica)* is rounder in shape and is generally sweeter than the nagami. There's also the meiwa *(F. crassifolia)*, which, with its pale-coloured, thick skin and often seedless flesh, is the best type for eating raw.

caramelized kumquats
with honey parfait

Put the honey in a small saucepan and bring to the boil. Whisk the egg yolks in a bowl until thick and pale, then add the hot honey in a slow stream, whisking constantly. Allow to cool, then gently fold in the cream and liqueur. Pour the mixture into six 125 ml (4 fl oz/ 1/2 cup) ramekins or pudding moulds (basins). Freeze for 4 hours, or until firm.

Wash the kumquats and prick the skins with a skewer. Put the kumquats in a large saucepan, cover with boiling water and simmer for 20 minutes. Strain the kumquats and reserve 500 ml (17 fl oz/2 cups) of the liquid. Return the liquid to the saucepan, add the sugar and stir over medium heat until the sugar has dissolved. Increase the heat and boil for 10 minutes. Add the kumquats and simmer for 20 minutes, or until the kumquats are soft and the skins are smooth and shiny. Remove from the heat and set aside to cool. Lift the kumquats out of the syrup, reserving the syrup.

To serve, dip the moulds in hot water for 5–10 seconds before inverting the parfait onto serving plates. Serve with the caramelized kumquats alongside and syrup spooned over the top.

note Kumquats in syrup also make a delicious topping for ice cream, sponge cakes and puddings.

90 g (3 1/4 oz/ 1/4 cup) honey
4 egg yolks, at room temperature
300 ml (10 1/2 fl oz) pouring
    (whipping) cream, whipped
1 tablespoon orange liqueur,
    such as Grand Marnier
500 g (1 lb 2 oz) kumquats
350 g (12 oz/1 1/2 cups) caster
    (superfine) sugar

citrus ■ kumquat

A Cantonese native, the kumquat is associated in China (and other Asian nations, such as Vietnam) with prosperity; its name in Chinese, jingua, means 'gold melon'.

lemon

fruit ■ citrus
season ■ peak season winter–spring

selection and storage

Choose lemons that have firm, unblemished, glossy yellow skin. Avoid buying lemons that are wrinkled, have cuts or soft spots or are still green—the flavour of the latter will not be fully developed. Avoid too, any fruits that are damp, as this causes mould to quickly grow and spread among other lemons that sit nearby.

Lemons will store for up to 2 weeks in the refrigerator or up to 1 week at cool room temperature.

The lemon is surely one of the kitchen's most useful and versatile fruits, lending its unmistakable, sharp-sweet fragrance to myriad dishes; in fact, we take the lemon quite for granted. Its juice and finely grated zest spike dressings and drinks, sauces both sweet and savoury, and a plethora of desserts, cakes, fillings and preserves. Its juice can be used for everything from preventing discoloration in other fruits and vegetables given to oxidation (apples, pears, bananas, quince, artichokes), to 'cooking' fresh raw seafood, as in the famous raw fish dishes of Central and South America.

Lemons are believed to have originated in northern India; from there it was a short step to adoption into Arabic cuisines, from which language it got its name—*limun*. Arabs planted the fruit in Andalusia and Sicily, regions still famed for the quality and profusion of their lemons. Christian crusaders also helped spread the lemon far and wide; today about a quarter of the world's lemons are grown in California.

Lemons are stunningly nutritious—aside from their high vitamin C content, they are high in flavonoids, an antioxidant thought to help fight off cancer and heart disease. The membrane between lemon segments are a rich source of pectin, a fibre that can be helpful in controlling blood cholesterol.

varieties

The two most common lemon varieties are the lisbon and the eureka, both almost identical in size and shape. Oblong, with vivid yellow skin and acidic, juicy flesh, these are the workhorses of the lemon world; they can be used in any recipe where lemons, their juice or zest are called for.

The meyer lemon is a 'sweet' variety, with thin, yellow-orange skin and oceans of deeply lemony, slightly sweet juice. Its flesh is a rich yellow-orange colour. Meyer lemons are worth seeking out for their fabulously full flavour and particularly high yield of juice. These lemons, thought to be a lemon-orange hybrid, are particularly good in drinks, such as home-made lemonade, and Middle Eastern-style raw lemon salads, relishes and desserts.

preparation

Check with your supplier whether lemons have been waxed or not, and scrub very lightly before use if they have. If you have a surplus of lemons, the juice can be frozen for several months; heat the fruit in a bowl of hot water before juicing as this will greatly boost the yield.

To use the zest of a lemon, grate it using the finest holes of a grater, applying light pressure and turning the fruit as you go so that you don't grate any of the bitter white pith.

Use a small, sharp knife to remove the peel in slices, working from the top to the bottom of the lemon, having first cut off the ends of the fruit to give it a stable base as you work. Lay the strips, pith side up, on a work surface and use the knife, held at a deep angle, to remove all remaining pith from them, then cut the peel into super-thin shreds. It is a good idea to briefly blanch fine strips of zest in boiling water before using (especially in desserts), as this will remove some of the more volatile, harsher flavours.

culinary uses

The culinary world is dotted with lemon classics: French tarte au citron, English lemon curd, North African preserved lemons, Greek avgolemono soup (and sauce) and the Italian liqueur limoncello, for example.

There are also many food partnerships that rely for success on the jolt of lemon: think of simply-cooked fish eaten with a good dousing of lemon juice; tender veal slices napped in a creamy lemon sauce; billowy, meringue-topped pie saved from sickly sweetness by its bracing, lemony layer; and a cup of perfectly brewed black tea with its finishing float of sliced fresh lemon.

preserved lemons

8–12 thin-skinned lemons
315 g (11 oz/1 cup) rock salt
500 ml (17 fl oz/2 cups) lemon
   juice
½ teaspoon black peppercorns
1 bay leaf
1 tablespoon olive oil

citrus ■ lemon

Wash and scrub the lemons in warm water to remove any wax coating. Cut each lemon in half lengthways, stopping just before the base and keeping the base intact, then make another cut to form four attached quarters. Open each lemon, remove any visible pips and pack 1 tablespoon of the salt against the cut edges of each lemon. Push the lemons back into shape and pack into a 2 litre (70 fl oz/8 cup) sterilized airtight jar. Depending on their size, you may not need all 12 lemons—they should be firmly packed and the jar should be full.

Add 250 ml (9 fl oz/1 cup) of the lemon juice, the remaining rock salt, the peppercorns and bay leaf to the jar. Fill the jar to the top with the remaining lemon juice. Seal and shake to combine all the ingredients. Leave in a cool, dark place for 6 weeks, inverting the jar each week. The liquid will be cloudy initially, but will clear by the fourth week.

To test if the lemons are ready, cut through the centre of one of the quarters. If the pith is still white, the lemons are not ready. Re-seal and test again in another week.

Once the lemons are preserved, cover the brine with a layer of olive oil. Preserved lemons can be stored for up to 6 months in a cool, dark place.

note To prepare preserved lemons for cooking, remove the required number from the jar with a fork, separate into quarters and rinse under cold running water. Remove and discard the pulp (you can add it to dishes, if you wish, but use it sparingly as it has a bitter taste). Rinse the rind, pat dry with paper towels and finely slice. Replace the oil each time you remove some of the lemon. Refrigerate a jar once it has been opened.

warm olives with lemon and herbs

serves 6

350 g (12 oz/2 cups) black
  kalamata olives
80 ml (2½ fl oz/⅓ cup) olive oil
1 teaspoon fennel seeds
2 garlic cloves, finely chopped
1 pinch cayenne pepper
finely grated zest of 1 lemon
juice of 1 lemon
1 tablespoon finely chopped
  flat-leaf (Italian) parsley
1 tablespoon finely chopped
  coriander (cilantro) leaves

Rinse the olives, drain and place in a saucepan with enough water to cover. Bring to the boil and cook for 5 minutes, then drain in a sieve.

Add the olive oil and fennel seeds to the saucepan and heat until fragrant. Add the garlic, drained olives, cayenne pepper, lemon zest and juice. Toss for 2 minutes, or until the olives are heated through.

Transfer to a bowl and toss with the parsley and coriander. Serve hot as part of an antipasti selection or with crusty bread to soak up the juices.

lemon cake with sugar crust

serves 6–8

250 g (9 oz) unsalted butter,
  softened
200 g (7 oz/1 scant cup) caster
  (superfine) sugar
2 teaspoons finely grated lemon
  zest
4 eggs, lightly beaten
250 g (9 oz/2 cups) self-raising
  flour
1 teaspoon baking powder
2 tablespoons lemon juice

sugar crust
125 g (4½ oz/½ cup) sugar
60 ml (2 fl oz/¼ cup) lemon juice

Preheat the oven to 170°C (325°F/Gas 3). Lightly grease and line a 22 cm (8½ inch) square cake tin with baking paper.

Cream the butter and sugar in a small bowl until pale and fluffy. Beat in the lemon zest, then gradually add the egg in stages, beating well after each addition. Transfer to a large bowl. Using a metal spoon, fold in the combined sifted flour, baking powder and 1/4 teaspoon salt. Stir in the lemon juice, mixing until smooth.

Spoon the mixture into the cake tin and smooth the surface. Bake for 1 hour 20 minutes, or until a skewer inserted into the centre of the cake comes out clean. Remove from the tin and turn out onto a wire rack.

To make the topping, mix together the sugar and lemon juice and quickly brush over the top of the warm cake. Allow to cool before serving (the crust forms as the cake cools).

lemon delicious

Preheat the oven to 180°C (350°F/Gas 4). Grease a 1.25 litre (44 fl oz/5 cup) ovenproof ceramic dish.

Using an electric beater, beat the butter, the sugar and grated zest together in a bowl until the mixture is pale and fluffy. Gradually add the egg yolks, beating well after each addition. Fold in the flour and milk alternately to make a smooth, thin batter. Stir in the lemon juice; don't worry if the batter looks separated.

Whisk the egg whites in a clean, dry bowl until firm peaks form then, with a large metal spoon, fold a third of the whites into the batter to loosen. Gently fold in the remaining egg whites, being careful not to overmix.

Pour the batter into the prepared dish and place in a large roasting tin. Pour enough hot water into the tin to come one-third of the way up the side of the dish. Bake for 55 minutes, or until the top of the pudding is golden, risen and firm to touch. Leave for 5 minutes before serving. Dust with icing sugar and serve with cream.

60 g (2¼ oz) unsalted butter, at room temperature
185 g (6½ oz/¾ cup) sugar
2 teaspoons finely grated lemon zest
3 eggs, separated
30 g (1 oz/¼ cup) self-raising flour
185 ml (6 fl oz/¾ cup) milk
80 ml (2½ fl oz/⅓ cup) lemon juice
icing (confectioners') sugar, to dust
thick (double/heavy) cream, to serve

citrus ■ lemon

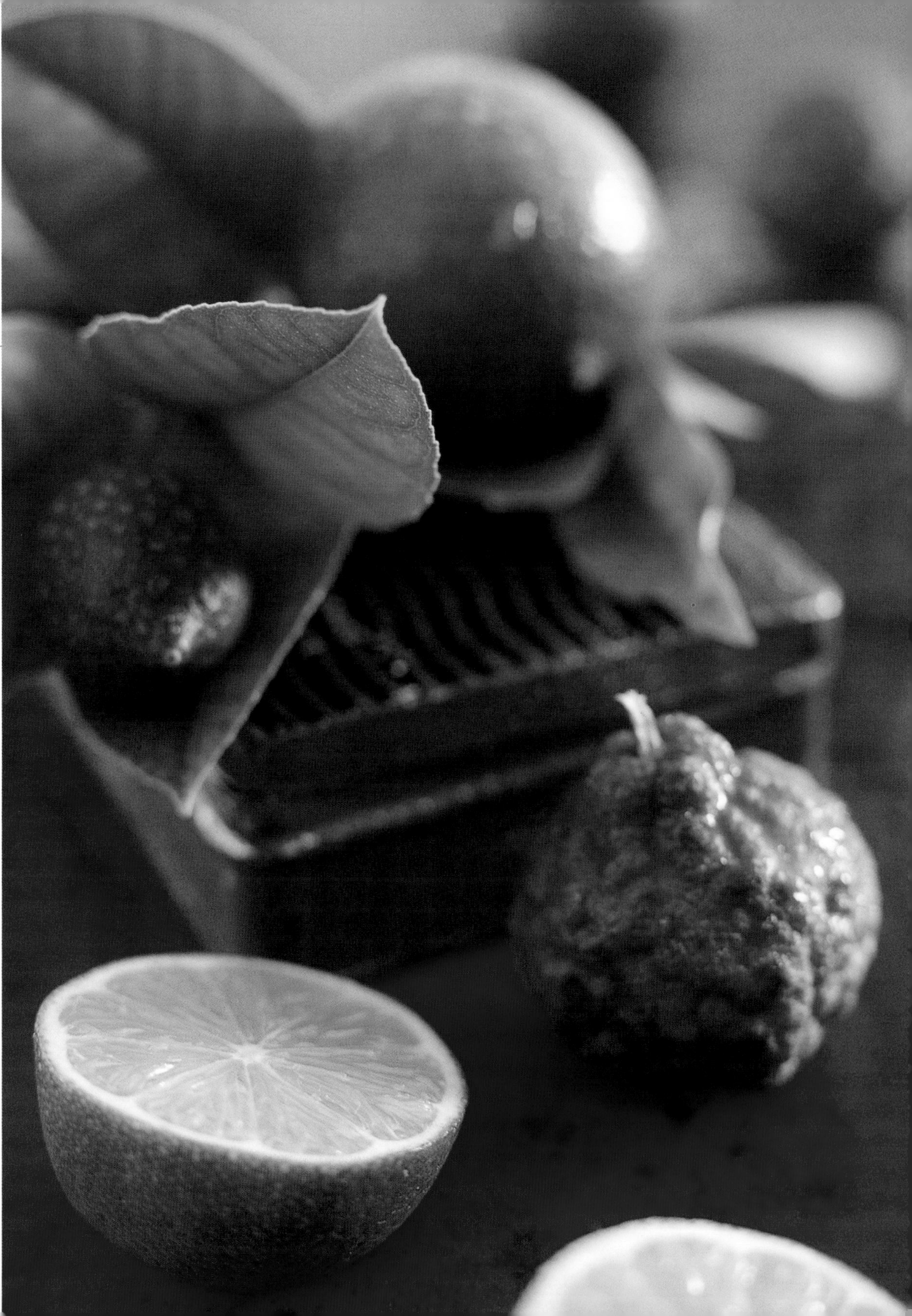

lime

fruit ■ citrus
season ■ peaking late summer–autumn

makrut (kaffir) lime

Could there be a brighter, purer, more alluring smell than that of a just-cut lime? And where would the culinary world be without them—their penetrating flavour spikes everything from drinks (margaritas, mojitos, daiquiris, limeade) to Latin staples such as guacamole, ceviche, salsa, and the legendary Floridian key lime pie. Their juice perks up low-acid tropical fruits (papaya, mango, custard apple) like nothing else and imagine, if you will, the tequila-salt-lime ritual without this crucial citric element.

The origins of the lime, a close lemon relative, are quite obscure but it is generally believed they are native to modern-day Malaysia or Indonesia. The 'original' lime is the key lime—smaller, sourer and more difficult to pick than today's common Tahitian lime hybrid, but with a far more rewarding and complex flavour. Limes have long been an important feature of Middle Eastern and Persian cookery—there is even a reference from the stories of the famed Arabian Nights to 'Egyptian limes' which dates back to 1450 AD.

Limes can be used interchangeably with lemons, but remember that their flavour is much more assertive than lemon so less is generally required. Hence, lime marmalade, lime curd, lime meringue pie, lime syrup cakes and lime dressings and sauces are all as delicious as their lemony prototypes.

selection and storage

Limes are picked and sold while still under-ripe as this is when their flavour is best—when fully ripe their skin turns yellow and they lose that hallmark fragrant acidity. Look for fruits that are bright darkish green, glossy-skinned, feel firm and are heavy for their size. There should be no spots or brown, soft patches.

Store limes for up to 2 weeks in the refrigerator or for 1 week at cool room temperature. Lime juice and the finely grated zest can be frozen for up to 3 months.

varieties

key lime Lime etymology is a little confusing. It's thought the 'original' lime is the key lime, which is really the Mexican lime (also known as the West Indian lime). Native to the East Indies, this lime is golf-ball small with highly acidic, intensely flavoured, juicy flesh. It is difficult to source outside of the Florida Keys area in the United States, from where it derived its common name.

tahitian The Tahitian or Persian lime is the fruit you are most likely to encounter at the fruit stand. It is thought to be a hybrid of the original East Indian lime and was developed early in the twentieth century. Seedless and thin-skinned, the pale, juicy flesh is not as forceful or aromatic as that of its Mexican cousin.

makrut Also known as kaffir limes, makruts are dispersed throughout Southeast Asia, have thick, knobby skin, highly aromatic leaves and very little juice. They are not strictly a lime at all but rather a citrus subspecies—the word *kaffir* is Arabic for 'unbeliever' or 'infidel' and has racist connotations in South Africa, so increasingly the fruit goes by the Thai name, makrut.

preparation

Lime juice brings out many flavours and can be used as a part-substitute for salt in cooking. To make the juice easier to extract, first submerge the limes in very hot water for 1 minute. Drain well and allow to cool slightly, then roll them on a hard surface, using the palm of your hand and applying firm pressure. Halve the limes and squeeze the juice, which should flow quite readily.

Lime juice is very useful in meat marinades as it has a natural tenderizing effect and will 'cook' the diced flesh of fresh fish and other tender seafoods when used in quantity. As a useful guide, 1 lime will yield about 40 ml (1¼ fl oz/ 2 tablespoons) of juice and 1½ teaspoons of finely grated zest.

Don't cook limes in aluminium or iron cookware as the acids will react with the metal, causing changes in the colour and taste of your food.

lime pie (in the style of key lime)

Sift the flour and ¼ teaspoon salt into a large bowl. Add the butter and rub it into the flour using your fingertips until the mixture resembles fine breadcrumbs. Fold in the sugar.

Make a well in the centre, add nearly all the water and mix with a flat-bladed knife, using a cutting rather than a stirring action. The mixture will come together in small beads of dough. If necessary, add more water, a teaspoon at a time, until the dough comes together. Test the dough by pinching a little piece between your fingers—if it doesn't hold together, it needs more water. Gather the dough together and lift out onto a lightly floured surface. Press the dough into a ball and then flatten it slightly. Cover in plastic wrap and refrigerate for 20–30 minutes.

Preheat the oven to 180°C (350°F/Gas 4). Grease a 23 cm (9 inch) loose-based tart tin. Roll the dough out between two sheets of baking paper until it is large enough to fit into the tin. Remove the top sheet of paper and invert the pastry into the tin. Use a small ball of pastry to help press the pastry into the tin, allowing any excess to hang over the sides. Use a small sharp knife to trim away excess pastry.

Line the pastry shell with baking paper and pour in some baking beads or rice. Bake for 10 minutes, remove the paper and beads and return the pastry to the oven for a further 5 minutes, or until the base is dry to touch. Leave to cool.

Using electric beaters, beat the egg yolks, condensed milk, lime juice and zest in a large bowl for 2 minutes, or until well combined. Pour into the pastry shell and smooth the surface. Bake for 20–25 minutes, or until set. Allow the pie to cool, then refrigerate for 2 hours, or until well chilled. Garnish with lime slices, dust with sifted icing sugar and serve with whipped cream.

sweet shortcrust pastry
250 g (9 oz/2 cups) plain (all-purpose) flour
125 g (4½ oz) chilled butter, cut into cubes
2 tablespoons caster (superfine) sugar
2–3 tablespoons iced water

filling
4 egg yolks
395 g (14 oz/1¼ cups) tinned condensed milk
125 ml (4 fl oz/½ cup) lime juice
2 teaspoons grated lime zest
lime slices, to garnish
icing (confectioners') sugar, to dust
whipped cream, to serve

citrus ▪ lime

makes 2.25 litres
(79 fl oz/9 cups)
lime marmalade

lime (or kumquat) marmalade

1 kg (2 lb 4 oz) limes
2 litres (70 fl oz/8 cups) water
2.25 kg (5 lb/10¼ cups) sugar,
  warmed (see note)
10 cm (4 inch) square of muslin
  (cheesecloth)

makes 1.75 litres
(61 fl oz/7 cups)
kumquat marmalade

1 kg (2 lb 4 oz) kumquats
1.25 litres (44 fl oz/5 cups) water
60 ml (2 fl oz/¼ cup) lemon juice
1.25 kg (2 lb 12 oz/5⅔ cups)
  sugar, warmed (see note)
10 cm (4 inch) square of muslin
  (cheesecloth)

For other lime recipes see:

Scrub the limes (or kumquats) under running water to remove any wax. Cut the fruit in half lengthways, reserving any pips, slice thinly and place in a large non-metallic bowl with the water. Tie any pips securely in the muslin (cheesecloth) and add to the bowl. Cover and leave overnight.

Put two small plates in the freezer. Put the fruit, water and muslin bag in a large saucepan. (If making kumquat marmalade, add the lemon juice to the pan.) Bring slowly to the boil, then reduce the heat and simmer, covered, for 30–45 minutes, or until the fruit is tender.

Add the warmed sugar and stir over low heat, without boiling, for 5 minutes, or until dissolved. Return to the boil and boil rapidly, stirring often, for 20 minutes. Remove any scum during cooking with a slotted spoon. When the syrup falls from a wooden spoon in thick sheets, test for setting point.

To do this, remove from the heat, put a little marmalade onto one of the cold plates and place in the freezer for 30 seconds. A skin should form on the surface and the marmalade should wrinkle when pushed with your finger. If not, return to the heat and retest a few minutes later with the other plate. Discard the muslin bag.

Transfer to a heatproof jug and immediately pour into hot sterilized jars and seal. Allow to cool, then label and date each jar. Store in a cool, dark place for 6–12 months. Refrigerate after opening for up to 6 weeks.

note To warm the sugar, preheat the oven to 150°C (300°F/Gas 2). Spread the sugar evenly in a baking dish and heat in the oven for 10–15 minutes. To save time you can warm the sugar while you are cooking the jam. Do not add the sugar until the fruit has softened. If sugar is added before the fruit has fully softened, it will stay firm.

mandarin and tangerine

fruit ■ **citrus**
season ■ **early autumn–late spring**

With their characteristic baggy, easy-peel skin, segments that fall neatly and messlessly apart, thin pith and (mostly) sweet, sweet flesh, there's much to like about the mandarin. It's another native of China where for centuries it was reserved exclusively for the privileged classes, or Mandarins, which is, some speculate, how it acquired its name.

Visitors to China, where it was cultivated as early as 300 BC, would take seeds of the fruit back home with them, hence its early spread to Japan and the Philippines. It wasn't until the nineteenth century that the mandarin found its way to Europe, North and South America, Australia and North Africa.

The first mandarins imported into Europe came in through the Moroccan port city of Tangiers, giving rise to the name 'tangerine'. This nomenclature causes confusion today—all tangerines are varieties, sub-varieties or hybrids of the mandarin, but not all mandarins are tangerines, even though the names are often used interchangeably. Indeed 'differences' between tangerine types of mandarins are subtle, at best. David Arthur and Daemmon Reeve (*Perfumer and Flavorist* magazine) state differences in juice flavour and essential oil characters, which took careful scientific analysis to detect. In general though, tangerines have a darker, red-orange skin than non-tangerine types of mandarin.

selection and storage

Mandarins are often, but not always, sold by variety. As with all citrus, select fruits that are heavy for their size and, if possible, try before you buy.

Avoid mandarins with overly puffy skin as this indicates over-ripeness; also avoid fruits with any soft or weepy areas.

Mandarins don't keep as well as other citrus. Store them in the refrigerator for up to 10 days or up to 1 week at cool room temperature.

varieties

clementine A cross between a mandarin and a bitter, seedless orange, the clementine was discovered by Father Clement Rodier in Algeria in 1902. Generally, but not always, the clementine has seedless flesh and loose, smooth, bright reddish orange skin. The flesh is juicy and deep-flavoured.

honey mandarin A cross between a mandarin and sweet orange hybrids, these are classified as a tangerine. They are thin-skinned and have a smooth and shiny peel that hugs the flesh and is particularly sweet, juicy and meaty. In some countries they are called murcotts. Tangerine types are classified by their large size and have deep orange-red skin.

satsuma The satsuma originated in Japan centuries ago. There are over 70 varieties of satsumas, most of which are seedless, with loose, easily removed peel. Their flavour should be slightly tart, perfumed and sweet.

tangelo A cross between a mandarin and a grapefruit, tangelos are orange-sized with a thin, tapering stem-end. Their bright orange skin is easily peeled and their flesh is at once acid, sweet and fragrant.

tangor Another hybrid, this time between a mandarin and a sweet orange, the tangor is a largish fruit with close-fitting skin and sweet, perfumed, juicy flesh.

culinary uses

Mandarin juice is a flavoursome alternative to orange juice and the segments are worthy additions to fruit salads and compotes. Mandarins make fabulous marmalade, either on their own or in tandem with other citrus fruits, and can also be put to excellent use in home-made ice creams, sorbets and other ices. Use their grated zest and juice in baking recipes (cakes, puddings and pies) that usually call for orange and enjoy the fragrant difference.

tangerine gelato

Whisk the egg yolks and half the sugar together until pale and creamy. Put the milk, tangerine zest and remaining sugar in a saucepan and bring to the boil. Pour over the egg mixture and whisk to combine. Pour the custard back into the saucepan and cook over low heat, stirring continuously until the mixture is thick enough to coat the back of a wooden spoon—do not allow the custard to boil.

Strain the custard into a bowl, add the tangerine juice and cream and then cool over ice. Churn in an ice-cream maker following the manufacturer's instructions. Alternatively, pour into a plastic freezer box, cover and freeze. Stir every 30 minutes with a whisk during freezing to break up the ice crystals and give a better texture. Keep in the freezer until ready to serve.

5 egg yolks
125 g (4½ oz/½ cup) sugar
500 ml (17 fl oz/2 cups) milk
2 tablespoons grated tangerine zest
185 ml (6 fl oz/¾ cup) tangerine juice
3 tablespoons thick (double/heavy) cream

citrus ■ mandarin and tangerine

mandarin soda

makes 560 ml
(19¼ fl oz/2¼ cups) syrup

Put the sugar and water in a large saucepan. Dissolve the sugar over low heat, stirring occasionally. Bring to the boil and cook, uncovered, for 5 minutes.

Add the fresh mandarin juice and boil for a further 5 minutes. Allow to cool, then pour into a hot sterilized airtight jar and refrigerate for 1 hour. Dilute about 2–3 tablespoons of syrup per glass and top up with soda or sparkling mineral water and ice cubes.

250 g (9 oz/1 heaped cup) sugar
600 ml (21 fl oz/2½ cups) water
375 ml (13 fl oz/1½ cups) mandarin juice
soda water or sparkling mineral water, to serve
ice cubes, to serve

orange

fruit ▪ citrus
season ▪ peaking in winter

selection and storage

Oranges should feel heavy with juice for their size, firm to the touch and give when gentle pressure is applied. They should not be shrivelled, bruised or mouldy and should have no soft spongy spots.

A winter fruit, oranges can be stored at room temperature for 3 days or will keep for up to 2 weeks in a loosely sealed plastic bag in the crisper section of the refrigerator.

A wake-up glass of freshly squeezed orange juice, with its bracing acid-sweetness and healthy wallop of vitamin C, is a morning ritual the world over. But, while orange juice may hold the fruit's flavour, the zest encapsulates its heady essence.

A most prosaic fresh fruit, thanks to year-round availability and the competition from so many more 'interesting' fruits, the orange is hardly associated with high gastronomy. But this wasn't always the case. The French, for example, who were introduced to the sweet orange around the fifteenth century, have contributed some of the most enduring, sophisticated orange dishes to the culinary lexicon. Think of duck à l'orange, that apotheosis of rich-flesh-meets-tangy-citrus, or the iconic crêpes suzette, where flaming pancakes are infused with the orange's bright aromas and flavour. In England oranges star in traditional festive dishes, the juice in Cumberland sauce for ham and the grated zest stirred into dense fruitcake batter.

Widely known for its rich vitamin C content, a single orange contains more than 100 per cent of the recommended daily intake. Oranges also contain vitamin A, dietary fibre, thiamine, folate, potassium, antioxidants and, surprisingly, a little protein. They aid the body in healing, in absorbing iron and in boosting immunity.

citrus ■ orange

bitter and sweet

Oranges can roughly be divided into two groups: bitter and sweet. Bitter oranges, such as sevilles and bergamots, are too tart to eat out of hand and are most often used for marmalades, general cooking and to add zing to mixed drinks. They are also prized for their peel, which is often candied, and their essential oils, which are used in making the liqueur Curaçao. In the Middle East, the blossoms of bitter oranges are distilled then transformed into the fragrantly floral orange-blossom water.

Sweet oranges are those that are eaten as a table fruit, added raw to salads and used for juice. Generally large, they have skins that are relatively difficult to peel and include navels, valencias and the exceptionally sweet and richly flavoured blood oranges. Sweet oranges can have seeds or be pip-free.

blood oranges

varieties

blood orange The red pigmentation varies depending on growing conditions—those blood oranges from cooler climates seem to be redder than those from warmer areas. With their complex, spicy, almost berried flavours and ruby good looks, blood oranges are a favourite choice for use in salads, fresh drinks and the classic pinkish French sauce, maltaise (a derivative of hollandaise sauce).

hamlin This orange has sweet, pale and juicy flesh and, while not the world's most interesting orange, is tasty and useful nonetheless. It is widely grown in Florida.

navel So-named for the distinctive, navel-shaped dimple on its base, the popular navel orange is actually a secondary fruit, produced at the blossom end of the primary fruit—in Portugal and Spain they were once called pregnant oranges. They are also characterized by their rich-coloured skin (particularly washington navels), juicy, sweet and almost always seedless flesh, and ability to peel easily.

pineapple With hints of pineapple flavour in its flesh, the pineapple orange is a deeply-flavoured, brightly-coloured, heavily-juicy orange, perfect for eating, juicing or using in cooking—its only shortcoming is the large number of seeds, which require straining out.

seville A cooking orange, on account of its very bitter flavour, the seville is thick-skinned and contains many seeds. It is the best orange for most savoury recipes requiring orange juice, and for marmalade.

valencia The classic juicing orange and a late-ripening variety, the valencia is a large fruit with more seeds than a navel and often green-tinged skin. This greening in no way affects their flavour—oranges need a cool temperature to retain their orange skin colour and valencias harvested in summer may lose some colour as a result.

preparation

To segment an orange, cut off the base and top to create flat ends. Put the orange, flat side down, on a work surface. Using a small, sharp knife and working from the top of the orange to the base, remove peel in strips, taking care to remove all the bitter, white pith. Holding the orange over a bowl to catch juices, cut between the white membranes to remove sections of flesh—the leftover membranes can be squeezed to extract more juice, then discarded.

Orange zest can first be removed with a small sharp knife or using the fine holes of a grater; either way it is important to remove as little of the bitter white pith as possible. This is a tricky job and involves placing strips, skin side down, on a work surface and cutting away the pith on an angle. When preparing oranges for candying the zest or making orange confit (cooking unpeeled slices for a very long time in dense sugar syrup until translucent and semi-candied), it is best to first blanch the fruit in several changes of boiling water, as this both softens the fruit and eliminates excess bitterness.

culinary uses

Like their lemon cousins, oranges lift the flavour of ingredients they are cooked with and go particularly well with chocolate, almonds, walnuts, duck liver, cumin, ginger, Madeira, Marsala, pork, cardamom, pumpkin (winter squash), spinach, witlof (chicory/Belgian endive) and beetroot (beets).

As with all premium ingredients, the simplest treatments are often the best—a bowl of cinnamon-infused caramelized oranges is an ode to this maxim. Or to take it up a notch, slice some peeled blood oranges and serve them with a sublime chocolate mousse or in an airy, blood orange rind-flecked soufflé. Oranges are also greatly used in confectionery and desserts in glacé or crystallized form and they have contributed their inimitable flavour to some of the world's most famed liqueurs—Grand Marnier, Cointreau and Triple Sec.

Moving away from desserts to more savoury offerings, an orange, avocado and watercress salad is an excellent combination. Chillies are a surprisingly good partner for oranges, used to great effect in Mexico, where their juice is excellent in prawn ceviche. Regularly baste a turkey with a mixture of orange juice and zest, sherry, oregano and garlic, or drizzle orange and dijon mustard vinaigrette over a baby beetroot, spinach and feta salad, or any beetroot-based salad or soup for that matter, as the two have a special affinity.

makes 315 ml
(10¾ fl oz/1¼ cups)

orange hollandaise sauce

175 g (6 oz) butter
4 egg yolks
2 tablespoons orange juice

Melt the butter in a small saucepan. Skim any froth from the top and discard; cool the melted butter. Combine 2 tablespoons of water and the egg yolks in a separate saucepan. Whisk for about 30 seconds, or until the mixture is pale and creamy.

Put the pan over very low heat and continue whisking for 3 minutes or until thick and foamy; remove from the heat. (Make sure the saucepan does not get too hot or you will end up with scrambled eggs.)

Add the cooled butter slowly, a little at a time at first, whisking well between each addition. Keep adding the butter in a thin stream, whisking continuously, until all of the butter has been used. Try to avoid using the milky white whey in the bottom of the pan, but don't worry if a little gets in. Stir in the orange juice and season with sea salt and white pepper.

variation To make a basic hollandaise sauce replace the 2 tablespoons of orange juice with 1 tablespoon of lemon juice. (Strain through a fine sieve to remove any pulp before measuring.)

In Scotland, chunky bittersweet seville marmalade was invented by accident in 1700, when a Spanish ship took refuge in Dundee harbour and its entire load of oranges was purchased by an enterprising local— he discovered them to be too bitter to eat so his wife turned them into a sweetened preserve.

orange, hazelnut and goat's cheese salad

Preheat the oven to 180°C (350°F/ Gas 4). Put the hazelnuts on a tray and roast for 5–6 minutes, or until the skins turn dark brown. Wrap the hazelnuts in a clean tea (dish) towel and rub them together to remove the skins.

To make the dressing, combine the nuts, orange juice, lemon juice and a pinch of salt in a food processor. With the motor running, gradually add the olive oil a few drops at a time. When about half the oil has been added, pour in the remainder in a steady stream.

Remove the stems from the watercress and place the leaves in a bowl with the spinach, orange segments and 2 tablespoons of the dressing. Toss to combine and season with sea salt and freshly ground black pepper. Arrange the salad on four plates.

Heat a small non-stick frying pan over medium–high heat and brush lightly with olive oil. When hot, carefully press each slice of goat's cheese firmly into the pan and cook for 1–2 minutes, or until a crust has formed on the cheese. Carefully remove the cheese from the pan and arrange over the salads, crust side up. Drizzle over the remaining dressing, to serve.

35 g (1¼ oz/¼ cup) hazelnuts
1 tablespoon orange juice
1 tablespoon lemon juice
125 ml (4 fl oz/½ cup) olive oil
250 g (9 oz) watercress, rinsed and dried
50 g (1¾ oz/1 cup) baby English spinach leaves, rinsed and dried
24 orange segments (about 2 oranges)
300 g (10½ oz) firm goat's cheese, sliced into 4 equal portions

citrus ■ orange

A source of nutrition for Christopher Columbus and his sailors, the orange undoubtedly contributed to their seafaring success. Columbus took the seeds of oranges, lemons and citrons with him to Haiti and the Caribbean, where they took root to become an integral ingredient of the local cuisine. As long as oranges have been eaten, they have been associated with fertility—perhaps because they come from an evergreen tree that can simultaneously produce foliage, flowers and fruit.

orange and almond cake

Lightly grease a 22 cm (8½ inch) spring-form cake tin and line the base with baking paper.

Scrub the oranges under warm running water to remove any wax coating from the skins. Put the whole oranges in a saucepan, cover with water and boil for 1 hour. Remove from the water and set aside to cool.

Preheat the oven to 180°C (350°F/Gas 4). Using a plate to catch any juice, cut the cooled oranges into quarters and remove any seeds. Blend the orange quarters, including the skin, in a food processor or blender until they turn to a pulp.

Beat the eggs in a large bowl with electric beaters until light and fluffy. Add the orange pulp and any reserved juice to the bowl with the almonds, sugar and baking powder. Mix thoroughly to combine.

Pour the cake batter into the tin. Bake for 1 hour, or until the cake is firm to touch and lightly golden. Cook the cake a little longer if it is still wet. Cool in the tin before turning out onto a wire rack to cool completely. Dust with sifted icing sugar before serving.

Contrary to popular belief, the word 'orange' actually refers to the fruit's aroma, not its colour, as it comes from the Sanskrit word naranga, *meaning 'fragrant'. The fruit itself is thought to have come from China and perhaps India, as the name would suggest. From there it travelled west to the Mediterranean, and Arab, Dutch, Portuguese and Spanish sailors planted oranges along the shores of their trade routes to guard against scurvy.*

2 large oranges
5 eggs
250 g (9 oz/2½ cups) ground
   almonds
220 g (7¾ oz/1 cup) sugar
1 teaspoon baking powder
icing (confectioners') sugar, sifted,
   to dust

citrus ■ orange

For other orange recipes see:

blackberries

fruit ▪ soft
season ▪ late summer–autumn

selection and storage

Blackberries remain sour long after they turn black and are not truly ripe and ready to eat until they are soft. Consume them quickly, as they lose their flavour fast. Blackberries should be plump and their stems removed—attached stems are a sign that they were picked too early and may be under-ripe and tasteless.

Like all berries, blackberries can be frozen. To freeze berries so they 'free-flow' (as opposed to being frozen in a lump), spread them in a single layer on trays lined with baking paper, then freeze solid. Transfer to an airtight container or freezer bag, pressing all the air out of the bag, then seal and use within 6 months.

Once considered a noxious weed, blackberries have gained in popularity over the years and their price has risen accordingly. Growing on bushes and made up of a congregation of smaller fruits called drupelets, blackberries are botanically not classified as berries at all, but are part of the rose (Rosaceae) family.

Wild blackberries grow freely throughout the English, European and US late summer countryside. Smaller than their cultivated cousins, they are more intensely flavoured, but do lose their flavour quickly. The cultivation of the blackberry has resulted in the complete elimination of the thorny branches which once made the wild crop difficult to harvest. Blackberries are a good source of calcium, iron, potassium and vitamin C.

culinary uses

Containing high levels of pectin, slightly under-ripe blackberries are ideal for making jams, jellies and preserves—a few drops of geranium water is an excellent addition. If you are lucky enough to have a surplus of blackberries, then purple-stained blackberry butter takes minutes to make and is divine over crumpets, pancakes and scones—simply combine the blackberries, a little icing (confectioners') sugar and some softened, unsalted butter in a food processor until smooth. Blackberries can be macerated in sweetened Prosecco (a sparkling wine) and served with a dollop of mascarpone cheese, or, with the addition of some softened gelatine they can be poured into champagne glasses to set, becoming elegantly jellied.

serves 4

venison with blackberry sauce

60 g (2 1/4 oz) clarified butter
12 baby onions, peeled with root
   left intact
150 g (5 1/2 oz/1 cup)
   blackberries or blackcurrants
3 tablespoons redcurrant jelly
sixteen 50 g (1 3/4 oz) venison
   medallions
60 ml (2 fl oz/1/4 cup) red wine
410 ml (14 1/2 fl oz/1 2/3 cups)
   ready-made beef stock
1/2 tablespoon butter, softened
2 teaspoons plain (all-purpose)
   flour

Heat half the clarified butter in a saucepan. Add the onions, cover and cook for 20–25 minutes, stirring occasionally, until the onions are browned and softened. Set aside. Put the berries in a separate saucepan with the redcurrant jelly and 3 tablespoons water. Boil for 5 minutes, or until the fruit is softened and the liquid reduced and syrupy. Set aside.

Season the venison with sea salt and freshly ground black pepper, heat the remaining clarified butter in a frying pan and cook the medallions in batches over high heat for 1–2 minutes, turning once. Transfer the venison to a plate, cover loosely with foil and keep warm in a 120°C (235°F/Gas 1/2) oven.

Add the wine to the reserved juices in the frying pan and boil for 30 seconds. Add the stock and boil until reduced by half. Mix together the butter and flour separately to make a smooth paste and whisk into the stock. Boil, stirring constantly to avoid lumps forming, for 2 minutes, or until slightly thickened.

Drain the syrup from the fruit into the stock to make a sauce. Stir well, season and serve with the venison and onions, using the drained fruit as a garnish.

Called brambles in the United Kingdom, local folklore has it that blackberries should not be picked after 29 September (Michaelmas or the feast of St Michael), when it is said that the devil claims them for his own evil uses.

blackberry and apple jam

Peel, core and chop the apples. Put the apple pieces in a large saucepan with the berries and 125 ml (4 fl oz/½ cup) water. Cook, covered, over medium heat, stirring often, for 30 minutes, or until the fruit has softened.

Add the warmed sugar to the fruit and stir, without boiling, for 5 minutes, or until all the sugar has dissolved.

Put two small plates in the freezer. Bring the jam to the boil and boil for 20 minutes, stirring often. Stir across the base of the pan to check that the jam is not sticking or burning. When the jam falls from a wooden spoon in thick sheets without dripping, start testing for setting point. To do this, remove from the heat, put a little jam onto one of the cold plates and place in the freezer for 30 seconds. A skin should form on the surface and the jam should wrinkle when pushed with your finger. If not, continue to reduce the syrup over heat and use the second testing plate to test for setting point.

Transfer to a heatproof jug and immediately pour into hot sterilized jars and seal. Allow to cool, then label and date each jar. Store in a cool, dark place for 6–12 months. Refrigerate after opening for up to 6 weeks.

note To warm sugar, preheat the oven to 150°C (300°F/Gas 2). Spread the sugar evenly in a baking dish and warm in the oven for about 10–15 minutes, or until warmed through. Do not overheat the sugar or it will start to lump together. To save time you can warm the sugar while cooking the jam. Do not add the sugar until the fruit has softened. If sugar is added before the fruit is fully soft, the fruit will stay firm.

750 g (1 lb 10 oz or about 5) green apples
1 kg (2 lb 4 oz/8 cups) fresh blackberries, boysenberries or raspberries
1.5 kg (3 lb 5 oz/7 cups) sugar, warmed (see note)

soft fruit ■ blackberries

blackcurrants

fruit ▪ **soft**
season ▪ **high summer**

Blackcurrants are the jewels of the summer fruit bowl their shiny, tiny, purple-black looks adding a glamorous touch to any dish they grace. They have a unique, astringent, somewhat musky sourness, and are one of the few fruits that require cooking to render them palatable. With their tartness tempered by sugar, blackcurrants make garnet-hued jellies, preserves, sauces and syrups. Of all the blackcurrant-based alcohols, the French liqueur crème de cassis, the essential ingredient in the champagne cocktail kir royale, is the most famed. Offering manganese, vitamin C, dietary fibre, folate and bioflavonoids that reduce blood pressure, blackcurrants are extremely nutritious too.

selection and storage

Choose currants that are plump, firm and show no signs of crushing.

Currants are best kept refrigerated, covered tightly, for up to 4 days, then washed just prior to using. They can also be frozen for up to 3 months.

culinary uses

Explore the culinary potential of blackcurrants by adding handfuls to a mixed berry clafoutis (see page 83), stirring some through a citrus-scented pound cake mixture, or scattering them over a blackcurrant-tea-infused crème brûlée.

On a savoury note, gently heat blackcurrants in warmed butter until they just burst, add a spoonful of blackcurrant jelly, a splash of balsamic vinegar and brown sugar, then spoon over slices of roast pork, pan-fried duck breasts or pot-roasted guinea fowl. The flavour of blackcurrants is complemented by flavours found in Northern European cuisines, such as juniper berries, cinnamon, cloves, nutmeg, dark chocolate, vanilla beans and venison.

summer pudding

Put all the berries except the strawberries in a large saucepan with 125 ml (4 fl oz/½ cup) water and heat gently until the berries begin to collapse. Add the strawberries and turn off the heat. Add sugar to taste (the amount you need will depend on how ripe the fruit is). Set aside to cool.

Line a 1 litre (35 fl oz/4 cup) pudding basin (mould) with bread, cutting a large circle out of one slice for the base and slicing the rest into fingers to line the sides. Drain a little juice off the fruit mixture. Dip one side of each piece of bread in the juice before fitting it, juice side down, into the basin, leaving no gaps. Do not squeeze or flatten the bread or it will not absorb the juices well.

Fill the centre of the mould with the fruit, reserving any leftovers, and add a little juice. Cover the top with a layer of dipped bread, juice side up, and cover with plastic wrap. Put a plate which fits tightly inside the basin onto the plastic wrap to weigh it down. Refrigerate overnight. Carefully turn out the pudding and serve with any reserved berry mixture and cream.

150 g (5½ oz/1¼ cups) blackcurrants
150 g (5½ oz/1¼ cups) redcurrants
150 g (5½ oz/1¼ cups) raspberries
150 g (5½ oz/1¼ cups) blackberries
200 g (7 oz/1⅓ cups) strawberries, hulled and halved
caster (superfine) sugar, to taste
6–8 slices good-quality day-old sliced white bread, crusts removed
pouring (whipping) cream, to serve

soft fruit ■ blackcurrants

Currants are relatives of the gooseberry family—redcurrants were domesticated in the sixteenth century in Scandinavia, with whose cuisines they are largely associated (although they are the key component in the singularly British cumberland sauce). Redcurrants and their many hybrids, of which the pretty, transclucent white currant is one, have thinner skins and sweeter flesh then blackcurrents and can be eaten raw. They are often used in Northern European-style soups, plus jellies, drinks and summer desserts.

For other blackcurrant recipes see:
venison with blackberry sauce 42

blueberries

fruit ▪ **soft**
season ▪ **late spring–summer**

selection and storage

Look for plump, firm, uniform-sized blueberries that are coated with a dusty, silver-white bloom—as well as indicating freshness, this is their natural protection against the sun.

Blueberries are generally sold in punnets, so check there are no squashed or mouldy berries lurking at the bottom of the storage container.

If not using immediately, transfer any unwashed blueberries to an absorbent paper-lined dish, cover with plastic wrap and refrigerate for up to two days. Blueberries can be frozen for up to 6 months—do not wash them before freezing, as this tends to toughen their skin.

Blueberries are one of the few fruits native to North America. It is hardly surprising then that the very best blueberry recipes—blueberry-studded muffins, velvety blueberry cheesecakes and homely pies spilling sticky juices—come from there too.

Their deep indigo blue exterior covers sweet, greenish flesh, containing tiny, almost invisible seeds. For baking or making jams, pancakes and salads, blueberries work well with the flavours of lemon (which can turn them red), cinnamon, cloves, pecans, almonds, peaches, yoghurt and fromage frais.

Containing cholesterol-lowering compounds, antioxidants, vitamin C, potassium, folate and dietary fibre, blueberries are now regarded as one of the so-called 'super foods'; it is even thought that their consumption can have anti-aging effects.

preparation

Blueberries are one of the easiest fruits to eat, requiring absolutely no preparation—no peeling, stoning, topping or tailing. Just wash them immediately before eating, then drain on paper towels. If adding blueberries to cake and muffin batters, do this at the very last moment to prevent their vibrant juices from streaking the mixture. When including them in pancakes, scatter over half-cooked batter in the pan before turning, to minimize the risk of over-cooking them and to seal in their luscious juices. Lightly heated with sugar and a splash of brandy, blueberries make a wonderful topping for waffles with vanilla ice cream.

blueberry muffins

makes 12

375 g (13 oz/3 cups) plain
   (all-purpose) flour
1 tablespoon baking powder
165 g (5¾ oz/¾ cup) firmly
   packed soft brown sugar
125 g (4½ oz) butter, melted
2 eggs, lightly beaten
250 ml (9 fl oz/1 cup) milk
185 g (6½ oz/1¼ cups)
   blueberries

Preheat the oven to 210°C (415°F/Gas 6–7). Grease two trays of six 125 ml (4 fl oz/½ cup) muffin holes.

Sift the flour and baking powder into a large bowl. Stir in the sugar to combine and make a well in the centre. Working quickly, pour the combined melted butter, eggs and milk into the well and stir until just combined. Do not overmix; the batter should look quite lumpy.

Fold in the blueberries. Spoon the batter into the prepared muffin tins. Bake for 20 minutes, or until golden brown. Cool on a wire rack or serve warm.

hot blueberry sauce

makes 500 ml
(17 fl oz/2 cups)

500 g (1 lb 2 oz/3¼ cups)
   blueberries
60 g (2¼ oz/¼ cup) sugar
1 tablespoon balsamic vinegar
vanilla ice cream or warm
   chocolate cake, to serve

In a non-metallic bowl, combine the blueberries, sugar and balsamic vinegar. Allow to marinate for 30 minutes.

Place the berry mixture in a saucepan with 2 tablespoons water and stir over low heat for 4–5 minutes, or until sugar dissolves. Bring to the boil and simmer for 5 minutes. Serve warm with vanilla ice cream or warm chocolate cake.

blueberry cheesecake

Grease a 20 cm (8 inch) spring-form cake tin and line the base with baking paper. Melt the butter in a saucepan, add the oats and biscuit crumbs and mix well. Stir in the sugar. Press half the biscuit mixture into the base of the tin in an even layer and gradually press the remainder around the sides, but not quite all the way up to the rim, using a glass to firm it into place. Refrigerate for 10–15 minutes.

Preheat the oven to 180°C (350°F/Gas 4). To make the filling, beat the cream cheese, ricotta cheese, sugar and sour cream with electric beaters until smooth. Beat in the eggs, orange zest and flour. Put the cake tin on a flat baking tray to catch any drips. Pour the filling into the crust and bake for 40–45 minutes, or until the filling is just set. Remove from the oven and leave in the tin to cool to room temperature.

To make the topping, scatter the blueberries on top of the cheesecake. Push the jam through a sieve into a small saucepan with the cherry brandy. Stir over medium heat until smooth and then simmer for 2–3 minutes. Carefully brush the hot mixture over the blueberries. Refrigerate for several hours or overnight, until well chilled.

variation Other berries, such as blackberries, raspberries or strawberries can be used instead of blueberries for the topping—just substitute the same weight in berries. If using strawberries they need to be quartered or sliced first.

Blueberries were a key source of nutrition to the American Indian population, who added them to soups, stews and meat dishes and dried them for nourishment during the harsh winter months. Colonizing pilgrims did likewise, contributing to their survival in their new home, and since then blueberries have become an ingrained part of the American diet.

125 g (4½ oz) butter
100 g (3½ oz/1 cup) rolled (porridge) oats
100 g (3½ oz/¾ cup) wholemeal biscuits (graham crackers), finely crushed
2 tablespoons soft brown sugar

filling
375 g (13 oz/1½ cups) light cream cheese
100 g (3½ oz/⅓ cup) ricotta cheese
90 g (3¼ oz/⅓ cup) caster (superfine) sugar
125 g (4½ oz/½ cup) sour cream
2 eggs
1 tablespoon finely grated orange zest
1 tablespoon plain (all-purpose) flour

topping
250 g (9 oz/1⅔ cups) blueberries
240 g (8½ oz/¾ cup) blackberry jam
60 ml (2 fl oz/¼ cup) cherry brandy

soft fruit ∎ blueberries

boysenberries

selection and storage

Boysenberries should be firm and uniform in size, with no signs of mould or shrivelling. Highly perishable, they should be gently wiped with a damp cloth before eating, preferably on the day of purchase. Alternatively, put them unwashed and in a single layer on absorbent paper towels in an airtight container and refrigerate for up to 2 days. If faced with a glut, you can freeze boysenberries for up to 3 months; they'll only be good for cooking; use them for greatest effect in preserves, sauces, sorbets or granitas.

Shaped like an elongated blackberry but lacking its gritty seeds, with the deep purple colour and acid note of loganberries and hints of the aromatic flavour of raspberries, boysenberries feature the best characteristics of these three delectable berries. Named after American horticulturalist Rudolph Boysen, who hybridized them in 1923, boysenberries can be used interchangeably or in combination with any of their progenitors.

Boysenberries taste delicious when pureed with caster (superfine) sugar, a little grated orange zest and Grand Marnier for a quickly prepared crepe filling, or paired with pistachio and vanilla gelato for a grown-up sundae. Scattered over the base of a small baking dish, splashed with crème de cassis, slathered with crème fraîche and topped with soft brown sugar, they can be placed under a hot grill (broiler) to create a bubbling boysenberry gratin. Or, for an extremely easy dessert, stir boysenberries through whipped cream with some ground almonds, soft brown sugar, lemon juice and natural vanilla extract, spoon into glasses and serve.

Rich in fibre, vitamin C and potassium, their luscious sweet-sour flavour marries especially well with vanilla or other berry ice creams, citrus flavours, chocolate, apples, mangoes, pastry and meringue.

boysenberry (or blackberry) pie

Sift the flour and 1/4 teaspoon salt into a large bowl. Add the butter and rub it into the flour using your fingertips until the mixture resembles fine breadcrumbs. Fold in the sugar.

Make a well in the centre, add nearly all the water and mix with a flat-bladed knife, using a cutting rather than a stirring action. The mixture will come together in small beads of dough. If necessary, add more water, a teaspoon at a time, until the dough comes together. Test the dough by pinching a little piece between your fingers—if it doesn't hold together, it needs more water. Gather the dough together and lift out onto a lightly floured surface. Press the dough into a ball and then flatten it slightly. Cover in plastic wrap and refrigerate for 20–30 minutes.

Preheat the oven to 180°C (350°F/Gas 4). Grease a 26 x 20 cm (10¼ x 8 inch) pie dish. Roll half the dough out between two sheets of baking paper until it is large enough to fit into the dish. Remove the top sheet of paper and invert the pastry into the dish. Use a small ball of pastry to help press it down, allowing it to hang over the sides. Use a small sharp knife to trim away excess pastry.

Toss the boysenberries, sugar and cornflour together in a bowl until well combined, then transfer to the pie dish. Roll out the remaining pastry between two sheets of baking paper until large enough to cover the pie. Moisten the rim of the pie base with milk and press the pastry lid firmly into place. Trim and crimp the edges. Brush with egg and sprinkle with the extra sugar. Pierce the top of the pie with a knife.

Bake on the bottom shelf of the oven for 10 minutes, then move the pie to the centre shelf. Bake for another 30 minutes, or until golden on top. Cool before cutting into wedges and serving with cream or ice cream.

sweet shortcrust pastry
400 g (14 oz/3¼ cups) plain (all-purpose) flour
180 g (6½ oz) chilled butter, cut into cubes
2 tablespoons caster (superfine) sugar
3–4 tablespoons iced water

filling
500 g (1 lb 2 oz/4 cups) boysenberries or blackberries
160 g (5¾ oz/⅔ cup) caster (superfine) sugar
2 tablespoons cornflour (cornstarch)
milk, to brush
1 egg, lightly beaten
caster (superfine) sugar, extra, to sprinkle
pouring (whipping) cream or vanilla ice cream, to serve

soft fruit ■ boysenberries

For other boysenberry recipes see:
blackberry and apple jam....................43

fig

One of the most sensual of all fruits, with their velvety skins, succulent rose-tinted, seedy flesh and delicate, distinctly musky flavour, it's no wonder figs have long been associated with temptation. They achieved mythological status in ancient Rome and Greece, where they were not only a chief source of sustenance for the original Olympians, but so important to the Greek diet that it became illegal to export them. The ancient Greeks were certainly onto something, as modern research indicates that figs have one of the highest combined mineral counts of any popular cultivated fruit. Rich in calcium, potassium, phosphorus and iron, they are also packed with dietary fibre.

While fig trees are extremely hardy and flourish in tough conditions, the fruit is extremely delicate and must be handled with care. Figs must be picked when completely ripe, for once they are picked they will not ripen further, and can't be kept very long in cold storage before spoiling. The difficulty of getting them to market in prime condition makes it hardly surprising that fig aficionados eagerly anticipate their autumnal appearance and will search to find a supplier of quality, ripe fruit.

selection and storage

There are hundreds of varieties of figs; all are highly perishable, ranging in skin colour from purple, brown, green to white, with flesh colour from crimson and pinkish brown to amber.

Choose figs that feel yielding but not squashy, and that have no splits, bruises, black spots, leaking or wrinkling on their skin. Ripe figs are sometimes coated with a natural, light whitish bloom; this is desirable.

Store figs on an uncovered tray or plate in the refrigerator for 2–3 days, but be sure to allow them to come to room temperature before eating, as chilling tends to dull their glorious flavour.

varieties

black genoa A large purple-skinned fruit with sweet, pulpy, deep pink flesh.

brown turkey Another large fig with copper-brown skin, brown-pink flesh and a mild flavour.

mission Also known as franciscan figs, these are the mainstay of Californian fig-growing with deep purple-black skin and pink flesh which has a coarse texture but sweet, lush flavour.

white adriatic Characterized by a vivid green skin and a flame-red interior, these figs have a brightly pronounced flavour.

preparation

Figs do not need to be washed before eating, just lightly wiped with a damp cloth. Some figs have thicker skins than others and it may be necessary to peel these—use a peeler for this or just pull the skin off gently using a paring knife to assist, working from the stem end down. Always trim off the stem as this contains an oozy white substance which is unpleasant to eat.

culinary uses

Flavour lightly poached figs with orange-blossom water and they'll need little more than some honeyed yoghurt and a scattering of crushed walnuts. A most luscious dessert consists of nothing more than halved, ripe figs doused in sweetened whipped cream into which has been folded plenty of pureed raspberries.

Dried figs are perfect on a cheese platter, add texture and character to a sticky golden syrup pudding, make a glorious sweet compote (cook them in a red wine and fresh thyme-flavoured syrup), and are the vital ingredient in the eponymous American cookie, the fig newton. Figs can be roasted or baked, or halved, brushed with olive oil and carefully grilled (broiled).

Other worthy companions for this luscious fruit include honey, walnuts, pistachios, yoghurt, citrus, rosewater, raspberries and cheeses, especially those of the blue and soft goat's varieties.

chicken stuffed
with figs and fennel

To make the stuffing, heat 4 tablespoons of olive oil in a saucepan. Add the pancetta and onion and cook over medium-high heat, stirring often, for 5 minutes, or until golden. Add the fennel and potato and cook for another 2 minutes. Add the garlic and rosemary and season with sea salt and freshly ground black pepper. Stir in the wine, reduce the heat and cover. Cook for about 15 minutes, or until the potato is tender and has absorbed the wine. Remove the saucepan from the heat and add the orange zest and figs. Set aside to cool if not using immediately. Stuffing can be made several hours in advance.

Preheat the oven to 250°C (500°F/Gas 9). Season the cavity of the chicken, then fill with the stuffing. If there is any stuffing left over, add it to the roasting tin 15 minutes before removing the chicken from the oven.

Put the chicken, breast side up, in a roasting tin, drizzle over the remaining oil and cook for 15 minutes. Remove the chicken from the oven and turn it over, then cook for another 15 minutes. After this time, remove from the oven again and turn it on its back, reduce the heat to 180°C (350°F/Gas 4), and cook for a further 30 minutes.

Check that the chicken is cooked by piercing the thickest part of the thigh with a skewer—the juices should run clear. Check that the stuffing is cooked through by pushing a skewer into the cavity for 3 seconds—the skewer should feel very hot when you pull it out. If it isn't, cover the chicken with aluminium foil and cook for another 10–15 minutes, or until stuffing is heated through. Remove from the oven and rest for 10 minutes before serving. Serve with any extra stuffing and pour over any juices.

170 ml (5½ fl oz/⅔ cup) olive oil
140 g (5 oz) smoked pancetta, diced
1 onion, chopped
1 head of fennel, chopped
1 large potato, cut into 2 cm (¾ inch) cubes
2 garlic cloves, chopped
1 tablespoon chopped rosemary
125 ml (4 fl oz/½ cup) white wine
zest of 1 large orange
4 figs, chopped
2 kg (4 lb 8 oz) whole chicken

soft fruit ■ fig

For other fig recipes see:

grilled figs in prosciutto

25 g (1 oz) unsalted butter
1 tablespoon orange juice
12 small ripe figs
12 sage leaves
6 slices prosciutto, trimmed and
   halved lengthways

Put the butter in a small heavy-based saucepan. Melt the butter over low heat, then cook for 8–10 minutes, or until the froth subsides and the milk solids appear as brown specks on the bottom of the saucepan. Strain the butter through a sieve lined with paper towels into a clean bowl, then stir in the orange juice.

Wash the figs gently and pat them dry with paper towels. Cut each fig into quarters, starting from the stem end and cutting almost to the base, then gently open out—figs will open like a flower. Put a sage leaf in the opening of each fig, then wrap a piece of prosciutto around each one, tucking the ends under the base of the fig. Arrange the figs, cut side up, in a shallow ovenproof dish and brush with the butter mixture.

Put the tray of figs under a hot grill (broiler) and cook for 1–2 minutes, or until the prosciutto is slightly crisp. Serve warm or at room temperature.

figs with rosewater, almonds and honey

12 purple-skinned figs
50 g (1¾ oz/⅓ cup) blanched
   almonds, lightly toasted
3–4 teaspoons rosewater
1–2 tablespoons honey

Wash the figs gently and pat them dry with paper towels. Cut each fig into quarters, starting from the stem end and cutting almost to the base, then gently open out—figs will open like a flower. Put on a serving dish, cover with plastic wrap and chill in the refrigerator for 1 hour, or until required.

Coarsely chop the toasted almonds and set aside. Carefully drizzle about ¼ teaspoon of rosewater into the centre of each fig, then sprinkle over 1 teaspoon of the chopped almonds. Drizzle a little honey over the nuts, to serve.

gooseberries

fruit ■ **soft**
season ■ **summer**

Gooseberries have opaque, finely veined skins, which can be either furry or smooth. They are highly popular in Britain and Northern Europe, where their pleasing acidity and unique taste are utilized in tarts, pies, sauces, desserts and preserves. Gooseberries are an old-fashioned fruit, with recipes for their use included in cookbooks dating back to the 1700s.

Depending on their cultivar and state of ripeness gooseberries can be red, yellow or green. Boasting high levels of vitamin C, potassium and citric acid, they always require some sweetening ingredient, even when used in savoury dishes. In England, they are traditionally associated with Whitsuntide, a time when they are made into gooseberry pies or the elderflower-scented Wiltshire Whitsun cake.

selection and storage

Gooseberries do continue ripening after picking, unlike other berries. Look for shiny, firm berries, which show no signs of crushing or bruising, then handle them as little as possible.

They must be 'topped and tailed' before using. Gooseberries will keep for 1–2 days at room temperature, or for about 1 week in the refrigerator. Gooseberries can be frozen for later use— remove stems, put in a flat layer in an airtight freezer bag and seal; use within 6 months.

culinary uses

Gooseberries are one of the few fruits that are not eaten raw and the only berry at its finest when unripe. This quality makes them perfect for cutting the richness of oily fish, as the numerous recipes for smoked or pan-fried mackerel with gooseberry sauce attest. High in pectin, gooseberries make delightful jams and conserves, and spiced gooseberry chutney is great with roast goose and game. Gently sauté sliced gooseberries with a splash of sherry vinegar, thyme and brown sugar, then serve with pan-fried duck breasts, pork chops, or use to top a sweet crème fraîche or crème patissière-filled tart.

gooseberry cream shortcake

To make the pastry, combine the flour and sugar in a large bowl and stir to mix well. Add the butter and rub it in until the mixture resembles coarse breadcrumbs. Add the egg and, using a fork, mix until a soft dough forms. Form the dough into a flat disc, wrap in plastic wrap then refrigerate while you prepare the filling.

To make the filling, combine the gooseberries and 230 g (8½ oz/1 cup) sugar in a saucepan. Bring slowly to the boil over medium heat and cook, uncovered, for 10–15 minutes, or until berries are cooked and liquid is thick and syrupy. Remove from the heat and cool.

Using an electric mixer or food processor, mix the cream cheese, sour cream and remaining sugar together until mixture is smooth. Stir in the flour and egg yolk until well combined.

Preheat the oven to 180°C (350°F/Gas 4). On a lightly-floured surface, roll out two-thirds of the pastry to cover the base and side of a 25 cm (10 inch) loose-based tart tin. Press the pastry into the tin using a small ball of dough, trimming excess pastry.

Spoon the gooseberry mixture into the tin, then spoon the cream cheese mixture over the berries. Roll the remaining pastry out onto a floured surface to about 5 mm (¼ inch) thick and cut into 1.5 cm (⅝ inch) strips. Arrange strips on a slight diagonal over the top to form a lattice pattern, trimming and joining pieces of pastry as needed.

Mix egg yolk with 2 teaspoons of water then brush strips of pastry with mixture. Bake the shortcake for 35–40 minutes or until pastry is firm and golden. Cool tart then serve warm or at room temperature with whipped cream.

pastry
300 g (10½ oz/2½ cups) self-raising flour
80 g (2¾ oz/⅓ cup) caster (superfine) sugar
125 g (4½ oz) unsalted butter, cut into cubes
1 egg, lightly beaten

550 g (1 lb 4 oz/3 cups) gooseberries, topped and tailed
285 g (10 oz/1¼ cups) caster (superfine) sugar
150 g (5½ oz/⅔ cup) cream cheese
60 ml (2 fl oz/¼ cup) sour cream
1 tablespoon plain (all-purpose) flour
1 egg yolk
whipped cream, to serve

soft fruit ▪ gooseberries

grapes

Whether classified as white or black, red or green, all grapes have smooth skins surrounding translucent, juicy flesh, some with seeds and others without. Grapes are actually true berries, unlike many fruits bearing that moniker, such as strawberries.

There are over 8000 grape varieties in existence, although the vast majority of cultivated grapes are used for making wine rather than eating out of hand, and this has long been the case.

Archaeological evidence suggests that not long after grapes were first found growing in the Fertile Crescent (an historical region in the Middle East and the world's original 'fruit bowl', from where many other fruits originated), people quickly realized their juice could be fermented into wine. This fortuitous discovery has been appreciated by civilizations ever since, and utilizes grape varieties that are generally too tart for eating.

Used to make vinegar, verjuice, jam, jelly, grapeseed oil and even the leavening agent cream of tartar, the versatility of grapes make them an extremely valuable crop, second only to olives as the most widely cultivated temperate-climate fruit.

Containing vitamins B and C, dietary fibre, some potassium, protein and a cancer-inhibiting compound called resveratrol, grapes are also rich in tannins, as any fan of red wine will appreciate.

selection and storage

Developing sugar as they ripen, grapes do not sweeten further after picking—bunches of table grapes are hand harvested to preserve their fruit-laden clusters.

Choose grapes that are well-coloured for their variety, plump, and still firmly attached to their stems—a gentle shake will show whether the bunch is too old, as grapes will tellingly fall from their stems. Green grapes should have a slightly pale, yellowish hue rather than be grassy green, whereas red varieties are at their best when deeply coloured.

Store unwashed grapes in a plastic bag in the refrigerator for 5–7 days. Wash grapes and gently pat dry just before eating.

varieties

There are many table grapes produced and these are differentiated by skin thickness and colour, shape, juiciness, intensity of flavour and sweetness and whether the variety is seeded or seedless. Seedless types are increasingly preferred by consumers, although most experts agree that seeded grapes have better flavour.

flame seedless A dark red, seedless grape with a juicy somewhat 'crisp' flesh with a tart edge.

muscat An ancient grape that is used for making wine, raisins and as a table fruit. There are many varieties: the muscat of Alexandria has yellowish skin, is large and seeded, with a very sweet and juicy flesh; muscat Hamburg is a blue-black grape with oval, medium–large fruit. The flesh is pleasantly winey in flavour, is sweet and seeded.

red globe An extremely large, round red grape with subtle flavour, mealy flesh and a large seed.

thompson seedless Popular for processing into raisins, the medium-sized thompson seedless have yellowish green skin and a pronounced sweet flavour.

preparation

Although eating peeled grapes is associated with indolent Roman aristocracy, for some uses (in sauces to go with meats, for example), particularly if the skins are tough and tannic, peeling is necessary. To do this, cut a small incision at the stem end, then simply pull the skin off carefully. For particularly thick-skinned grapes, put them in a bowl, add boiling water to cover, then refresh in iced water and peel.

Similarly, if seeds are large and chewy, remove these by simply cutting grapes in half and picking them out.

culinary uses

Generally, there's no beating the classics—the Italians got it right with schiacciata, a flat bread studded with red or black grapes, as did the Spanish with ajo blanco (see page 160), the almond-based gazpacho topped with a few refreshing green grapes.

A handful of grapes tossed into a poached chicken, tarragon and watercress salad makes memorable summer fare, as does an idea from Umbrian vintners—slow-roasting pork sausages with muscatel grapes until they become a delicious, crimson mass. Serve this as a satisfying lunch to combat autumn's chill.

Perfect, sweet grapes served with freshly cracked walnuts and a delicious chunk of soft cheese (something decadent like a triple cream or an oozing brie) is an unbeatable way to end a meal.

grape fritters
with cinnamon sugar

To make the cinnamon sugar, combine the sugar and cinnamon in a bowl. Set aside.

Whisk the egg yolks with the vanilla extract and sugar until pale and creamy. Slice each grape into four and stir into the egg yolk mixture. Sift the flour into the mixture and stir to combine. Beat the egg whites in a separate bowl until soft peaks form. Gently fold half of the egg whites into the grape mixture with a metal spoon until just combined and then fold in the remaining egg whites.

Melt 2 teaspoons of butter in a frying pan over low heat. Drop 6 heaped teaspoons of the batter separately into the pan, and cook over low–medium heat for 2–3 minutes, turning carefully when the base becomes firm and bubbles appear around the edges. Cook for a further 2 minutes, or until golden. Remove to a plate and keep warm, covered, in a 120°C (235°F/Gas ½) oven. Repeat to make 24 fritters. Dust the fritters with cinnamon sugar and serve immediately.

cinnamon sugar
2 tablespoons caster (superfine) sugar
1 teaspoon ground cinnamon

fritters
2 eggs, separated
½ teaspoon natural vanilla extract
60 g (2¼ oz/¼ cup) caster (superfine) sugar
150 g (5½ oz/¾ cup) large seedless red or black grapes
40 g (1½ oz/⅓ cup) self-raising flour
40 g (1½ oz) unsalted butter

soft fruit ■ grapes

The ancient Greeks and Romans were the first to dry grapes, the precursors of dried currants, sultanas and raisins; their very reduced juices were widely used as a sweetening agent before the advent of sugar. Italians also distil grape skins, seeds and stems (the 'waste' product of wine-making) to make a type of clear brandy called grappa.

schiacciata con uva
(sweet grape flat bread)

serves 6

100 g (3½ oz/¾ cup) raisins
90 ml (3 fl oz) sweet Marsala
150 ml (5 fl oz) milk
7 g (¼ oz or 2 teaspoons)
    instant dried yeast
125 g (4½ oz/½ cup) caster
    (superfine) sugar
300 g (10½ oz/2½ cups) plain
    (all-purpose) flour
olive oil
500 g (1 lb 2 oz/2¾ cups)
    black seedless grapes

Combine the raisins and Marsala in a bowl. Warm the milk and put in a small bowl. Stir in 1 teaspoon of sugar, sprinkle over the yeast and set aside in a draught-free place for 7 minutes, or until the mixture becomes foamy.

Put the flour, 90 g (3¼ oz/⅓ cup) sugar and a pinch of salt in a bowl and mix together. Add the yeast mixture and mix until a dough forms. Transfer to a lightly floured surface and knead for 6–8 minutes, or until smooth and elastic. Add a little more flour or a few drops of warm water if necessary to give a soft, but not sticky, dough.

Lightly oil the inside of a large bowl with olive oil, add the dough and roll to coat. Cut a cross on the top of the ball of dough with a sharp knife. Leave the dough in the bowl, cover with plastic wrap and stand in a draught-free place for 1 hour, or until doubled in size.

Preheat the oven to 180°C (350°F/Gas 4). Drain the raisins and squeeze them dry. Lightly dust a baking tray with flour. Punch down the dough and divide in two. Shape each half into a flattened round about 20 cm (8 inches) in diameter and place one round on the tray. Scatter half the grapes and half the raisins over the dough, and then cover with the second round of dough. Scatter the remaining grapes and raisins over the top. Cover loosely with a tea (dish) towel and leave in a draught-free place for 1 hour, or until doubled in size.

Sprinkle the dough with the remaining sugar. Bake for 40–50 minutes, or until golden. Serve warm or at room temperature, cut into thick slices.

raspberries

fruit ▪ **soft**
season ▪ **late summer**

Squiggles of raspberry coulis became an over-used 1980s menu staple, adorning everything from chocolate mud cake and brownies to duck liver pâté. These days, cooks are rediscovering the simpler delights of raspberries, as the resurgence in popularity of dishes such as peach melba, with its essential raspberry sauce, and squidgy summer pudding, can attest.

The red raspberry and its rarer golden relative both hail from the Caucasus, while the lesser-known black version is indigenous to North America. If you are fortunate enough to spy yellow raspberries at the market, try them, as they have a particularly concentrated flavour. Like all berries, raspberries are rich in vitamins A and C, potassium and iron.

culinary uses

Although raspberries are undoubtedly one of the finest-flavoured of the berries and do not need too many competing flavours, they are luxurious when paired with dark or white chocolate, almonds, hazelnuts, vanilla, lavender, rosewater, coconut, sparkling wine, rosé or crème de framboise.

Showcase their glorious colour and flavour by using them in simple, classic desserts, such as eton mess, a sherry-sodden trifle, a Sauternes syllabub or a humble berry crumble. For a very lush dessert, top raspberries with fresh clotted cream. Raspberries, in the form of raspberry vinegar, can add a special note to savoury food, such as a dressing for spinach or beetroot-based salads, or splashed into a sauce destined for pairing with a roasted duck.

selection and storage

Labour intensive to harvest, due to their extreme fragility, raspberries should be eaten within 2 days of purchase and stored in the refrigerator.

Choose deeply-coloured raspberries, as these are the most strongly flavoured, and do try to buy those that have escaped spraying as they won't need washing (raspberries don't respond well to drenching in water).

When purchasing, look to see that the hulls have been removed when picked, leaving the characteristic hollow centre; if still there it's an indication that the berries were picked when under-ripe and will be sour. Raspberries can be frozen for up to 3 months.

duck breast with raspberries and cassis

serves 4

four 200 g (7 oz) duck breasts
2 teaspoons ground cinnamon
1 tablespoon raw (demerara)
    sugar
250 ml (9 fl oz/1 cup) red wine
150 ml (5 fl oz) crème de cassis
1 tablespoon cornflour
    (cornstarch) or arrowroot
250 g (9 oz/2 cups) raspberries

Using a sharp knife, score the duck breasts through the skin and fat, taking care not to cut into the meat. In a frying pan, cook the duck breasts over medium-high heat for 4–5 minutes, skin side down, until the skin browns and the fat runs out. Remove the meat from the pan and drain excess fat, reserving pan.

Combine the cinnamon, sugar and 2 teaspoons sea salt in a small bowl. Sprinkle over the skin of the duck breasts, then press in with your hands. Season with black pepper. Reheat the frying pan and cook the duck breasts, skin side up, for 10 minutes, or until the duck is cooked through but still a little pink in the middle. Remove from pan and leave to rest on a carving board, reserving pan and about 2 tablespoons of cooking juices. Preheat the grill (broiler).

Meanwhile, mix together the red wine and cassis in a jug. Pour about 100 ml (3½ fl oz) of the liquid into a small bowl and mix in the cornflour or arrowroot, then pour this back into the jug.

Return the pan with the cooking juices to the heat and pour in the red wine mixture. Simmer for 2–3 minutes, stirring constantly, until the sauce has thickened. Add the raspberries and simmer for another minute to warm the fruit through. Season to taste.

Grill (broil) the duck breasts, skin side up, for 1 minute, or until the sugar mixture starts to caramelize. Remove from heat, slice the duck breasts thinly, pour a little of the hot sauce over the top and serve the rest of the sauce separately in a jug.

white chocolate and raspberry mousse

Melt the white chocolate in a heatproof bowl over a saucepan of simmering water, making sure that the water does not touch the bowl. Cool slightly, then stir in the cream. Stir the yolks into the white chocolate and mix well.

Whisk the egg whites until stiff peaks form. Fold a third of the egg whites into the chocolate mixture to loosen them. Fold in the remaining egg white until just combined. Fold in the raspberries, then divide among four serving bowls. Refrigerate for at least 4 hours. Decorate with extra fresh raspberries to serve.

150 g (5½ oz) good quality white chocolate
150 ml (5 fl oz) pouring (whipping) cream
4 eggs, separated
250 g (9 oz/2 cups) raspberries, crushed
raspberries, extra, to serve

soft fruit ■ raspberries

fig and raspberry cake

serves 6–8

Preheat the oven to 180°C (350°F/Gas 4). Grease a 23 cm (9 inch) spring-form cake tin.

Cream the butter and sugar in a bowl until light and pale. Add the egg and egg yolk and beat again. Sift the flour and baking powder into the bowl and add a pinch of salt. Stir to combine. Chill for 15 minutes, or until firm enough to roll out.

Divide the dough in two equal halves and roll out one half large enough to fit the base of the tin. Cover with the figs, orange zest and raspberries. Roll out the remaining dough and place it over the filling. Lightly brush the top with water and sprinkle with sugar. Bake for 30 minutes, or until a skewer inserted into the centre of the cake comes out clean. Cut into slices and serve with cream or mascarpone cheese.

185 g (6½ oz) unsalted butter
185 g (6½ oz/¾ cup) caster (superfine) sugar
1 egg
1 egg yolk
335 g (11¾ oz/2⅔ cups) plain (all-purpose) flour
1 teaspoon baking powder
4 figs, quartered
grated zest of 1 orange
200 g (7 oz/1⅔ cups) raspberries
2 tablespoons sugar, extra
pouring (whipping) cream or mascarpone cheese, to serve

strawberries

fruit ■ **soft**
season ■ **summer**

Arguably the most beloved of all the soft fruits, strawberries belong to the rose family, so it's no surprise that adding a few judicious drops of rosewater enhances their floral flavour. Strawberries are the only fruit whose seeds grow around the exterior rather than interior. While their botanic name, *Fragaria*, means 'fragrance', describing perfectly their perfumed essence, strawberries had romantic associations long before chocolate-dipped fruits and strawberries floating in champagne became Saint Valentine's Day staples. Once regarded as an aphrodisiac in provincial France, they are also the symbol of Venus, goddess of love, due to their ruby colour and unique heart shape.

Cultivated strawberry varieties abound, ranging in colour from scarlet to yellow and even white. The smaller, sweeter wild strawberries, known in France as *frais de bois*, meaning 'strawberries of the woods', are the most highly prized, on account of their exquisite, concentrated flavour.

Strawberries contain more vitamin C than oranges. A good source of potassium and folic acid, they also contain ellagic acid, a compound that guards against cancer. Be warned though: strawberries can cause a severe allergic reaction in babies, so it is best to wait until they are over one year old before introducing them to the fruit.

preparation

Don't wash or hull strawberries before storing or soak them in water before using, as they readily absorb moisture, which dilutes their flavour. Wash just before eating, then remove leaves and stems with a small sharp knife or strawberry huller.

culinary uses

Who can resist a luscious bowl of sun-ripened strawberries? Imagine the ritual of afternoon tea without scones adorned with lashings of strawberry jam and cream, or Neapolitan ice cream minus the obligatory strip of strawberry. The marriage of strawberries and cream may have evolved into more refined expressions, but the original combination remains one of summer's purest pleasures.

Take a cue from the Italians and sprinkle perfect strawberries with caster (superfine) sugar, then drizzle with a little aged balsamic vinegar; finish with a light grinding of black pepper and lashings of mascarpone cheese. Crush strawberries with sugar and a dash of orange-flower water or rosewater, then fold through whipped cream and serve as a fool, or use as a filling for sponge cake or a pavlova topping (see page 109). Along with sliced cucumber, lemon, lime and mint, strawberries are a vital ingredient in an authentic Pimm's No. 1 Cup. Strawberries' sweetness offsets rhubarb's tartness; together the pair make excellent pies, crumbles, jams and preserves.

selection and storage

As delicate as the hearts they resemble, strawberries should be handled with care. They do not ripen further after picking but just soften.

Choose strawberries that are plump, fragrant and firm, with no signs of bruising, leaking or mould festering in the bottom of the container and no greenish white 'shoulders' at the stem end. Carefully store and handle them—ideally eat them on the day of purchase.

A glut of strawberries will be best used by making jam or freezing for up to 6 months for later use—hull them first and freeze them in a single layer on trays before transferring to freezer bags or containers.

soft fruit ■ strawberries

serves 6

balsamic strawberries

500 g (1 lb 2 oz/3⅓ cups) strawberries, hulled and halved
60 ml (2 fl oz/¼ cup) balsamic vinegar
2 tablespoons caster (superfine) sugar
2 teaspoons lemon juice
small handful mint leaves
vanilla ice cream, to serve

Put the strawberries in a glass bowl. Combine the balsamic vinegar, caster sugar and lemon juice in a small saucepan and stir over medium heat for 5 minutes, or until sugar dissolves. Remove from the heat and cool.

Pour the balsamic mixture over the strawberries, add the mint leaves and toss together. Cover with plastic wrap and refrigerate for 1 hour to allow the flavours to develop. Serve with vanilla ice cream.

makes 500 ml
(17 fl oz/2 cups)

strawberry curd

250 g (9 oz/1⅔ cups) strawberries, hulled and roughly chopped
185 g (6½ oz/¾ cup) caster (superfine) sugar
125 g (4½ oz) unsalted butter, softened
1 teaspoon grated lemon zest
1 tablespoon lemon juice
4 egg yolks

Put the strawberries in a saucepan with the sugar, butter, lemon zest and lemon juice. Stir over low heat until the butter has melted and the sugar dissolved. Simmer gently for 5 minutes, then remove from the heat.

Lightly beat the egg yolks in a large bowl then, stirring constantly, slowly add the strawberry mixture in a thin stream. The mixture will thicken as you add it.

Return to low heat and cook for 2 minutes, stirring constantly. Do not allow the mixture to boil or the curd will separate. Pour into hot sterilized jars and seal while hot. Curd will keep in the refrigerator for up to 2 months. Once opened curd will keep, refrigerated, for 5 days.

apricot

fruit ▪ **stone**
season ▪ **summer**

If you have only ever eaten supermarket-supplied apricots, on the whole sadly tasteless specimens, you could be forgiven for wondering what the fuss over apricots is about. All too often, this eagerly anticipated summer fruit, which should brim with sweet, fragrant juices and have satisfyingly lush flesh, has all the mouth-appeal of the boxes it arrives in and is rather similar in taste. The fact is, the highly perishable apricot doesn't travel well when ripe and doesn't much ripen once picked, although a few days at room temperature will improve flavour a little. The best way to obtain full-flavoured fruit is to buy it sun-ripened and just picked from a caring supplier. Only then will the 'fuss' become apparent as there can be few lovelier experiences than eating a juicy apricot, warm with the flavours of high summer.

The apricot hails from China where it has been cultivated for over 4000 years. Marco Polo is credited with the westward spread of the fruit, via the legendary Silk Road. This was a highly successful migration; assorted Turkish, Spanish, Arab and other Mediterranean cooks have, over time, embraced the fruit with great enthusiasm, producing some of the most memorable apricot recipes, including savoury preparations where the fruit is cooked with lamb, chicken or rice and a plethora of exotic sweet spices, such as cardamom, ginger and cinnamon.

preparation

There is no need to peel apricots; this would be tediously difficult anyway. They split in half easily and neatly along their natural crease. Do beware, the flesh will oxidize (turn brown) on contact with the air, so work quickly and if serving raw, prepare just before you plan to serve them.

culinary uses

Fresh apricots make sublime jam and if you are blessed with an excess, they are perfectly suited to being bottled in syrup. They are fabulous in tarts, pies, cakes (upside-down cake springs to mind) and crumbles; they can be poached, pureed and even stuffed and roasted—there, the classic Italian filling for stuffed roast peaches, comprising chopped almonds, chocolate and amaretti biscuits, translates perfectly to apricots.

Their flavour also goes particularly well with those of vanilla beans, almonds, hazelnuts and pistachios, fresh rosemary, honey, saffron, some cheeses (camembert, brie and mascarpone, for example), dessert wines and orange-flower and rose waters. Simple desserts can be made by lightly poaching apricots in syrup spiked with one (or some) of these flavours—saffron-poached apricots served with yoghurt and pistachios are delicious, as are honey and rosemary poached apricots served chilled with dollops of mascarpone cheese.

selection and storage

Buy directly from a grower, then you'll know what apricot variety you are purchasing; otherwise it's something of a lottery. If possible, seek out older varieties like blenheim or the peerless moorpark, a large apricot with particularly fine flavour.

Buy fruits that are firm but not hard, and ones with clear, unblemished skin. They should feel slightly soft when pressed and have a faintly sweet fragrance; they should be a deep, clear orange and some may blush with red.

Once purchased, apricots should be consumed within 1–2 days and stored carefully at cool room temperature (chilling masks their flavour); cradled in a single layer on several layers of paper towel is the best way.

serves 4

chicken with apricots and honey

40 g (1½ oz) butter
1 teaspoon ground cinnamon
1 teaspoon ground ginger
⅛ teaspoon cayenne pepper
four 175 g (6 oz) chicken breasts,
    trimmed
1 onion, sliced
250 ml (9 fl oz/1 cup) ready-
    made chicken stock
6 sprigs coriander (cilantro), tied
    in a bunch
500 g (1 lb 2 oz or about 10)
    apricots, halved and stones
    removed
2 tablespoons honey
2 tablespoons slivered almonds,
    toasted, to serve
couscous, to serve

Melt the butter in a large frying pan. Add the spices, season
with freshly ground black pepper and stir over low heat
for about 1 minute, or until fragrant. Increase the heat to
medium and add the chicken breasts. Cook for 1 minute
on each side, taking care not to let the spices burn.

Add the onion and cook for 5 minutes, stirring the onion
and turning the chicken occasionally. Add the stock and
coriander sprigs and season to taste. Reduce the heat to low,
cover and simmer for 5 minutes, turning the chicken once.

Transfer the chicken to a serving dish, cover and rest for
2–3 minutes. Put the apricots, cut side down, into the pan
with the juices and drizzle with honey. Cover and simmer
for 7–8 minutes, turning the apricots after 5 minutes.
Remove the coriander and discard.

Spoon the apricots and sauce over the chicken, scatter with
almonds and serve with couscous passed separately.

*Apricot kernels, found inside the hard stone, look somewhat like
an almond and, when blanched and used sparingly, impart a delicious
bitter almond flavour—this is particularly lovely in apricot jam, stewed
or poached apricots. Beware however, as apricot kernels can be toxic
eaten in any quantity—always use just a few (4 kernels in a large batch
of jam or 3 in a brew of poached fruit to serve 6–8), and retrieve them
before serving.*

makes 750 ml
(26 fl oz/3 cups)

apricot jam

1 kg (2 lb 4 oz or about 20) apricots, halved and stones removed
1 kg (2 lb 4 oz/4½ cups) sugar, warmed (see note)

Put the apricots in a large saucepan with 375 ml (13 fl oz/1½ cups) water. Bring to the boil, stirring, for 20 minutes, or until the fruit has softened.

Put two plates in the freezer. Add the sugar and stir, without boiling, for 5 minutes, or until all the sugar has dissolved. Return to the boil and boil for 20 minutes, stirring often. Remove any scum during cooking with a slotted spoon. When the jam falls from the back of a tilted wooden spoon in thick sheets without dripping, start testing for setting point. To do this, remove from heat, put a little jam onto one of the cold plates and place in the freezer for 30 seconds. A skin will form on the surface and the jam will wrinkle when pushed with your finger. If not, return to the heat for a few minutes and retest with the other plate.

Transfer to a heatproof jug and immediately pour into hot sterilized jars and seal. Allow to cool, then label and date each jar. Store in a cool, dark place for 6–12 months. Refrigerate after opening for up to 6 weeks.

note To warm the sugar, preheat the oven to 150°C (300°F/Gas 2). Spread the sugar evenly in a baking dish and heat in the oven for 10–15 minutes. To save time you can warm the sugar while you are cooking the jam. Do not add the sugar until the fruit has softened. If sugar is added before the fruit is fully soft, the fruit will stay firm.

apricot meringue torte

Combine 375 ml (13 fl oz/1½ cups) of water, 125 g (4½ oz/heaped ½ cup) of sugar, the cinnamon stick and 1 teaspoon of the vanilla extract in a large saucepan. Stir over low heat until the sugar has dissolved, then increase the heat and simmer for 15 minutes. Add the quartered apricots and simmer over low heat for another 20 minutes, or until very soft. Set aside to cool.

Preheat the oven to 150°C (300°F/Gas 2) and draw a 22 cm (8½ inch) circle on two sheets of baking paper. Put the sheets, pencil side down, on two baking trays.

Using electric beaters, whisk the egg whites in a bowl until stiff peaks form. Add the remaining sugar, a little at a time, and continue beating until the mixture is stiff and glossy. Beat in the vinegar and remaining vanilla extract. Gently fold in the ground hazelnuts.

Divide the meringue mixture between the two circles on the prepared trays and smooth the surface. Bake for 35–40 minutes, or until the meringues are firm and dry. Turn off the oven and leave the meringues in the oven to cool completely.

Peel off the baking paper and place one meringue on a serving plate. Whip the cream until stiff peaks form. Discard the cinnamon stick from the syrup and drain the apricots. Gently stir the apricots through the whipped cream and then spread over the meringue. Put the second meringue on top of the apricot cream and dust with icing sugar to serve.

375 g (13 oz/1⅔ cups) caster (superfine) sugar
1 cinnamon stick
2 teaspoons natural vanilla extract
450 g (1 lb or about 9) apricots, quartered and stones removed
6 egg whites, at room temperature
1½ teaspoons white vinegar
35 g (1¼ oz/⅓ cup) ground hazelnuts
300 ml (10½ fl oz) thickened (whipping) cream
icing (confectioners') sugar, to dust

stone fruit ■ apricot

cherries

fruit ▪ **stone**
season ▪ **summer**

No fruit epitomizes lazy, hazy summer days like cherries, those cheerful, shiny and ruby-red (or pink or yellowish) globes that seem to come and then go all too quickly. Even in these days of year-round produce supply, cherries remain stubbornly seasonal, making them a highly anticipated treat. Divinely juicy and addictively sweet, cherries are at their best eaten out of hand, although they can also lend their subtle but unmistakable flavour to any number of sweet and savoury preparations.

It seems too, that cherries are not just delicious—they burst with good things for the body. Particularly rich in cancer-fighting antioxidants, cherries also contain anti-inflammatory compounds plus abundant quantities of melatonin, which helps regulate the body's circadian rhythms. Cherry consumption is being credited with everything from helping arthritis and gout sufferers to preventing diabetes and heart disease.

A venerable fruit, the first recorded mention of the cherry was in Theophrastus' (372–287 BC) *History of Plants*, where he suggests the Greeks had been cultivating the fruit, a native of Asia Minor, for centuries. The Romans spread the cherry throughout Europe, leaving it in the wake of their conquests, and it is thought to have been an important part of the Legionnaires' diet.

varieties

Cherries can be divided into two basic categories—sweet and sour. Some of the most popular and well-known sweet cherry varieties are the bing (large and very dark red-black fruit), napoleon, florence and ranier—these latter three types have yellowish skins that blush pink when ripe.

Perhaps the two most popular sour varieties are the maraschino (used to produce the classic preserved cherry used in desserts) and the morello. Sour cherries, with their complex flavour and slightly tart edge, are perfectly suited for cooking (in fact they're too tart to eat raw) and are the cherry behind some of the world's most beloved cherry preparations—think black forest cake, Hungarian-style chilled cherry soup, the liqueur kirsch and sour cherry strudel. Sweet cherries also work well when cooked; witness the timeless cherry clafoutis from France, that fabulous batter-based pudding which is utterly delicious and particularly easy to prepare.

preparation

Cherry stones contain kernels which can contribute a complementary, slightly bitter-almond flavour to cherry dishes. If you want this flavour, leave them in when freezing or, if dealing with fresh fruit, crack a few kernels, tie them in a piece of muslin (cheesecloth) and add them to the cooking liquid or poaching syrup when making jam, compotes or puddings.

culinary uses

Cherries are such a special treat that it is unlikely you will have to deal with a glut. However, if fortunate enough to be in possession of more fruit than you can possibly use, they can be made into gorgeous jams or pickled in a lightly spiced, vinegared syrup to serve with smoked meats, such as ham, pâtés and terrines.

selection and storage

Buy cherries with the stalk still on—they'll keep better. Make sure the fruits have been kept cool as their flavour and texture degrade if they have been exposed to warmth. Ripe sweet cherries will last for 2–3 days in a plastic bag in the refrigerator. Sour cherries keep for up to 2 weeks, refrigerated.

Both sweet and sour types can be frozen successfully and if doing this, consider investing in a cherry pitter to remove stones before freezing so they'll be easier to deal with once thawed.

Always take the time to choose your own cherries from the piles typically heaped high at markets. Pick out fruit that is unblemished, shiny, large (cherries gain 30 per cent of their flavour and volume in the last week before picking), heavy and with no soft, wrinkled, spotted or burst patches. Generally, the deeper the skin colour (according to variety), the riper the fruit.

serves 8

cherry and cream cheese strudel

250 g (9 oz/1 cup) cream
  cheese, at room temperature
100 ml (3½ fl oz) pouring
  (whipping) cream
60 g (2¼ oz/¼ cup) caster
  (superfine) sugar
1 tablespoon brandy or cherry
  brandy
1 teaspoon natural vanilla extract
150 g (5½ oz or 10 sheets)
  ready-made filo pastry
75 g (2½ oz) unsalted butter,
  melted
35 g (1¼ oz/⅓ cup) dry
  breadcrumbs
35 g (1¼ oz/⅓ cup) ground
  almonds
2 tablespoons caster (superfine)
  sugar, extra
425 g (15 oz/1¼ cups) cherries,
  pitted
icing (confectioners') sugar,
  to dust

Preheat the oven to 200°C (400°F/Gas 6). Lightly grease a large baking tray. Put the cream cheese, cream, sugar, brandy and vanilla extract in a bowl and beat with electric beaters until smooth.

Take one sheet of filo pastry. Keep the rest covered with a damp tea (dish) towel to prevent drying out. Brush with some of the melted butter and sprinkle with some of the combined crumbs, almonds and sugar. Put another sheet of pastry on top. Repeat brushing and sprinkling until all the sheets are used.

Spread the cream cheese mixture evenly over the pastry, leaving a 4 cm (1½ inch) border all around. Brush butter over the border. Arrange the cherries over the cream cheese.

Roll the pastry from one long side and fold in the ends as you roll. Form into a firm roll and place, seam side down, on the greased tray. Brush all over with the remaining butter. Bake for 10 minutes, then reduce the oven to 180°C (350°F/Gas 4) and continue to bake for 30 minutes, or until crisp and golden. Cool on a wire rack. To serve, dust liberally with icing sugar and cut into slices, using a sharp serrated knife.

cherry clafoutis

Preheat the oven to 180°C (350°F/Gas 4). Put the cream in a small saucepan. Scrape out the seeds of the vanilla bean and add the seeds and scraped bean to the cream. Heat gently for 2–5 minutes, then remove from the heat, add the milk and cool. Strain to remove the vanilla bean and seeds.

Whisk the eggs with the sugar and flour, then stir into the cream. Add the kirsch and cherries and stir well. Pour into a 23 cm (9 inch) round baking dish and bake for 30–35 minutes, or until golden on top. Dust with icing sugar and serve.

note It is traditional to leave the stones in the cherries when you make a clafoutis (they add a bitter, almost-almond flavour during the cooking), but you should point this out when you're serving the pudding.

185 ml (6 fl oz/¾ cup) thick (double/heavy) cream
1 vanilla bean, halved lengthways
125 ml (4 fl oz/½ cup) milk
3 eggs
55 g (2 oz/¼ cup) caster (superfine) sugar
85 g (3 oz/⅔ cup) plain (all-purpose) flour
1 tablespoon cherry brandy, such as kirsch
450 g (1 lb/2¼ cups) sweet black cherries
icing (confectioners') sugar

stone fruit ■ cherries

Today, much of the world's sweet cherry crop is produced in Turkey, Iran, the United States, Italy and Spain, while Russia and Poland grow huge quantities of sour cherry varieties.

date

fruit ■ **stone**
season ■ **autumn–winter**

selection and storage

Select dates which haven't been pre-packaged (typically on small trays, wrapped tightly in plastic wrap) as it is difficult to tell their condition. Choose dates that are plump, with unbroken, slightly wrinkled skins. Avoid any with sugary surfaces as this indicates their sugars are crystallizing (due to inappropriate storing or age).

Store dates in a sealed container in the refrigerator. Fresh dates will keep for 12 months—they can also be frozen for several years.

With a sugar content of around 60 per cent, it's little wonder that dates taste so good! They are one of the world's oldest food crops; some believe they were cultivated as early as 8000 BC. Known as 'the tree of life' in the Arab countries where they flourish, date palms are also one of the world's most useful crops. Legendarily the palm has 800 uses—the sap is drunk, the fibre woven, the stones are ground and used for camel fodder, the palm-hearts are eaten and the bark is used as building material, to name a few.

Aside from the usual sweet uses for dates (in scones, cakes and muffins, for example), dates also star in salads, tagines, sauces, rice and grain dishes; even in an intriguing rice-based stuffing for fish.

varieties

There are countless varieties of dates; they are rarely sold by name but the two sorts most likely to be encountered are the famous medjool (crinkly-skinned, mellow, sticky and sweet) and the noble deglet noor, 'date of light', which has a translucent, smooth skin, chewy texture and delicate flavour.

Usually we buy dates by type—namely, 'soft', 'semi-dry' or 'dry'. Soft dates, which are very fresh, have soft flesh, with a high moisture content and relatively low sugar levels. 'Semi-dry' (which are often erroneously labelled 'fresh dates') have firmer but still softish flesh, lower moisture and higher sugar content; these are 'soft' dates that have been partially dried to develop the sugars and extend shelf-life. 'Dry' or 'bread' dates, are quite hard and contain little moisture and loads of sugar. Dry dates are usually packaged and used extensively in western countries for baking.

trout stuffed with dates

serves 4

4 medium-sized trout
140 g (5 oz/1 cup) chopped fresh
  dates
45 g (1½ oz/¼ cup) cooked rice
1 onion, finely chopped
4 tablespoons chopped
  coriander (cilantro) leaves
¼ teaspoon ground ginger
¼ teaspoon ground cinnamon
50 g (1¾ oz/⅓ cup) roughly
  chopped blanched almonds
40 g (1½ oz) butter, softened
ground cinnamon, to dust

Preheat the oven to 180°C (350°F/Gas 4). Rinse the trout under cold running water and pat dry with paper towels. Season with sea salt and freshly ground black pepper.

Combine the dates, rice, half the onion, the coriander, ginger, cinnamon, almonds and half the butter in a bowl. Season well.

Spoon the stuffing into the fish cavities and put each fish on a well-greased double sheet of foil. Brush the fish with the remaining butter and divide the remaining onion among the four parcels. Wrap the fish neatly and seal the edges of the foil. Put the parcels on a large baking tray and bake for 15–20 minutes, or until cooked to your liking. Serve dusted with cinnamon.

dates poached in earl grey syrup

serves 2–4

2 Earl Grey tea bags
250 g (9 oz/1 cup) sugar
12 fresh dates
thick (double/heavy) cream or
  mascarpone cheese, to serve

Infuse the tea bags in 250 ml (9 fl oz/1 cup) of boiling water for 30 minutes.

Discard the tea bags and place the liquid in a small saucepan with the sugar. Stir over medium heat until the sugar has dissolved. Bring to the boil, then reduce heat and simmer for 10 minutes, without stirring.

Add the dates and cook for 2–3 minutes, turning once, until dates are tender. Serve with thick cream or mascarpone cheese.

sticky date pudding with caramel sauce

Preheat the oven to 180°C (350°F/Gas 4). Grease a deep 23 cm (9 inch) round spring-form cake tin and line the base with baking paper. Chop the dates and put them in a saucepan with 435 ml (15¼ fl oz/1¾ cups) water. Bring to the boil, then remove from the heat, add the bicarbonate of soda and ginger and leave to stand for 5 minutes.

Cream together the butter, sugar and 1 egg. Beat in the remaining eggs one at a time, mixing well after each addition. Fold in the sifted flour and mixed spice, add the date mixture and stir until well combined. Pour into the tin and bake 55–60 minutes, or until a skewer inserted into the centre of the pudding comes out clean. Cover with foil if overbrowning during cooking. Leave to stand for 5 minutes before turning out onto a serving plate.

To make the caramel sauce, stir all the ingredients in a saucepan over low heat until the sugar has dissolved. Simmer, uncovered, for about 3 minutes, or until thickened slightly. Brush some sauce over the top and sides of the pudding until well-glazed. Serve the pudding immediately with extra sauce and a dollop of crème fraîche.

370 g (13 oz/2 cups) fresh dates
1½ teaspoons bicarbonate of
   soda (baking soda)
1 teaspoon grated fresh ginger
90 g (3¼ oz) unsalted butter
250 g (9 oz/1 heaped cup) caster
   (superfine) sugar
3 eggs
185 g (6½ oz/1½ cups)
   self-raising flour
½ teaspoon mixed (pumpkin pie)
   spice
crème fraîche, to serve

caramel sauce
150 g (5½ oz) unsalted butter,
   cut into cubes
230 g (8 oz/1¼ cups) soft brown
   sugar
80 ml (2½ fl oz/⅓ cup) golden
   (maple) syrup
185 ml (6 fl oz/¾ cup) pouring
   (whipping) cream

stone fruit ∎ date

The date palm takes 30 years to mature, grows up to 30 metres (100 feet) and can live for up to 150 years—if it doesn't topple over first, which is commonly the way date palms die.

peach and nectarine

fruit ▪ **stone**
season ▪ **summer**

Raw fruit perfection doesn't come any more complete than a ripe, fragrant peach or nectarine, served in simple slices or eaten, complete with the inevitable drips and mess, out of sticky hands. Like apricots, these fragile stone fruits taste best when purchased as near to where they grow as possible as they bruise easily when transported and are most scrumptious when ripened on the tree.

Nectarines are no more than a subspecies of the peach and not, as is often supposed, a cross between a peach and a plum; essentially, the nectarine is a fuzz-free peach. Nectarine and peach trees are virtually indistinguishable from each other, producing the same leaves, buds and flowers. In fact, no more than a single recessive gene (the one for 'fuzzlessness') separates the two fruit. Nectarines and peaches come with either white or yellow flesh—purists claim that white fruits have a finer flavour.

varieties

In general, mid-to-late summer peach and nectarine varieties taste better than those first fruits of summer. There are dozens of types cultivated commercially and yet all too often, they are not sold by variety. Many of these stone fruits have very, very brief seasons, so as one disappears from the stands, another will take its place—you will need to purchase what's around and go back for more if you particularly love a variety you've discovered.

freestone Peaches and nectarines are classified as either freestone (slipstone) or clingstone. Freestone varieties, as the name implies, separate easily from their stone—all that is needed is to cut through to the stone, all the way around the fruit, then gently twist the cut halves in opposite directions and pull them off the stone. Freestone fruits are perfect when you wish to poach whole halves or if you want to roast, stuff or bake intact halves. If you plan to bottle quantities of fruits or make preserves, such as jams, chutneys or relishes, freestone fruits make preparation a breeze.
clingstone Clingstones will not yield their stones at all and the flesh must be cut away to separate it. Clingstones are fine when you want to serve whole, poached peaches, require a puree or wish to cook something else that doesn't require neat halves.

preparation

Nectarines don't need to be peeled, but fuzzy peaches do, especially if served poached or in pies, jams or ice creams. To peel clingstones, score a tiny cross at the base of each peach and plunge, a few at a time, into boiling water for 15–20 seconds. Using a slotted spoon, transfer each one carefully to a bowl of iced water to cool then peel away the skin.

To peel freestones, score the peach through the skin all the way around and right through to the stone then plunge into boiling water and iced water as above—the skin will easily peel off.

culinary uses

If they are to be cooked (and with the exception of a few chutney, salsa and savoury salad recipes), peaches and nectarines are best suited to sweet recipes. They are complemented well by the flavours of almonds, champagne, vanilla, raspberries, wine (poached in either white or red wine, these fruits are transcendental), dashes of cinnamon or cardamom, yoghurt and cream.

selection and storage

Choose unblemished specimens that give slightly to gentle pressure but don't feel too soft. Peaches in particular should smell sweetly fragrant when ripe so follow your nose when selecting them.

Both peaches and nectarines will soften at room temperature but not ripen once they are picked. Refrigerate ripe fruits for a day or so only and bring them to room temperature before serving, as their flavour is diminished by chilling.

stone fruit ■ peach and nectarine

makes 8

nectarine feuilletées

2 sheets butter puff pastry,
50 g (1¾ oz) unsalted butter,
  softened
55 g (2 oz/½ cup) ground
  almonds
½ teaspoon natural vanilla
  extract
5 large nectarines
55 g (2 oz/¼ cup) caster
  (superfine) sugar
110 g (3¾ oz/⅓ cup) apricot or
  peach jam, warmed and sieved

Preheat the oven to 200°C (400°F/Gas 6). Line two large baking trays with baking paper.

Cut the pastry sheets into eight 12 cm (4½ inch) rounds and put on the prepared trays. Combine the butter, ground almonds and vanilla extract, then stir to form a paste. Divide the paste among the pastry rounds and spread evenly, leaving a 1.5 cm (⅝ inch) border around the edge of each.

Halve the nectarines, remove the stones, then cut into 5 mm (¼ inch) slices. Arrange the nectarine slices over the pastry rounds, overlapping the slices and leaving a thin border. Sprinkle the sugar over the nectarines.

Bake for 15 minutes, or until the pastry is puffed and golden. Brush the nectarines and pastry with the warm jam while still hot. Serve hot or at room temperature.

serves 6

cointreau-glazed peaches

6 peaches
1–2 tablespoons soft brown
  sugar
80 ml (2½ fl oz/⅓ cup)
  Cointreau
250 g (9 oz/1 heaped cup)
  mascarpone cheese
ground nutmeg, to dust

Line a grill tray with foil and lightly grease the foil. Preheat the grill (broiler) to medium. Cut the peaches in half, remove the stones and place the peaches, cut side up, on the tray.

Sprinkle peaches with the sugar and Cointreau and grill for 6 minutes, or until the peaches are soft and the tops are glazed.

Serve immediately with dollops of mascarpone cheese, dusted lightly with ground nutmeg.

bottled peaches

Using a small sharp knife, score a small cross in the base of each peach. Put the peaches in a heatproof bowl and cover with boiling water. Leave for 30 seconds, then transfer to a bowl of cold water. Peel the peaches, cut in half and remove the stones. Cut each peach into 1.5 cm (5/8 inch) slices. Arrange the fruit in six 500 ml (17 fl oz/2 cups) hot sterilized airtight bottles.

To make a sugar syrup, put the sugar and 1.25 litres (44 fl oz/5 cups) water into a saucepan over low heat. Stir for 8–10 minutes, or until the sugar has dissolved. Bring to the boil and boil for 3 minutes. Cover the fruit with the hot syrup. Tap the bottles while filling to remove any air bubbles and carefully close the lids.

Put a folded tea (dish) towel on the base of a stockpot. Fill the pot with enough warm water to cover the bottles. Gradually bring the water to simmering point—this may take 30–35 minutes—then simmer steadily for 15 minutes. Do not allow the water to boil. Check the water level regularly and top up with boiling water, if required.

Remove the stockpot from the heat. Wear rubber gloves or use tongs to remove the bottles. Do not put any pressure on the lids. Allow to cool overnight, then label and date each bottle.

It is quite easy to breathe sweet life into slightly under-ripe peaches or nectarines or those lacking in flavour. Cut unpeeled seeded fruit into wedges, then pour boiling sugar syrup over them in a bowl—they will cook as they cool. Make the syrup interesting by making it half red wine and half water, and add a sprig of fresh rosemary and a cinnamon stick, or a few whole cloves and a couple of star anise.

2.5 kg (5 lb 8 oz) freestone (slipstone) peaches
375 g (13 oz/1¾ cups) sugar

stone fruit ■ peach and nectarine

poached vanilla peaches with raspberry puree and passionfruit sauce

serves 4

350 g (12 oz/1½ cups) caster (superfine) sugar
1 vanilla bean, halved lengthways
4 freestone (slipstone) peaches
100 g (3½ oz/heaped ¾ cup) raspberries
4 scoops vanilla ice cream

passionfruit sauce
60 ml (2 fl oz/¼ cup) passionfruit pulp (from about 4 passionfruit)
2 tablespoons caster (superfine) sugar

Put the sugar, vanilla bean and 625 ml (21½ fl oz/2½ cups) of water in a large saucepan. Stir over low heat for 8–10 minutes, or until the sugar has dissolved. Bring to a slow boil, then add the peaches and simmer for 5 minutes, or until the peaches are just tender and softened. Cool the peaches in the syrup, then remove with a slotted spoon. Peel and halve the peaches, removing the stones.

Put the raspberries in a food processor and process until pureed. Push the puree through a sieve, discarding the pulp.

To make the passionfruit sauce, combine the passionfruit pulp and the sugar in a small bowl and stir until the sugar has dissolved.

To serve, divide the raspberry puree between 4 glasses. Arrange a scoop of ice cream and two peach halves on top. Spoon over the passionfruit sauce and serve immediately.

The word peach is a corruption of the Latin persica, *meaning 'Persian', whereas nectarine comes from the Greek* nektar, *meaning 'sweet'. Both fruits are thought to have originated in China, where even today, mythology and symbology shroud the delicious peach. It is a potent symbol there for long life, and the word peach in Chinese was once slang for 'young bride'.*

plum

fruit ▪ **stone**
season ▪ summer–early autumn

In China, where they are believed to have first been cultivated, plums symbolize good fortune—the tree is favourably associated with age and wisdom.

Plums are a varied bunch. The skins of some are green, some yellow; others are pink, red or blue-black. The flesh varies widely in colour, texture, sweetness and juiciness; and depending upon variety, the fruit size and shape do too. Hence there are elongated and ovular or rotund and plump plums.

From damsons to mirabelles, gages to satsumas, the plum world is populated with a startling selection of fruits. They star in all manner of sweet and savoury dishes around the globe, from the ubiquitous pork in plum sauce found on many a Chinese restaurant menu, to Germany's repertoire of plum cakes. In the Balkans, plums are distilled to make the local high-octane beverage of choice, *slivovitz* (a brandy or schnapps made from bluish plums); the French use mirabelles to make an *eau de vie* (a clear brandy distillate made from fermented fruit juice, translating from the French as 'water of life') of the same name.

Nutritionally, plums are a good source of calcium, magnesium, vitamin A, iron, potassium and dietary fibre.

selection and storage

If lucky enough to find plums still covered with a silver, powdery bloom, snap them up as this indicates extreme freshness. Wash them just before using. When ripe, a plum should feel firm but not hard and be blemish-free.

Store ripe plums in the refrigerator and eat within a few days; unripe plums can be softened at room temperature, although they won't develop any more sweetness or flavour.

Choose larger, sweeter plum varieties for eating fresh or for use in desserts and baking—smaller, tart varieties are best used for savoury recipes or for preserving in sugar syrup.

The skins of all varieties can be sour, but will easily slip off, like those of tomatoes. To skin a plum, make a small cross-shaped incision at the base with a sharp knife, then plunge briefly into boiling water. Transfer to ice water immediately and gently pull back the skin.

Although plums freeze for up to 3–4 months, the stones can impart a strong bitter-almond aftertaste, so are best removed before freezing.

prunes

In dried form, plums are known as prunes. Unfortunately, prunes have come to be associated with bowel regulation (for which they were notoriously used by previous generations) and suffer a terrible image problem as a result. They are, however, utterly delicious and very versatile, and can be utilized in everything from a Persian-inspired savoury rice pilaf, stuffing for the Christmas turkey, a lightly-spiced fruit compote, or paired with almonds or hazelnuts in a fancy tart. Try plumping prunes in brandy, drain, then pat them dry and dip them in dark chocolate—you'll quite forget they're so good for you.

varieties

There are hundreds of cultivated plum varieties, which broadly fall into two main camps: European plums, which are said to come from the Caucasus and are mostly used for preserving and drying (making prunes, that is); and Japanese plums, which are actually the ones from China. The latter can be either eaten fresh or used in cooking. Japanese plums are generally round or heart-shaped and include all the blood plum varieties.

preparation

Plums can be peeled by first making a small, cross-shaped incision in their base, then plunging them briefly (in batches if dealing with quantities) in boiling water. Drain the plums, cool in a bowl of iced water and the skins will easily slip off. Depending on the size of the plums and their intended use, it may not be necessary to bother—when making puree or jam, for example, the skins can simply be sieved out. To remove the stones, most varieties require the flesh to be cut away, although some types have stones which, once the fruits are halved, are quite easily lifted out.

culinary uses

While juicy, sun-ripened plums require little embellishment, they also pair well with sweet spices, especially cardamom, cloves, ginger and star anise. More unusually, but just as successfully, plums team well with herbs such as mint, thyme and rosemary.

Plums also make wonderful pies, tarts, crumbles and can be baked into certain butter cakes. Pickled plums are excellent with pâtés and terrines, and their sweet, puckery flavour also complements the richness of pork, rabbit and duck. Plums make excellent jam but they don't contain much pectin, which helps jam set. When using them for jam, crack a few stones and remove their kernels, tie these in a muslin (cheesecloth) bag and add to the cooking jam to assist in setting.

plum sauce

makes 1 litre
(35 fl oz/4 cups)   97

Peel, core and chop the apple and place in a large saucepan with 125 ml (4 fl oz/½ cup) water. Cover and simmer for 10 minutes, or until the apple is soft. Cut the chillies in half lengthways. Remove the seeds then chop chillies finely. Add the plums, sugar, vinegar, onion, soy sauce, ginger, garlic and chilli to the saucepan.

Bring the mixture to the boil and cook, uncovered, over low heat for 45 minutes, stirring often. Remove the sauce from the pan and, using a wooden spoon, push it through a coarse sieve over a large bowl. Discard the solids. Rinse the pan, then return sauce to pan and bring to a boil.

Simmer the sauce over medium-high heat for 20 minutes, or until it has thickened slightly. The sauce will thicken even further on cooling. Pour immediately into hot sterilized jars and seal. Label and date each jar. Leave for 1 month for the flavours to develop. Store in a cool, dark place for up to 12 months. Once opened, sauce will keep in the refrigerator for up to 6 weeks. Plum sauce is delicious with beef or pork spareribs, or Chinese barbecued pork and duck.

1 large green apple
2 red chillies
1.25 kg (2 lb 12 oz) plums, halved and stones removed
460 g (1 lb/2½ cups) soft brown sugar
375 ml (13 fl oz/1½ cups) white wine vinegar
1 onion, grated
60 ml (2 fl oz/¼ cup) soy sauce
2 tablespoons fresh ginger, finely chopped
2 garlic cloves, crushed

stone fruit ■ plum

makes 1

plum and rosemary flat bread

60 ml (2 fl oz/1/4 cup) warm milk
7 g (1/4 oz or 2 teaspoons)
   instant dried yeast
115 g (4 oz/1/2 cup) caster
   (superfine) sugar
2 eggs, lightly beaten
grated zest of 1 lemon
2 teaspoons finely chopped
   rosemary
185 g (61/2 oz/11/4 cups) white
   bread (strong) flour
150 g (51/2 oz) usalted butter, cut
   into cubes, softened
10 plums, halved and stoned
whipped cream or mascarpone
   cheese, to serve

Grease a 25 cm (10 inch) spring-form cake tin or loose-based tart tin with butter. Combine the milk and yeast in the bowl of an electric mixer. Stir in 55 g (2 oz/1/4 cup) of the sugar, the eggs, lemon zest and 1 teaspoon of the rosemary, then add the flour. Using the beater attachment, mix for 1 minute, or until a soft dough forms. Add the butter, then continue mixing for a further minute, or until the dough is smooth and shiny. Alternatively, mix the dough by hand using a wooden spoon.

Spoon into the prepared tin and cover with plastic wrap. Leave in a draught-free place for 11/2–2 hours, or until doubled in size.

Knock back the dough by punching it gently. Dampen the palms of your hands with water and press the dough into the edge of the tin. Arrange the plums, cut side up, over the top, pressing them gently into the dough. Leave for 30 minutes. Meanwhile, preheat the oven to 200°C (400°F/Gas 6).

Sprinkle the plums with the remaining sugar and scatter over the remaining rosemary. Bake for 10 minutes, then reduce the oven to 180°C (350°F/Gas 4) and bake for a further 20 minutes, or until light golden and slightly spongy when pressed in the centre. Serve warm, cut into wedges, with cream or mascarpone cheese.

plum cobbler

Preheat the oven to 180°C (350°F/Gas 4). Lightly grease a 2 litre (70 fl oz/8 cup) baking dish. Cut the plums into quarters, discarding the stones.

Put the plums in a saucepan with 60 g (2¼ oz/¼ cup) sugar and 1 tablespoon of water. Stir over low heat for 5 minutes, or until the sugar dissolves and the fruit softens slightly. Spread the plum mixture into the prepared dish.

Sift the flours into a bowl, add the remaining sugar and stir to combine. Rub in the butter, using your fingertips, until the mixture is fine and crumbly. In a separate bowl, combine the egg and milk and whisk until smooth. Stir into the flour mixture until a soft dough forms.

Drop large spoonfuls of mixture on top of the plums, until the plums are covered or all the mixture has been used. Bake for 30–40 minutes, or until the top is golden and cooked through. Dust with icing sugar before serving.

750 g (1 lb 10 oz or about 10) plums
120 g (4¼ oz/½ cup) caster (superfine) sugar
125 g (4½ oz/1 cup) self-raising flour
60 g (2¼ oz/½ cup) plain (all-purpose) flour
125 g (4½ oz) unsalted butter, chopped
1 egg
125 ml (4 fl oz/½ cup) milk
icing (confectioners') sugar, to dust

stone fruit ■ plum

banana

fruit ■ tropical
season ■ available year-round

selection and storage

Bananas are harvested when they register about 20 per cent starch content and one per cent sugar content and continue to ripen until their starches have all converted to fructose, sucrose and glucose. So you can buy quite green fruit and it will quickly turn to sunny yellow at ambient room temperature.

Bananas are at their most flavoursome when the skin is lightly flecked with black spots. Fruit that has become over-ripe (very brown or verging on black) is perfect for baking in cakes, breads or muffins.

Bananas can be refrigerated although this does turn the skin an unappealing black colour—very ripe fruit can also be pureed then frozen and used, thawed, in baking.

If possible, store bananas away from other ripe fruits, as they produce ethylene, which will cause fruit or vegetables sitting near them to ripen prematurely.

How exotic the banana must have appeared to those Europeans who first encountered them and who so enthusiastically helped their global infiltration. Bananas are believed to be native to Malaysia, from where they travelled to India. It is here that Alexander the Great is reputed to have tasted them around 327 BC and subsequently introduced them to the Western world. The Portuguese, slave dealers, Arabic traders (the word *banan* is Arabic for 'finger')—everyone, it seems, had a hand in their spread.

Technically, the banana tree is a herb, the world's largest in fact, and is related to plants like grasses, palms and orchids.

varieties

The vast majority of bananas available are the cavendish variety. This is a longish, thin-skinned, pale-fleshed and sweet banana that is favoured by growers because it is particularly disease-resistant, although it does bruise easily. Other varieties include red bananas, with the reddish-brown skin and red-tinged, firm flesh, and the particularly sweet, flavoursome and fragrant lady's finger.

The vast majority of commercially-produced bananas are plantains, the hard, green-skinned cooking banana. In many cultures they are treated as a vital starch food crop in a similar fashion to the way the potato is in other cuisines. Plantains have tough flesh that turns from green to black as they ripen, although they can be cooked whether ripe or unripe—they just can't be eaten raw.

tropical fruit ■ banana

banana and plum crumble

serves 4

30 g (1 oz/¼ cup) plain
(all-purpose) flour
50 g (1¾ oz/½ cup) rolled
(porridge) oats
30 g (1 oz/½ cup) shredded
coconut
45 g (1¾ oz/¼ cup) soft brown
sugar
finely grated zest of 1 lime
100 g (3½ oz) unsalted butter,
cut into cubes
2 bananas, peeled and halved
lengthways
4 plums, halved and stones
removed
60 ml (2 fl oz/¼ cup) lime juice
pouring (whipping) cream or
vanilla ice cream, to serve

Preheat the oven to 180°C (350°F/Gas 4). Combine the flour, rolled oats, coconut, sugar and zest in a small bowl. Add the butter and, using your fingertips, rub the butter into the flour mixture until crumbly.

Put the bananas and plums in a 1.25 litre (44 fl oz/5 cup) capacity ovenproof dish, pour over the lime juice and then toss to coat. Sprinkle the crumble mixture evenly over the fruit. Bake for 25–30 minutes, or until the crumble is golden. Serve hot with vanilla ice cream or cream.

bananas foster

serves 4

2 bananas, thickly sliced
1 tablespoon unsalted butter
1 tablespoon soft brown sugar
1 tablespoon rum
vanilla ice cream, to serve

Melt the butter in a large frying pan, add the bananas, then cook over medium-high heat, turning bananas to coat. Add the sugar and fry until bananas are caramelized. Sprinkle with the rum. Divide the bananas between bowls and serve with vanilla ice cream.

banana bread

Preheat the oven to 180°C (350°F/Gas 4). Grease and line the base and side of a 23 x 13 x 6 cm (9 x 5 x 2½ inch) loaf (bar) tin. Sift together the flour, baking powder, mixed spice and ¼ teaspoon salt into a bowl.

In a separate bowl, cream the butter and sugar using electric beaters until pale and fluffy. Add the eggs gradually, mixing well after each addition, and beat until smooth. Mix in the banana. Add the dry ingredients in several batches and stir the mixture until smooth.

Pour into the prepared loaf tin and bake on the middle shelf of the oven for 35–45 minutes, or until a skewer inserted into the centre of the bread comes out clean. Cool in the tin for 10 minutes before turning out onto a wire rack. Serve warm or at room temperature. Bread will keep for up to 3 days covered in plastic wrap in an airtight container.

250 g (9 oz/2 cups) plain (all-purpose) flour
2 teaspoons baking powder
1 teaspoon mixed (pumpkin pie) spice
150 g (5½ oz) unsalted butter, softened
185 g (6½ oz/1 cup) soft brown sugar
2 eggs, lightly beaten
240 g (8½ oz/1 cup) mashed very ripe banana

tropical fruit ■ banana

Americans first sampled the banana in 1876, in Pennsylvania, as part of the celebrations for the 100th anniversary of the signing of the Declaration of Independence. The Domestic Cyclopaedia of Practical Information, *published in the 1870s, advised that bananas should be 'eaten raw … with sugar and cream or wine and orange juice. They are also roasted, fried or boiled and are made into fritters, preserves and marmalades.'*

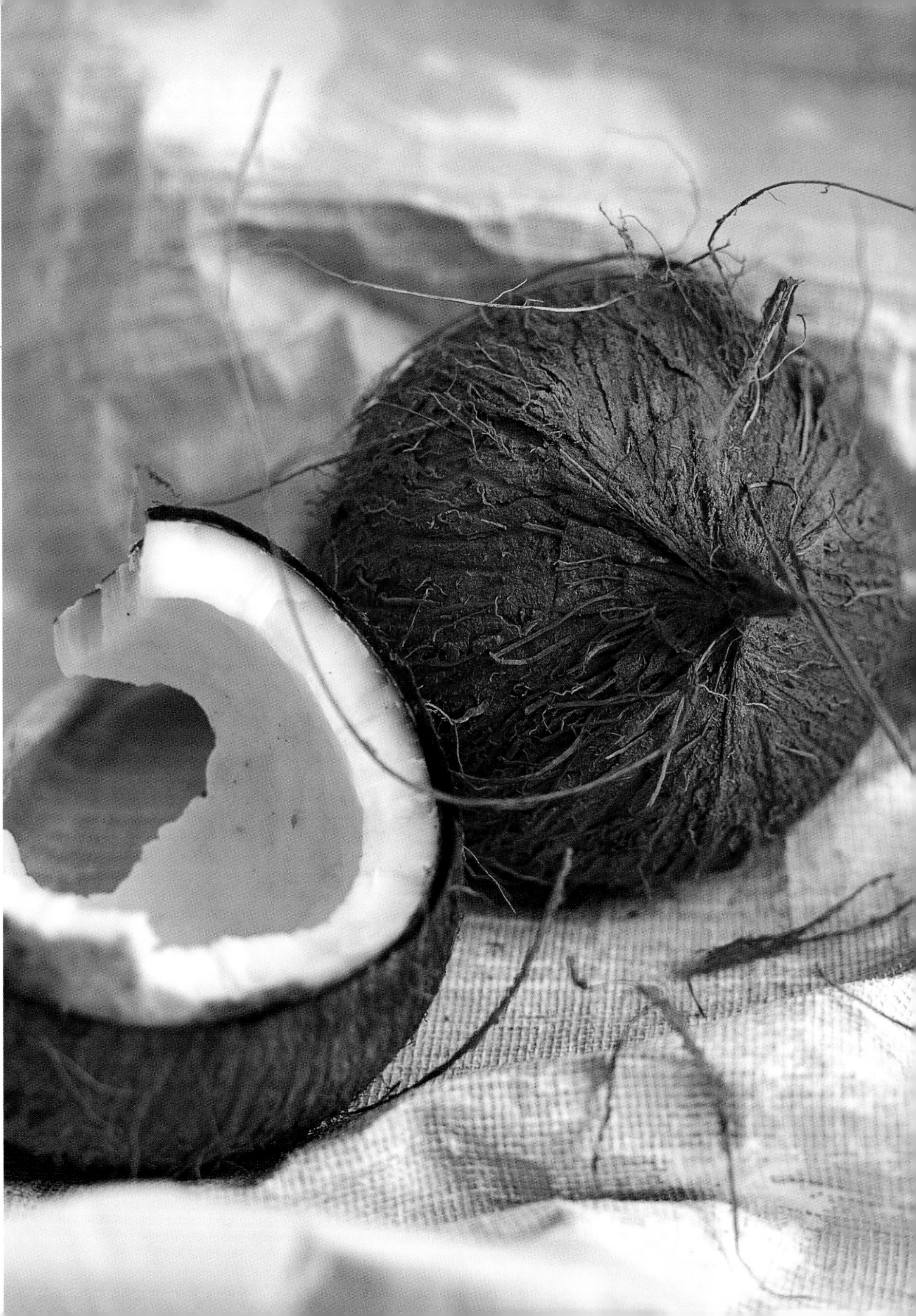

coconut

The coconut is a culinary marauder. It started life in India then, thanks to ocean currents and its ability to bob over vast stretches of water, made its way around the world, insinuating itself into every tropical region one could care to name. The Portuguese introduced the coconut to Brazil and the Spanish took it to the Caribbean, thereby completing the worldwide coconut invasion. Today, there are about 10 million hectares (25 million acres) of the nut planted around the world.

preparation

Punch through two of the 'eyes' (place a screwdriver in each hole and deal it a heavy blow with a hammer) then drain it of the liquid, which can be used for drinking or in cooking. To facilitate the easy removal of the flesh, bake the coconut in a 180°C (350°F/Gas 4) oven for 20 minutes, then cool. Crack the coconut open using a hammer. Peel away the brown skin from the meat using a potato peeler or small, sharp knife—partially frozen pieces are particularly easy to peel using this method.

culinary uses

Coconuts can be eaten when young (about six months old) when their meat is soft and has a fruity, nutty flavour. In this form, coconuts are commonly used in drinks, desserts or just scraped out and eaten with a spoon. Mature coconut flesh, intrinsic to many Asian cuisines, is used (mainly grated) in salads, fresh chutneys, curries, soups and coconut milk. Freshly grated it is wonderful in cakes, biscuits and desserts, being infinitely sweeter and mellower in flavour than its dried counterpart.

selection and storage

Choose a coconut that feels heavy and sloshes with liquid when you shake it. Coconuts take about 12 months to mature on a plam tree, after which time they weigh about 2.5 kilograms (5 lb 8 oz), although half of this weight is shell and husk. The three 'eyes' on top of the nut should be uniformly dark and there should be no mould on the husk.

The meat can be used immediately or stored, frozen in plastic bags, for up to 1 month.

A coconut of average size will yield about 300 g (10½ oz) of grated fresh coconut.

coconut chutney

1 teaspoon gram lentils
  (chana dhal)
1 teaspoon black lentils
  (black urad dhal)
½ coconut, flesh grated
2 green chillies, seeded and
  chopped
½ teaspoon salt
1 tablespoon oil
1 teaspoon black mustard seeds
5 curry leaves
1 teaspoon tamarind puree

Soak the lentils in cold water for 2 hours, then drain well.

Put the grated coconut, chillies and salt in a food processor, or in a mortar with a pestle, and process or pound to a smooth paste.

Heat the oil in a small saucepan and add the black mustard seeds and the lentils, then cover and shake the pan until the seeds pop. Add the curry leaves and fry for 1 minute, or until the lentils brown. Combine with the coconut mixture and add the tamarind puree, stirring to mix well. Serve on the side with spicy meat dishes.

mango and coconut salad

300 g (10½ oz) grated coconut
  (about 1 coconut)
2 dried chillies, seeded and
  chopped
1 tablespoon grated palm sugar
  (jaggery) or soft brown sugar
300 g (10½ oz) ripe mango
  flesh, cut into cubes
1 tablespoon oil
½ teaspoon coriander seeds
½ teaspoon black mustard
  seeds
6 curry leaves

Put the coconut, chilli and palm sugar in a blender then process with just enough water to make a thick, coarse paste. If you don't have a blender, crush everything together in a mortar using a pestle, adding a little water as necessary. Transfer the paste to a bowl, add the mango and toss to combine. Season to taste, cover with plastic wrap, then refrigerate.

Heat the oil in a small frying pan over low heat and add the coriander, mustard seeds and curry leaves. Cover and shake the pan until the seeds start to pop. Pour the oil and seeds over the mango mixture and stir to coat mango. Serve with southern Indian-style curries or as an accompaniment to grilled fish or chicken.

coconut cream and milk

makes 125 ml (4 fl oz/1/2 cup)
coconut cream or 250 ml
(9 fl oz/1 cup) coconut milk   107

300 g (10½ oz) grated coconut
(about 1 coconut)

Drain the coconut by punching a hole in two of the dark-coloured eyes. Drain out the liquid and use it as a refreshing drink. Holding the coconut in one hand, tap around the circumference firmly with a hammer or pestle. This should cause the coconut to split open evenly. If the coconut doesn't crack easily, put it in a 150°C (300°F/Gas 2) oven for 15 minutes. This may cause it to crack as it cools. If it doesn't it will crack easily with a hammer.

If you don't have a coconut grater, prise the flesh out of the shell, trim off the hard brown outer skin and either grate by hand on a box grater or chop in a food processor. If you would like to use a coconut grater, the easiest ones to use are the ones that you sit on at one end, then scrape out the coconut from each half on the serrated edge, catching the grated coconut meat in a large bowl. Grated coconut can be frozen in small portions until it is needed.

Mix the grated coconut with 125 ml (4 fl oz/½ cup) hot water and leave to steep for 5 minutes. Pour the mixture into a container through a sieve lined with muslin (cheesecloth), then gather the muslin into a ball to squeeze out any remaining liquid. This will make a thick coconut milk, which is usually called coconut cream.

Repeat this process with another 250 ml (9 fl oz/1 cup) hot water to make a thinner coconut milk.

tropical fruit ■ coconut

For other coconut recipes see:

kiwi fruit

The kiwi fruit is properly called the Chinese gooseberry and is native to China, but New Zealand growers and marketers who championed the fruit and produced the first serious commercial offerings of it are responsible for the name we all know today. Kiwi fruit grows on vines and is typically harvested in autumn when still hard—the fruit can be cool-stored for up to 6 months and travels well, continuing to ripen to full softness after picking.

There are two types of kiwi fruit available—the furry-skinned sort with its startlingly green interior and the less common yellow-fleshed kiwi fruit, which is a recently developed cultivar. This type has smooth, bronze-coloured skin and a pointed cap at one end.

selection and storage

Buy kiwi fruit quite firm and you'll be able to keep them in the refrigerator for 4–5 weeks—bring them out to ripen at room temperature when you want sweet, soft, lush fruit.

To speed ripening, put kiwi fruit in a paper bag at room temperature with a banana or an apple, as these fruits produce ethylene gas which accelerates fruit ripening.

When ripe, kiwi fruit should give slightly when pressed and can be eaten simply cut in half and the flesh scooped out with a teaspoon. Steer clear of overly soft fruit or any whose skins are wrinkled, as this indicates they are well and truly past their prime.

preparation

Use kiwi fruit in breakfast drinks such as smoothies, in fruit salads, or sliced to decorate sponge cake, fruit tarts or pavlova. An excess can be turned into jam or chutney but use ever-so-slightly under-ripe fruit for the best flavour. Kiwi fruit contains an enzyme that dissolves protein—hence it is used commercially as a meat tenderizer. Never use it uncooked (cooking destroys the enzyme) in dairy-based recipes; it will attack milk proteins and turn them bitter.

pavlova with kiwi fruit

Preheat the oven to 160°C (315°F/Gas 2–3). Line a 32 x 28 cm (13 x 11¼ inch) baking tray with baking paper.

Put the egg whites and a pinch of salt in a large, clean, dry stainless steel or glass bowl—any hint of grease will prevent the egg whites foaming. Using electric beaters, whisk slowly until the whites start to become foamy, then increase the speed until the bubbles in the foam have become small and even-sized. Continue whisking until stiff peaks form, then add the sugar gradually, whisking constantly after each addition, until the mixture is thick and glossy and all the sugar has dissolved. Don't overbeat or the mixture will become grainy.

Using a metal spoon, fold in the sifted cornflour and the vinegar. Spoon the mixture into a mound on the prepared tray. Lightly flatten the top of the pavlova and smooth the sides; pavlova should have a cake shape and be about 2.5 cm (1 inch) high. Bake for 1 hour, or until pale cream and crisp on the outside. Remove from the oven while warm, carefully turn upside down onto a plate and cool to room temperature.

Lightly whip the cream until soft peaks form and spread over the pavlova. Decorate with passionfruit pulp and sliced kiwi fruit. Cut into wedges to serve.

note The addition of cornflour and vinegar gives the meringue a marshmallow-soft centre.

4 egg whites, at room
    temperature
250 g (9 oz/1 cup) caster
    (superfine) sugar
2 teaspoons cornflour
    (cornstarch)
1 teaspoon white vinegar
250 ml (9 fl oz/1 cup) pouring
    (whipping) cream
pulp from 3 passionfruit,
    to decorate
2 kiwi fruit, skinned and sliced,
    to decorate

tropical fruit ■ kiwi fruit

For other kiwi fruit recipes see:
tropical sprout salad 275

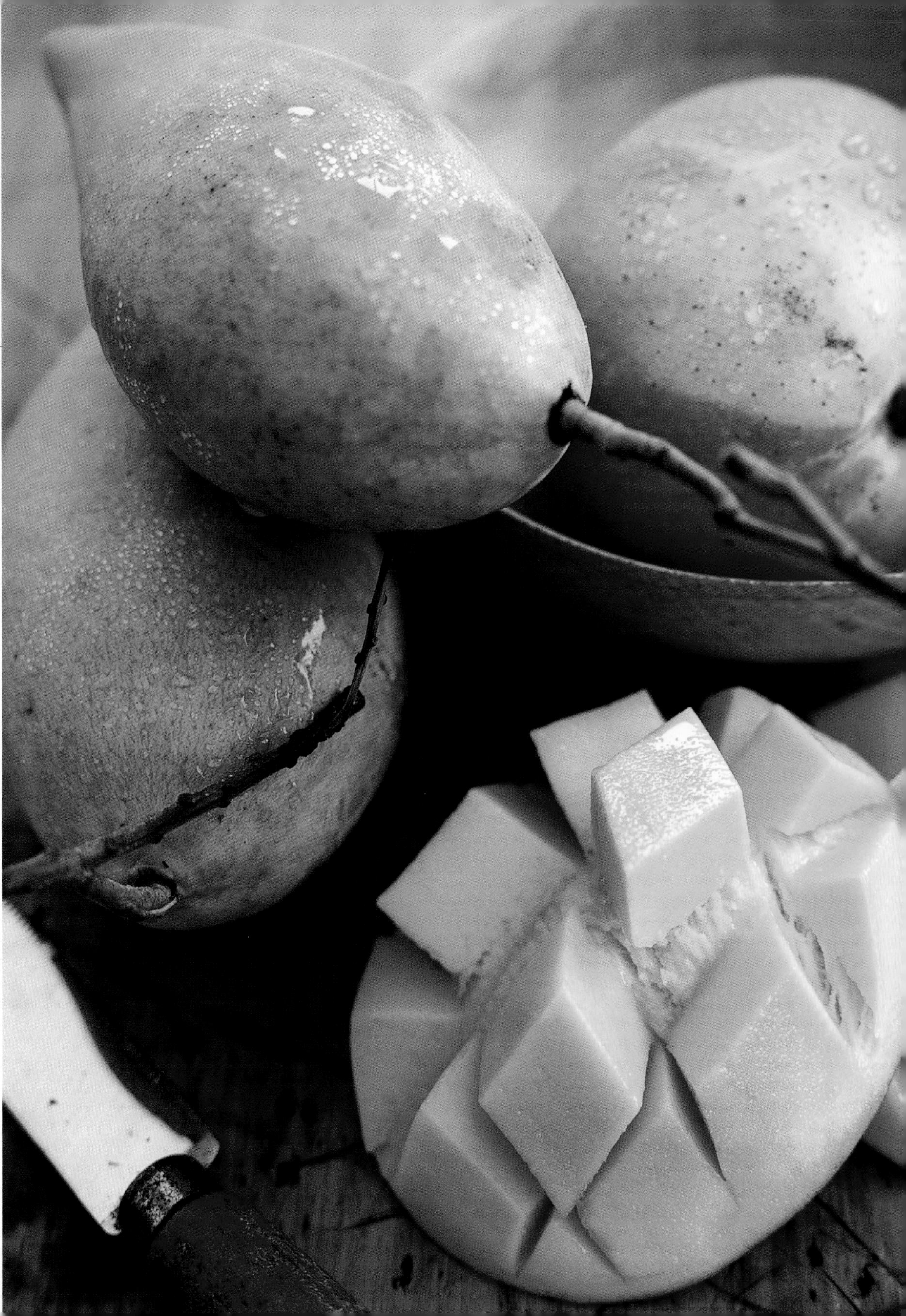

mango

The mango is referred to as 'the king of fruits' and rightly so. 'For taste, the nectarine, peach and apricot fall short', exclaimed Englishman Dr John Fryer upon sampling a mango in seventeenth-century India, and fans of the fruit have been heaping on the accolades ever since.

There are hundreds of varieties of mango in existence and these vary in size from plum-small to the gigantic keitt mango, whose fruit weigh in at around 2 kilograms (4 lb 8 oz). Mango skin ranges in hue from yellow, orange, red, blush-pink, green to a patchy mix of these colours. The majority of the world's mangoes are grown in India where they play a sacred role and are considered a potent symbol of love; on holy days, Hindus even brush their teeth with twigs from the mango tree.

Mangoes don't just taste glorious, they are terribly good for you too. Low in calories, extremely high in fibre, mangoes are also rich sources of betacarotene plus minerals like potassium, magnesium and antioxidants as well as vitamins A, B and C. They contain an enzyme, similar to papain in papaya, that aids digestion and is reputed to add to that undeniable feeling of contentment that eating a mango brings.

selection and storage

The size of a mango depends upon type, not quality or ripeness, so check the varietal characteristics with your supplier.

When ripe, mangoes should yield slightly to pressure and their stem end should emit sweet, fragrant, tropical smells. According to type, the skin colour will deepen and may develop pink or red patches. Black speckles on the skin can indicate damaged flesh underneath or over-ripeness; avoid fruits with loose or wrinkled skin as these are past their best.

Under-ripe fruit will continue to ripen at room temperature, and once ripe, should be stored in the refrigerator and used within 1–2 days.

green mangoes

In Southeast Asia green mangoes are used in refreshing salads, curries, chutneys and other savoury preparations. Green-skinned, with hard, pale flesh, they are prepared by peeling off the skin with a small sharp knife then either coarsely grating the flesh or cutting it off the stone in very thin slices and then into fine matchsticks.

Green mango has a pleasantly tart, fruity flavour which combines well with lime juice, palm sugar (jaggery), prawns, chicken, peanuts, chilli and fresh Asian herbs such as coriander and Thai basil. Amchoor (mango powder), a fragrant Indian seasoning made from ground, dried green mangoes, is also used widely as a meat tenderizer.

Green mangoes can be used in the same ways as green papaya (see pages 116–117).

varieties

It is estimated there are about 350 varieties of mangoes cultivated commercially—these are sometimes, but not always, sold by variety so if not, ask your supplier to identify the type. The variables between varieties are their sweetness, amount of fibre in their flesh, the flesh-to-stone ratio and their size. Some of the more popular varieties are listed below.

keitt An Indian strain of mango producing prodigiously large fruit with an oval shape and a slightly tapering protruberance above the tip. It has lush, firm flesh, minimal fibre and thick skin that remains green even when it is fully ripe.

kensington pride Also known as bowen, this orange-skinned variety (blushing red when ripe) is popular in Australia. Fruits are large with particularly juicy flesh and have a slightly tangy flavour. The flesh has minimal fibre.

kent Fruits are large with plum cheeks and form a regular oval shape. When ripe the skin is yellow with red shoulders, while the flesh is very sweet, fibre-free and butter-soft.

nam doc mai This mango is small-medium in size and has a fattish, slipper shape with a long, thin stone. Traditionally used green in salads, curries and chutneys, this mango is also prized for its deep, slightly acid and sweet flavours when fully ripe.

R2E2 A recently-developed Australian hybrid, initially exported to Asia, R2E2 is an enormous fruit with thin orange skin. It has a very sweet flavour with a high flesh-to-stone ratio.

tommy atkins One of the most common mango varieties, with oval, medium to large fruit that has thick skin, a mild flavour and more fibrous flesh than most others.

preparation

The mango has a large, central seed that clings to the flesh—you need to cut the 'cheeks' away from this. The most effective method is to hold the mango with a narrow side facing you. Using a large, sharp serrated knife, cut from the top down to the base of one side, feeling with your knife for the stone as you go and trying to cut as close to the stone as possible to remove the cheek. Repeat with the other side of the mango—the flesh left clinging to the stone is generally considered the 'cook's treat'.

Use a sharp knife to score deep parallel cuts in the flesh of each cheek, then score the flesh in the other direction to form square-shapes—the mango cheek can then be pushed inside out and the little squares easily removed for further preparation or just eaten as is, with a teaspoon.

mango, coconut and almond tart

To make the pastry, put the flour, sugar, ground almonds and butter in a food processor. Process until the mixture resembles fine crumbs. Add the egg yolks and process until smooth. Add the water, ½ teaspoon at a time, until a firm dough forms. Flatten the dough to a rectangle shape, wrap in plastic wrap and refrigerate for 30 minutes.

Preheat the oven to 190°C (375°F/Gas 5). Grease a 19 x 27 cm (7½ x 10¾ inch) loose-based tart tin.

To make the filling, cream the butter and sugar with electric beaters for about 3 minutes. Add the eggs, one at a time, beating well after each addition. Fold in the ground almonds, flour and desiccated coconut. Gently stir in the coconut cream and coconut liqueur.

Roll out the pastry on a sheet of baking paper until large enough to line the base and side of the tin. Ease it into the tin, pressing gently to fit, and trim any excess. Line the pastry with baking paper and pour in some baking beads or uncooked rice. Bake for 10 minutes, remove the paper and beads and bake for another 5 minutes. Reduce the temperature to 170°C (325°F/Gas 3).

Cut the cheeks from the mango, remove the cheek from each piece with a large spoon and cut the flesh into 3 mm (⅛ inch) thick slices. Spread the filling in the pastry case and arrange the mango slices in two rows down the length of the filling. Scatter the flaked coconut over the top and press it into the exposed filling with your fingertips, giving an uneven surface. Bake for 30 minutes, or until the coconut begins to brown, then cover loosely with foil. Bake for another 35 minutes, or until the filling is set and the top is golden brown. Serve warm with ice cream.

almond pastry

210 g (7½ oz/1⅔ cups) plain (all-purpose) flour
60 g (2¼ oz/¼ cup) caster (superfine) sugar
25 g (1 oz/¼ cup) ground almonds
150 g (5½ oz) unsalted butter, chilled and cut into cubes
2 egg yolks, at room temperature
1–2 tablespoons iced water

filling

185 g (6½ oz) unsalted butter, softened
185 g (6½ oz/heaped ¾ cup) caster (superfine) sugar
2 eggs, at room temperature
70 g (2½ oz/⅔ cup) ground almonds
60 g (2¼ oz/½ cup) plain (all-purpose) flour
90 g (3¼ oz/1 cup) desiccated coconut
2 tablespoons coconut cream
1 tablespoon coconut liqueur
1 mango
30 g (1 oz/½ cup) shaved coconut
ice cream or whipped cream, to serve

mango ice cream

serves 6

400 g (14 oz) fresh mango flesh
125 g (4½ oz/⅔ cup) caster
   (superfine) sugar
3 tablespoons mango or apricot
   nectar
250 ml (9 fl oz/1 cup) pouring
   (whipping) cream
mango slices, extra, to serve

Put the mango in a food processor and process until smooth. Transfer the mango puree to a bowl and add the sugar and nectar. Stir until the sugar has dissolved.

Beat the cream in a small bowl until stiff peaks form and then gently fold into the mango mixture. Spoon into a shallow loaf (bar) tin, cover and freeze for 1½ hours or until half frozen. Quickly spoon the mixture into a food processor and process for 30 seconds, or until smooth. Return the mixture to the tin or a plastic container, then cover and freeze completely. Remove the ice cream from the freezer 15 minutes before serving to allow it to soften a little. Serve the ice cream in scoops with some extra fresh mango if desired.

mango lassi

serves 4

2 large mangoes
500 g (1 lb 2 oz/2 cups) Greek-
   style yoghurt
2 teaspoons lemon juice
3–4 tablespoons caster
   (superfine) sugar, to taste
ice cubes, optional, to serve
extra diced mango, to serve

Prepare the mangoes by slicing off the cheeks with a sharp knife. Using a large spoon, scoop the flesh from the skin. Cut the flesh into chunks and put in a blender with the yoghurt, lemon juice and 3 tablespoons of sugar.

Add 185 ml (6 fl oz/¾ cup) of cold water and blend for 40–60 seconds, or until smooth. Taste for sweetness and add extra sugar, if desired.

Put some ice cubes, if using, in the bottom of four glasses. Pour the lassi over the top and serve immediately, topped with diced mango.

papaya

The papaya plant (technically not a tree but a rather tall herb) is a prolific bearer of fruit. Hanging like pendulous melons under a canopy of leaves, from a slim, branchless trunk, the fruit varies in size and skin colour—from green to pink, orange or yellow.

Papayas grow prodigiously throughout tropical and semi-tropical regions of the world from where they are exported widely to cooler climates. They are a thin-skinned fruit and susceptible to damage so are harvested unripe, for travel.

There are two main varieties you will likely encounter—the larger, pear-shaped yellow papaya, with its orange, slightly pungent-smelling flesh and the smaller, sweeter, rose-fleshed type.

culinary uses

The taste of a ripe papaya is unforgettable—at once musky, sweet, the merest touch bitter, and distinctly floral. The crinkly black seeds, which tend to be discarded, are perfectly edible, and possess a black-pepper flavour. The soft flesh is best enjoyed raw, tossed through fruit salads, whipped into orange-based drinks or just spooned directly from its skin.

Papaya has a particular affinity for the flavours of lemon, lime, chilli and ginger. Like mango, hard, unripe green papaya is much-used throughout Southeast Asia as a vegetable; it mainly appears shredded in salads, dressed, like green mango, with the tart, spicy, sweet flavours of lime juice, fish sauce, palm sugar (jaggery), chilli and garlic. Once skinned and seeded it can be used in the same ways as green mangoes (see page 112).

selection and storage

Before buying papaya be aware that it is often marketed as 'pawpaw'—the pawpaw is in fact a wild American fruit completely unrelated to the papaya—the confusion is likely to have sprung from the fact that throughout the Caribbean, papayas are called 'pawpaws'.

Papayas continue to ripen once picked (leave in a dark place at room temperature for several days to ripen) but their flavour suffers when not fully tree-ripened. When ripe, the skin, which will have lost all trace of green and may have a spotty appearance, will yield to gentle pressure (about the same amount as that of a ripe avocado).

Use ripe papaya within 2 days, storing it in the refrigerator and covering any cut portions in plastic wrap.

green papaya and peanut salad

Pound the dried shrimp in a mortar using a pestle, or chop finely.

Cook the beans in a saucepan of boiling water for 2 minutes. Drain and then plunge them into iced water; drain again. Shred the lettuce and arrange it on a serving plate. Top with the shrimp, beans and papaya.

Combine the lime juice, fish sauce, sugar and chilli in a small bowl; mix well. Pour over the salad and sprinkle the peanuts and extra chilli over the top.

note When grating papaya, lightly oil your hands or wear gloves as it can be very sticky and hard to wash off.

50 g (1¾ oz) dried shrimp
100 g (3½ oz) green beans, trimmed and cut into short pieces
1 head lettuce
½ green papaya or green mango, peeled and grated
60 ml (2 fl oz/¼ cup) lime juice
2 tablespoons fish sauce
2 teaspoons soft brown sugar
1–2 teaspoons chopped red chilli
80 g (2¾ oz/½ cup) unsalted roasted peanuts, chopped
1 small red chilli, extra, finely chopped

tropical fruit ∎ papaya

papaya lime fool

serves 4

Peel the papayas, remove the seeds and mash the flesh until smooth. Do not do this in a food processor or the puree will be too thin. Add the lime juice and vanilla sugar, to taste— the amount will vary according to the sweetness of the fruit.

Whisk the cream until soft peaks form, then fold through the mashed papaya. Spoon into serving glasses and chill until ready to serve.

variation 500 g (1 lb 2 oz) stewed rhubarb can be substituted for the papaya. If using rhubarb, replace the lime with the same amount of orange juice.

2 ripe papaya
1–2 tablespoons lime juice
3 tablespoons vanilla sugar
315 ml (10¾ fl oz/1¼ cups) pouring (whipping) cream

For other papaya recipes see:
tropical sprout salad 275

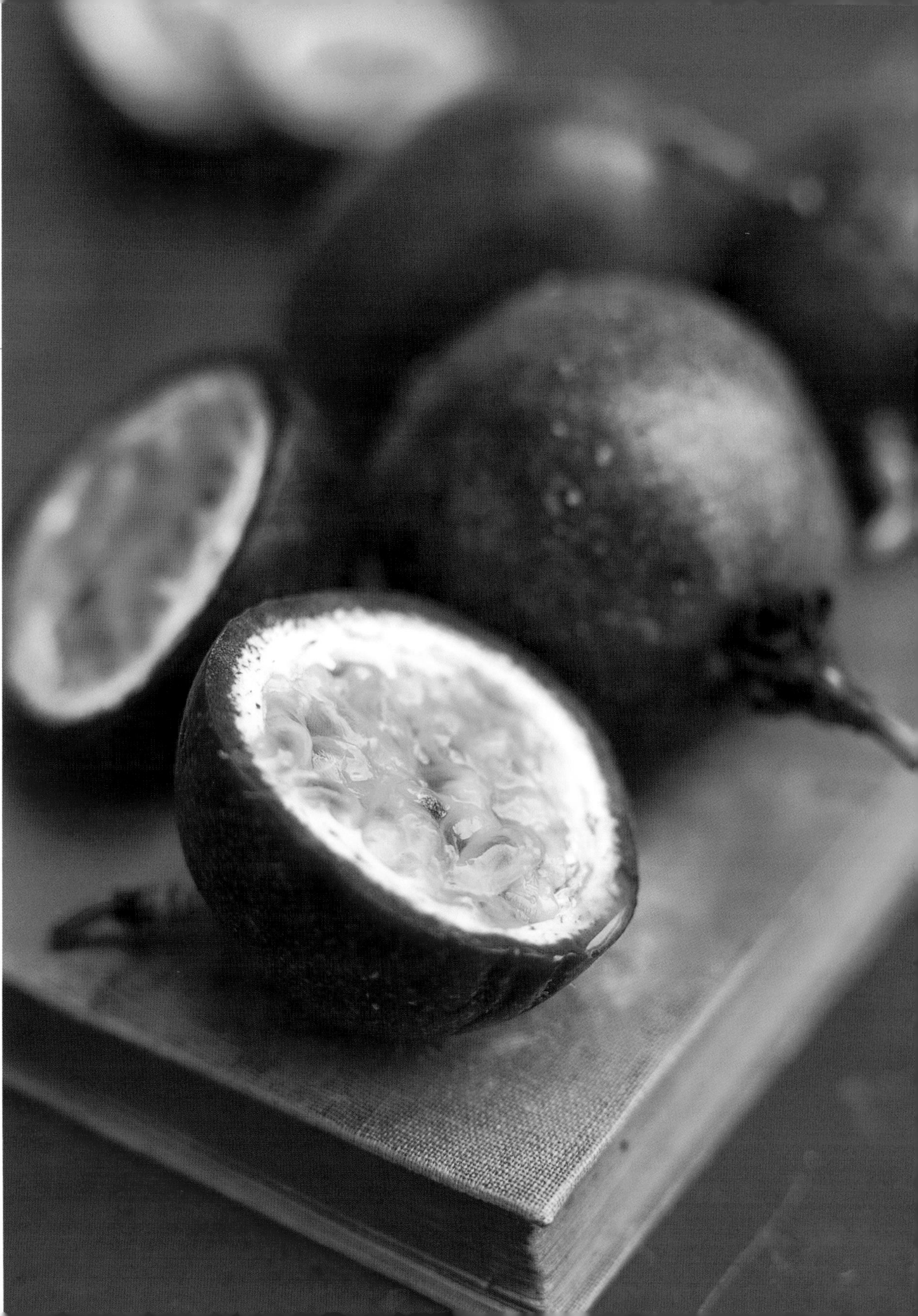

passionfruit

fruit ▪ tropical
season ▪ late summer–early autumn

The haunting flavour of the passionfruit defines for many the true taste of the tropics. This most unusual fruit, with its tough, protective exterior and seed-filled, pulpy and intensely fragrant interior, is known to us via a couple of edible varieties—there are many more in South America but these either don't travel well or are poisonous (the *Passiflora* genus is associated with cyanide). There's the small purple sort, also called 'purple granadilla', and the smoother-skinned yellow variety, which is larger but has less flavour than the purple passionfruit.

preparation

Although the seeds are perfectly edible, for some recipes it is necessary to strain them out; this can be done by simply pushing the pulp through a sieve using a ladle or the back of a spoon, pressing firmly on the seeds to extract as much juice as possible.

Roughly speaking, 10 ripe passionfruit will yield around 250 g (9 oz/1 cup) of pulp and about 125 ml (4 fl oz/1/2 cup) of strained juice.

culinary uses

Passionfruit can be halved and eaten directly from the shell. Their concentrated, fruity flavours are a wonderful addition to drinks, icing for sponge or banana cake, to shortbread dough and fruit salads. The pulp is also great dribbled over yoghurt, ice cream and other creamy desserts. A little passionfruit goes a long way—its powerful flavours quickly pervade whatever it is added to.

selection and storage

Passionfruit grows on a vine, from which it drops when the fruit is ready. Purple passionfruit should be avoided if the skin is smooth, as they will be too tart to enjoy—when ripe their skin thins a little and becomes wrinkled.

Ripe passionfruit will keep at cool room temperature for about 1 week and up to 3 weeks if refrigerated. Both passionfruit pulp and the strained juice can be frozen.

serves 4

hot passionfruit soufflé

2 egg yolks
125 g (4½ oz/½ cup)
    passionfruit pulp, from about
    10 passionfruit
2 tablespoons lemon juice
90 g (3¼ oz/¾ cup) icing
    (confectioners') sugar
6 egg whites
passionfruit sauce (see page 92),
    to serve
icing (confectioners') sugar,
    to dust, optional

Preheat the oven to 210°C (415°F/Gas 6–7). Place a collar of baking paper to come about 3 cm (1¼ inches) above the outside of four small 125 ml (4 fl oz/½ cup) ramekins. Tie collars securely with string. Lightly grease the ramekins (including the paper) and sprinkle with caster sugar; shake out any excess.

Combine the egg yolks, pulp, lemon juice and half the icing sugar in a large bowl. Whisk until well combined.

Using electric beaters, whisk the egg whites in a separate bowl until soft peaks form. Gradually add the remaining icing sugar, beating well after each addition. Using a large metal spoon, fold the egg white mixture, in batches, into the passionfruit mixture. Divide the mixture among the four ramekins. Using a flat-bladed knife, cut through the mixture in a circular motion 2 cm (¾ inch) from the edge.

Put the ramekins on a large baking tray and bake for 20–25 minutes or until the soufflé is well-risen and cooked through. Cut the collars from the dishes and serve the soufflés immediately, drizzled with passionfruit sauce and dusted with sifted icing sugar.

Hailing from tropical South America, the passionfruit was named by Spanish missionaries who saw in its flower various references to Christ's passion—the five wounds in the anthers, the three nails in the stigmas and the crown of thorns in the filaments.

pineapple

fruit ■ tropical
season ■ peaking spring–summer

Pineapple has become ubiquitous; think of the mountains of canned rings swimming in syrup that fill supermarket shelves, or those piles of the fresh fruit that often hover on the wrong side of ripeness and, when eaten, are disappointingly sour.

But what a revelation this curiously spiny, spiky South American native must have been to Christopher Columbus when he first saw it on the island of Guadeloupe in 1493—it is recorded that his men were 'astonished and delighted' when they sampled it. And, if further reminders are needed of what we should expect from this incredible fruit, it's worth noting that the indigenous South American name, *ananas*, translates as 'fragrant excellent fruit'.

If you buy a pineapple that is neither fragrant nor excellent, you've been short-changed. The problem is that the pineapple doesn't continue to ripen after picking and, for convenience of transport and storage, is often harvested a little early.

Generally, pineapples aren't sold by variety. Rather, they fall into one of two categories—the 'rough-leafed' or the 'smooth-leafed'. The former are typified by small, sweet, deep-golden-fleshed fruit, which are particularly aromatic, while the latter are large, very juicy when ripe, but are not as sweet as 'roughies'.

preparation

To trim and peel a pineapple, you need a sharp, sturdy knife. Cut off the leafy top, a little below the leaves, and cut off the base. Then, with the pineapple standing firmly on a cut end, run your knife down the fruit, cutting off the thick skin in strips. To remove the 'eyes', use a small, sharp knife to cut v-shaped grooves that follow the pattern of the eyes around the fruit. Slice the pineapple in half lengthways, and cut out the tough core. The pineapple is now ready to be sliced, diced or chopped.

culinary uses

Luscious, juicy pineapple needs little to improve upon its raw perfection and is best enjoyed in sweet, dripping slices after a meal, or as an easy snack. However it is undeniably delicious when caramelized in a hot pan in the company of some butter and sugar and, perhaps, a dash of cardamom, then served as a warm dessert. It marries beautifully with other tropical fruits in a fruit salad and benefits too from a splash of kirsch or Grand Marnier.

If lucky enough to find yourself with an excess of pineapples, they do make terrific jam and, in combination with the bracing influence of lime or lemon, marmalade too. Pineapple is also sublime in certain curries and other Asian dishes as it has a special affinity for the flavours of those places, such as coriander (cilantro), coconut milk, chilli, spices and fish sauce.

Pineapple is rich in the enzyme bromelin, which attacks protein and turns it to mush. Therefore, never use raw pineapple in gelatin-based desserts as they won't set, nor combine it with cream or yoghurt (unless stirred in just before serving) as it will cause them to separate. Heat destroys the enzyme so you can make jellies and uncooked cheesecakes with pineapple that has first been cooked.

selection and storage

In choosing good pineapple, let your nose be your guide—ripe, rich, sweet aromas should waft from within. There should be no soft spots or dark patches whatsoever. The colour of the skin doesn't necessarily indicate the ripeness of the fruit either—depending on the variety, the skin can be golden, reddish yellow or even green-tinged.

Fully ripe pineapples are quite perishable—store at room temperature for no longer than 1–2 days, or in the refrigerator for up to 4 days, in a plastic bag and with the leaves still attached.

coriander pork with fresh pineapple

serves 4

400 g (14 oz) pork loin or fillet, trimmed
¼ pineapple, peeled and trimmed
1 tablespoon oil
4 garlic cloves, chopped
4 green onions (scallions), chopped
1 tablespoon fish sauce
1 tablespoon lime juice
1 large handful coriander (cilantro) leaves
1 large handful chopped mint
steamed rice, to serve

Partially freeze the pork until it is just firm and slice it thinly. Cut the pineapple flesh into bite-sized pieces.

Heat the oil in a wok or heavy-based frying pan. Add the garlic and green onion and cook over medium-high heat for 1 minute. Remove from the wok.

Heat the wok to very hot; add the pork in batches and stir-fry for 2–3 minutes or until just cooked. Return the garlic and green onion to the wok and then add the pineapple pieces, fish sauce and lime juice. Toss to combine and cook for 1 minute or until pineapple is heated through. Add coriander and mint, toss to combine. Serve immediately with steamed rice.

sweet drunken pineapple

serves 6

1 large pineapple
oil, for brushing
40 g (1½ oz/¼ cup) coarsely grated palm sugar (jaggery) or soft brown sugar
2½ tablespoons rum
2 tablespoon lime juice
3 tablespoons small mint leaves
thick (double/heavy) cream, to serve

Preheat a barbecue grill plate or chargrill pan (griddle). Trim the ends from the pineapple, remove the skin and cut into quarters lengthways. Brush the hot grill plate or chargrill pan with oil, over medium heat, add the pineapple quarters and cook for about 10 minutes, turning to brown all the cut sides.

Take the pineapple off the heat and cut each quarter into 1.5 cm (⅝ inch) thick slices. Overlap the slices on a large serving plate.

Combine the sugar, rum and lime juice in a small jug, mixing well to dissolve the sugar. Pour the mixture evenly over the warm pineapple slices, then cover with plastic wrap and refrigerate for several hours. Serve at room temperature, sprinkled with the mint leaves and a dollop of cream.

pineapple and mango jam

Remove the skin and tough eyes from the pineapple.
Cut pineapple into quarters lengthways, remove the core
and chop the flesh into 1 cm (½ inch) pieces. Peel the
mangoes and cut each cheek from the stones. Using a large
spoon, scoop the flesh from the skin and cut into 1 cm (½ inch)
pieces. Put the pineapple, mango, 1 teaspoon lemon zest,
lemon juice and sugar in a large saucepan. Stir over medium
heat for 5 minutes, or until the sugar has dissolved.

Put two small plates in the freezer. Put the reserved lemon
seeds and remaining zest on the muslin and tie up securely
with string. Add to the pan. Bring mixture to the boil, then
reduce the heat and simmer, stirring often, for 30–40 minutes.
When the jam falls from a tilted wooden spoon in thick sheets
without dripping, start testing for setting point. To do this,
remove from the heat, put a little jam onto one of the cold
plates and place in the freezer for 30 seconds. A skin should
form on the surface and the jam should wrinkle when pushed
with your finger. If not, return to the heat for a few minutes
and test again with the other plate.

Transfer to a heatproof jug and immediately pour into hot
sterilized jars and seal. Allow to cool, then label and date
each jar. Store in a cool, dark place for 6–12 months.
Refrigerate after opening for up to 6 weeks.

note To warm the sugar, preheat the oven to 150°C
(300°F/Gas 2). Spread the sugar evenly in a baking dish
and warm in the oven for about 10–15 minutes, or until
warmed through. Do not overheat the sugar or it will start
to lump together.

1 pineapple
2 large mangoes
zest of 1 lemon
80 ml (2½ fl oz/⅓ cup) lemon
  juice, reserving the seeds
10 cm (4 inch) square of muslin
  (cheesecloth)
1.25 kg (2 lb 12 oz) warmed
  sugar (see note)

tropical fruit ■ pineapple

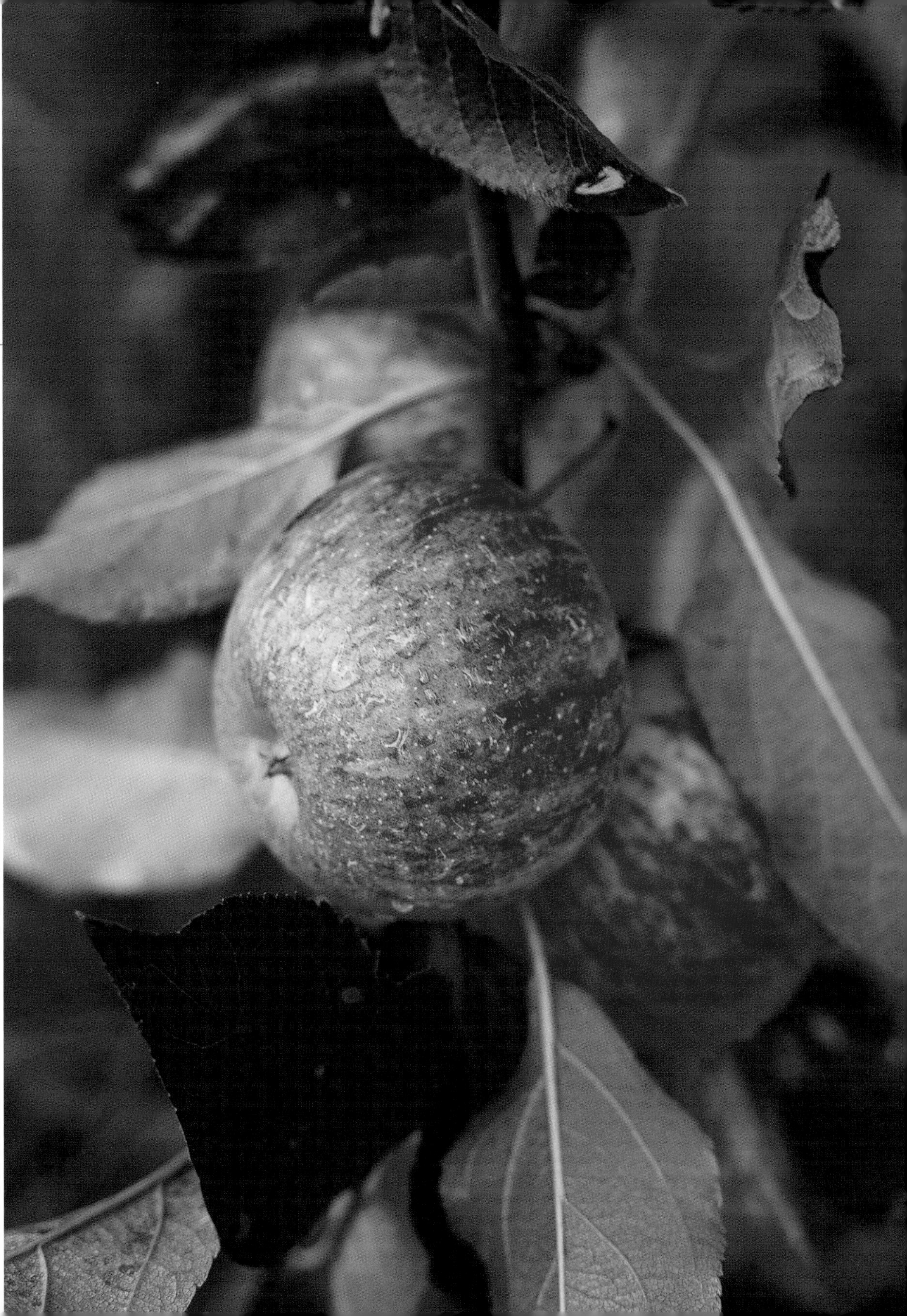

apple

Only a small proportion of the 8000 named apple varieties are commercially cultivated. However, all modern day cultivars can trace their roots back to the earliest form of apple, the wild, sour crab apple that originated in the Caucasus, in what is now Kazakhstan. Along with pears and quinces, which also hail from this region, apples belong to the rose sub-family branch *Maloideae*.

Large-scale commercial growing and the advent of cold storage have driven demand for apple uniformity. Consistent size, colour and shape have become the predominant concern for farmers, as large retailers demand these qualities. They also favour those varieties that are disease-resistant and that travel and store well. In response to such standardization (and long storage), which has resulted in some quite 'boring' and mealy fruit, there is a revival of interest in seasonally available heirloom apple varieties.

With so many apple varieties, there are significant differences in nutritional value between them. However, the most commonly available varieties generally have decent amounts of vitamins A, B and C, magnesium, iron and manganese.

selection and storage

Apples kept in cold storage eventually lose flavour, juiciness and crispness, their most desirable qualities. It is best to either buy apple varieties as they come into season, or purchase fruit from farmer's or grower's markets and roadside stalls that dot the landscape of apple-orchard territory. Buying this way may also provide an opportunity to sample some lesser-known varieties.

Favour firm, smooth and shiny-skinned apples that feel heavy for their size. Apples should still have their stalk intact and have dry, tight skin. Bruised apples deteriorate rapidly, so are best trimmed, then used immediately.

Apples slowly continue ripening after picking, so keep them in a ventilated plastic bag in the refrigerator crisper for up to 1 week. To store quantities of apples for out-of-season use, wrap firm fruit, individually, in tissue paper then spread on slatted wooden boxes (or similar). They need to be stored in a cool, dry, well-ventilated place where they will keep for several months (check them occasionally for signs of deterioration).

varieties

While many apple varieties are multifunctional, there is a traditional division between cooking and eating apples, generally based on sugar and acid levels. Unpalatable as an eating fruit, the acidic, green-skinned British bramley is perfectly suited to cooking—rich in pectin, it is excellent made into jellies and jams, and, as it collapses into a smooth puree, is ideal for sauces. Elsewhere, the tart, green granny smith is a cooking favourite. The French traditionally use the pomme reinette for tarte tatin, but also favour the golden delicious when the former is not available. Golden delicious holds its shape without emitting too much moisture, making it the perfect pie or tart apple.

Like the golden delicious, others retain their shape, flavour and moisture when cooked (gala, jonagold and pink lady, for example) so are suitable for stuffing and baking whole; they can also be poached or used in tarts, cakes and pies. As a general rule, apples containing high sugar levels hold their shape better when cooked; however, these often need to be peeled before using, as their skins are prone to toughening when cooking with sugar.

In contrast, apple varieties best suited to eating raw are generally firm-textured, crisp and juicy, with some acidity to counterbalance their sweetness. Red delicious and gala apples fall into this camp and are not suited to cooking at all.

braeburn The braeburn apple was developed in New Zealand. It has firm, juicy flesh, is a medium-large apple, and has red-blushed skin with a delicate sweet-sour flavour. As such, braeburns are an ideal eating apple, best reserved for table eating or adding raw to salads. They are at their crunchy best at the start of apple season, from autumn to early winter.

cox's orange pippin Created by Englishman and retired brewer Richard Cox in 1825 by crossing a ribston pippin with a blenheim orange, this heirloom mid-season English apple variety is generally small and round, with greenish yellow skin flushed with some red russeting and creamy flesh. Its crisp, juicy, firm texture and sweet flavour is balanced by a little acidity. While this is an all-purpose apple, it is best when simply eaten out of hand and are at their peak in autumn.

fuji Originally from Japan and named after Mount Fuji, fuji apples have juicy, crisp flesh and a high sugar content, which makes them one of the sweetest of all the cultivated apples. Their reddish pink skins often have golden yellow highlights. With an appealing, highly perfumed aroma, they are the perfect eating apple. Holding their texture well, they are also suited to baking whole and adding to pies. Fujis are a late season variety.

golden delicious With yellowy green skin, golden freckles and tender sweet flesh, golden delicious apples maintain their shape during cooking, making them the perfect choice for caramelized apple desserts, tarts, and sautéing when cut into slices. Discovered in West Virginia in 1914, they are also a fine eating apple and, with a long season, are available in excellent condition throughout the winter months. Although it shares part of its name with the red delicious, the only relationship between the two is that the same people, the Stark brothers, marketed them.

granny smith Named after Australian Maria Ann Smith (aka 'granny' Smith), who found the seedlings growing in a spot in her suburban Sydney garden where she had thrown some apple cores. Mrs Smith recognized their cooking potential and began marketing these unusual new apples, said to be derived from French crab apples. Featuring thick, freckled, apple-green skin and hard, crisp, tart, white flesh, the medium-large granny smith is a great all-rounder, suiting both eating and cooking. As their flesh collapses upon cooking, they are the apple of choice for apple purees and sauces and their slightly sour flavour is the perfect foil for pork, goose and duck. This quality makes them not so desirable for recipes requiring quarters or chunks.

pink lady Another Australian apple, the pink lady is one of the newest apple varieties. First grown in 1979 in the Margaret River region of Western Australia, it was the natural result of cross-pollination between the golden delicious and lady williams apples. Characterized by a distinct, pink-blushed skin surrounding crisp, juicy, sweet flesh, pink ladies are an excellent multi-purpose fruit. Great for either eating or cooking, they are aromatic with a unique sugar-acid balance, so are ideal for baking whole and using in pies. Pink ladies are a late season apple.

red delicious First appearing in an Iowa orchard in 1880, this ubiquitous, elongated apple has thick, tough, deep red shiny skin and distinct ridged bumps at its base. With crisp, juicy, white flesh and a low level of acidity, red delicious is a good eating apple, due to its tender flesh, but does not suit cooking at all. An early season variety, red delicious tends towards flouriness when stored for too long, so buy it in winter months.

As one of the oldest and most prolific cultivated fruits, apples have been the subject of legend, myth and scientific discourse for centuries. The earliest records of apple cultivation go back to 8000 BC—dried apple slices dating to 2500 BC were found in the excavated tomb of an ancient Persian queen near Basra in modern-day Iraq. Apples are mentioned in Homer's Odyssey *and Pliny the Elder recorded 20 apple varieties in his definitive tome* Naturalis Historia. *In 1655, a falling apple inspired Sir Isaac Newton to discover the law of gravity, while the familiar edict of 'an apple a day keeps the doctor away' has been repeated to children ever since first stated in a speech by JT Stinson in 1904.*

preparation

If coring quantities of apples, a purpose-made apple corer can be purchased for the job. Peeled, cored and cut apples should either be placed in a bowl of acidulated water (water with lemon juice added) or lightly brushed with lemon juice to prevent them from browning.

culinary uses

A juicy ripe apple is the ultimate fast food—but served with a selection of cheese it becomes perfect picnic or after-dinner fare. Apples are a welcome addition to savoury winter salads: a crisp salad of sliced apple, shaved cucumber, torn witlof and dill is a refreshing textural counterpoint to an extravagant whole poached salmon or cider-poached trout. A heart-warming plate of bangers and mash makes the transformation from homely country staple to urbane sophisticate when reinvented as pork and fennel sausages with celeriac (or potato) and apple mash (see page 193).

Apple dessert possibilities are endless, from Austrian apple strudel and old-fashioned pastry-wrapped apple dumplings to the English cheddar-pastry-wrapped apple pie. Apples can also be used in muffins, cheesecakes, preserves (chutneys, jams, mincemeat), yeast-raised sweet breads, sweet omelettes, sorbets (particularly good here with mint), chilled mousses, hot soufflés and the classic tarte tatin (see variation, page 139).

Flavours that complement apples in cooking include Calvados, cider, brandy, allspice, cinnamon, cloves, nutmeg, cheese, maple syrup, muscovado sugar, caramel, golden syrup, raisins, blackberries, pears, pastry, butter, lemon, pork, pickled herrings, horseradish, rhubarb, walnuts, almonds, vanilla beans and cream. Or more adventurously, but equally compatibly, apples complement thyme, sage, quince, rabbit, pancetta, prosciutto, radicchio, endive, mayonnaise, mint, star anise, caraway, coriander seeds, polenta, parsnips, venison, hot-smoked trout and beetroot.

layered potato and apple bake

Preheat the oven to 180°C (350°F/Gas 4). Grease a large, shallow baking dish. Peel the potatoes and cut into thin slices. Peel, halve and core the apples, then cut into thin slices. Slice the peeled onion into very fine rings.

Layer the potatoes, apples and onions in the prepared dish, finishing with a layer of potatoes. Sprinkle evenly with cheese, then pour over the cream.

Sprinkle with nutmeg and black pepper, to taste. Bake for 45 minutes or until golden brown. Remove from the oven and allow to stand for 5 minutes before serving.

note To prevent potatoes and apples browning before assembling dish, put in a bowl of cold water with a squeeze of lemon juice. Drain and pat dry with paper towels before using.

2 large potatoes
3 green apples
1 onion
60 g (2¼ oz/½ cup) finely grated cheddar cheese
250 ml (9 fl oz/1 cup) pouring (whipping) cream
¼ teaspoon ground nutmeg

pome fruit ■ apple

traditional apple sauce

serves 6–8

Put the apple, sugar, cloves, cinnamon stick and 125 ml (4 fl oz/½ cup) of water in a small saucepan. Cover and simmer over low heat for 10 minutes, or until the apple is soft. Remove from the heat and discard the cloves and cinnamon stick.

Mash the apple, or press through a sieve for smooth-textured sauce. Stir in the lemon juice, to taste. Serve warm or cold with roast pork, pork chops or pan-fried pork fillet. Will keep for 4 days stored, covered, in the refrigerator.

4 green apples, peeled, cored and chopped
2 teaspoons caster (superfine) sugar
2 cloves
1 cinnamon stick
1–2 teaspoons lemon juice

apple galette

serves 4–6

1 sheet ready-made puff pastry
80 g (2¾ oz/¼ cup) apricot jam
1 cooking apple, such as granny smith
2 teaspoons raw (demerara) sugar

Preheat the oven to 210°C (415°F/Gas 6–7). Trim the corners from the pastry to make a neat 24 cm (9½ inch) circle (use a large plate as a guide if you like).

Put the jam in a small saucepan and stir over low heat until melted. Strain the jam, discarding any solids, then brush over the puff pastry, leaving a 1.5 cm (⅝ inch) border.

Peel, quarter and core the apple, and cut into 2 mm (1/16 inch) thick slices. Arrange over the pastry in an overlapping circular pattern, leaving a 1.5 cm (⅝ inch) border around the edge. Sprinkle evenly with the sugar. Carefully place the galette on a lightly greased tray and bake for 35 minutes, or until the edge of the pastry is well browned and puffed.

apple and passionfruit crumble

serves 4–6

4 passionfruit
4 green apples
135 g (4¾ oz/⅔ cup) caster (superfine) sugar
60 g (2¼ oz/1 cup) shredded coconut
90 g (3¼ oz/¾ cup) plain (all-purpose) flour
80 g (2¾ oz) unsalted butter, softened

Preheat the oven to 180°C (350°F/Gas 4). Grease a 1 litre (35 fl oz/4 cup) baking dish.

Sieve the passionfruit, discarding the pulp, and place the juice in a bowl. Peel, core and thinly slice the apples and add to the passionfruit juice, along with 50 g (1¾ oz/¼ cup) sugar. Mix well, then transfer the mixture to a prepared dish.

Combine the shredded coconut, flour, remaining sugar and butter in a bowl and rub together until the mixture resembles coarse crumbs. Pile evenly over the apple mixture.

Bake the crumble for 25–30 minutes, or until the topping is crisp and golden.

pear

fruit ▪ **pome**
season ▪ **peaking autumn–end of winter**

'The pear is the grandfather of the apple, its poor relation, a fallen aristocrat …' So said François Pierre de La Varenne (one of the greatest chefs and culinary writers of the seventeenth century) and perhaps that quite sums up how many of us feel about the pear. It isn't the satisfying daily staple that a crunchy apple is, nor does it have the treat value of, say, a mango or a bag of cherries. Once, however, the pear basked in star-status.

The pear is thought to have originated in the Caucasus thousands of years ago but it wasn't taken seriously until European gardeners such as Louis XIV's own, Jean de la Quintinie (1626–1688)—the man responsible for the kitchen gardens of Versailles—showed some interest and gave us some of the buttery, creamy-fleshed varieties we have today. In fact, nobles at the French court could once find favour with the King by introducing delicious new varieties. By 1842, the English Horticultural Society had demonstrated the existence of over 700 types—today there are around 6000 named varieties.

It could be we under-value this fruit today because so often we experience them as under-ripe, bland and hard, and it's true it can be tricky to know just when a pear is properly ripe. But when they are, they drip with juices and have sublimely sweet, aromatic flesh; a good pear is an irresistible thing.

nashi pear

varieties

Pears belong to the diverse Rosaceae family and are therefore related to apples and quinces. They fall into two basic groups —European pears and Asian pears.

European pears are classically 'pear-shaped' (or pyriform) and have sweet, buttery, slightly gritty flesh that is balanced by an amount of acid. Asian pears, also called nashi (which simply means 'pear' in Japanese), are round in shape and have extremely crisp, juicy, non-acidic sweet flesh that is very mild in flavour. More people worldwide eat nashi pears than the European varieties yet they are relatively little-known outside Asia.

beurre bosc An elegant pear with a long, tapering neck, the beurre bosc has greenish to brown skin and creamy, dense, full-flavoured flesh. This pear will ripen at room temperature in 3–8 days but because it is a harder variety, will not become as burstingly soft as other types. This makes the beurre bosc an excellent choice for cooking—it keeps its shape beautifully when poached either whole or halved, sliced and sautéed or halved and roasted for use in sweet or savoury dishes.

doyenne du comice This pear is regarded as one of the finest, with its excellent, smooth texture, rich aromas and intense pear flavour. It bruises very easily, so in some places, where more hardy, transportable varieties reign, it may be difficult to find. Fruits are large and squat, with pale green-yellow skin that blushes red when ripe. The comice is best enjoyed raw and is perfect on the cheese board.

nashi The nashi is also known as the 'pear apple' or 'sand pear', the latter on account of the slight grittiness which often characterizes the texture of the flesh. Its consumption was once reserved for the Chinese ruling classes and to sink your teeth into its thirst-quenching flesh is to understand why— it is indeed a princely fruit. It comes from the Eastern regions of China, Korea and Japan in which places it is wildly popular still—increasingly, it is becoming available in Western markets.

packham's triumph Also just called packham, this variety was developed in Australia in 1896. It bears many similiarities to the williams but has knobbly skin; it is reputedly the best-selling variety in the world. A large pear, the skin colour changes from green to pale yellow when ripe and the flesh is white and juicy. Eat this pear ripe out of hand, or use for general cooking, but only when still on the firm side. Hard packhams will ripen in 6–8 days at room temperature.

williams bon chrétien Also known as bartlett or simply, williams. Green when unripe but maturing to a light yellow with (sometimes) a reddish blush, this widely planted pear is

storage

As pears vary in colour from green, yellow, brown, crimson to russet (and in shape and size), colour is not necessarily an indicator of ripeness. Buy pears that are unblemished and firm, then ripen at room temperature—depending upon the variety, this could take anything from 3–10 days.

Unripe pears will keep in the refrigerator for several weeks but just make sure there is air circulating around them (don't seal them in plastic) or they may rot. Ideally, store pears in a single layer; if stacked, they will bruise. Asian pears store exceptionally well and will keep, refrigerated, for up to 2 weeks.

one of the world's most popular. They are medium-large in size with a thick neck and have sweet, buttery flesh that is quite juicy. These pears ripen quickly off the tree and will soften and sweeten at room temperature over 3 days. A red-skinned variety, which tastes the same, is variously called red bartlett, red williams or red sensation. This all-purpose pear is a good eating pear but can also be poached, baked and used in fruit, or leafy, salads.

winter nelis Originally from Belgium, winter nelis is not the prettiest of pears, with its squat shape and dull, rusted, yellow-green skin. Medium to small in size, the nelis is however a useful pear, with sweet, slightly spicy flesh that lends itself to cooking and to eating raw, although it does have a tough skin.

culinary uses

European pears are versatile fruits. As noted above, they can be poached whole or halved (peel first), roasted in unpeeled halves, quarters or wedges then used in sweet or savoury dishes; they can also be sautéed, stewed or simply sliced and used raw. Their flavour has an affinity with spices like ginger, nutmeg, cardamom, saffron, star anise, cloves and cinnamon.

Pears are excellent poached in a red wine syrup, or in port or white dessert wine. Firm, poached, cooled pear halves work even better than raw pears in upside-down cakes and sweet tarts. Firmer pears, such as beurre bosc, make an admirable tarte tatin in place of the usual apple.

Pears team beautifully with cheese, either in a salad or cheese course—partner them with parmesan or blue cheese, a washed-rind or goat's cheese. Nuts such as walnuts, hazelnuts, almonds and pistachios also complement pears, as do salad leaves like radicchio, cress, spinach and rocket (arugula). Like melon, pear also goes well with prosciutto and firmer varieties are wonderful in braises with chicken, duck or pork.

selection

Pears are picked when mature but still hard, then transferred to cool storage to cure for a period (the length of time here depends upon variety) and then, finally, bought to room temperature to complete ripening. During ripening, the starches are converted to sugars, and the pear, unusually, ripens from the inside out.

When allowed to fully tree-ripen, pears are fit to eat for a few days only, after which their flesh turns dry and mealy. Perhaps this is why, before the days of commercial cool storage, Ralph Waldo Emerson declared that, 'There are only ten minutes in the life of a pear when it is perfect to eat'.

To tell if a pear is ripe, it should give slightly when pressed (use your thumb) at the base of the 'neck'; some varieties will also smell a little fragrant. Asian pears are the exception to the above rules as they are picked when ready to eat.

pome fruit ■ pear

pear and walnut salad
with blue cheese dressing

dressing

100 g (3½ oz) creamy blue
   cheese
60 ml (2 fl oz/¼ cup) olive oil
1 tablespoon walnut oil
1 tablespoon lemon juice
1 tablespoon pouring (whipping)
   cream
2 teaspoons finely chopped sage

salad

100 g (3½ oz/1 cup) walnut
   halves
4 small firm pears
2 tablespoons lemon juice
2 witlof (chicory/Belgian endive),
   trimmed and leaves separated
100 g (3½ oz/1 cup) shaved
   parmesan cheese

To make the dressing, process the blue cheese in a small processor until smooth, then add the olive oil, walnut oil and lemon juice, and blend until combined well. With the motor running, slowly add 2 teaspoons warm water. Stir in the cream and sage, and season with sea salt and freshly ground black pepper.

Preheat the grill (broiler) to medium-hot. Place the walnuts in a bowl and cover with boiling water. Stand for 1 minute, then drain well. Spread the walnuts on a baking tray and place under the grill for 3 minutes, or until lightly toasted. Chop coarsely.

Slice unpeeled pears widthways to make thin rounds; discard the seeds. As each pear is sliced, brush slices with a little lemon juice to prevent browning.

Arrange three pear slices in a circle on a serving plate. Top with a scattering of walnuts, a few witlof leaves, then a few more walnuts and some parmesan cheese. Repeat this layering, finishing with a layer of parmesan cheese and some walnuts. Spoon some dressing over each stack. Serve as a first course, or as an accompaniment to simple meat dishes.

pear tarte tatin

Preheat the oven to 220°C (425°F/Gas 7). Place a 22 cm (8½ inch) heavy-based frying pan with ovenproof handle over medium heat. Add the sugar and heat, shaking the pan constantly, until the sugar is a dark caramel colour. Add the butter, ginger and cinnamon and stir to combine. Arrange the pears on top, spoon over the syrup to coat, then reduce the heat to low and cook, covered, for 5 minutes, or until the pears just begin to soften.

Remove the frying pan from the heat and arrange the pears over the base of the pan, overlapping them so they fit tightly and will look neat when turned out. Leave to cool slightly.

Roll out the pastry on a lightly floured work surface to a 24 cm (9½ inch) round. Put the pastry over the pears in the frying pan, tucking the edges around the pears so they are enclosed in pastry. Bake for 20–25 minutes, or until the pastry is golden and puffed. Leave for 10 minutes, then run a knife around the edge of the pan to loosen the tart and invert it onto a serving platter. Serve warm with cream. The tart is best served on the day it is made.

variation You can make an apple tarte tatin by following the recipe instructions and substituting the pears for 2–3 green apples, such as granny smiths.

145 g (5 oz/⅔ cup) caster (superfine) sugar
50 g (1¾ oz) butter, cut into cubes
½ teaspoon ground ginger
½ teaspoon ground cinnamon
3 beurre bosc pears, peeled, cored and cut into wedges widthways
450 g (1 lb) ready-made block puff pastry
thick (double/heavy) cream, to serve

pome fruit ■ pear

pears in red wine

serves 6

1 tablespoon arrowroot
750 ml (26 fl oz/1 bottle) red wine
110 g (3¾ oz/½ cup) sugar
1 cinnamon stick
6 cloves
zest of 1 small orange
zest of 1 small lemon
6 large firm pears
cream or crème fraîche, to serve

Combine the arrowroot with 2 tablespoons of wine in a small bowl and stir to form a smooth paste. Heat the remaining wine in a saucepan with the sugar, cinnamon stick, cloves and citrus zest. Simmer gently for 2–3 minutes, or until the sugar has dissolved.

Peel the pears, leaving stalks intact. Add pears to the saucepan, cover and cook over medium heat for 25 minutes, turning pears occasionally. When the pears are very tender, lift out with a slotted spoon and put in a deep serving dish.

Strain the spiced wine, discarding solids, then return the wine to the saucepan. Stir the arrowroot and add to the hot wine. Simmer gently, stirring occasionally, until thickened. Pour over the pears and allow to cool. Serve with cream or crème fraîche.

pear and raspberry crumble

serves 4

1.5 kg (3 lb 5 oz or about 6 large) ripe but firm pears
2 tablespoons caster (superfine) sugar
3 star anise
125 g (4½ oz/1 cup) raspberries
125 g (4½ oz/1 cup) plain (all-purpose) flour
95 g (3½ oz/½ cup) soft brown sugar
100 g (3½ oz) unsalted butter, cut into cubes
vanilla ice cream, to serve

Preheat the oven to 190°C (375°F/Gas 5). Peel, quarter and core the pears, then cut each piece in half lengthways. Put into a large saucepan and sprinkle the sugar over. Add 1 tablespoon of water and the star anise. Cover and bring to the boil. Cook, covered, over medium-low heat for 10 minutes, stirring occasionally, until the fruit is tender, but still holds its shape. Drain the pears and discard the star anise. Transfer to a 1.5 litre (52 fl oz/6 cup) capacity baking dish. Scatter the raspberries over the pears.

Combine the flour, sugar and butter in a bowl. Use your fingertips to rub the butter into the flour until the mixture resembles coarse breadcrumbs. Sprinkle over the fruit, then bake for 20–25 minutes, until golden brown. Stand for 5 minutes, then serve with vanilla ice cream.

quince

fruit ▪ **pome**
season ▪ **late autumn–winter**

The quince is an unpromising looking fruit, rock-hard (yet prone to bruising), thick-skinned, yellow and covered with a strange fuzz. But the smell of quince (a complex, sweet perfume that invades your house with even a few of the fruit in a bowl), hints at the glorious flavours within, which require long, patient cooking to be fully unlocked.

An ancient fruit (one theory suggests that it was a quince or pomegranate that was Eve's downfall and not the apple), the quince originated around the Black and Caspian Seas and, after making its way westward, became a firm favourite throughout Mediterranean Europe, Northern Africa and Portugal.

Quinces, like apples and pears, are a member of the Rosacaea, or rose family, and in times past was a popular tree in household orchards—in fact, it has been noted that seventeenth century English cookbooks have more quince recipes than any other fruit. Over recent years, the quince has been 'rediscovered', becoming something of a winter favourite among professional chefs and enthusiastic home cooks alike. And little wonder—when cooked (quince can't be eaten raw as it is too astringent), the flesh takes on a glorious, rosy colour and a deep haunting flavour.

preparation

Wash quince well to get rid of any fuzz. If making jelly (and, with its particularly high pectin content, quince is ideal for this), don't bother to peel or core as the flavour will be better and the flotsam gets strained out anyway. Otherwise, peel and core your quinces—the flesh turns brown quickly on contact with air so if preparing a lot of the fruit put the pieces in acidulated water (water with lemon juice) as you go. Be sure to remove any brown patches—it's hard to tell if a quince is bruised until you come to peel it, so look out for soft, damaged spots at this stage.

culinary uses

Quinces are suited to poaching, baking, stewing, preserving in syrup, or being made into jam or dense, sweet quince paste—perfect to eat with cheese. They can also be pot-roasted, whole and unpeeled, in a very sweet, spiced syrup—this takes several hours and the fruit must be turned every now and then so it cooks evenly—the results of this treatment are especially luscious.

Quinces complement apples and pears and these other fruits can be used to extend your supply of quinces as, when cooked together, the quinces' flavour overpowers the more neutral ones of apples and pears. Although most often used in sweet preparations, Moroccan, Spanish and Persian cooks also incorporate them into savoury stews and tagines where they are an unexpected complement the flavours of lamb, chicken or fish.

selection and storage

There's little chance you'll get to buy quince by variety—generally you take what you can get—although pineapple quince (an early-ripening variety with large, yellow fruit) and smyrna (a smaller quince with a very pronounced flavour and which doesn't break up even when cooked for a very long time) are two common varieties.

Choose fruit that has bright yellow or gold skin, with no signs of green or of discoloration. Riper fruit tends to have less fuzz on its skin although the amount of fuzz present can also be a feature of the variety.

Ripe quince will keep at cool room temperature for 10–14 days and for up to 3 weeks in the refrigerator. If choosing this option, seal the fruit in a large plastic bag to prevent their aroma permeating the entire contents of your refrigerator.

Called marmelos *by the Portugeuse and* membrillo *by the Spanish, the quince is the source of the English word 'marmalade'—initially this jam was made using quinces.*

lamb tagine with quince

serves 4–6

1.5 kg (3 lb 5 oz) boned lamb
    shoulder
2 large handfuls coriander
    (cilantro) leaves, chopped
2 large onions, diced
1/2 teaspoon ground ginger
1/2 teaspoon cayenne pepper
1/4 teaspoon ground saffron
    threads
1 teasoon ground coriander
1 cinnamon stick
500 g (1 lb 2 oz) quinces
40 g (1 1/2 oz) butter
100 g (3 1/2 oz/1/2 cup) dried
    apricots
1 tablespoon caster (superfine)
    sugar
coriander (cilantro) leaves, extra,
    to garnish
couscous or rice, to serve

Cut the lamb shoulder into 3 cm (1 1/4 inch) pieces. Put the lamb in a heavy-based, flameproof casserole dish. Add the coriander, half the onion, ginger, cayenne pepper, saffron threads, ground coriander and cinnamon stick. Season with sea salt and freshly ground black pepper.

Cover with cold water and bring to the boil over medium heat. Lower the heat and simmer, partly covered, for 1 1/2 hours, or until the lamb is tender.

Meanwhile, core the quinces and cut them into thick wedges. Melt the butter in a heavy-based frying pan over medium heat and cook the quinces and remaining onion for 15 minutes, or until lightly golden. When the lamb has been cooking for 1 hour, add the quince mixture, dried apricots and sugar.

Taste the sauce and adjust the seasoning if necessary. Transfer to a warm serving dish and sprinkle with the extra coriander. Serve immediately with couscous or rice.

'There is no fruit growing in this land that is of so many excellent uses as (the quince).' — John Parkinson (herbalist to King James I), 1629.

quince paste

Line a 28 x 18 cm (11 x 7 inch) rectangular cake tin or dish with plastic wrap. Wash the quinces, place in a saucepan, cover with water and simmer for 30 minutes, or until tender, then drain. Peel and core the quinces then push them through a sieve or potato ricer.

Put the pulp in a heavy-based saucepan and add the sugar. Cook over low heat, stirring occasionally, for 3½–4½ hours, or until very thick. Pour into the prepared tin. Allow to cool. Quince paste can be kept for several months in a tightly sealed container in the refrigerator. Serve before a meal with cheese and crackers, as part of an antipasti selection or with game such as pheasant.

note The amount of sugar will vary depending on the size of the quinces. The amount of sugar you use should equal the weight of quince pulp. You can measure this once strained.

3 large quinces
800 g (1 lb 12 oz/3⅔ cups)
  sugar (see note)

pome fruit ■ quince

slow-baked quinces in honey

serves 8

Preheat the oven to 150°C (300°F/Gas 2). Use half the butter to grease a shallow ovenproof dish large enough to hold the halved quinces in one layer, overlapping slightly.

Peel and halve the quinces. Don't worry about them discolouring as they will turn very dark during cooking. Remove cores. Put them, cut side up, in the prepared dish.

Drizzle the honey and wine over the quinces and dot with remaining butter. Cover with foil and bake for 2 hours, turn the quinces and bake for a further 2 hours. The quinces should be a rich maroon red and the juices caramelized. Serve hot or warm with cream or softened vanilla ice cream.

60 g (2¼ oz) unsalted butter,
  softened
8 quinces
2 tablespoons honey
125 ml (4 fl oz/½ cup) sweet
  white dessert wine, such as
  Sauternes
pouring (whipping) cream or
  vanilla ice cream, to serve

melons

fruit ▪ other
season ▪ cantaloupe, watermelon and rockmelon
(netted muskmelon) peaking in summer; honeydew
in autumn

A French poet is credited as saying, 'there are three things which cannot support mediocrity—poetry, wine and melons'. Indeed, an unsatisfactory melon is quite horrible; there is no disguising any absence of the gentle flavours, voluptuous fragrance or that sweet juiciness for which melons are so prized.

Melons are one of those fruits that are technically a vegetable, related as they are to other trailing, vine-borne crops such as pumpkins, gourds, cucumbers and squash. They come from the cucurbit family, which includes many vegetables commonly used throughout Asia (bitter gourd, winter melon and fuzzy melon, for example), where the words 'gourd' and 'melon' are virtually interchangeable.

Sweet melons fall into two broad groups—the genus *Cucumis melo* includes cantaloupe, rockmelon (also known as netted melon or muskmelon) and the honeydew; it is thought these originated in Persia, Afghanistan or Armenia. The watermelon is from the *Citrullus lanatus* grouping; these are native to the Kalahari Desert of Africa.

Melons comprise around 90 per cent water and it goes without saying they are very low in calories. Their nutritional profile varies according to type, but generally they provide generous quantities of vitamin C, betacarotene, with orange-fleshed varieties providing more than others.

cantaloupe

True cantaloupes are grown more widely in Europe (they take their name from a town near Rome called Cantalupo) and the Middle East than they are in North America or Australia—often what passes for cantaloupes in these latter countries are actually rockmelons (netted melons/muskmelons).

True cantaloupes are smaller and rounder than these and have tougher skin that is marked in clear sections—either smooth or slightly scaly, but never netted. The legendary charentais and ogen melons are regarded as the aristocrats of the cantaloupe. They possess fine, full-flavoured and deep orange flesh. Charentais are smallish, with smooth, grey-green rind. The ogen, which hails from Israel, has green flesh and an orange-green rind with dark green demarcations.

honeydew

The honeydew is distinguished by its smooth, creamy, thin skin and sweet green flesh. The Japanese adore honeydews—theirs is the fragrance supposedly encapsulated by Midori liqueur. The honeydew, which is unpleasantly bland when under-ripe, will continue to develop some flavour after picking, when stored at room temperature. It's a little tricky to tell when honeydews are ripe; some claim the skin turns yellow when ripe while others insist it should be creamy or pale green; unlike other melons, honeydews will continue to ripen once harvested.

With many varieties of this melon now available (even orange-fleshed ones have been developed), the most reliable method of determining ripeness is to lightly press the stem end; it should be slightly soft when the fruit is mature. Store ripe honeydews in the refrigerator for up to 4 days, taking care to completely cover all cut surfaces, as the smell of melon permeates everything in its proximity. Bring honeydews back to room temperature before eating though, as chilling dulls their flavour.

other fruit ■ melons

rockmelon

Also called 'netted' melon (because of the raised webbing on its skin) or muskmelon on account of its glorious smell when ripe, the rockmelon has deep, peachy-coloured flesh which is rich in betacarotenes (vitamin A). Round or slightly ovoid in shape, these melons have a netted skin with lengthwise demarcations, called sutures.

Select rockmelons with a deep, sweet aroma and pronounced netting on the skin—the background skin colour should be beige to golden. A ripe melon should also have a paler, slightly flattened side where it rested on the ground before harvesting, and the stem end should be a little damp.

Rockmelons are rather perishable; ripe ones (and these don't continue to ripen once picked, so select with care) should be eaten immediately. They will store for 1–2 days at cool room temperature or 2 days in the refrigerator. Avoid any melons that have soft, shrivelled or sunken patches as this indicates spoilage.

watermelon

There are over 1000 varieties of watermelon grown, ranging in skin colour from pale green and faintly striped, to dark green with bold veining and stripes, to nearly black and unmarbled. Watermelons are rounded or oval in shape, although the Japanese, wishing to develop a melon that will fit cooperatively into a refrigerator, have even developed a square melon!

Under the skin of a watermelon lies a layer of thick, protective white rind which isn't edible raw, although certain culinary cultures either pickle or candy it. The many seeds contained in the flesh (large specimens can harbour over 1000) can also be roasted for snacking, thereby making edible use of every part of the melon. In Russia, they even brew a beer from watermelon juice.

To tell if a watermelon is ripe, inspect the pale patch where it rested on the ground—it should be yellow, not white or light green. The skin should be matt and have a waxy rather than shiny appearance and the fruit should be large for its type and feel heavy for its size. If you tap the fruit it should sound a little hollow. Many suppliers will let you taste from a cut specimen before you buy.

Don't store watermelon for too long (2–3 days maximum, covered in plastic wrap in the refrigerator). With age, the flesh takes on a deeper colour, glassy appearance and dry, almost gritty texture and, needless to say, is not so pleasant to eat.

Melons have extremely venerable origins; depictions of them have been found on Egyptian walls dating back to 5000 BC. The Romans imported melons in great quantity from the Near Eastern reaches of their Empire, although these melons were tiny, orange-sized specimens, not the large ones we are familiar with today. In the fourteenth century, well after the Roman Empire had collapsed, the Italians finally began cultivating the fruit themselves and, as a result of their efforts, melons began to expand in size and weight. In seventeenth-century France, melons were called sucrins, *meaning 'sweet', and little wonder, as gardeners hydrated them with honeyed water to make them even more so.*

culinary uses

A perfect melon demands little more than to be simply sliced, seeds removed, and served with a teaspoon for scooping— or in fleshy wedges to be eaten out of hand. There are, however, some utterly timeless dishes involving melon which deserve consideration. There's Italian prosciutto with melon— cantaloupe or rockmelon are best used as the perfumed sweetness is somehow the perfect foil for the salty, rich meat. From French cooking came the idea of melon (usually honeydew or cantaloupe, cut into balls with a special cutter which can be purchased from specialist kitchen stores) doused with port. Greeks hit upon the combination of feta and watermelon; sublime when tossed into a refreshing salad with sliced Spanish onions, mint and olives. Fragrant rockmelon also goes well in cold dishes with smoked chicken, ham and roast duck and with sweet crustaceans (prawns, lobsters, crab), too.

In recent years it has become fashionable to fill a whole watermelon with vodka (using a funnel to poke through a small hole cut in the melon, the flesh absorbs great amounts of the alcohol) which is served in chilled, spirit-sodden wedges. Any melon will greatly enhance a fruit salad and they have an affinity for the flavour of ginger and rum.

Puree seeded melons and use in frappés and frozen ices— pureed rockmelon, mixed with a little chicken stock, garlic, ground almonds and sherry vinegar, makes an extremely pleasant gazpacho-style chilled soup.

other fruit ■ melons

makes 1 litre
(35 fl oz/4 cups)

melon and lemon conserve

6 lemons
10 cm (4 inch) square of muslin
  (cheesecloth)
2.5 kg (5 lb 8 oz) honeydew
  melon, peeled, seeded and cut
  into 1 cm (½ inch) cubes
1 tablespoon brandy
1.25 kg (2 lb 12 oz) sugar,
  warmed (see note)

Scrub the lemons under hot running water to remove any wax, then cut in half widthways. Juice the lemons, strain the juice, reserving the seeds, then place in a large saucepan. Roughly chop the lemon skins. Put the seeds on the muslin and tie up securely with string. Add the seeds to the pan along with the chopped lemon skins, melon, brandy and 750 ml (26 fl oz/3 cups) water. Bring to the boil and boil for 40 minutes, or until the fruit is soft.

Put two small plates in the freezer. Add the sugar to the pan and stir over low heat, without boiling, for 5 minutes, or until the sugar has dissolved. Bring to the boil and boil, stirring often, for 30 minutes. As the mixture thickens and starts to darken, reduce the heat and simmer, stirring frequently, for 20–30 minutes. When the conserve falls from a tilted wooden spoon in thick sheets without dripping, start testing for setting point. To do this, remove from the heat, put a little conserve onto one of the cold plates and place in the freezer for 30 seconds. A skin should form on the surface and the conserve should wrinkle when pushed with your finger. If not, return the pan to the heat for a few minutes and re-test using the second plate. Discard the muslin bags. Remove any scum from the surface.

Transfer to a heatproof jug and immediately pour into hot sterilized jars and seal. Allow to cool, then label and date each jar. Store in a cool, dark place for 6–12 months. Refrigerate after opening for up to 6 weeks.

note To warm the sugar, preheat the oven to 150°C (300°F/Gas 2). Spread the sugar evenly in a baking dish and put in the oven for about 10–15 minutes, or until warmed through. To save time warm the sugar while cooking the conserve. Do not add the sugar until the fruit has softened. If sugar is added before the fruit is fully soft, the fruit will stay firm.

watermelon granita

Put the sugar in a saucepan with 250 ml (9 oz/1 cup) water and stir over low heat without boiling until the sugar has dissolved. Increase the heat and bring to the boil, then reduce the heat and simmer, without stirring, for 5 minutes. Pour into a large bowl to cool.

Remove the rind from the watermelon, cut flesh into chunks and place in a food processor. Process melon until a puree forms, then strain, discarding seeds and fibre. Mix the watermelon puree with the sugar syrup and pour into a shallow metal dish. Freeze for 1 hour, or until ice crystals start to form around the edges. Scrape frozen edges back into the mixture with a fork. Repeat this process at least twice more, or until the mixture has large, even-sized ice crystals. For refreshing extra flavour, add 2 tablespoons chopped mint when freezing the last time.

Serve immediately or beat well with a fork and refreeze until ready to serve. Scrape the granita into serving dishes with a fork, or serve in scoops in tall glasses.

250 g (9 oz/1 heaped cup) caster (superfine) sugar
1.5 kg (3 lb 5 oz) watermelon
2 tablespoon chopped mint, optional

other fruit ■ melons

Watermelons are by far the largest of the sweet melons; the 1996 Guinness Book of Records *documents one that weighed in at 120 kg (262 lb), although generally, anywhere between 2.25–18 kg (5–40 lb) is normal. Not surprisingly, watermelon flesh comprises a whopping 92 per cent water—even today, in some parts of Africa, it is relied upon to satisfy thirst in times of water scarcity.*

pomegranate

fruit ■ **other**
season ■ **autumn**

Pomegranates, also called Chinese apples, are an old, old fruit. The word 'pomegranate' derives from the Latin meaning 'apple with many seeds' and it is true that, under the tough, red, leathery skin of a pomegranate, lie hundreds of small seeds encased in cranberry-red sacs of juice. The fleshy seeds have a tart-sweetness and make a refreshing drink. So unique is the pomegranate, that it is in a botanical family, *Punicaceae*, all its own; there are a few varieties but the differences are slight—skin may be darker, fruit may be larger or seeds may be slightly sweeter.

selection and storage

As with many juicy fruits, it is important to choose pomegranates that feel heavy for their size—this indicates the presence of a lot of juice. Generally, larger pomegranates have sweeter flesh with well-developed flavour.

Store pomegranates at cool room temperature for up to 3 weeks or, if in good condition (with firm, unblemished skin), up to 8 weeks in the refrigerator; the skin becomes tougher and more leathery with time but is an effective protector of the fruits' interior. The seeds and juice can also be frozen for up to 6 months.

preparation

Whichever way you approach it, dealing with a pomegranate is going to require patience and a gentle hand. Avoid getting the juice on your clothes—it is such an effective stain that it is still used as a dye in the manufacture of Persian carpets.

The most effective way of extracting the seeds is to cut off the crown (top) of the pomegranate then cut the fruit into quarters. Put in a bowl of cold water then carefully bend the skin back to open up the membranes, prising out the seeds—the bitter white membrane and skin will float to the top of the water, making for efficient disposal, while the seeds will sink (simply strain off water to retrieve the seeds).

To extract the juice, process the seeds briefly in a food processor then strain off the juice. As a rough guide, a medium pomegranate should yield 185 ml (6 fl oz/3/4 cup) of seeds and about 125 ml (4 fl oz/1/2 cup) juice.

pomegranate, green olive and walnut salad

Soak the walnut halves in boiling water for 3–4 minutes, or until the skins peel off readily. Drain, peel and pat dry. Lightly toast, shaking often, under a medium grill (broiler) for 8 minutes, or until golden. Cool, then roughly chop.

Combine the olive oil, pomegranate syrup and chilli flakes in a screw top jar and shake well.

Put the olives, pomegranate seeds, onion, walnuts and parsley in a bowl and toss. Just before serving, pour the dressing over, season with sea salt and freshly ground black pepper, and combine well.

note Pomegranate syrup is available from specialist Middle Eastern food stores and good delicatessens.

100 g (3½ oz/1 cup) walnut halves
125 ml (4 fl oz/½ cup) olive oil
1½ tablespoons pomegranate syrup
½ teaspoon chilli flakes
350 g (12 oz/2 cups) green olives, pitted and cut in halves
175 g (6 oz/½ cup) pomegranate seeds
1 large red onion, chopped
1 large handful flat-leaf (Italian) parsley

other fruit ■ pomegranate

Pomegranates have been found buried in ancient Egyptian tombs and are mentioned frequently throughout the Old Testament. They require serious heat in which to ripen to juicy sweetness, hence they grow best in the Middle East, to whose cuisines they are mainly connected, although they are native to Central Asia (Persia and Afghanistan).

For other pomegranate recipes see:
radicchio and figs with ginger
   vinaigrette 311

tamarillo

selection and storage

Tamarillos will ripen at room temperature—when fully ripe, they should feel slightly soft and rather heavy for their size. Select fruit that has tight skin with no blemishes or wrinkles.

Once fully ripe, tamarillos should be stored in the refrigerator, where they will keep for about 10 days. When cutting a tamarillo, take care that the juice doesn't splash your clothing as it will stain.

The most common, commercially available varieties of tamarillo, which are elegant, tapered globes about 7.5 cm (3 inches) long, are rich red or yellow skinned, with apricot coloured flesh. The numerous seeds, contained in the centre of the fruit in a large, pulpy, gel-like core, are perfectly edible but the bitter thin skin is not. Tamarillos can be enjoyed raw, although they need to be very ripe as their flesh can be somewhat tart—the yellow-skinned varieties being less acidic than the red. The fruit is highly nutritious, yielding good quantities of vitamins A, B6, C and E, and is also rich in iron and potassium.

preparation

Tamarillos are most effectively peeled by blanching in boiling water—prepared this way, they can then be poached whole. Using a small, sharp knife, make a tiny criss-cross incision in the base of the fruit. Plunge the fruit (about six at a time; don't crowd the pot) into a saucepan of boiling water for 30 seconds, then transfer to a bowl of iced water to quickly cool. Drain them well; the skin should easily peel away.

culinary uses

Tamarillos make suburb jam, are wonderful stewed (perhaps with a few apples, or chopped dates and bananas, to cut the acid) then baked under a crisp crumble topping, or served sweetened and warmed with good vanilla ice cream or custard on the side. The whole, peeled fruit, still with their stems intact, make for a dramatic presentation when poached whole in a lightly spiced sugar syrup.

poached tamarillo with vanilla bean cream pots

Put six 125 ml (4 fl oz/½ cup) ramekins in a large baking dish. Put the cream and vanilla bean in a saucepan, bring slowly to the boil then reduce the heat and simmer for 5 minutes. Remove from the heat, split the bean, scrape out the seeds and return the bean and seeds to the cream. Cover and set aside for 30 minutes. Strain.

Preheat the oven to 160°C (315°F/Gas 2–3). Whisk the eggs, yolks and sugar in a jug. Whisk in the cream, then pour into the ramekins and cover each securely with foil. Pour hot water into the baking dish to come halfway up the ramekins. Bake for 30 minutes, or until just set. Refrigerate, covered, for 4 hours or overnight.

To poach the tamarillos, score a cross in the base of the fruit, plunge them into boiling water for 10 seconds, then transfer to iced water and peel away the skins, leaving the stalks attached. Put the sugar in a saucepan with 750 ml (26 fl oz/ 3 cups) water and the orange peel. Stir to dissolve the sugar. Bring to the boil and boil for 3 minutes. Reduce the heat to a simmer and add the tamarillos. Poach for 6–8 minutes, depending on their ripeness. Turn off the heat, add the liqueur and leave the fruit in the syrup to cool.

Remove the fruit from the pan, then bring the syrup to the boil and boil for 5–10 minutes, or until reduced and thickened. Pour into a jug, cover and cool. Cut each tamarillo in half, leaving the stalk end intact, and serve with the sauce and vanilla bean cream.

The tamarillo originates from the Peruvian and Bolivian Andes and is a relative of the potato, eggplant (aubergine) and capsicum (pepper). We have New Zealand to thank for its commercialization and renaming (originally it was known as the tree tomato). It became popular there during the lean, food-rationed years of World War II.

vanilla bean cream
700 ml (24 fl oz) pouring (whipping) cream
1 vanilla bean
2 eggs
2 egg yolks
2 tablespoons caster (superfine) sugar

poached tamarillos
6 tamarillos with stalks
375 g (13 oz/1⅔ cups) caster (superfine) sugar
5 cm (2 inch) piece of orange peel
2–3 tablespoons kirsch or cherry liqueur, optional

other fruit ■ tamarillo

nuts

almonds
chestnuts
hazelnuts
macadamias
peanuts
pecans
pistachios
walnuts

almonds

selection and storage

If purchased in their shells, almonds will keep for up to 1 year, stored in a cool dark place. Shelled nuts, as prone to rancidity as all other nut types, should be stored in an airtight container in the refrigerator for several months or in the freezer, for up to a year. Avoid any that show signs of mould, cracking or holes in their shells—if purchasing shelled almonds, look for ones that are plump and unwrinkled.

produce ▪ nuts
season ▪ harvested in summer

Almonds are the most widely planted nut tree. They are part of the *Prunus* (plum, cherry, peach) genus, native to North Africa, West Asia and the Mediterranean—it is thought the earliest almonds travelled along the Silk Road with explorers.

The word 'almond' derives from the Greek word '*amygdalon*' which, via Latin, has become the botanical name for the species. The almond is a fruit, or drupe. It grows inside a hard, oval shell enclosed in a green-grey husk. The husks split open when the kernels, or nuts, are mature. In certain Mediterranean cultures the immature kernels, still moist, soft, pale and cosseted in their furry green coat, are enjoyed with salty white cheese as an appetizer or snack.

varieties

There are two types of almonds—the common sweet almond and the bitter almond, a native to Asia although now virtually naturalized around the Mediterranean. The flavour of the bitter almond will be familiar thanks to the widespread use of natural almond extract (the making of which is one of bitter almond's main uses) in baking and confectionery. Bitter almond is also the defining flavour of Italian amaretti biscuits and, also from Italy, amaretto liqueur. Bitter almonds contain a poisonous compound (cyanide, essentially) that dissipates during processing, however they are very toxic when raw—about 20 kernels will kill an adult. Having said this, the taste of a raw bitter almond is so disagreeable that it is unlikely that anyone would eat enough of them to become seriously ill.

There are many varieties of the more familiar sweet almond, with over 100 different types grown in California alone. These are widely used in sweet and savoury dishes the world over; whole, blanched, chopped, sliced or ground. Their mild, milky flavour goes particularly well with vegetables, fish and chicken—however they are used, a light roasting before use will accentuate their flavour. Almond milk, made by finely grinding whole almonds in water then straining the mixture of solids, has long been appreciated as an alternative to cows' milk—one of the first European uses for this was during the Middle Ages, in making of the original blancmange.

preparation

shelling The best way to extract kernels from their shells is to use a nutcracker. The shells are not particlularly hard so lots of force is not necessary.

roasting A light roasting significantly enhances the flavour of almonds and is easy to do. The most effective method is oven-roasting. Spread whole, shelled kernels (or blanched whole kernels) on a single layer in a roasting dish, then cook in a 180°C (350°F/Gas 4) oven for 8–10 minutes, or until light golden all the way through and fragrant.

blanching To blanch whole raw almonds, put almonds in a bowl then cover them with boiling water. Stand for 1 minute and then drain well. Rinse under cold water and drain, then dry almonds using a clean tea (dish) towel—skins should just slip off.

almond milk To make almond milk, combine 155 g (5½ oz/ 1 cup) of chopped, blanched almonds and 250 ml (9 fl oz/1 cup) water in a food processor and process until a smooth paste forms. Gradually add 2 cups water with the motor running. Strain mixture through a sieve lined with muslin (cheesecloth). Gather up cloth and nut solids and wring tightly to extract all liquid, discarding the solids. Almond milk can be used in smoothies, blancmange, custards and ice creams, or sweetened with honey to make a delicious milk jelly.

tamari roasted almonds with spicy green beans

serves 4–6

125 g (4½ oz/¾ cup) almonds
tamari, for soaking
1 tablespoon oil
3 tablespoons sesame oil
500 g (1 lb 2 oz/2½ cups) rice
1 litre (35 fl oz/4 cups) boiling water
1 long red chilli, seeded and
    finely chopped
2 cm (¾ inch) piece ginger,
    peeled and grated
2 garlic cloves, crushed
375 g (13 oz) green beans, cut
    into 5 cm (2 inch) lengths
125 ml (4 fl oz/½ cup) hoisin sauce
1 tablespoon soft brown sugar
2 tablespoons mirin

Soak the unpeeled almonds in a bowl with enough tamari to cover, for 30 minutes. Drain and dry with paper towels. Heat a non-stick frying pan with oil. Toss the almonds for 2–3 minutes, then drain. Roughly chop and set aside.

Preheat the oven to 200°C (400°F/Gas 6). Heat 1 tablespoon of sesame oil in a deep baking dish, add the rice and stir until well coated. Stir in the boiling water. Cover and cook for 20 minutes, or until all the water is absorbed. Keep warm.

Meanwhile, heat the remaining sesame oil in a wok or large frying pan and cook the chilli, ginger and garlic for 1 minute. Add the beans, hoisin sauce and sugar, and cook for a few minutes. Stir in the mirin and cook for 1 minute, or until the beans are just tender; they should be a little crunchy. Remove from the heat and stir in the almonds. Serve with the rice.

ajo blanco

serves 4–6

1 loaf day-old white Italian bread,
    crusts removed
155 g (5¾ oz/1 cup) blanched
    almonds
3–4 garlic cloves, chopped
125 ml (4 fl oz/½ cup) extra
    virgin olive oil
80 ml (2½ fl oz/⅓ cup) dry sherry
310 ml (10¾ fl oz/1¼ cups)
    ready-made vegetable stock
2 tablespoons olive oil, extra
75 g (2¾ oz) day-old white
    Italian bread, extra
200 g (7 oz) seedless green grapes

Soak the bread in cold water for 5 minutes, then squeeze out any excess liquid. Chop the garlic and almonds in a food processor until well ground. Add the bread and continue to process until smooth. With the motor running, add the oil in a slow steady stream until the mixture resembes thick mayonnaise. Slowly add the sherry and stock. Season to taste. Refrigerate for at least 2 hours.

When ready to serve, heat the extra oil in a frying pan, add the bread cubes and toss over medium heat for 3 minutes, or until golden. Drain on paper towels. Serve the soup very cold—you may need to add extra stock or water to thin it. Garnish with the grapes and bread cubes.

almond, orange and cardamom biscotti

Preheat the oven to 160°C (315°F/Gas 2–3). Line a baking tray with baking paper.

Beat the eggs and sugar in a bowl until pale and creamy. Sift the flours into the bowl, then add the almonds, orange zest and cardamom and mix to a soft dough.

Turn out the dough onto a lightly floured work surface. Divide the mixture into equal portions, shaping it into two 5 x 20 cm (2 x 8 inch) loaves.

Bake for 35–40 minutes, or until lightly golden. Transfer to a wire rack to cool. Cut the loaves into 1 cm (1/2 inch) diagonal slices with a large serrated bread knife. The biscotti will be crumbly on the edges so work slowly and, if possible, try to hold the sides as you cut.

Arrange the slices on a baking tray in a single layer (you may need to use two trays or do this in batches). Return to the oven for 10 minutes on each side. Don't worry if they don't seem fully dry as they will become crisp on cooling. Transfer to a wire rack to cool. Store in an airtight container for up to 3 weeks.

2 eggs
155 g (5 1/2 oz/3/4 cup) soft brown sugar
125 g (4 1/2 oz/1 cup) self-raising flour
90 g (3 1/4 oz/3/4 cup) plain (all-purpose) flour
125 g (4 1/2 oz/1 cup) almonds
1 tablespoon finely grated orange zest
1/4 teaspoon ground cardamom

nuts ▪ almonds

chestnuts

produce ■ **nuts**
season ■ **harvested in autumn**

selection and storage

Mature chestnuts simply fall to the ground when ready for eating and need only to be gathered up. When buying chestnuts, choose those with glossy and smooth shells (their prickly outer casing will generally have been removed) and that feel heavy for their size.

Avoid nuts that rattle in their shells as this indicates they are starting to dry out. Store fresh chestnuts for up to 1 month in a perforated plastic bag in the refrigerator; they'll also be fine frozen, for up to 4 months. Cooked chestnut flesh can also be frozen successfully for up to 4 months.

With their low fat and calorie content, sweet, starchy flesh and quite significant vitamin C levels, the chestnut is hardly a typical nut. In fact, many food cultures have long used the chestnut as a vegetable, mashing the mealy flesh like potato, braising it with meats or cooking it with cabbage or Brussels sprouts. Chestnuts also star in traditional sweet preparations. Think of monte bianco where piles of sweetened chestnut puree are pushed through a mouli into long strands then lavished with cream, or the hopelessly luxurious marrons glacés (candied chestnuts) from France. Chestnuts are also dried, made into flour for baked goods and widely enjoyed roasted as a hot snack.

As well as starch (they contain twice as much as potatoes), chestnuts are rich in potassium and contain reasonable amounts of vitamin B.

preparation

Chestnuts contain high levels of tannic acid so do need to be fully cooked—never eat them raw. To prepare chestnuts make a cross-shaped incision in their flat side with a small, sharp knife. Boil the nuts in water for 15–20 minutes then peel them while still hot—the tough inner skin will come off more easily than when cold. Work with a few nuts at a time, keeping remaining nuts warm in their cooking water.

To roast chestnuts, make the same incision then cook them in a 200°C (400°F/Gas 6) oven for 20 minutes, or until soft, then peel.

chestnut, pancetta and cabbage soup

Cook the cabbage in 1.5 litres (52 fl oz/6 cups) boiling salted water over high heat for about 10 minutes. Drain, reserving the water. Cool cabbage slightly and finely chop.

Heat the oil in a large saucepan, add the onion and pancetta and cook over medium-high heat for 4–5 minutes, or until the onion is soft and the pancetta lightly browned. Add the garlic and rosemary and cook for a few minutes more.

Using your hands, break up the chestnuts and add to the pan with the cabbage. Stir to combine, season to taste, then add the wine. Bring to the boil and cook for 2 minutes. Add the cabbage water, reduce the heat and simmer for 15 minutes. Remove half the soup mixture from the saucepan and allow to cool slightly before blending to a puree in a food processor. Return puree to heat and stir to combine. Serve with a drizzle of extra virgin olive oil.

100 g (3½ oz) savoy cabbage, roughly chopped
2 tablespoons olive oil
1 large onion, finely chopped
185 g (6½ oz) pancetta, diced
3 garlic cloves, crushed
2 tablespoons chopped rosemary
300 g (10½ oz/2 cups) cooked peeled chestnuts
150 ml (5 fl oz) red wine
extra virgin olive oil, to serve

chestnut cake

serves 8

Preheat the oven to 180°C (350°F/gas 4). Grease and flour a 20 cm (8 inch) round cake tin. Boil the chestnuts in a saucepan of water over high heat for 15–20 minutes, or until tender. Drain and peel the chestnuts while still hot. Put peeled chestnuts into a food processor and puree. Push the puree through a sieve so that the mixture is smooth.

Whisk the egg yolks and sugar until light and fluffy. Add the butter, lemon zest, chestnut puree, ground almonds and flour and stir well. Whisk the egg whites until soft peaks form and fold into the mixture. Pour into the tin and bake for 50–60 minutes. Turn out onto a wire rack to cool. Serve with whipped cream.

400 g (14 oz) chestnuts
5 egg yolks
200 g (7 oz/heaped ¾ cup) caster (superfine) sugar
100 g (3½ oz) unsalted butter
1 tablespoon grated lemon zest
150 g (5½ oz/1½ cups) ground almonds
2 tablespoons plain (all-purpose) flour
4 egg whites
whipped cream, to serve

nuts ■ chestnuts

hazelnuts

selection and storage

Purchase hazelnuts that feel full and heavy in their shells—the nuts inside should be plump; the fine brown skin that covers it should be tight. Hazelnuts, like all nuts, are highly perishable so store them away from heat and humidity—in the refrigerator is ideal.

produce ■ nuts
season ■ harvested in summer

Hazelnut lore is legion—ancient Greek texts assert the nut is effective as a cure for colds as well as for hair loss. Some people in Spain still insist that a dozen hazelnuts eaten before sleep will discourage bed-wetting. The Romans burned torches of hazelnut wood at weddings as a fertility rite and magicians' wands are traditionally made of hazelnut wood, a member of the birch (Betulaceae) family.

Today, much of the world's hazelnut crop is supplied by Turkey, although the state of Oregon in the United States claims it grows the world's best. Italy has given us some of the most adored hazelnut treats—the hazelnut-flavoured liqueur Frangelico and *gianduja* (a divine chocolate-hazelnut paste used in desserts and confectionery). Hazelnuts, as the Italians discovered, have a special affinity with chocolate and are delicious in all manner of chocolate cakes, biscuits, tarts, sauces and sweets.

preparation

Shelled hazelnuts benefit from the removal of their fine skin as this is slightly bitter. To do this, roast the nuts in a 180°C (350°F/Gas 4) oven for 10–12 minutes or until skins are beginning to lift. Transfer them to a paper towel (or tea towel) and wrap them in this to steam for several minutes, then rub vigorously to remove skins—not all will be removed but most will come off.

chocolate and hazelnut semifreddo

serves 10   165

Line a 1.5 litre (52 fl oz/6 cup) loaf (bar) tin with two long strips of foil. Heat 200 ml (7 fl oz) cream in a small saucepan. Combine the sugar, cocoa and egg yolks in a bowl. Pour the hot cream on top and mix well. Pour the mixture back into the saucepan and cook over low heat, stirring continuously, until the mixture is thick enough to coat the back of a wooden spoon—do not allow the custard to boil. Stir in the brandy and remove from the heat. Cover the surface with plastic wrap and cool.

Using electric beaters, whisk the egg whites in a clean dry glass bowl until stiff peaks form. Add the icing sugar and continue whisking until stiff and glossy. Whip the remaining cream in a large bowl until soft peaks form. Lightly fold the chocolate custard into the whipped cream, then fold in the egg whites. Gently fold through the hazelnuts. Spoon into the tin, smooth the surface and cover with foil. Freeze for at least 24 hours. Leave at room temperature for 5 minutes before serving in slices. Semifreddo will keep, frozen, for up to 5 days.

500 ml (17 fl oz/2 cups) thick (double/heavy) cream
150 g (5½ oz/⅔ cup) caster (superfine) sugar
50 g (1¾ oz/½ cup) unsweetened cocoa powder
4 eggs, separated
3 tablespoons brandy
3 tablespoons icing (confectioners') sugar
150 g (5½ oz/1¼ cups) skinned, roughly chopped hazelnuts

nuts ▪ hazelnuts

Confusingly, in the United States hazelnuts are also called 'filberts', while in Europe 'filbert' and 'cob' are used to indicate varieties of cultivated hazelnuts, possibly because they are harvested around St Philbert's feast day on 20 August.

For other hazelnut recipes see:
orange, hazelnut and goat's cheese salad....................................37
mixed nut tartlets.............................171

macadamias

produce ■ **nuts**
season ■ **available year-round**

Macadamia nuts are native to Australia, where the indigenous peoples had eaten them long before European settlement. In fact, the colonizers of Australia initially paid little notice to the macadamia and it wasn't until the 1880s that the first orchard was planted. By then the nut had already been taken to Hawaii where it was found to grow spectacularly well—today, Hawaii is a significant producer of quality macadamias.

selection and storage

The macadamia has the hardest shell of all commercially grown nuts and indicates its ripeness by falling to the ground after the green husk that surrounds it has split—it is then collected, dried and then shelled. Because of their very high oil content (up to 80 per cent), macadamias can quickly turn rancid, so store them in an airtight container in the refrigerator for up to 6 months, or in the freezer for up to 1 year.

preparation

Macadamias are difficult to shell at home and are generally purchased out of their shell, although a nutcracker has been developed specifically for this purpose. Macadamias are relatively expensive as their nut yield in relation to their weight when unshelled is quite high—about 25 kg (55 lb) of unshelled nuts yields an average amount of 6–7 kg (13–15 lb) nut meat.

culinary uses

With their subtle, rich, buttery taste and singularly smooth texture, macadamias are quite unlike any other nut. A light roasting brings out their flavour, as does a sprinkling of salt, in which state they make an indulgent snack to eat with drinks. Their delicate, creamy flavour and silky texture make macadamias an ideal partner for other nuts and tropical fruits and, intruigingly, white chocolate. They can be chopped and tossed through salads and can also be used in a crust for chicken or fish—finely ground and combined with breadcrumbs, parsley and a touch of grated lemon or lime zest, the mixture can be used to coat chicken or firm white fish fillets before shallow-frying for a delicious outcome.

macadamia-crusted chicken bites

Cut the chicken into strips and dust with the flour. Dip the strips in the egg, then coat them in the combined nuts and breadcrumbs. Refrigerate for at least 30 minutes to firm the crust.

Fill a large heavy-based saucepan one-third full of oil and heat to 180°C (350°F), or until a cube of bread dropped into the oil browns in 15 seconds. Cook the chicken strips in batches for 2–3 minutes, or until golden brown all over, taking care not to burn the nuts. Drain well on paper towels. Serve warm with mango salsa.

12 chicken tenderloins
seasoned plain (all-purpose)
   flour, for coating
2 eggs, lightly beaten
240 g (8¾ oz/1½ cups)
   macadamias, finely chopped
160 g (5¾ oz/2 cups) fresh
   breadcrumbs
oil, for deep-frying
mango salsa (see page 417),
   to serve

nuts ■ macadamias

macadamia blondies

makes 25 pieces

Preheat the oven to 180°C (350°F/Gas 4). Lightly grease a 20 cm (8 inch) square tin and line with baking paper, leaving the paper hanging over on two opposite sides.

Put the butter and white chocolate in a heatproof bowl. Half fill a saucepan with water and bring to the boil. Remove from the heat. Put the bowl over the saucepan, making sure the base of the bowl does not touch the water. Stir until the butter and chocolate have melted and are smooth.

Put the caster sugar into the bowl and gradually stir in the eggs. Add the vanilla extract, fold in the flour and macadamia nuts, then pour into the tin. Bake for 35–40 minutes. If the top starts to brown too quickly, cover with foil. When cooked, cool in the tin before lifting out, using the paper as handles, and cutting into squares to serve.

100 g (3½ oz) unsalted butter,
   cubed
100 g (3½ oz/⅔ cup) chopped
   white chocolate
125 g (4½ oz/heaped ½ cup)
   caster (superfine) sugar
2 eggs, lightly beaten
1 teaspoon natural vanilla extract
125 g (4½ oz/1 cup) self-raising
   flour
80 g (2¾ oz/½ cup)
   macadamia nuts, roughly
   chopped

peanuts

selection and storage

Like all nuts, peanuts contain a high ratio of oil and are prone to rancidity so need to be stored carefully. Buy them in their shells (look closely for any sign of mould as this is common in peanuts) and store them in a well-aerated bag (not in plastic or they could turn mouldy).

produce ▪ nuts
season ▪ harvested autumn–winter

The peanut isn't a nut at all but rather a legume, related to peas and beans. Peanuts are technically seeds in pods, which grow on tendrils below the ground, hence their common name, groundnut.

To say the peanut is a significant worldwide food crop is something of an understatement—an estimated half a billion people, mainly in Africa, rely on peanuts as their main protein. From the satay sauces of Southeast Asia, to the peanut-based stews and soups of Africa and the Caribbean, to the spicy stir-fries of Sichuan in China's southwest and the ever-popular peanut butter, the peanut is a truly global food. Nutritionally, it's a powerhouse, offering 26 per cent of its mass as protein and containing a veritable smorgasbord of vitamins and essential minerals.

preparation

roasting To roast peanuts in their shell, simply spread them on a baking tray, in a single layer, and bake them for 30 minutes in a 180°C (350°F/Gas 4) oven, turning them often and testing after about 20 minutes. They can be served hot, warm or at room temperature.

blanching To blanch shelled peanuts, put them in a bowl, pour boiling water over them, stand for 5 minutes then drain well. The skins should just slip off. In China peanuts are boiled, either in their shells or skins. Simmered for 40 minutes in water fragranced with star anise, cinnamon, cloves, Sichuan pepper, fennel seed and salt, they swell, soften and absorb the delicious flavours, making a wonderfully different snack.

satay sauce

Put the peanuts in a food processor and process until finely chopped.

Heat the oil in a frying pan. Add the onion and cook over medium heat for 5 minutes or until softened. Add the garlic, ginger, chilli powder, curry powder and ground cumin, and cook, stirring, for 2 minutes. Add the coconut milk, soft brown sugar and the chopped peanuts. Reduce the heat and cook for 5 minutes or until the sauce thickens. Add the lemon juice, season with sea salt and freshly ground black pepper. Serve as a dip or a sauce for barbecued meats, pork, lamb, beef or chicken.

note For a smoother sauce, wait until the mixture has cooled slightly and process in a food processor for 30 seconds. Then, return to heat to warm the sauce.

160 g (5¾ oz/1 cup) unsalted peanuts, roasted
2 tablespoons oil
1 onion, chopped
2 garlic cloves, crushed
2 teaspoons grated fresh ginger
½ teaspoon chilli powder
2 teaspoons curry powder
1 teaspoon ground cumin
420 ml (14½ fl oz/1⅔ cup) coconut milk
3 tablespoons soft brown sugar
1 tablespoon lemon juice

king prawns with peanuts

serves 4

Peel and devein the prawns, leaving the tails intact.

Combine the prawns with the green onion, garlic, ginger, sambal oelek, coriander, turmeric, lemon zest, lemon juice and peanuts. Cover and refrigerate for 1 hour.

Heat the oil in a frying pan; add the prawn mixture and stir-fry over high heat for about 3 minutes or until the prawns are cooked. Serve with rice.

1.25 kg (2 lb 12 oz) raw king prawns
4 green onions (scallions), chopped
1 garlic clove, crushed
1 teaspoon grated fresh ginger
1 teaspoon sambal oelek
1 teaspoon ground coriander
½ teaspoon ground turmeric
1 teaspoon grated lemon zest
1 tablespoon lemon juice
110 g (3¾ oz/⅔ cup) chopped unsalted roasted peanuts
2 tablespoons peanut oil

nuts ▪ peanuts

pecans

produce ■ nuts
season ■ harvested autumn

A North American native, the pecan was an important food for the indigenous peoples; the Algonquin called it *paccan*, which French settlers later turned into 'pecan'. Botanists assumed, because of the huge numbers growing there, that the pecan tree was originally from Illinois—hence the scientific name *Carva illinoinensis*, although its original home is more likely to have been Texas or Louisiana.

There are hundreds of varieties of pecan grown today, many of which have been specially developed to produce large nuts with thin shells, generally better-tasting and with a longer shelf life than their ancestors. Pecans are grown now in Australia, Israel, Brazil and South Africa although the United States still grows most of the world's supply.

Like other nuts, pecans are incredibly nutritious. They contain no less than 19 different vitamins and minerals, including high levels of zinc, which helps in the generation of testosterone. They also contain antioxidants

culinary uses

Pecans are used in similar ways to their walnut relative, although their flavour is somewhat smoother and sweeter. Toss them into salads or include them in breads, cakes, tarts and stuffing for meats, although they are arguably at their most memorable in decadent classics such as pecan pie and butter pecan ice cream.

selection and storage

The freshest pecans are those available in autumn, when the nut meat is sweet and moist. Keep the nuts cool as their high monounsaturated fat content (around 75 per cent) can quickly cause rancidity.

Shelled nuts are best stored in the refrigerator where they will maintain freshness for up to 3 months. Unshelled nuts will store at cool room temperature for up to 3 months—for longer storage times, both shelled and unshelled nuts should be frozen.

mixed nut tartlets

Preheat the oven to 180°C (350°F/Gas 4). Spread the nuts on a baking tray and roast for 7 minutes, or until light golden.

Put the sifted flour and butter in a food processor. Pulse for 10 seconds, or until the mixture resembles fine breadcrumbs. Add about 80 ml (2 1/2 fl oz/ 1/3 cup) water and process until the mixture just comes together. Add another tablespoon of water if needed, but do not over-process as pastry will be tough. Turn out onto a lightly floured surface and gather into a ball. Refrigerate for 20 minutes.

Divide the pastry into 10 equal-sized portions. Roll each portion out on a lightly floured surface to fit a fluted 8 cm (3 1/4 inch) tartlet tin. Trim any excess pastry, then refrigerate the pastry cases for 10 minutes. Put the tins on two baking trays. Cut sheets of baking paper to line the base and side of each tin. Put baking beads or rice in the tins and bake for 10 minutes. Remove the beads and paper and bake for a further 10–12 minutes, or until dry to touch and golden.

Divide the nuts among the pastry shells. Whisk together the soft brown sugar, white sugar, corn syrup, butter and eggs, and drizzle the mixture over the nuts. Bake for 15–20 minutes, or until just set and golden. Cool completely before serving.

300 g (10 1/2 oz/2 cups) mixed nuts (pecans, macadamias and hazelnuts)
375 g (13 oz/3 cups) plain (all-purpose) flour
230 g (8 oz) butter, chopped
3 tablespoons soft brown sugar
2 tablespoons white sugar
3 tablespoons light corn syrup
30 g (1 oz) butter, extra, melted
2 eggs, lightly beaten

nuts ■ pecans

Perhaps no dish is associated with a particular nut as is pecan pie, that staple of the American south. Its invention was suprisingly recent—it wasn't mentioned in cookbooks until the 1940s. Composed of pastry and a corn-syrup based, pecan studded filling, pecan pie is incredibly sweet and best enjoyed ocassionally and in thin slices.

pistachios

produce ▪ nuts
season ▪ harvested late summer–early autumn

selection and storage

Some processors open their pistachios mechanically, so make sure any nuts you buy have been allowed to open naturally on the tree, as their flavour will be superior. Once the pistachios' shell has split, they have a limited shelf life, so store them carefully. This is best done in a container in the refrigerator (for up to 3 months) or frozen, for up to 6 months.

The Queen of Sheba knew a good thing when she saw it—she decreed that all pistachios grown in her domains be sent for the exclusive use of her court. An ancient food, the pistachio nut is just one of two nuts given mention in the Old Testament (the other is the almond) and is reputed to have been a feature of Nebuchadnezzar's fabled Hanging Gardens of Babylon. Certainly the pistachio was a founding crop in the Fertile Crescent of today's Middle East region where until recent decades it was almost exclusively grown—most notably in Iran.

Technically, the pistachio does not produce nuts at all but rather drupes, of which the pale green 'nuts', or kernels, are the edible seeds. These grow in grape-like clusters and are enclosed in a pale shell. When the kernels ripen, they expand inside their shells causing these to split open at one end (prompting the Chinese to call them the 'happy nut' and the Arabs the 'smiling pistachio')—they are ready to eat when this happens.

Good pistachios should taste delicately sweet and buttery and be quite green—their characteristic pigment comes from chlorophyll and the greener the pistachios are the better the flavour. The brownish skin which covers the kernels is perfectly edible but can be removed by blanching in boiling water, if desired.

pistachio, yoghurt and cardamom cake

Preheat the oven to 180°C (350°F/Gas 4). Grease a 20 cm (8 inch) round cake tin and line the base with baking paper. Put the pistachios and cardamom in a food processor and using the pulse action, process the mixture until pistachios are coarsely chopped. Add the butter, flour and caster sugar and pulse for 20 seconds, or until crumbly. Add the combined eggs and yoghurt and pulse for 10 seconds, or until just combined. Spoon into the tin and smooth the surface.

Bake for 45–50 minutes, or until a skewer comes out clean when inserted into the centre of the cake. Allow to cool in the tin for 10 minutes before turning out onto a wire rack.

To make the syrup, peel the zest off the lime with a vegetable peeler—remove any white pith from the zest. Put the caster sugar and 100 ml (3½ fl oz) water in a saucepan and stir over low heat until the sugar has dissolved. Bring to the boil, then add the lime zest and cook for 5 minutes. Strain and cool slightly. Put the cake on a serving plate, pierce with a skewer and pour the hot syrup over the cooled cake.

150 g (5½ oz/1 cup) unsalted pistachio nuts
½ teaspoon ground cardamom
150 g (5½ oz) unsalted butter, chopped
185 g (6½ oz/1½ cups) self-raising flour
185 g (6½ oz/¾ cup) caster (superfine) sugar
3 eggs
125 g (4½ oz/½ cup) plain yoghurt

syrup
1 lime
125 g (4½ oz/heaped ½ cup) caster (superfine) sugar

nuts ▪ pistachios

Fresh, soft, immature pistachios are available, fleetingly, in late summer and early autumn. Their soft pink shell is stripped away to reveal a soft, sweet, green kernel. Serve these as a snack with a snifter of arak (a Lebanese liqueur that tastes of aniseed) or toss them through Middle Eastern-style salads.

walnuts

produce ▪ **nuts**
season ▪ **available year-round**

selection and storage

Buy walnuts with undamaged shells and shake them first—if any rattle, it means the meat has withered inside the shell. The shells protect the meat from insects and light and the nuts will keep, unshelled, for up to 1 year stored in a cool, dark place. Shelled nuts should be refrigerated for up to 3 months or frozen for up to 6 months.

Purchase walnuts in the shell, crack them yourself and taste the sweet difference—the majority of shelled, packaged nuts are bitter and less than fresh, giving this delicious and versatile nut a bad reputation. The walnut fruits are classified as drupes. The nut we are most familiar with is that produced by the *Juglans regia* tree, one of over a dozen edible species of *Juglans*, of which the *regia* walnut is the largest and the most easily cracked. The name derives from the latin *Jovis glans*, meaning 'regal nut of the Gods' although the name 'walnut' is an English corruption of Gaul (or French) nut.

preparation

For certain uses (for pickling in the English manner or infusing into alcohol to make the delicious Italian digestive Nocino, for example) walnuts are picked while the shell is soft and immature and surrounded by a fleshy, green layer. Generally though, walnuts are used when fully mature and completely dried after harvesting. As a rough guide, 500 g (1 lb 2 oz) of walnuts in the shell will yield about 200 g (7 oz/2 cups) nut meat.

culinary uses

The world of cookery is awash with ways to use this delicious nut. In Italy it turns up in a version of pesto, whole in honey to spoon over gorgonzola and, in the north, in regional tarts and breads. Everyone knows the Greek sweet baklava, and is familiar with the English notion of serving cracked walnuts with stilton cheese and port. In Asia and the Middle East the walnut is used in numerous sauces, including the famous taratoor.

walnut taratoor

Finely chop the walnuts in a blender or food processor.
Set aside ½ teaspoon of the walnuts for a garnish. Add the
breadcrumbs, garlic, vinegar and 3 tablespoons water and
blend well. With the motor running, gradually add the olive
oil in a thin steady stream until smooth. Add a little more
water if the sauce appears to be too thick. Season to taste,
then transfer to a serving bowl and refrigerate. Combine
the reserved walnuts and parsley and sprinkle on top. Serve
with seafood, salads, fried vegetables or bread.

variation A taratoor can be made with almonds,
hazelnuts or pine nuts instead of the walnuts. Lemon
juice can be used as a substitute for the vinegar.

250 g (9 oz/2½ cups) shelled
  walnuts
80 g (2¾ oz/1 cup) fresh white
  breadcrumbs
3 garlic cloves
60 ml (2 fl oz/¼ cup) white wine
  vinegar
250 ml (9 fl oz/1 cup) olive oil
fresh parsley, chopped,
  to garnish

nuts ▪ walnuts

walnut and cheddar soda bread

makes 1 loaf

Preheat the oven to 180°C (350°F/Gas 4). Line a baking tray
with baking paper.

Sift the flours, baking powder and bicarbonate of soda into
a large bowl (tip any husks from the wholemeal flour left in
the sieve back into the mixture). Stir in the sugar, walnuts
and cheese. Make a well in the centre. Combine the butter,
eggs and buttermilk in a bowl and pour into the well. Stir
with a wooden spoon until a soft dough forms, then turn
out onto a lightly floured work surface. Knead briefly just
until smooth, then shape the dough into a 20 cm (8 inch)
round. Transfer to the baking tray.

Using a sharp knife, cut a 1 cm (½ inch) deep cross into the
top of the loaf. Bake for 30–40 minutes, or until golden.
Allow to cool and serve cut into slices, with butter.

250 g (9 oz/2 cups) plain
  (all-purpose) flour
225 g (8 oz/1½ cups) wholemeal
  (whole-wheat) flour
1 tablespoon baking powder
1 teaspoon bicarboate of soda
  (baking soda)
1 tablespoon soft brown sugar
60 g (2¼ oz/½ cup) walnuts,
  chopped
175 g (6 oz/1½ cups) grated
  mature cheddar cheese
40 g (1½ oz) butter, melted and
  cooled
2 eggs, lightly beaten
250 ml (9 fl oz/1 cup) buttermilk

beetroot (beet)
carrot
celeriac
ginger
horseradish
jerusalem artichoke
kohlrabi
parsnip
potato
radish
sweet potato
taro
turnip and swede
   (rutabaga)
asparagus
celery
fennel
garlic
green onion (scallion)
leek
onion
rhubarb
shallot
sprouts
artichoke
broccoli
cauliflower
asian greens
brussels sprout
cabbage
lettuce
radicchio
rocket (arugula)
silverbeet (swiss chard)
spinach
sorrel
watercress
witlof (chicory/belgian endive)
avocado
capsicum (pepper)
chilli
cucumber
eggplant (aubergine)
pumpkin (winter squash)
tomato
zucchini (courgette)
zucchini flower
broad (fava) beans
green beans
okra
peas
soya beans
sugar snap and snowpeas (mangetout)
sweet corn
cultivated mushrooms
exotic mushrooms

vegetables

beetroot
(beet)

Beetroot, also known as beets, are believed to be a vegetable from pre-history, once occurring wild over vast swathes of the northern hemisphere, from Britain all the way to India. Initially, it was just their leaves that were appreciated—the Romans and Greeks consigned the roots to medicinal uses and Pliny the Elder (23–79 AD) referred to them as 'those crimson, nether parts'.

It wasn't until the third century AD that the roots were declared to taste 'better than cabbage', as was noted at the time. And little wonder they were pronounced so good—beetroot contain more sucrose than any other vegetable.

Beets, although generally rounded, come in less-common elongated varieties and, increasingly, in 'baby' golf-ball sizes. Recent hybrids have golden orange or white interiors while others, known as chioggia, are layered inside with concentric rings of pink and white. These hybrids have a more delicate flavour than the standard red sort, whose startling carmine colour is due to the pigment betacyanin, to which some people are intolerant. In these individuals, the maroon colour passes all the way through their systems without being absorbed, which, given its resemblance to blood, can prove a little disconcerting.

selection and storage

Always buy beetroot with the stems and leaves attached. These should look fresh and bright—a sign that the beets have been recently dug.
Try to choose bulbs that are approximately the same size (otherwise they'll all have different cooking times) and that have smooth, unblemished, tight skin.
Avoid any that are very big as these may be woody inside.

Use the leaves and stems within 2 days of purchase—these are delicious when chopped and stewed in olive oil with garlic, anchovies, currants and a splash of red wine vinegar. Trimmed beetroot will keep, stored in a plastic bag in the refrigerator, for up to 10 days.

preparation

Sweet, earthy beetroot are unavoidably messy to prepare, leaving vivid, hard-to-remove trails of deep red on whatever their juices touch; chopping boards, hands, bench tops. They also take what seems like an age to cook and perhaps this is why many people know beets only from their more user-friendly tinned guise—which is a great pity, as these are but a pallid stand-in for the real thing.

Beetroot can be boiled, roasted or steamed. It is advisable to cook them in their skins, as this preserves both flavour and colour (much of the colour bleeds out into cooking water if peeled). Don't cut off the long roots and only peel beetroot if you are using them in certain soup recipes that demand this.

Of all the ways to cook beetroot, baking or roasting results in the sweetest, most intense flavour as this dry method of cooking concentrates the flavours. Once tender, beetroot can be sliced, diced, or cut into wedges and used in salads, risottos, dips and vegetable side dishes. Not all recipes require beetroot to be pre-cooked, though. Certain soups, chutneys and even thin, crisp-fried 'chips' are prepared using the raw vegetable, while finely grated, raw beetroot is often the basis for deliciously fresh-tasting salads. Whichever method of cooking you opt for, the preparation is identical. Simply cut off the stems and leaves, reserving these for some other use. Scrub the beets to remove all dirt; if roasting, pat dry.

boiling Cook large-medium beetroot in simmering, salted water for up to 1½ hours or until tender all the way through—a thin skewer is perfect for testing them. Baby beetroot will only take 20–30 minutes to cook. Drain well and allow to cool, then use your hands to slip the skins off (a pair of rubber gloves is useful here).

roasting Put beetroot in a roasting tin in a single layer and brush lightly with olive oil. Cook in a 180°C (350°F/Gas 4) oven for about 1½–2 hours, depending on size, or until tender when tested with a knife. Peel when cool enough to handle but still quite warm. Beetroot can also be wrapped tightly in foil before baking, which has a steaming effect—the beets won't shrivel as much and will be easier to peel but won't have the same, concentrated flavour (see recipe on page 182).

steaming Cook beetroot over boiling water in a perforated, double-boiler arrangement or an electric steamer—large ones will take around 1¼ hours to reach tenderness, while baby beetroot will take about 20 minutes.

beetroot hummus

Put the chickpeas in a large bowl, cover with cold water and soak overnight.

Drain the chickpeas and put them in a large heavy-based saucepan with the onions. Cover with water and bring to the boil. Cook for 1 hour, or until the chickpeas are very soft. Drain, reserving 250 ml (9 fl oz/1 cup) of cooking liquid. Allow the chickpeas to cool.

Cook the beetroot in a large saucepan of boiling water for 1½ hours, or until tender. Drain and allow to cool slightly before removing skins.

Chop the beetroot and place in a food processor, in batches if necessary. Add the chickpea and onion mixture, tahini, garlic, lemon juice and cumin; process until smooth. Slowly add the reserved cooking liquid and olive oil while the machine is running. Blend until mixture is thoroughly combined. Drizzle with a little olive oil to serve.

250 g (9 oz/1 cup) dried
  chickpeas
1 large onion, chopped
500 g (1 lb 2 oz) beetroot
125 ml (4 fl oz/½ cup) tahini
  (sesame seed paste)
3 garlic cloves, crushed
60 ml (2 fl oz/¼ cup) lemon juice
1 tablespoon ground cumin
60 ml (2 fl oz/¼ cup) olive oil

roots and tubers ■ beetroot (beet)

beetroot chips

serves 4 as a snack

Use a sharp knife to cut the beetroot into paper-thin slices. Preheat the oven to 120°C (235°F/Gas ½).

Heat the oil in a frying pan over high heat and cook the beetroot slices, in batches, until they are crisp and browned. Drain on paper towels and keep warm in a 120°C (235°F/Gas ½) oven while cooking the remainder.

Serve the beetroot chips with aïoli.

500 g (1 lb 2 oz) beetroot, peeled
750 ml (26 fl oz/3 cups)
  vegetable oil, to fry
aïoli (page 253), to serve

serves 4–6

roasted beetroot with horseradish cream

8 beetroot
2 tablespoons olive oil
2 teaspoons honey
½ quantity horseradish cream
  (see page 199), to serve
chopped parsley, to garnish

Preheat the oven to 200°C (400°F/Gas 6). Scrub and peel the beetroot, trim the ends and cut into quarters. Put the oil and honey in a small bowl and mix well. Season with salt and freshly ground black pepper. Divide the beetroot pieces among four large squares of foil and drizzle with the honey mixture, turning to coat well. Wrap the beetroot loosely in the foil. Bake for 1 hour, or until the beetroot are tender when pierced with a skewer.

Once the beetroot are cooked, remove from the oven and leave in the foil for 5 minutes. Remove from the foil and serve with a generous dollop of horseradish cream, and parsley to garnish.

serves 4

beetroot and goat's cheese salad

dressing
1 tablespoon red wine vinegar
2 tablespoons extra virgin
  olive oil
1 garlic clove, crushed
1 tablespoon salted capers,
  rinsed, drained and chopped

4 beetroot bulbs, with leaves
200 g (7 oz) green beans
100 g (3½ oz/⅔ cup) crumbled
  goat's cheese

To make the dressing, put all the ingredients into a screw-top jar, season with sea salt and freshly ground black pepper and shake. Trim the leaves from the beetroot. Scrub the bulbs and wash the leaves. Simmer the whole bulbs in a large saucepan of boiling water, covered, for 30 minutes, or until tender.

Meanwhile, bring a separate saucepan of water to the boil, add the beans and cook for 3 minutes, or until just tender. Remove with a slotted spoon and plunge into a bowl of cold water. Drain well. Add the beetroot leaves to the same saucepan and cook for 3–5 minutes, or until leaves and stems are tender. Drain and plunge into a bowl of cold water, then drain again. Peel the skins off the beetroot and cut into thin wedges.

To serve, put the beans, beetroot leaves and beetroot wedges into a serving bowl. Crumble the goat's cheese over the top and drizzle with the dressing.

carrot

vegetable ▪ **roots and tubers**
season ▪ **available year-round**

Carrots are essential to kitchens the world over; there is barely a cuisine that does not rely on their sweet, earthy presence in stocks, soups, stews, salads, stir-fries and sauces. Even in drinks (consider the recent mainstream popularity of carrot juice), preserves, cakes and baked desserts, carrots are an indispensable ingredient. And, unlike many other root vegetables, carrots are as delicious raw as they are cooked.

While we think of the carrot as a distinctively orange-hued vegetable, the original carrots (including some wild and heirloom varieties available today) were white, yellow, pink, black or purple. Believed to have originated in Afghanistan, carrots moved gradually westward over the centuries, eventually ending up, via Arab traders, in twelfth-century Spain. It is believed that the purple carrot was being cultivated in Italy and other corners of Europe in the fourteenth century—the orange version, so familiar to us now, didn't come on the scene until the 1700s. The orange carrot was developed by the Dutch, motivated, it is believed, out of patriotism for the ruling House of Orange.

The high vitamin A content of carrots (it contains more than any other vegetable) is, among other things, beneficial for retinal function.

baby carrots

Baby carrots, sometimes called Dutch carrots, are those which have been specially bred to mature when small, or are a larger variety that have been thinned out of the main crop. Most often these are sold in bunches with their green, feathery tops still on. You do not need to peel baby carrots, just give them a good scrub—with their cute size and sweet, juicy interior, they are perfect for serving raw or steaming whole.

preparation

roasting Although we tend to boil carrots, they are delicious when roasted, as this concentrates their sugars, which caramelize in dry heat. To do this, peel then cut them into 'pennies'. Put them in a roasting tin with olive oil to coat and roast them for about 35 minutes, turning once, in a 180°C (350°F/Gas 4) oven, or until deep golden. Serve them at room temperature, doused in balsamic vinegar and sprinkled with sea salt and a handful of chopped mint.

culinary uses

Carrots generally play a support role in cookery, as one of many components in sauces, stews or soups. Examples do abound though, of dishes where carrots are the star feature. In North Africa, a coarse, highly spiced and lemony puree of carrot is served as an appetizer. The Indians make a carrot-based halva, a concentrated sweet dessert involving highly reduced, thickened milk, loads of grated carrot and sweet spices.

A pureed carrot soup is delicious flavoured with a little orange juice and finished with a cream. To make such a soup, sauté 1 chopped onion and 1 kg (2 lb 4 oz) peeled, chopped carrots in a large saucepan over medium-low heat for 20–25 minutes, or until completely tender. Cooking in their own juices renders carrots much sweeter than if they are simply boiled to softness in stock. Add 800 ml (28 fl oz) ready-made chicken or vegetable stock and 500 ml (17 fl oz/2 cups) orange juice, and simmer for 10 minutes. Puree the soup, adding more stock or juice if necessary. Season with sea salt and freshly ground black pepper and nutmeg, and finish with a dash of pouring (whipping) cream.

Although there are few flavour scenarios the versatile carrot won't fit into, it has a special affinity with the following—dill, parsley, mint, butter, cream, walnuts, honey, raisins, cinnamon and nutmeg.

selection and storage

Today, carrots are bred for consistency of colour and size. Gone, it seems, are the days of wiggly, misshapen carrots—they all seem to be uniformly straight and thick. Choose mature carrots with smooth, unblemished skin, exhibiting no soft, shrivelled, brown or wrinkled spots. The deeper the orange colour, the higher in betacarotene the carrots are.

Avoid any with green 'shoulders' as these have been exposed to sunlight and will be bitter. Don't buy overly-large carrots either as these will have a tough, woody core and not taste as sweet.

Generally, carrots are marketed without their luxurious, green tops—if you do happen to buy some with tops on, which should be green and fresh-looking with no signs of wilting or yellowing, cut these off for storage as they will drain the carrots of nutrients and moisture. Greens from extremely fresh young carrots have a distinctive, spicy taste and can be eaten chopped and tossed into a salad or soup.

serves 4

carrot and pumpkin risotto

90 g (3¼ oz) butter
1 onion, finely chopped
250 g (9 oz) pumpkin, diced
2 carrots, diced
2 litres (70 fl oz/8 cups) ready-
    made vegetable stock, heated
440 g (15½ oz/2 cups) risotto
    (arborio) rice
90 g (3¼ oz/1 cup) shaved
    romano or parmesan cheese
¼ teaspoon freshly grated
    nutmeg

Heat 60 g (2¼ oz) of butter in a large, heavy-based frying pan. Add the onion and fry for 1–2 minutes, or until soft. Add the pumpkin and carrot and cook for 6–8 minutes, or until tender. Mash slightly with a potato masher. In a separate saucepan heat the stock over medium heat and keep the stock at simmering point.

Add the rice to the vegetables and cook for 1 minute, stirring constantly, until the grains are translucent. Ladle in 125 ml (4 fl oz/½ cup) of hot stock and stir well. Reduce the heat and add the stock little by little, stirring constantly for 20–25 minutes, or until the rice is tender and creamy. You may not need to add all the stock, or you may run out and need to use a little water—every risotto is different.

Remove from the heat, add the remaining butter, the cheese and nutmeg, season with freshly ground black pepper and stir thoroughly. Cover and leave for 5 minutes before serving.

The original, wild carrots were quite bitter and their first uses were medicinal. Their seeds were used as a spice, hardly surprising given that close carrot relatives include caraway, cumin and coriander. In ancient Greek and Roman times, carrots were used as a cure for everything from ulcerous sores, snakebite and tumours, to bladder infections; during the Middle Ages they were thought to be a remedy for a miscellany of ills from syphilis to dog bite.

carrot and coriander soup

serves 4

2 tablespoons olive oil
1 onion, chopped
800 g (1 lb 12 oz) carrots, chopped
1 bay leaf
1 teaspoon ground cumin
1 teaspoon cayenne pepper
1 teaspoon ground coriander
2 teaspoons paprika
1.25 litres (44 fl oz/5 cups)
 ready-made vegetable stock
250 g (9 oz/1 cup) Greek-style
 yoghurt
coriander (cilantro) leaves, to serve

Heat the olive oil in a saucepan, add the onion and carrot and cook over low heat for 30 minutes.

Add the bay leaf and spices and cook for another 2 minutes. Add the stock, bring to the boil, then reduce the heat and simmer, uncovered, for 40 minutes, or until the carrot is tender. Cool slightly, then blend in batches in a food processor. Return to the saucepan and gently reheat. Season with sea salt and freshly ground black pepper.

Mix the yoghurt with the fresh coriander leaves. Pour the soup into bowls and top with a dollop of the yoghurt mixture.

carrot pesto bake

serves 4

50 g (1¾ oz) butter
60 g (2¼ oz/¼ cup) plain
 (all-purpose) flour
750 ml (26 fl oz/3 cups) milk
160 g (5½ oz/⅔ cup) sour
 cream
100 g (3½ oz/¾ cup) grated
 cheddar cheese
4 eggs, lightly beaten
2 tablespoons pesto (see
 page 411)
750 g (1 lb 10 oz) carrots, grated
250 g (9 oz or about 15) instant
 lasagne sheets
50 g (1¾ oz/⅓ cup) grated
 cheddar cheese, extra

Grease a 30 x 20 cm (12 x 8 inch) baking dish . Heat the butter in a large saucepan; add the flour. Stir over low heat until mixture is bubbling. Gradually add the combined milk, sour cream and 1 teaspoon freshly ground black pepper. Stir constantly over medium heat for 5 minutes until mixture boils and thickens. Remove from heat, stir in the cheese and cool slightly. Gradually add the beaten eggs, stirring constantly.

Preheat the oven to 150°C (300°F/Gas 2). Pour one-third of the sauce into a separate bowl and set aside. Add the pesto and grated carrot to the remaining sauce, stirring to combine.

Put one-third of the carrot mixture into the dish, followed by an even layer of lasagne sheets. Repeat this layering twice more, finishing with a layer of lasagne sheets. Spread reserved sauce evenly over the top. Sprinkle with extra cheese and bake for 40 minutes. Remove from the oven and set aside for 15 minutes before serving.

carrot cake with lemon icing

Preheat the oven to 160°C (315°F/Gas 2–3). Lightly grease a 23 cm (9 inch) round cake tin and line the base and side with baking paper.

Sift the flours, spices and bicarbonate of soda into a large bowl and make a well in the centre. Whisk together the oil, sugar, eggs and golden syrup in a jug until combined. Add this mixture to the well in the flour and gradually stir into the dry ingredients with a metal spoon until smooth. Stir in the carrot and nuts, mixing thoroughly.

Spoon the batter into the prepared tin and smooth the surface. Bake for 1½ hours, or until a skewer comes out clean when inserted into the centre of the cake. Leave the cake in the tin for at least 15 minutes before turning out onto a wire rack to cool completely.

To make the lemon icing, beat the cream cheese and butter with electric beaters until smooth. Gradually add the icing sugar alternately with the vanilla and lemon juice, beating until light and creamy. Spread the icing over the cooled cake using a flat-bladed knife. As an option you can serve it sprinkled with freshly grated nutmeg.

The carrot was a favourite of the English Queen Elizabeth I (1533–1603). During the reign of James I, carrot leaves and flowers became a fashion statement—ladies even wore them in their hair and festooned their clothing with them. Carrots were also once favoured as a powerful love potion—their effects were thought to make men more passionate and women more willing.

- 125 g (4½ oz/1 cup) self-raising flour
- 125 g (4½ oz/1 cup) plain (all-purpose) flour
- 2 teaspoons ground cinnamon
- 1 teaspoon ground ginger
- ½ teaspoon ground nutmeg
- 1 teaspoon bicarbonate of soda (baking soda)
- 250 ml (9 fl oz/1 cup) oil
- 185 g (6½ oz/1 cup) soft brown sugar
- 4 eggs
- 175 g (6 oz/½ cup) golden syrup (dark corn syrup)
- 400 g (14 oz/2½ cups) grated carrot
- 60 g (2¼ oz/½ cup) chopped pecans or walnuts

lemon icing

- 175 g (6 oz/¾ cup) cream cheese, softened
- 60 g (2¼ oz) butter, softened
- 185 g (6½ oz/1½ cups) icing (confectioners') sugar
- 1 teaspoon natural vanilla extract
- 1–2 teaspoons lemon juice
- freshly ground nutmeg (optional), to dust

roots and tubers ▪ carrot

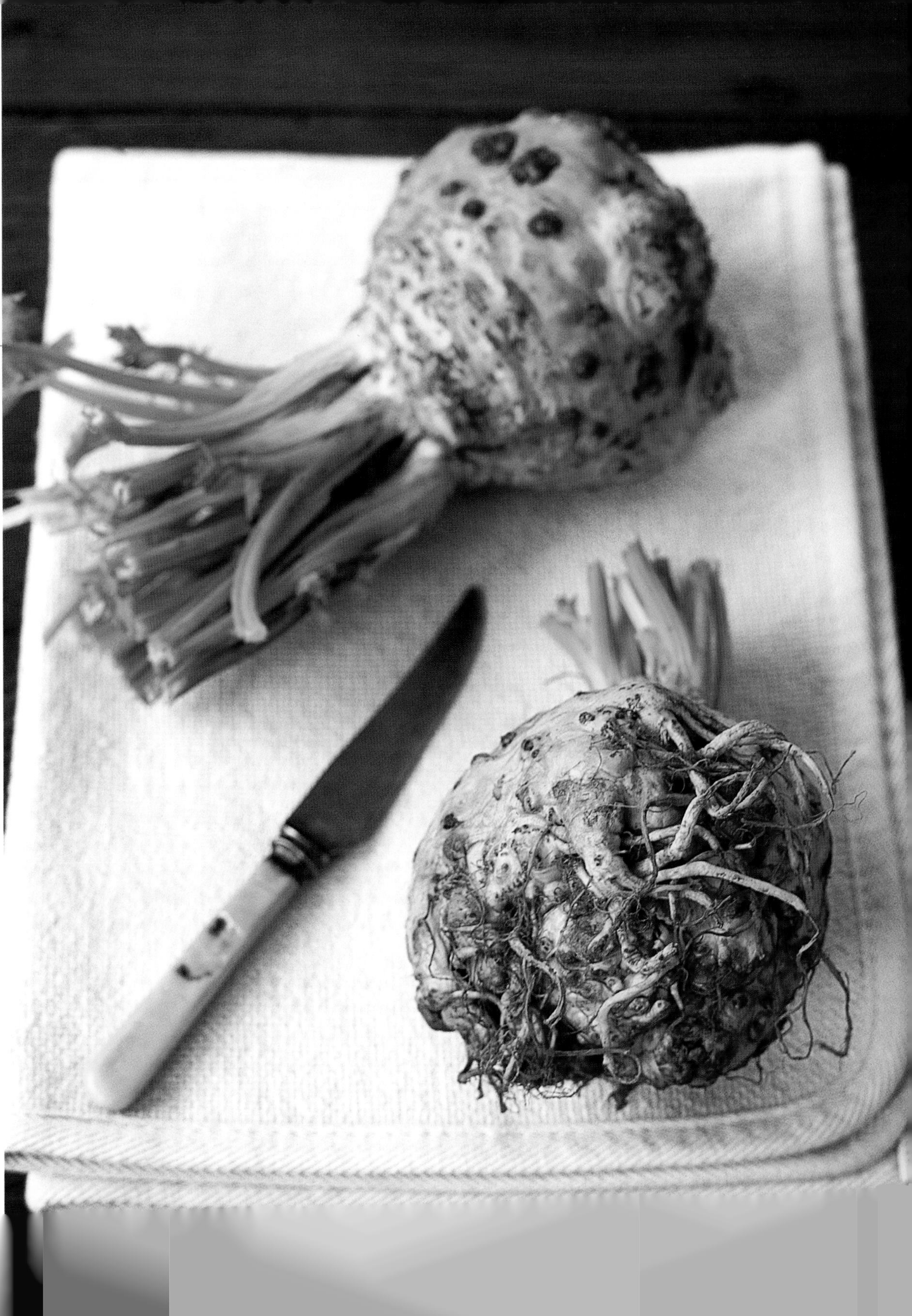

celeriac

A relative of the carrot family, as is celery, celeriac is an unpromising-looking brute of a vegetable. It has a bumpy surface, a brackish-coloured skin, and tough, largely inedible stalks sprouting from its top, balanced by a hairy tangle of roots at its base. But with its subtle, celery-like flavour, celeriac is thoroughly delicious and suited to a range of cooking purposes.

It is believed celeriac was first cultivated in the Mediterranean, where it was used medicinally until the seventeenth century, and then as a food only sparingly. Somewhere along the food-history line, however, somebody discovered the possibilities of this root—celeriac makes dreamy puree, either solo or in tandem with potato, ditto creamy gratins and smooth soups (celeriac and chestnut soup is simply heavenly).

Celeriac is also extremely delicious raw, cut into matchsticks and tossed with mayonnaise, mustard, lemon juice and parsley (as in the classic French salad, celeriac remoulade), or cut into very thin slices and fried, to become chips.

selection and storage

Celeriac keeps well, in fact it will keep in the ground long after the stalks are killed off by the first frosts.

Avoid buying celeriac that are overly large, as these tend to have cottony centres. Select bulbs that are very heavy for their size, that feel firm and are about the size of a baseball; these will have the crispest, most dense interior. If they still have their leaves, these should be bright green and bulbs that are freshly harvested will have a green tinge around their tops.

Celeriac bulbs, trimmed of their stalks, will keep in a bag in the coolest part of the refrigerator for up to 10 days.

preparation

To prepare celeriac you need to remove and discard the stalks and leaves, then remove all of the thick skin with a sharp knife. This can seem like quite a wasteful exercise, as rather a lot of trimming is necessary to get rid of all the root material at the base. Put cut or sliced pieces of celeriac into a bowl of acidulated water (water with lemon juice) as you go, as the flesh quickly oxidizes on contact with the air.

Celeriac can be grated or cut into matchsticks for putting in salads—good partners for its aniseed taste include watercress, crumbled goat's or blue cheese, walnuts, hazelnuts, apples, capers, anchovies, olives, boiled eggs and oranges. As its flavour tends to dominate, celeriac can be tempered by a quick blanching in boiling salted water before tossing through a salad.

boiled Peeled chunks of celeriac can be boiled in salted water for about 15 minutes, or until tender. They can then be mashed with butter and cream or tossed with a little butter and black pepper and served as a side dish with sausages, smoked meats, chicken or fish. Celeriac can also be cut into matchsticks and deep-fried in hot oil until golden and crisp. If using this method, it is best to par-boil the celeriac first for quicker cooking. The matchsticks go well served with fish, chicken or beef.

roasted Celeriac can be roasted much like potatoes, in olive oil or butter. Peel celeriac, then cut into 1.5 cm (5/8 inch) wedges. Toss generously in olive oil to coat, then arrange in a large roasting dish in a single layer. Cook in a 200°C (400°F/Gas 6) oven for 20–25 minutes, or until tender and golden.

culinary uses

Celeriac mash is brilliant—you can also cook celeriac and potato together, then mash them for a milder flavour or, cook peeled and cored granny smith apples with celeriac and mash together for a sweet-tasting variant. Either of these scenarios also make for winning soups of the pureed, creamy sort.

celeriac remoulade

To make the mustard mayonnaise, whisk the egg yolks, vinegar and mustard together. Add the oil, drop by drop from the tip of a teaspoon, whisking constantly until it begins to thicken, then add the oil in a very thin stream. If you're using a food processor, pour the oil in a thin stream with the motor running. Season with sea salt and freshly ground black pepper and, if necessary, thin with a little warm water. Set aside until required.

To make the remoulade, put 1 litre (35 fl oz/4 cups) of cold water in a large bowl and add half the lemon juice. Roughly grate the celeriac and place in the acidulated water. Bring a saucepan of water to the boil over high heat and add the remaining lemon juice. Drain the celeriac and add to the saucepan. After 1 minute, drain again and cool under running water. Pat dry with paper towels. Toss with the mayonnaise, capers, gherkins and parsley. Serve with a baguette.

mustard mayonnaise
2 egg yolks
1 tablespoon white wine vinegar
  or lemon juice
1 tablespoon dijon mustard
150 ml (5 fl oz) light olive oil

juice of 1 lemon
2 celeriac, trimmed and peeled
2 tablespoons capers, rinsed and
  drained
5 gherkins (cornichons),
  chopped
2 tablespoons finely chopped
  parsley
baguette, to serve

celeriac mash

serves 4

Put 500 ml (17 fl oz/2 cups) cold water in a large bowl and add half the lemon juice. Chop the celeriac into the same size cubes as the potatoes and put in the water until ready to use.

Put the potato and celeriac in a saucepan with the milk and bring to the boil over high heat. Cover and cook for 15 minutes, or until the celeriac and potato are tender. Mash together with the milk. Season with sea salt and freshly ground black pepper and stir in the butter to serve.

variation To make celeriac and apple mash, add 2 peeled, cored and coarsely choped apples to the potato and celeriac; boil with the milk and continue as above.

juice of ½ lemon
1 celeriac, trimmed and peeled
1 potato, cut into cubes
250 ml (9 fl oz/1 cup) milk
1 tablespoon butter

ginger

vegetables ▪ roots and tubers
season ▪ available year-round

Ginger is one of the world's most popular spices and has been known and used for so long that its wild origins are not clear. It is believed to be native to the south of India, from where it spread to the Western world at least 2000 years ago; the Romans traded in ginger and by the time of the Norman Conquest in 1066 it was familiar to the tables of England. Botanically, the edible part of the ginger plant is a fat rhizome, which creeps under the ground, sprouting new stalks as it goes. The plant produces no seeds, and one theory about this is that it has been cultivated for so long the plant has forgotten how!

Ginger has some powerful culinary, medicinal and preservative properties. Its ability to combat nausea is legendary, hence the use of ginger ale or ginger tea to treat mild gastro illnesses, motion and morning sickness, and recent research shows it can also play a role in reducing cholesterol. It contains a substance called protease, a protein-digesting enzyme, which tenderizes meats, while powerful antioxidants in ginger have been shown to retard food spoilage. This, it has been conjectured, is why ginger was initially used so heavily in baked items in England and Europe—not only does gingerbread in its many guises taste sensational, it is also extremely long-keeping as well.

selection and storage

Ginger should feel solid and heavy—the harder the rhizomes are, the better. Don't purchase ginger that is soft, shows signs of withering (indicating dryness and old age) or mould.

The age of the ginger when harvested has a distinct bearing on flavour. Young or 'early-harvest' ginger has a light, thin, tan-coloured skin with pinkish tips, and is juicier, crisper and milder than more mature ginger. Ginger that has a late harvesting has thicker and dark-tan skin, with hard, quite fibrous flesh and a far stronger flavour.

The size of the 'hands' of ginger are not indicative of quality or age but are the result of where, and under what conditions, the vegetables were grown.

Ginger will store in an airtight container in the refrigerator for several weeks.

preparation

Fresh ginger bears little resemblance to its dried, powdered counterpart which is only good for baking. Fresh ginger can be sliced, cut into matchsticks, chopped, grated or ground to a paste.

Unless you have very young ginger, it is necessary to peel it before use—a small, sharp paring knife is best for this. To cut ginger into matchsticks, slice ginger thinly then stack the slices on top of each other, in batches, and cut these into fine strips. To chop these, turn the strips 90 degrees on your board and, holding them together, cut them into very small pieces.

Alternatively, use the finest hole of a grater to grate ginger; you can also purchase purpose-made ginger graters from Asian food stores or kitchenware shops. These are generally either wooden or ceramic. A small food processor is ideal for reducing chopped ginger to a fine paste, as is often required when making Indian or Southeast Asian curries.

Some recipes call for ginger juice—this is easily extracted by placing freshly-grated ginger in a piece of muslin (cheesecloth) and squeezing firmly to collect juices.

culinary uses

Fresh ginger is most useful in Asian-style dishes; it is a vital component of stir-fries, curries, condiments and braises from Burma to Beijing, Seoul to Surabaya. Generally it is sautéed first, perhaps with garlic or onion, which tempers its hot edge somewhat.

The longer ginger cooks, the mellower it becomes. Fine shreds of young ginger can be sprinkled over fish to be briefly steamed or added to a quick-cooking stir-fry, while older, hotter tasting ginger is best used in slow-simmering dishes such as curries and braises. Raw, it adds a healthy zing to freshly-made juices, such as carrot, apple and ginger juice.

fish in ginger broth

Heat the oil in a large saucepan, add the green onions and ginger and cook over low heat for 2 minutes, stirring occasionally. Add the fish sauce, sugar and 1.5 litres (52 fl oz/6 cups) water and bring to the boil. Reduce the heat, add the fish and poach gently for 3–4 minutes, or until the fish is just cooked and flakes easily when tested with a fork. Lift the fish out with a slotted spoon and put in a warm shallow bowl. Cover with foil to keep warm.

Bring the liquid in the saucepan to the boil, reduce the heat and simmer until reduced by half. Add the lime juice.

Cook the peas in a separate saucepan of boiling water for 5 minutes, or until tender, then drain well. To serve, put the fish in bowls, ladle the broth over the top, then divide the peas among the bowls. Garnish with coriander leaves.

1 tablespoon oil
8 green onions (scallions), sliced diagonally
2 tablespoons finely chopped fresh ginger
80 ml (2½ fl oz/⅓ cup) fish sauce
4 tablespoons grated palm sugar (jaggery) or soft brown sugar
four 200 g (7 oz) salmon or ocean trout fillets
2 tablespoons lime juice
200 g (7 oz/1⅓ cups) fresh peas, about 400 g (14 oz) unpodded
fresh coriander (cilantro) leaves, to garnish

pickled ginger

makes 260 g (9¼ oz/1 cup)

Cut the ginger into 2.5 cm (1 inch) pieces. Sprinkle with 2 teaspoons salt, cover and refrigerate for 1 week.

With a sharp knife, cut the ginger into paper-thin slices across the grain. In a saucepan over low heat, dissolve the sugar in the rice vinegar and 2 tablespoons water. Bring to the boil and simmer for 1 minute.

Put the ginger into a hot sterilized jar, cover with the marinade, seal and refrigerate for 1 week before using. The ginger will turn pale pink or it can be coloured using 1 teaspoon grenadine. Store in the refrigerator for up to 3 months.

125 g (4½ oz) fresh ginger, or about 12 cm (4½ inch) piece
2 tablespoons sugar
125 ml (4 fl oz/½ cup) rice vinegar
1 teaspoon grenadine, optional

roots and tubers ■ ginger

horseradish

Horseradish belongs to the mustard family, which will hardly surprise anyone acquainted with its hot, peppery flavour. Generally sold in jars, often prepared as a creamy condiment to eat with roast beef, horseradish is available in limited supply fresh each season and is well worth trying in this form. It presents as a hard, gnarly root—sometimes so hard and fibrous it can barely be cut with a knife.

selection and storage

Fresh horseradish is usually sold in short sections—entire roots measure up to 50 cm (20 inches) in length and 2.5–5 cm (1–2 inches) in diameter. Choose roots, or sections of them, that are very firm with no damp or mouldy patches, nor any green or shrivelled-looking areas. Horseradish needs to be stored in the refrigerator, in a sealed plastic bag in the crisper section, where it will last for 7–10 days, although it will decrease in pungency somewhat during storage.

preparation

Before using horseradish you need to peel off the tough skin and, if the roots are older, remove the fibrous central core, as well as any green bits. Horseradish is best used finely chopped or grated and, in common with garlic and onions, the finer it is chopped, the more volatile compounds it releases and the stronger it tastes. Horseradish devotees insist that it should be prepared just before it is needed as the flavour starts to dissipate the moment the cut flesh has contact with the air. Perhaps the easiest way to finely chop horseradish is in the food processor, after first cutting it into pieces; the vapours from it can seriously hurt your eyes and throat, so beware of breathing these in.

culinary uses

Horseradish can be used in soups and stews (cooking renders it quite mild so add it near the end of cooking if you want a mustardy hit of flavour) although it is, arguably, at its best in sauces and condiments to accompany meats and fish. Grated horseradish in a vinaigrette dressing is great over raw oysters or a salad with beef, beetroot, spinach leaves and walnuts or one with dill in a potato, fennel, steamed mussel and watercress salad. An apple sauce spiked subtly with horseradish is sublime with smoked eel, smoked mackerel or smoked trout.

horseradish cream

To make the horseradish cream, whip the cream until starting to thicken, then fold in the horseradish, lemon juice, sugar and a pinch of salt. Don't overwhip the cream as the acid from the lemon juice and horseradish will act as a thickener—if the cream is heavily whisked from the start it may split. Store in a hot sterilized jar and serve with beetroot, smoked salmon or roast beef dishes.

150 ml (5 fl oz) thick
 (double/heavy) cream
2 tablespoons grated fresh
 horseradish
2 teaspoons lemon juice
1 pinch sugar

If you have more fresh horseradish than you can easily use, you have a few options. One is to finely grate the flesh and freeze it in small, usable quantities—it will lose some pungency in the freezer but will last for 6–8 weeks. Another is to finely grate or process it and to add a little sugar, some salt and a good slosh or two of white wine vinegar, stir to mix well, then store in a tightly-sealed jar in the refrigerator. It will keep for 4–5 weeks and you can use it in sauces, condiments and dressings as you would fresh.

roots and tubers ■ horseradish

jerusalem artichoke

vegetables ▪ **roots and tubers**
season ▪ **late autumn–early spring**

In a reverse of the usual trend, the Jerusalem artichoke was sent to the Old World in 1616 by North American settlers who thought the Europeans might like it. They were quite right and now this tuber is more popular there than in its homeland, where native Indians had cultivated it for aeons.

The name is confusing—it is not an artichoke at all but a member of the sunflower family, nor is there any connection to Jerusalem—this is an English corruption of the Spanish *gerasol* and Italian *girasole*, which mean 'turn to the sun', or 'sunflower'. Whatever the etymology, the Jerusalem artichoke, also called the sunchoke, has a deliciously sweet, nutty and earthy flavour and, when raw, a pleasantly crisp texture. It has a high calcium content and appreciable levels of vitamins A, C and some of the B group, plus the minerals iron, magnesium and phosphorus.

culinary uses

Jerusalem artichokes make delicious soup, especially when pureed with a finishing touch of cream. They can be roasted in butter, or boiled and mashed with potatoes. They can also just be boiled or steamed and served as an accompaniment to simple meat or fish dishes. They collapse when overcooked so check them regularly to guard against this. Jerusalem artichokes can be used raw in salads, as a crudite with dips, or pickled in vinegar. Peeled, cut into very thin rounds then patted dry, they can be deep-fried, salted and served as a snack with drinks.

selection and storage

Jerusalem artichokes look rather like large fresh ginger rhizomes, but with lighter, more translucent, thin skin. They can be plump, rounded and beige or longer, much knobbier and a reddish colour.

The very warty, protuberant ones can be time-consuming to prepare, as getting rid of all the skin (either by peeling or scrubbing) with its attendant detritus, takes patience. The skin, however, is perfectly edible so if you find smoother specimens a good wash and light scrub will suffice.

Choose tubers that are firm, of even size (so they will all be cooked at the same time) and show no signs of softness, green or sprouting. Store them, in a plastic bag, for up to 2 weeks in the refrigerator.

warm salad of jerusalem artichoke, radicchio and pastrami

Peel the artichokes. Cut any large ones to give pieces of roughly the same size. Put the artichokes in a non-reactive saucepan of boiling salted water with the lemon juice. Simmer for 12 minutes, or until tender, then drain. When cool, slice the artichokes on the diagonal.

Preheat the grill (broiler) to hot. Trim off any coarse outer leaves from the radicchio and quarter it lengthways. Put the radicchio, cut side up, in a medium shallow heatproof dish, scatter the walnuts on top and drizzle with half the oil. Grill (broil) for 1–2 minutes, or until the leaves start to pucker and the edges brown. Remove from the heat and set aside to cool for 2–3 minutes.

Cut off the radicchio stems and return the leaves to the dish. Add the artichokes, orange juice and parsley and season with salt and freshly ground black pepper. Toss lightly. Scrunch the pastrami pieces into loose balls and arrange them among the artichokes. Drizzle with the remaining walnut oil and return to the grill. Grill for 1–2 minutes, or until just beginning to brown. Top with the orange zest and serve immediately.

500 g (1 lb 2 oz) Jerusalem artichokes
juice of ½ lemon
1 treviso radicchio
40 g (1½ oz/⅓ cup) golden walnut pieces
60 ml (2 fl oz/¼ cup) walnut oil
zest of 1 orange
juice of 1 orange
1 tablespoon chopped parsley
100 g (3½ oz) slices pastrami, halved

roots and tubers ■ jerusalem artichoke

Like jicama, Jerusalem artichokes can be grated, sliced or cut into matchsticks and used raw in salads; their lovely flavour goes well with other nutty tastes (walnut, hazelnuts, pecans), with the sweetness of seafoods such as scallops, salmon and prawns, and with the bracing flavours of mint, lemon, chives or mustard—serve them tossed with mustard mayonnaise as a variation to the usual celeriac remoulade.

jicama

vegetables ▪ roots and tubers
season ▪ autumn–spring

selection and storage

Choose jicama with smooth, tight, silky skins that feel heavy and dense for their size. Blemished, raggy-looking tubers or those with dull skin are likely to be old—their interior will yield fibrous, tasteless, starchy flesh.

This vegetable keeps well and can be stored in the refrigerator for up to 2 weeks—do not store them in plastic as they need air to circulate around them.

Called yam bean in parts of Asia, on account of the pods that develop on the vine it grows on, jicama is a Central American native and its name (pronounced HEE-kama) is Mexican. Part of the morning glory family, the plant was taken by the Spanish to the Philippines from where it spread throughout Asia. There is, though, just one variety of jicama, which can come in a variety of sizes—from a 200 g (7 oz) to 2.5 kg (5 lb) smooth, tan-skinned tuber. The appeal of the jicama lies in its exceptionally crisp, juicy flesh. Ivory-white, the flesh is rather like that of a water chestnut but has a subtle, alluring flavour all its own. Jicama is most useful as a salad vegetable, when its delicious and refreshing crunch can be put to great use.

preparation

Jicama must first be peeled. If you have chosen your tubers well, the skin will be thin and come off easily. A paring knife is best for this as there is a layer of fibrous flesh just under the skin that also needs to be removed. In very fresh tubers the skin will simply pull off.

Unlike other root vegetables (such as potatoes or celeriac) jicama won't discolour with advance preparation so you can prepare it before you need it. Once peeled, you can slice it, grate it, fashion it into matchsticks, batons or cubes, depending on your requirements. Jicama can be used in stir-fries, braises and soups, or steamed with a selection of other vegetables—unusually, it absorbs flavours without losing its characteristic crunch.

tuna and jicama remoulade rolls

To make the jicama remoulade, combine the garlic, ginger, coriander and mayonnaise in a bowl and stir to mix well. Add the jicama, season with sea salt and freshly ground black pepper and stir to combine. Set aside until required.

Using a thin, sharp knife, cut the tuna into 2–3 mm (1/16–1/8 inch) thick slices. Place each slice on a work surface and, using the heel of your hand, gently flatten them. Divide the remoulade amongst the tuna slices, placing it down the middle of each piece, then roll the tuna around the filling to form tight rolls. Serve the tuna rolls immediately, with lime wedges and soy sauce passed separately.

jicama remoulade
1 garlic clove, crushed
2½ teaspoons very finely chopped ginger
1 large handful coriander (cilantro) leaves, chopped
125 ml (4 fl oz/½ cup) ready-made egg mayonnaise
750 g (1 lb 10 oz or about 2) jicama, peeled and cut into fine matchsticks

500 g (1 lb 2 oz) sashimi-grade tuna, blood line removed
lime wedges, to serve
soy sauce, to serve

roots and tubers ■ jicama

The jicama is used in Mexican cookery, where its blandness is complemented well by the flavours of chilli, lime juice, orange or coriander (cilantro). Elsewhere its crunch takes well to the textures of avocado, pineapple and peanuts. In Vietnam, the tuber is pickled and served as an accompaniment on the lunch or dinner table while in Indonesia and Malaysia it is included in the vigorously-flavoured salad rojak, *an intriguing mix of fruits and vegetables in a sweet-sour tamarind dressing.*

kohlrabi

vegetables ■ roots and tubers
season ■ peak season late summer–early winter

Kohlrabi, with its crisp texture and broccoli-stalk-crossed-with-cucumber flavour, is relatively young as far as vegetables go—the first record of it was in 1554 and today, in many parts of the world, it remains a little-known oddity. A curious-looking specimen, kohlrabi is one of the very few vegetables to have originated in Northern Europe.

It is technically not a root vegetable at all since the fleshy part isn't a tuber—rather, it is a swollen, above-ground stem. Kohlrabi is a member of the brassica family and theories abound that it, along with other family members (broccoli, brussels sprouts etcetera), is descended from wild cabbage. Over the centuries, selective breeding has emphasized aspects of the original plant (leaves, flowers, stems), depending on local preferences.

'Kohlrabi' is German for 'cabbage turnip' and, not surprisingly, that nation has the distinction of being the world's largest consumer of it. Kohlrabi has, historically, been used medicinally to strengthen and repair gums, teeth and bones. It does contain significant amounts of bone-building compounds (calcium, iron and phosphorus) as well as vitamins A and C.

It occurs in two colours—pale green and purple. The purple sort has a sweeter, more pronounced flavour—both varieties have pale greenish, crisp flesh.

selection and storage

Larger kohlrabi tend to be woody so select small to medium globes that are free of surface cracks, bruises or splits.

Leaves, if they have been left on, should be green and fresh-looking with no yellowing or wilting. The leaves are edible, but need to be stored separately so cut them off and store in a ventilated bag in the refrigerator.

The leaves will last just a few days, while the bulbs, stored in the same manner, will keep for several weeks.

preparation

Kohlrabi is enormously versatile; the only constant is that it needs to be peeled. Cut off stems, saving the tender leaves, if desired. Used raw, kohlrabi is delicious on a vegetable platter—slice it into half-moons or thick batons if using this way. Grated, finely diced, or cut into matchsticks, it is wonderful in salads, especially slaw-type ones that are dressed with rich, home-made mayonnaise.

blanching A quick blanching of prepared kohlrabi intensifies its flavour somewhat—blanch peeled, whole, small kohlrabi or halved, larger vegetables for 3–4 minutes in boiling water. Drain, then slice, dice or grate and use in salads or other cold dishes.

steaming Kohlrabi can be steamed or boiled. Depending on their size they will take 15–30 minutes to become tender. Once they are tender, they can be sautéed, stir-fried or added to soups and braises during the last 20 minutes of cooking.

culinary uses

Kohlrabi pairs well with creamy, cheesy sauces (gruyere and blue cheese especially), and can be hollowed out, stuffed (with meat and breadcrumb mixtures or rice, cheese and the blanched, chopped flesh and trimmed stems) then baked or braised in stock. Kohlrabi has also become popular in certain Asian cuisines, notably Vietnamese, where it is used in everything from salads to spring roll fillings, and in Chinese cookery where it is a winner in stir-fries and braises.

The leaves, trimmed of tough stems, can be blanched then sautéed in a little butter and served as a side dish with mushrooms. They can also be put to nutritious use in soups and stews and also in stuffings for baked kohlrabi, tasting not unlike Swiss chard.

sichuan-style kohlrabi braise

Dry-roast peppercorns in a heavy-based frying pan over low heat for 3 minutes or until fragrant—take care not to burn peppercorns. Using an electric spice grinder or in a mortar using a pestle, very finely grind the peppercorns. Set aside.

Heat 2 tablepoons of oil in a large frying pan, add half the pork and cook over medium-high heat for 5–6 minutes, turning often, or until golden all over. Transfer pork to a bowl. Add remaining pork and repeat this process, adding more oil to pan if necessary, then remove second batch of pork to bowl, reserving pan.

Add most of the stock, the wine, soy sauce, bean paste, rock sugar, star anise, ginger and garlic to the pan and slowly bring to the boil, stirring occasionally, until all the sugar is dissolved. Return the pork and a little more chicken stock to just cover, if necessary, reduce heat to low then gently simmer mixture for 1 hour, or until pork is tender. Add the kohlrabi, stir to combine then cook for a further 20 minutes, or until kohlrabi is cooked. Serve with steamed rice and Asian greens—braises taste better if left for a day, refrigerated, as the flavours will develop and deepen.

2½ tablespoons Sichuan peppercorns
peanut oil, to fry
1.25 kg (2 lb 12 oz) boneless, skinned pork leg or shoulder, trimmed and cut into 3 cm (1¼ inch) pieces
500 ml (17 fl oz/2 cups) ready-made chicken stock
100 ml (3½ fl oz) Shaoxing wine
1½ tablespoons soy sauce
80 ml (⅓ cup) Sichuan chilli-bean paste, or to taste
60 g (2¼ oz) Chinese rock sugar, coarsely crushed
1 star anise
5 garlic cloves, peeled and bruised
4 cm (1½ inch) piece of ginger, sliced
500 g (1 lb 2 oz or about 2 small) kohlrabi, trimmed, peeled and cut into 2 cm (¾ inch) pieces
steamed rice and Asian greens, to serve

roots and tubers ■ kohlrabi

parsnip

vegetables ■ roots and tubers
season ■ late autumn–winter

The parsnip is closely related to carrots and celeriac and has been utilized as a food for thousands of years. In fact, it was Europe's pre-eminent winter vegetable until the potato was introduced in the eighteenth century and ultimately usurped its position; from then on its popularity at the European table dwindled.

Like all produce of ancient origins, the parsnip has a fascinating history. Parsnips were so esteemed that the Roman emperor Tiberius had them bought to his Capri villa all the way from France and Germany. During the Middle Ages, parents gave their babies a parsnip to suck on when they needed pacifying—by this time the vegetable was enjoyed in savoury as well as sweet dishes. Colonists took the parsnip to the New World where the early settlers used it to make everything from wines, pies, breads and puddings, to chips and stews.

The parsnip has a unique, sweet-earthy flavour like that of no other vegetable, and it also has an interesting nutritional profile, being especially high in potassium, folacin and vitamin C.

preparation

Cut larger parsnips in half lengthways and inspect the core; larger ones are likely to have a woody core which is best removed before cooking. Peel parsnips just before cooking them as they discolour slightly on contact with the air; do not put them into acidulated water to prevent this or they will turn soggy.

While you may need to pre-boil parsnips in order to then use them in some other way (in a mash or baked into a gratin, for example), boiling isn't generally a good treatment for parsnips as they become water-logged and unpalatable.

steaming To steam parsnips, place peeled 5 cm (2 inch) thick rounds of parsnips in a steamer basket over boiling water. Cover and cook for about 10 minutes, or until tender.

roasting To roast parsnips, peel and halve them lengthways, then place in a large baking dish in a single layer and drizzle liberally with olive oil, tossing to coat. Cook in a 200°C (400°F/Gas 6) oven for 30–45 minutes (depending on size), or until golden and tender.

culinary uses

Home cooks tend to use parsnip largely as a roast vegetable to accompany meat or in a mash, classically, with potatoes or carrots. Parsnip has enjoyed something of a renaissance thanks to restaurant chefs rediscovering its sweet, nutty, earthy flavour, and putting it to more sophisticated uses.

Parsnips need richness to bring out their silky texture and nutty flavour; roasting in butter or olive oil, for example, or baking or pureeing with cream, are ideal. Roasted, cooled parsnips taste great in a salad—consider a combination such as roast parsnip tossed with rocket, walnuts and prosciutto. They also pair beautifully with rustic pork sausage, roasted or grilled (broiled) lamb or beef, bacon and certain seafoods (scallops and salt cod, for example) and take well to the flavours of nutmeg, gruyere cheese, ginger, orange, balsamic vinegar and curry.

selection and storage

Parsnips taste best during the colder months; their quality falls off once the weather warms up. They are always sold without their green tops as these contain an irritating juice that can cause a serious rash on some people.

The freshest parsnips will have smooth, creamy-beige skin; avoid any with browning on their skin or with tops that have started to sprout. The latter indicates they will be woody in the middle. Select ones that feel heavy for their size and try to pick them of a similar size so they will all cook at the same time. They should feel very hard and not be even slightly bendy, which indicates age.

Parsnips come in a variety of shapes—from very elongated and tapering, to fat, short and stumpy; maximize meatiness by choosing fatter, stumpy ones. Generally, toughness and the presence of fibres is due to long storage, and not size, so if possible, taste for sweetness and tenderness before you purchase. Parsnips will keep, refrigerated in a loosely sealed plastic bag, for up to 1 week.

serves 4–6

parsnip and leek puree

1 leek, white part only, thinly
  sliced
3 large parsnips, peeled and
  chopped
2 tablespoons snipped chives
30 g (1 oz) butter
3 tablespoons crème fraîche

Put the leek and parsnips in a saucepan of boiling salted
water. Cook for about 10 minutes, or until tender. Drain well
and allow to cool slightly before blending in food processor.
Combine to a smooth puree.

Put the puree in a clean saucepan and add the chives and
butter. Season with sea salt and freshly ground black pepper.
Cook until the puree is heated through. Remove from the
heat and stir through about 3 tablespoons of crème fraîche.
Serve with grilled lamb cutlets, roast beef or pork.

serves 4–6

parsnip and mustard soup

30 g (1 oz) butter
1 onion, chopped
750 g (1 lb 10 oz) parsnips,
  chopped
1 litre (35 fl oz/4 cups) ready-
  made vegetable stock
125 ml (4 fl oz/½ cup) milk
125 ml (4 fl oz/½ cup) pouring
  (whipping) cream
2–3 tablespoons wholegrain
  mustard
2 tablespoons chopped flat-leaf
  (Italian) parsley

Melt the butter in a large saucepan, add the onion and cook
over medium heat, stirring often, until soft but not brown.

Add the parsnip and stock and bring to the boil. Simmer,
covered, for 25 minutes, or until the parsnip is tender. Set
aside to cool slightly.

Blend the soup in batches in a blender or food processor.
Return to the pan, add the milk and cream and reheat gently,
but do not allow the soup to boil. Stir in the wholegrain
mustard and season to taste with salt and freshly ground
black pepper. Serve with fresh parsley as a garnish.

parsnip and pecan fritters

To make the dipping sauce, combine the sour cream, chives, lemon juice and sweet chilli sauce in a serving bowl. Add the Tabasco sauce to taste. Set aside.

Peel the parsnips, cut them into chunks and immediately place in a saucepan of water. Bring to the boil. Add ½ teaspoon salt, reduce the heat and simmer for 15–20 minutes, or until tender, then drain and allow to cool slightly.

Puree the parsnip with a potato ricer or mouli, discarding any tough bits. Transfer to a bowl and mix with the egg, flour, parsley, butter, milk, pecans and cayenne pepper. Season with sea salt and freshly ground black pepper.

Heat the oil in a non-stick frying pan over medium heat. Drop in large tablespoons of mixture, in batches, and flatten slightly with the back of a spoon. Cook, turning once, for 15–20 seconds on each side, or until golden. Remove with a slotted spoon and drain on paper towels. Serve hot, with the dipping sauce.

dipping sauce
200 g (7 oz/heaped ¾ cup) sour cream
1 tablespoon finely snipped chives
1 teaspoon lemon juice
2 tablespoons sweet chilli sauce
3–4 drops Tabasco sauce

3 parsnips
1 egg
30 g (1 oz/¼ cup) plain (all-purpose) flour
1 tablespoon chopped parsley
50 g (1¾ oz) butter, melted
60 ml (2 fl oz/¼ cup) milk
60 g (2¼ oz/⅔ cup) pecans, coarsely chopped
1 pinch cayenne pepper
250 ml (9 fl oz/1 cup) oil

The Romans adored parsnips—they ate them for dessert with honey and fruits and baked them into sweet cakes. According to the Roman epicure Apicius, parsnips were also combined with a sauce containing celery seed, honey, rue, raisin wine, stock and oil and, unusually, included in a vegetable sausage that they roasted and served with wine sauce.

potato

For such a poisonous plant (only the tubers are edible), the potato has made an incalculable impact on the global diet, providing more protein and energy than any other food crop, per unit of land. And who doesn't love the humble spud? From Chile to China, from Ireland to Idaho, potato dishes furnish countless societies with goodness, calories and comfort.

We have the sixteenth-century Spanish explorers to thank for bringing this nightshade (as in 'deadly') family member out from its South American obscurity and into the wider gastronomic world— although until it was discovered that their vitamin C content was a worthy cure for scurvy, potatoes were mainly fed to pigs.

The potato has come a long way since then. It's the 'little black dress' of the food world— or, as American food writer Linda Wells observed, it is to food 'what sensible shoes are to fashion'. Dependable and adaptable, with the ability to move between dressed-up glamour, and simple, satisfying understatement, the potato is equally tempting whether dolloped with caviar, smashed with cream to an unctuous puree, roasted with rosemary to crisped perfection, curried in a slew of exotic spices or simply baked to tenderness in its earthy jacket then topped with chips of cold butter.

selection and storage

Avoid potatoes that feel soft or spongy or have any discolouration, bruises or blemishes. Also, don't buy any that are showing signs of sprouting as these have simply been stored for too long.

Any green areas (and you may not detect these until you peel your potatoes), should be cut away and discarded—they contain a toxic substance called solanine. The greening occurs through excessive exposure to light; similiarly, cut off any eyes that are starting to sprout.

Light and humidity are enemies of the potato so for good storage, dark, dry conditions are best. Avoid refrigeration, plastic bags and sunlight at all costs as these promote softening, sprouting and spoiling.

During storage (and in the correct conditions potatoes will keep for 10–12 weeks), the starch in potatoes slowly converts to sugar. New potatoes, and small, thin-skinned varieties, should not be stored but used quickly within a few days.

new potatoes

'New' potatoes are those that are a little immature and have been harvested from plants that still have their green leaves, usually during the winter months. The skin of the new potato is fragile, thin and 'feathery'; their flesh dense, fresh-tasting and moist. The singular flavour and texture of new potatoes is best showcased by the simplest cooking methods—they require only boiling or steaming and perhaps enhancing with the flavours of mint, sea salt or butter.

nutrition

Potatoes are a rich source of vitamin B6, contain more vitamin C than your average orange, have very decent amounts of niacin, iodine, folic acid, copper and magnesium and offer around 5 per cent of their mass in protein.

Much of the potato's nutritional goodness is stored in (or just under) the skin, so don't peel unless necessary for aesthetic reasons (if making a potato salad, for example, or mash). Alternatively, boil potatoes whole first, in their skin, then cool slightly, peel and prepare. When boiled or baked whole with skins intact, potatoes retain most of their vitamins and nutrients.

Potatoes are a good source of complex carbohydrates, providing a steady, slow-burning source of energy—a perfect example of what is fashionably called a 'low GI' food.

varieties

Before exploring the names of specific potatoes it is worthwhile understanding the different 'types' of potatoes, which are quite separate to their variety. Floury potatoes are dry, have a low sugar content but are high in starch—these are perfect for baking, mashing and frying. Waxy potatoes have moist, dense flesh and are low in starch—ideal for boiling, using in salads and gratins or adding raw to stews, as they will not lose their shape when cooked. All-purpose potatoes (and many of the varieties commonly available from supermarkets fall into this category) have been specially bred to span all possible uses.

Most new potatoes, red-skinned potatoes and many of the fingerling varieties are waxy, while most old potatoes are floury. Because of starch, sugar and moisture variations (due to growing and storage conditions and the season a particular potato is harvested) there can be floury and waxy examples of the same variety available. With increasing 'heirloom' and 'boutique' potato varieties available, and more suppliers selling potatoes by named variety, it is easy to buy the best potato for the particular purpose (boiling, mashing, roasting, frying) you have in mind.

Varieties of potatoes and their growing seasons vary the world over but loosely, potatoes can be divided into the following categories.

blue-fleshed Although of ancient origin, blue and purple-fleshed potatoes are a novel addition to the modern potato scene and are a fun thing to serve at dinner parties—serve a lilac-hued mash and watch reactions around the table! These varieties vary in colour and texture enormously—the eccentric colour is their only commonality, so it may require some experimentation to see how they behave when cooked.

fingerlings These types are small and long and tend to have superior flavour and texture, making them ideal for steaming and boiling and for use in salads.

old potatoes

'Old' or maincrop potatoes are those harvested when their vines are blooming; the flesh of these specimens is drier and their skins thicker than their 'new' counterparts. They are generally stored in cool, dark conditions to extend their availability—the majority of potatoes purchased in supermarkets are 'old'. Any of the potato varieties, however, can be harvested new or old.

golden (tan-skinned) Within this category are an enormous number of varieties, which run the entire gamut of cooking and preparation possibilities from frying, boiling and mashing to roasting, baking and steaming.

red-skinned This group generally represent waxy, full-flavoured varieties that are great for boiling, baking or steaming.

preparation

Unless cooking them immediately, place peeled or cut potatoes into a bowl of water, as the flesh will discolour slightly.

boiling Place potatoes, either whole and unpeeled, cut and unpeeled (if very large) or peeled and cut, into a saucepan and cover with cold water. Add salt and bring to the boil, then simmer, uncovered, for 15–20 minutes (depending on size) until tender. Drain potatoes well the minute they are cooked or they will become unappetizingly soggy.

baking Scrub unpeeled potatoes, prick them several times with the point of a small, sharp knife then place directly on a rack in an oven at 200°C (400°F/Gas 6). Cook them until they are tender when tested with a thin, metal skewer—depending on the size and the variety, this will take between 50 minutes–1¼ hours. Do not wrap potatoes for baking in foil first as this will steam them, not bake them.

roasting Parboil small, unpeeled potatoes, or halved medium-size potatoes, for 20 minutes, or until tender but still quite firm. Drain them very well and stand in a colander for about 15 minutes to allow as much moisture as possible to evaporate. Toss potatoes into the roasting tin with whatever you are roasting (chicken, lamb, pork, beef), turning them occasionally to coat well in the rich cooking fats and juices and to let them brown and crisp on all sides—this will take about 45–55 minutes in a 180°C (350°F/Gas 4) oven. To roast them on their own, toss to coat in olive oil and cook them as above.

australia

chat
coliban
desiree
kipfler
nicola
pontiac
purple congo
sebago
toolangi delight
spunta

united kingdom

jersey royal
kerrs pink
king edward
maris piper
pink fir apple

united states

bintje
concord
early chio
german butterball
la ratte
purple peruvian
russet
yukon gold

serves 4 as a side dish

potato masala

2 tablespoons oil
1 teaspoon black mustard seeds
10 curry leaves
¼ teaspoon ground turmeric
1 cm (½ inch) piece of ginger,
    grated
2 green chillies, finely chopped
2 onions, chopped
500 g (1 lb 2 oz) waxy potatoes,
    cut into 2 cm (¾ inch) cubes
1 tablespoon ready-made
    tamarind puree

Heat the oil in a heavy-based frying pan, add the mustard seeds, cover and when they start to pop add the curry leaves, turmeric, ginger, chilli and onion. Cook, uncovered, for 5 minutes, or until the onion is soft.

Add the potato and 250 ml (9 fl oz/1 cup) water to the pan, bring to the boil, cover and cook until the potato is tender and almost breaking up. If there is any liquid left in the pan, simmer, uncovered, until it evaporates. If the potato isn't cooked and there is no liquid left, add a little more and continue to cook. Add the tamarind puree and mix throughly. Season with sea salt and freshly ground black pepper. Serve hot.

makes 12

potato croquettes

750 g (1 lb 10 oz) floury
    potatoes, coarsely chopped
2 tablespoons pouring (whipping)
    cream or melted butter
3 eggs, lightly beaten
¼ teaspoon nutmeg
plain (all-purpose) flour, for
    coating
150 g (5½ oz/1½ cups) dry
    breadcrumbs
oil, for deep-frying

Cook the potato in a saucepan of boiling salted water for 8–10 minutes, or until tender. Drain and return the potato to the hot pan and mash with a fork. Stir in the cream or butter, a third of the beaten egg and the nutmeg. Season with sea salt and cracked black pepper. Spread the potato mixture evenly on a baking tray, cover and place in the refrigerator for 30 minutes.

Divide the mixture into 12 equal portions and roll each portion into a sausage shape. Roll in the flour, shaking off the excess. Dip each croquette in the remaining egg, coat evenly in the breadcrumbs, shaking off any excess. Cover and refrigerate for at least 2 hours.

Half fill a deep heavy-based frying pan with oil and heat until a cube of bread dropped into the oil browns in 15 seconds. Cook the croquettes in batches for 5 minutes each, or until golden. Drain on paper towels and serve.

potato cake

Put the onion in a bowl, cover with cold water and leave for 1 hour. Drain well. Preheat the oven to 210°C (415°F/Gas 6–7). Line a 20 cm (8 inch) spring-form cake tin with foil. Grease the foil.

Melt the butter in a small saucepan, add the garlic and set aside. Put a layer of potato over the base of the tin, followed by layers of onion, butter, mozzarella cheese and parmesan cheese. Repeat the layers until you have used up all the ingredients, finishing with potato and keeping a bit of butter to drizzle over at the end. Season the layers as you go. Spoon the milk over the top.

Bake for 1 hour, or until the top is golden brown and the potatoes are tender. If the top is over-browning before the potatoes are done, cover with foil. Cool for 10 minutes before serving. Unclip the base of the tin, peel off the foil and transfer to a warm plate, to serve.

1 small onion, sliced into rings
75 g (2½ oz) butter
2 garlic cloves, crushed
1 kg (2 lb 4 oz) potatoes, thinly sliced
100 g (3½ oz/⅔ cup) mozzarella cheese, grated
50 g (1¾ oz/½ cup) shaved parmesan cheese
2 tablespoons milk

roots and tubers ■ potato

crisp potato wedges

serves 4

Preheat the oven to 220°C (425°F/Gas 7). Scrub and pat dry the potatoes and cut into thick wedges. Put in a single layer on a baking tray.

Brush the wedges lightly with olive oil, sprinkle with sea salt and sweet paprika (or chilli powder for a spicier flavour). Cook for 35–40 minutes, or until the wedges are crisp and golden. Serve with sweet chilli sauce or aïoli as a dipping sauce.

8 floury potatoes
olive oil, to brush
sweet paprika, to dust
sweet chilli sauce (see page 339) or aïoili (see page 253), to serve

serves 4

potato gnocchi
with pancetta and sage

gnocchi
1 kg (2 lb 4 oz) floury potatoes, unpeeled
2 egg yolks, lightly beaten
2 tablespoons grated parmesan cheese
185 g (6½ oz/1½ cups) plain (all-purpose) flour
extra plain (all-purpose) flour, to knead

sauce
1 tablespoon butter
80 g (2¾ oz) pancetta or bacon slices, cut into thin strips
8 very small sage or basil leaves
150 ml (5 fl oz) thick (double/heavy) cream
50 g (1¾ oz/½ cup) shaved parmesan cheese

Prick the potatoes all over, then bake for 1 hour, or until tender. Leave to cool for 15 minutes, then peel and mash, or put through a potato ricer or a mouli (do not use a blender or food processor).

Mix in the egg yolks and parmesan cheese, then gradually stir in the flour. When the mixture gets too firm to use a spoon, work with your hands. Once a loose dough forms, transfer to a lightly-floured surface and knead gently. Work in enough extra flour to give a soft, pliable dough that is damp to the touch but not sticky.

Divide the dough into six portions. Working with one portion at a time, roll out on the floured surface to make a rope about 1.5 cm (5/8 inch) thick. Cut the rope into 1.5 cm (5/8 inch) lengths. Take one piece of dough and press your finger into it to form a concave shape, then roll the outer surface over the tines of a fork to make deep ridges. Fold the outer lips in towards each other to make a hollow in the middle. Set aside and continue with the remaining dough.

Bring a large saucepan of salted water to the boil. Add the gnocchi in batches, about 20 at a time. Stir gently and cook for 1–2 minutes, or until they rise to the surface. Remove with a slotted spoon, drain and put the gnocchi in a greased shallow casserole dish or baking tray.

Meanwhile, preheat the oven to 200°C (400°F/Gas 6). To make the sauce, melt the butter in a frying pan and fry the pancetta until crisp. Stir in the sage leaves and cream. Season with sea salt and freshly ground black pepper and simmer for 10 minutes, or until thickened.

Pour the sauce over the gnocchi, toss gently and sprinkle the parmesan cheese on top. Bake for 10–15 minutes, or until the parmesan cheese melts and turns golden. Serve hot.

For other potato recipes see:

layered potato and apple bake........131
celeriac mash...................................193
aloo gobi...289
dry potato and pea curry.................385

radish

vegetables ▪ **roots and tubers**
season ▪ **peak season spring–autumn**

Radishes (*Raphanus sativus*), although a 'root'
vegetable, are members of the crucifer, or mustard
family—hence their distinctive peppery flavour.
Their hot, spicy jolt comes from enzymes in the
skin. Peeling a radish would reduce this effect and
indeed is necessary in 'winter' varieties, but really,
that distinctive, mustardy freshness is a large part
of the radish's attraction.

Radishes have been eaten, in some form or
another, for millennia. Red radishes were popular
in ancient Turkey and Persia. The ancient Greeks
thought much of the radish, even creating radish
replicas made from gold. Their modern name is
derived from *radix*, the Latin word for 'root'.

Today, the main types of radish you are likely to
encounter are the familiar round red sort, the long,
slender, white 'icicle' radish and the enormous
daikon—these can grow up to 50 cm (20 inches)
in length and over 10 cm (4 inches) in diameter.
Although daikon radish is firmly associated with
East Asia (the Japanese are reputed to grow more
of this vegetable than any other), they actually
originated in the Mediterranean. Some might be
fortunate enough to source the black radish,
which is popular in Eastern European countries
and has black skin, ivory flesh, and a dryish texture
with a pronounced, earthy flavour.

culinary uses

Radishes are very easy to grow, making them a favourite with home gardeners. In the main, it is the quick-growing, tender, crisp 'spring' varieties that are common—'winter' varieties are harder skinned and require peeling and tend to be cooked rather than consumed raw. Mostly, tender-skinned types of red radish are used raw; once trimmed, washed and sliced they generally get relegated to the green salad bowl.

Delicious though they are in this guise, they can be used in far more interesting ways. The French, for example, serve perfect little red radishes whole as an appetizer, accompanying them with quality, sweet, unsalted butter, sea salt and pepper. Sliced radish makes a delicious sandwich filling, especially with cream cheese, dill and slices of smoked salmon. Red radishes can also be steamed or roasted then served as a side dish with meats; cooking like this renders them soft and nutty. When braised in butter and raspberry or red wine vinegar, they become a sublime accompaniment to roast duck. In Middle Eastern cuisines they are variously pickled and used in colourful salad combinations, often with oranges and black olives, for example.

Black radishes, a winter vegetable, perform extremely well as a roast vegetable to serve with joints of meat, or can be grated raw to use as you would horseradish.

Daikon radishes are an Asian staple, particularly in Japan. Their name is Japanese for 'great root' and they come in green, yellow, pink and black varieties, too. They are said to aid the digestion of fatty foods and can be eaten raw (choose smaller specimens for this), though need to be peeled first, then grated or cut into very fine matchsticks. Daikon can also be used as one would a turnip, put into stews and soups where they provide a bright, refreshing note and offset the richness of meats. They can be stir-fried, finely grated and used as a garnish, pickled, baked or simmered. The Japanese claim that cooking daikon in rice-soaking water enhances their white colour and eliminates any sharp flavours.

selection and storage

Buy radishes with green, fresh-looking tops, as the tops will yellow and wilt very quickly. Not only do the tops indicate the roots are fresh, but they are delicious in their own right. Daikon tops, if you get them, are a rich source of vitamin C, betacarotene, calcium and iron and can be simmered in soups or blanched, then dressed and used in salads.

Small radish varieties as well as their large daikon cousins should have firm, smooth skin with no signs of growth cracks, browning or wrinkling.

Black radishes should feel very hard; any softness at all can indicate a 'woolly' interior. Once home, cut off radish tops and store these separately—this prolongs the life of the roots. Keep radishes for up to 1 week in the refrigerator, stored in a ventilated plastic bag.

crisp-skinned salmon with radish and cucumber salad

serves 4

salad
1 large cucumber
2 celery sticks, thinly sliced
1 shallot, diced
1 avocado, diced
20 red or white radishes, halved
1 small handful coriander
(cilantro) leaves

dressing
80 ml (2½ fl oz/⅓ cup) olive oil
2 tablespoons lime juice
1 teaspoon finely grated lime zest
1 garlic clove, crushed
1 teaspoon honey

4 small salmon fillets, skin on
2–3 tablespoons olive oil
1 small handful coriander
(cilantro) leaves

To make the salad, peel the cucumber and cut in half lengthways. Using a teaspoon, scoop out and discard the seeds. Slice very thinly into half-moon shapes and put in a large bowl. Add the celery, shallots, avocado, radishes and coriander.

To make the dressing, put the oil, lime juice, lime zest, garlic and honey in a small bowl and mix well. Season with sea salt and freshly ground black pepper. Set aside until ready to serve.

Brush the salmon fillets lightly with olive oil and sprinkle the skin with a little salt. Heat the remaining oil in a large frying pan over high heat. When hot, add the salmon, skin side down, and immediately hold a spatula or another frying pan on top of the fillets to keep them flat. Fry for 1–2 minutes, or until the skin is crisp and brown all over. Reduce the heat to medium and turn the salmon. Cook until just opaque, 2–3 minutes, depending on the thickness. Drain on paper towels.

When cool enough to handle, use kitchen scissors to cut each salmon fillet across the grain into 3 strips. Break each strip into bite-sized pieces. Add to the salad with the dressing and coriander. Toss gently to coat and serve immediately.

daikon salad with sashimi

To make the dipping sauce, stir the soy sauce, ginger and sugar in a small bowl until the sugar has dissolved. Set aside.

To make the salad, shave the daikon, cucumber and carrot lengthways into wide thin strips with a mandolin or a vegetable peeler and put in a large bowl. Cut the ginger into fine matchsticks and add to the bowl.

Just before you are ready to serve, add the green onion, sesame seeds, rice vinegar, soy sauce and mirin and toss to coat. Divide the salad among four serving plates.

Lightly roast the nori by holding the sheet 5 cm (2 inches) above a low flame, moving it around to toast evenly for 2–3 seconds. Cut the nori into thin strips using scissors and scatter some over each salad.

Using a very sharp knife, slice the salmon and tuna into even 5 mm (1/4 inch) thick strips. Divide among the plates, arranging them in neat rows. Add a dab of wasabi to the plates and serve immediately with the dipping sauce.

dipping sauce
125 ml (4 fl oz/1/2 cup) Japanese
   soy sauce
1 teaspoon grated fresh ginger
1 pinch sugar

daikon salad
150 g (5½ oz) daikon, peeled
1 Lebanese (short) cucumber
1 carrot, peeled
4 cm (1½ inch) piece ginger
3 green onions (scallions), thinly
   sliced on the diagonal
½ teaspoon sesame seeds,
   roasted
2 teaspoons rice vinegar
2 teaspoons Japanese soy sauce
2 teaspoons mirin
1 sheet nori

250 g (9 oz) piece sashimi-quality
   salmon
250 g (9 oz) piece sashimi-quality
   tuna
wasabi paste, to serve

roots and tubers ■ radish

The Egyptians were eating red, white and black radishes 4000 years ago; labourers working on the great pyramids were sustained by these and other vegetables. Meanwhile in Asia, the Chinese were cultivating the black sort and Indians and Indonesians were consuming white radishes.

sweet potato

vegetables ■ roots and tubers
season ■ available year-round

selection and storage

Most sweet potatoes are aged for some weeks in order for their sugars to develop—freshly harvested sweet potatoes are generally not sweet. Choose ones with smooth, unblemished skins, exhibiting no bruises, mould or soft spots.

Only buy as many sweet potatoes as you need because they don't last very long; store them at room temperature in a well-ventilated spot for 2–3 days and not in the refrigerator.

Not a relation to the potato at all, the sweet potato, or *Ipomoea batatas*, is a member of the morning glory family. Sometimes falsely called yams, sweet potatoes are native to tropical parts of Central and South America and are yet another vegetable that Columbus took to Europe during his voyages of exploration. While they were embraced by the Spanish, the sweet potato didn't really catch on throughout Europe and has come to be largely associated with the cooking of the Americas, the Pacific and the Caribbean. The Portuguese transported it to their Asian and African colonies where it rapidly spread, and today the sweet potato is an important staple in many countries in those regions.

Sweet potatoes are a troublesome lot to classify. There are several hundred different types and there is wide variance in their appearance and behaviour when cooked. Their skin may be extremely thin or tough and thick. Skin colour ranges from red to purple to orange to deep beige. Their flesh colour varies too, depending on type (some are yellow fleshed, some orange and some ivory or white), as does the texture of their flesh and their sweetness once cooked.

varieties

Orange-fleshed sweet potatoes tend to have a pumpkin-like flavour and become very soft when cooked. Their sweetness is variable, depending on where they were grown and the particular cultivar. Those with creamy-white flesh and smooth purplish or rosy skins are classified as 'oriental' types, as they were developed in the Far East. These are quite sweet when cooked—their flesh turns translucent yellow and they are also rather moist although they do hold their shape well.

Another sort, sometimes called the boniato, is large and heavy-looking with knobbly red-purple skin and pale flesh. This type is less sweet, and is fluffy and dry when cooked, with an appealing, slightly chestnut taste. Beige-skinned sweet potatoes, with their dark cream flesh, are a small, unprepossessing-looking vegetable but when baked, their flesh transforms into an incredibly sweet, moist substance.

preparation

Sweet potatoes can be boiled, mashed, roasted, baked, fried, made into fritters and even used in baking and desserts. When baking or roasting, which is the method that most concentrates their sweet, nutty flavours, sweet potatoes will hold their shape best if left unpeeled. They can be cooked in much the same way as potatoes (see page 215), but it is important to note that they will take a shorter time to cook—wedges of sweet potato or 2 cm (3/4 inch) slices will take about 40–45 minutes to cook in a 200°C (400°F/Gas 6) oven.

Similarly, when frying sweet potatoes, their high sugar content means they can easily burn so do this at a lower temperature than you would for regular potatoes. It is generally better to steam sweet potatoes than to boil them (unless you are making mash), making it much easier to peel the skin after cooking. Sweet potatoes are also delicious when chargrilled—thinly slice peeled sweet potatoes, brush them with oil then cook on a medium-hot chargrill plate for 2–4 minutes on each side until just tender.

culinary uses

Sweet potatoes are complemented well by the flavours of ginger, cinnamon and nutmeg, bacon, turkey, ham and chicken, and are luscious with butter, maple syrup or brown sugar. They also go well in curries, especially coconut-cream based ones. The sweet simplicity of a well-roasted sweet potato, cooked to the point of near-collapse, however, is extremely difficult to beat.

sweet potato ravioli

Preheat the oven to 220°C (425°F/Gas 7). Place the sweet potato on a baking tray and drizzle with oil. Bake for 40–45 minutes, or until tender. Transfer the sweet potato to a bowl with the ricotta, basil, parmesan cheese and one-third of the garlic and mash until smooth.

Line a baking tray with baking paper. Cover the won ton wrappers with a damp tea (dish) towel to stop them drying out. Place 2 level teaspoons of the sweet potato mixture into the centre of one won ton wrapper and brush the edges with a little water. Top with another wrapper, pressing edges together to seal. Place onto the prepared tray and cover with a tea towel. Repeat with the remaining ingredients to make about 60 ravioli, placing a sheet of baking paper between each layer on the tray.

Melt the butter in a frying pan. Add the green onion and remaining garlic and cook over medium heat for 1 minute. Add the cream, bring to the boil, then reduce the heat and simmer for 4–5 minutes, or until the cream has reduced and thickened. Keep warm.

Bring a large saucepan of water to the boil. Cook the ravioli in batches for 2–4 minutes, or until just tender. Drain well. Ladle the hot sauce over the top of the ravioli, garnish with the basil leaves and serve immediately.

500 g (1 lb 2 oz) orange sweet potato, cut into 2 cm (¾ inch) chunks
60 ml (2 fl oz/¼ cup) olive oil
150 g (5½ oz/⅔ cup) ricotta cheese
1 tablespoon chopped basil
2 tablespoons grated parmesan cheese
3 garlic cloves, crushed
500 g (1 lb 2 oz) ready-made egg won ton wrappers
60 g (2¼ oz) butter
4 green onions (scallions), sliced on the diagonal
310 ml (10¾ fl oz/1¼ cups) pouring (whipping) cream
baby basil leaves, to serve

roots and tubers ■ sweet potato

serves 4–6

beef tagine with sweet potato

1 kg (2 lb 4 oz) blade or chuck
  steak
60 ml (2 fl oz/¼ cup) olive oil
1 onion, finely chopped
½ teaspoon cayenne pepper
½ teaspoon ground cumin
1 teaspoon ground turmeric
½ teaspoon ground ginger
2 teaspoons paprika
2 tablespoons chopped flat-leaf
  (Italian) parsley
2 tablespoons chopped
  coriander (cilantro) leaves
2 tomatoes
500 g (1 lb 2 oz) orange sweet
  potatoes

Trim the steak of any fat and cut into 2.5 cm (1 inch) pieces. Heat half the oil in a saucepan and brown the beef in batches over high heat, adding a little more oil as needed. Set aside in a dish.

Reduce the heat to low, add the onion and the remaining oil to the pan and gently cook for 10 minutes, or until the onion is softened. Add the cayenne pepper, cumin, turmeric, ginger and paprika, cook for a few seconds, then add 1 teaspoon of sea salt and freshly ground black pepper. Return the beef to the pan, add the parsley, coriander and 250 ml (9 fl oz/1 cup) water. Cover and simmer over low heat for 1½ hours, or until the meat is almost tender.

Peel the tomatoes. To do this, score a cross in the base of each one using a knife. Put the tomatoes in a bowl of boiling water for 20 seconds, then plunge them into iced water to cool. Remove from the water and peel the skin away from the cross—it should slip off easily. Slice the tomatoes. Peel the sweet potatoes, cut them into 2 cm (¾ inch) dice and leave in water until required.

Preheat the oven to 180°C (350°F/Gas 4). Transfer the meat and its sauce to an ovenproof serving dish (the base of a tagine would be ideal). Drain the sweet potato and spread it on top of the beef. Top with the tomato slices. Cover with foil (or the lid of the tagine) and bake for 40 minutes. Remove the foil, increase the oven temperature to 220°C (425°F/Gas 7) and raise the dish to the upper oven shelf. Cook until the tomato and sweet potato are flecked with brown and are tender. Serve immediately.

sweet potato filo pie

Preheat the oven to 200°C (400°F/Gas 6). Cut the sweet potato into 2.5 cm (1 inch) cubes and put in a large roasting tin, along with the shallots and baby potatoes. Combine the olive oil, paprika, ginger, cumin and cinnamon in a small bowl and pour over the vegetables. Toss to coat. Roast for 25 minutes, then turn the vegetables and roast for a further 15 minutes. Remove from the oven and reduce the oven temperature to 180°C (350°F/Gas 4).

Add the spinach and sultanas to the vegetables. Toss lightly, then set aside for 5 minutes for the spinach to wilt. Transfer to a large bowl and add the almonds, pistachios and coriander. Put 2 tablespoons of the golden syrup, the yoghurt, chickpeas, garlic, cayenne pepper and lemon juice in a food processor and blend until smooth. Season with sea salt and freshly ground black pepper. Add to the vegetables and mix through.

Brush a 28 x 21 cm (11¼ x 8¼ inch) loose-based rectangular tart tin with butter. Brush a sheet of filo with butter and lay it on point over one end of the tin, so that three of the points stick out and the overhang at the end is about 10 cm (4 inches). Don't push the pastry into the rippled sides of the tin, just place it loosely on top. Brush another sheet of filo with butter and lay it similarly, at the opposite end of the tin. Brush a third sheet with butter and lay it in the middle of the tin. Continue in this way twice more, until all the filo is used.

Pile the sweet potato mixture in the centre of the tin. Starting in the middle, bring the opposite sides of the filo together, encasing the filling tightly but with the filo points sticking up. Brush carefully with the remaining butter and drizzle the remaining golden syrup in zigzags over the top. Place on the baking tray and bake for 30 minutes, or until golden. Set aside for 5 minutes before serving.

750 g (1 lb 10 oz) orange sweet potato, peeled
12 small shallots, peeled
6 baby potatoes, peeled and halved
125 ml (4 fl oz/½ cup) olive oil
1 teaspoon sweet paprika
1 teaspoon ground ginger
2 teaspoons ground cumin
¼ teaspoon ground cinnamon
100 g (3½ oz/2 cups) baby English spinach leaves
60 g (2¼ oz/½ cup) sultanas (golden raisins)
85 g (3 oz/⅔ cup) slivered almonds, toasted
100 g (3½ oz/⅔ cup) pistachio kernels, coarsely chopped
40 g (1½ oz/1 cup) coriander (cilantro) leaves, chopped
2½ tablespoons golden syrup (dark corn syrup)
80 g (2¾ oz/⅓ cup) plain yoghurt
400 g (14 oz/1½ cups) drained tinned chickpeas
3 garlic cloves, finely chopped
1 pinch cayenne pepper
60 ml (2 fl oz/¼ cup) lemon juice
125 g (4½ oz) butter, melted
9 sheets ready-made filo pastry

taro

vegetables ▪ roots and tubers
season ▪ available year-round

Taro is an old, old food plant, having been cultivated for longer than wheat or barley and predating rice as the starch of choice in parts of China and Southeast Asia. Taro is often sold as dasheen, a corruption of the French, *de la Chine*, meaning 'from China'. Taro is inedible raw; it contains the toxin calcium oxalate, present as crystals; these are destroyed by cooking. There is only one species but hundreds of varieties. All taro corms are either large, at 1.5 kg (3 lb 5 oz) or tiny at about 75 g (2¼ oz)—these smaller corms cluster around the 'mother' corm.

preparation

Small corms are blander in flavour and moister than the large ones. They are more suitable for plain boiling and steaming. Larger taro can be fibrous, dry and mealy when cooked, with a nutty sweetness. Expect their flesh to be cream-coloured or grey or lilac and, sometimes, flecked with purple or brown fibres.

Protect your hands with gloves when preparing taro as it contains irritating compounds. Remove the thick, slightly hairy skin with a sharp knife, then slip chunks of the vegetable directly into acidulated water, as it rapidly discolours. Taro can be cooked in much the same way as a potato (boil peeled and cut taro chunks in a saucepan of salted boiling water for 15–20 minutes, or until tender). Don't boil and then mash them as they will become inedibly gummy. Subsequent roasting after parboiling large chunks for 10 minutes in a 200°C (400°F/Gas 6) oven, lightens the texture of taro, rendering it pleasantly sweet, dry and chewy. When cooked in braises and stews, taro absorbs liquid, thus thickening the dish. Always serve taro while it is freshly-cooked and hot; as it cools it becomes unappealingly stolid.

selection and storage

Choose corms that are heavy for their size and check closely for blemishes, signs of mould or wrinkling; they should smell pleasantly fresh. As taro do not store well use them quickly once purchased, and store in the refrigerator for no longer than 2 days.

black sticky rice with taro

Put the rice in a bowl and pour in cold water to come 5 cm (2 inches) above the rice. Soak for at least 3 hours, or overnight if possible.

Drain the rice and add clean water. Scoop the rice through your fingers four or five times to clean it, then drain. Repeat two or three times with clean water to remove the unwanted starch. (The water will never be completely clear when using black rice, even when all the unwanted starch has gone.) Put the rice in a saucepan and add 625 ml (21½ fl oz/2½ cups) cold water.

Bring to the boil over high heat, stirring the rice frequently as it reaches boiling point. Reduce the heat to medium. Stir and simmer for 30–35 minutes or until nearly all the liquid has been absorbed. The rice should be very moist, but with hardly any water remaining in the bottom of the saucepan. Taste a few grains to check whether the rice is cooked.

Meanwhile, drain the taro, spread it on a plate and transfer it to a steamer. Taking care not to burn your hands, set the steamer over a saucepan of boiling water over high heat. Cover and steam for 8–10 minutes or until the taro is tender.

When the rice is cooked, add the sugar and gently stir until the sugar has dissolved. Add the taro and gently mix.

Mix the salt into the coconut milk. Divide the pudding among individual bowls and drizzle coconut milk on top. Serve warm.

200 g (7 oz/1 cup) black sticky (black glutinous) rice
280 g (10 oz) taro, cut into 1 cm (½ inch) squares and soaked in cold water
150 g (5½ oz) palm sugar (jaggery), chopped
1 teaspoon salt
185 ml (6 fl oz/¾ cup) coconut milk

roots and tubers ■ taro

turnip and swede (rutabaga)

vegetables ▪ roots and tubers
season ▪ peaking late autumn–early spring

selection and storage

The sweetest turnips are those that appear in spring and autumn. Winter turnips can have tough, thick skins and be on the large side but their flavour will still be good; it's not worth buying turnips in summer.

Try to buy turnips with their green tops still intact and fresh-looking—this will indicate they have just been harvested. Avoid any with shrivelled, wrinkled or damaged skins.

Turnips don't suit long storage as they quickly turn bitter, so try to use them within a few days and store them in a plastic bag in the refrigerator.

Swedes, on the other hand, will last for more than 1 month in the refrigerator; stored in a dry cellar and packed in sand or sawdust, they can keep for nearly a year.

Choose swedes that are heavy for their size as these will be juicy, and that have undamaged skins. If you see swedes with their tops still attached (and this is rare), snap them up as this means they have been freshly dug.

Close relatives (the turnip is *Brassica rapa* while the swede is *Brassica napus*), these vegetables are celebrated in the cuisines of certain countries, while spurned outright by others. The Scots wouldn't dream of serving haggis without their beloved 'bashed neeps' (mashed buttered swedes) and the French have made an art out of richly-flavoured turnip braises (although they do feed swede to cattle). Unfortunately however, many of us have been turned off these vegetables by memories of unappetising lumps of boiled turnips and swedes served during childhood.

In America, swedes are commonly called rutabagas, a dreadful name that has no doubt contributed as much to their poor image there as have bad cooking practices. The name 'swede' comes from the fact that this crop is common in Sweden. Swedes are not an ancient food; they are the result of a seventeenth-century crossing of a turnip with a cabbage. They have a delightfully sweet, earthy taste, pretty, pale orange flesh and, roughly the size of a baseball, have yellow-tan bases extending into mauve-coloured tops, above which sprout stems and leaves.

Turnips, on the other hand, are a very ancient food; experts in such things believe they were first cultivated by man about 5000 years ago.

roots and tubers ▪ turnip and swede (rutabaga)

preparation

Turnips should be peeled before cooking. Cut them into large chunks and boil in salted water, they can also be steamed in a double-boiler arrangement and either way will take the same time, about 15–20 minutes.

Swedes can be prepared and cooked in exactly the same ways as turnips, but will take slightly longer to cook—about 20–25 minutes. You can also slip uncooked chunks of swede or turnip into braises and stews and allow them to cook slowly in the liquid—give them extra time (almost twice as long) to reach complete tenderness.

culinary uses

Wonderfully versatile, there are many ways to use turnips and swedes. Both need to first be trimmed and peeled, although turnip greens can be lightly steamed or stir-fried, blanched then baked into gratins or incorporated into soups. If the flesh just under the skin is tough and fibrous, you will need to pare this away too.

Both turnips and swedes are delicious raw, served with other vegetables with a dip as an appetizer or, cut into very fine slices or matchsticks, tossed through salads (a winter slaw, for example). Both are delicious steamed until *al dente* then tossed with burnt butter or fruity olive oil—never overcook either vegetable as this ruins both their flavour and texture.

Both vegetables can also be added to the stew-pot (particularly great with lamb or beef) where they will impart sweetness as well as absorbing other flavours, while chunks of either are particularly good when roasted with a leg of lamb. Both vegetables will mash beautifully with potatoes or puree into unctuous, creamy soups. Combined in the latter with pumpkin, sweet potato or, unusually, pears or apples, even the most determined swede and turnip detractors will be won over.

duckling with turnips

Preheat the oven to 200°C (400°F/Gas 6). Put a roasting tin in the oven to heat up. Truss the duckling by tying the legs together behind the body. Prick all over, put the bouquet garni in the cavity and season.

Heat the clarified butter in a large frying pan and brown the duckling on both sides. Lift the duckling out of the pan and pour all but 1 tablespoon of the fat into a jug. Add the carrot, celery and onion to the pan and cook, stirring, for about 10 minutes, or until soft. Continue to cook until browned. Remove from the pan.

Add 2 tablespoons of the reserved duck fat to the frying pan over low heat. Add the sugar and cook until dissolved. Increase the heat and add the shallots and turnips. Caramelize over high heat, then remove from the frying pan. Pour in the white wine and boil, stirring, for 30 seconds to deglaze the pan.

Put the carrot, celery and onion in the middle of the hot roasting tin, place the duckling on top and pour in the white wine and stock. Add the turnips to the pan and roast for 45 minutes. Baste well, add the shallots and roast for a further 20 minutes. Baste again and roast for another 25 minutes.

Take out the duck, turnips and shallots and keep warm. Strain the sauce from the bottom of the tin, pressing the chopped vegetables through a sieve to extract the juices, then discard the chopped vegetables.

Pour the strained juice into a small saucepan and boil rapidly to reduce the mixture by half. Mix together the butter and flour. Whisk into the sauce and boil, stirring, for 2 minutes, or until thickened.

Put the duckling, turnips and shallots on a serving plate and pour the sauce over them to serve.

1.7 kg (3 lb 12 oz) whole duckling
bouquet garni (see page 413)
2 tablespoons clarified butter
1 carrot, chopped
1 celery stick, chopped
½ large onion, chopped
2 teaspoons sugar
8 shallots
8 baby turnips
80 ml (2½ fl oz/⅓ cup) white wine
500 ml (17 fl oz/2 cups) ready-made chicken stock
½ tablespoon butter, softened
½ tablespoon plain (all-purpose) flour

roots and tubers ▪ turnip and swede (rutabaga)

serves 4

spiced baby turnips

400 g (14 oz) small roma (plum) tomatoes
60 ml (2 fl oz/1/4 cup) olive oil
3 small onions, sliced
3 teaspoons ground coriander
1 teaspoon sweet paprika
350 g (12 oz) baby turnips, trimmed
1 teaspoon soft brown sugar
1 handful parsley
600 g (1 lb 5 oz/1/2 bunch) silverbeet (Swiss chard)

Score a cross in the top of each tomato, plunge into boiling water for 20 seconds, transfer to a bowl of iced water to cool, and then peel the skin and discard. Cut the tomatoes widthways into 1.5 cm (5/8 inch) slices and gently squeeze out most of the juice and seeds.

Heat the olive oil in a large frying pan over medium heat and fry the onion for 5–6 minutes, or until soft. Stir in the coriander and paprika, cook for 1 minute, then add the tomato, turnips, sugar and 80 ml (2 1/2 fl oz/1/3 cup) hot water. Season well. Cook over medium heat for 5 minutes. Cover the pan, reduce the heat to low and cook for 4–5 minutes, or until the turnips are tender.

Meanwhile, strip the silverbeet leaves off the stalks, reserving stalks for another use. Rinse under cold water and shake off the excess.

Stir the parsley and silverbeet into the pan, check the seasoning and cook, covered, for 4 minutes, or until the silverbeet is wilted. Serve hot.

Throughout the Middle East, turnips are turned into exceptionally delicious pickles (as they are in Japan, Korea and some parts of Russia) while in Finland a Christmas dish called tulaatiko, *where swede is baked into a buttery pudding and flavoured with nutmeg, cinnamon and allspice, is a hearty winter favourite.*

finnish creamy-baked swede

Preheat the oven to 180°C (350°F/Gas 4) and grease a shallow 18 x 30 cm (7 x 12 inch) baking dish.

Cook the swedes in boiling salted water for about 25 minutes, or until tender. Drain well, return to the saucepan and, using a potato masher, mash finely—mixture should still have some texture. Place a separate saucepan over medium heat and cook swede, stirring often, for 5–7 minutes or until excess liquid has evaporated. Remove from the heat and cool slightly.

Stir the cream, eggs, egg yolk, flour and spices into the swede to combine, then season with sea salt and freshly ground black pepper. Pour into prepared dish, smoothing the top.

Combine the breadcrumbs and butter in a food processor and process until fine clumps form, then sprinkle over swede mixture. Bake for 30–35 minutes, or until golden and set in the middle. Serve hot or warm as a side dish to accompany roast or grilled (broiled) meats.

variation You can substitute the same weight of turnips for swedes in this recipe if you prefer.

1.6 kg (3 lb 8 oz or about 4) swedes, peeled and cut into 4 cm (1½ inch) pieces
125 ml (4 fl oz/½ cup) pouring (whipping) cream
2 eggs, lightly beaten
1 egg yolk
35 g (1¼ oz/¼ cup) plain (all-purpose) flour
½ teaspoon freshly grated nutmeg
1 small pinch of ground cloves
105 g (3½ oz/1¼ cups) fresh breadcrumbs
50 g (1¾ oz) unsalted butter, cut into cubes

roots and tubers ■ turnip and swede (rutabaga)

By the time of Pliny the Elder in 23–79 AD, the Greeks had developed many types of turnips, some of which Pliny describes in his writings.
The Pantropheon *records the way the Romans developed particularly elaborate ways of dealing with turnips—'they were seasoned with cumin, rue, benzoin, pounded in a mortar, adding to it afterwards honey, vinegar, gravy, boiled grapes and a little oil …'*

asparagus

vegetables ▪ **stems, shoots and bulbs**
season ▪ **spring–early summer**

Resist all temptation to eat imported, out-of-season asparagus. This is a fragile vegetable, subject to moisture loss and damage, its sweetness slowly diminishing from the moment it is harvested. It is best eaten as close to the time and place of harvest as possible; which means waiting until spring, when the first tender spears appear at the market. Asparagus tips are actually leafy buds—if left to their own devices and not picked they develop into a very tall fernlike plant with bright red berries.

There are over 300 species of asparagus, including some wild varieties, which are highly esteemed in the Mediterranean regions where they grow. We are mostly familiar with green asparagus but there are also purple and white varieties. In many parts of Europe, 'asparagus' means the white sort, actually the same type as green except for the way it is grown.

White varieties are grown in deep soil trenches or black plastic tunnels, which protect the spears from sunlight, thus interrupting the greening process of photosynthesis. The technique, called 'blanching', is labour-intensive, making white asparagus an expensive treat. Purple asparagus, which turns green when cooked, doesn't taste much different to its green counterpart.

preparation

Bend asparagus at their base to find the point at which they naturally snap, break them, then discard the woody ends. Peel the lower few centimetres of green or purple asparagus using a paring knife or potato peeler, although if large, you may need to peel more—this depends how stringy they are. White asparagus spears always require peeling as their skin is tough and bitter. Take care when doing this as white asparagus is brittle and will easily break. Asparagus is traditionally boiled or steamed, then served as an accompaniment, or cooled and used in salads or other dishes.

boiling To boil asparagus, tie it into bundles of about 8 spears each, using string, then cook it in boiling salted water for about 5 minutes, or until tender. Drain well. Allow to cool without the use of cold water as this will just dilute its subtle flavour.

steaming To steam asparagus, cook it in bundles, covered, over boiling water for 6–7 minutes, or until tender. Hot, cooked asparagus is at its best when tossed in extra virgin olive oil, melted in butter or, of course, served with a dollop of hollandaise sauce variation (see page 36) or a beurre blanc (see page 273).

culinary uses

Roasting in a little oil or brushing with oil then grilling (broiling) or barbecuing asparagus concentrates the sweet, herbal flavours. Cooked this way, asparagus become an earthy addition to an antipasti selection and stands up well to robustly flavoured partners such as parmesan cheese, bacon, olives, anchovies or pesto. A platter of chargrilled asparagus goes well with aïoli (see page 253) as a party snack and makes an excellent addition to a big summer salad of other chargrilled vegetables such as capsicum (peppers), zucchini (courgette), eggplant (aubergine) and spanish onion.

selection and storage

Inspect the stem end and spurn any asparagus that is wrinkled, dried out or split. Tips should be tight, bright and clean—pass over ones that look weepy or floppy. Choose spears roughly the same size so they will cook at the same time.

Debate rages over the pros and cons of fat spears versus thin spears, with some claiming one to be vastly superior to the other—but this is not necessarily the case. By buying the freshest asparagus possible, you can't go too far wrong with either.

Store asparagus for no longer than 2 days in a plastic bag in the refrigerator.

serves 4

asparagus and mint frittata

6 eggs
35 g (1¼ oz/⅓ cup) grated
    pecorino or parmesan cheese
1 handful mint leaves, finely
    shredded
200 g (7 oz or about 16) baby
    asparagus spears
2 tablespoons extra virgin
    olive oil

Break the eggs into a large bowl, beat well, then stir in the cheese and mint and set aside. Trim the woody part of the asparagus, then cut on the diagonal into 5 cm (2 inch) pieces.

Heat the oil in a frying pan that has a heatproof handle. Add the asparagus and cook for 5 minutes, or until the asparagus is tender. Season, then reduce the heat to low. Pour the egg mixture over the asparagus and cook for 8–10 minutes. Use a spatula to pull the side of the frittata away from the side of the pan and tip the pan slightly so the uncooked egg runs underneath the frittata.

When the mixture is nearly set but still slightly runny on top, place the pan under a low grill (broiler) for 1–2 minutes, until the top is set. Serve warm or at room temperature.

tagliatelle with asparagus and herbs

serves 4–6

500 g (1 lb 2 oz) tagliatelle pasta
200 g (7 oz or about 16)
    asparagus spears, cut into
    short pieces
40 g (1½ oz) butter
1 tablespoon chopped parsley
1 tablespoon chopped basil
310 ml (10¾ fl oz/1¼ cups)
    pouring (whipping) cream
50 g (1¾ oz/½ cup) finely
    grated parmesan cheese
extra parmesan cheese, shaved,
    to garnish

Cook the pasta in a large saucepan of salted boiling water until *al dente*. Drain and return to the pan.

Heat the butter in a frying pan, add the asparagus and stir over medium heat for 2 minutes, or until just tender. Add the chopped parsley, basil, cream, salt and pepper. Cook for 2 minutes.

Add the parmesan cheese to the pan and stir well. When thoroughly mixed, add the sauce to the warm pasta and toss gently to distribute ingredients evenly. Serve in warmed bowls with shavings of parmesan cheese.

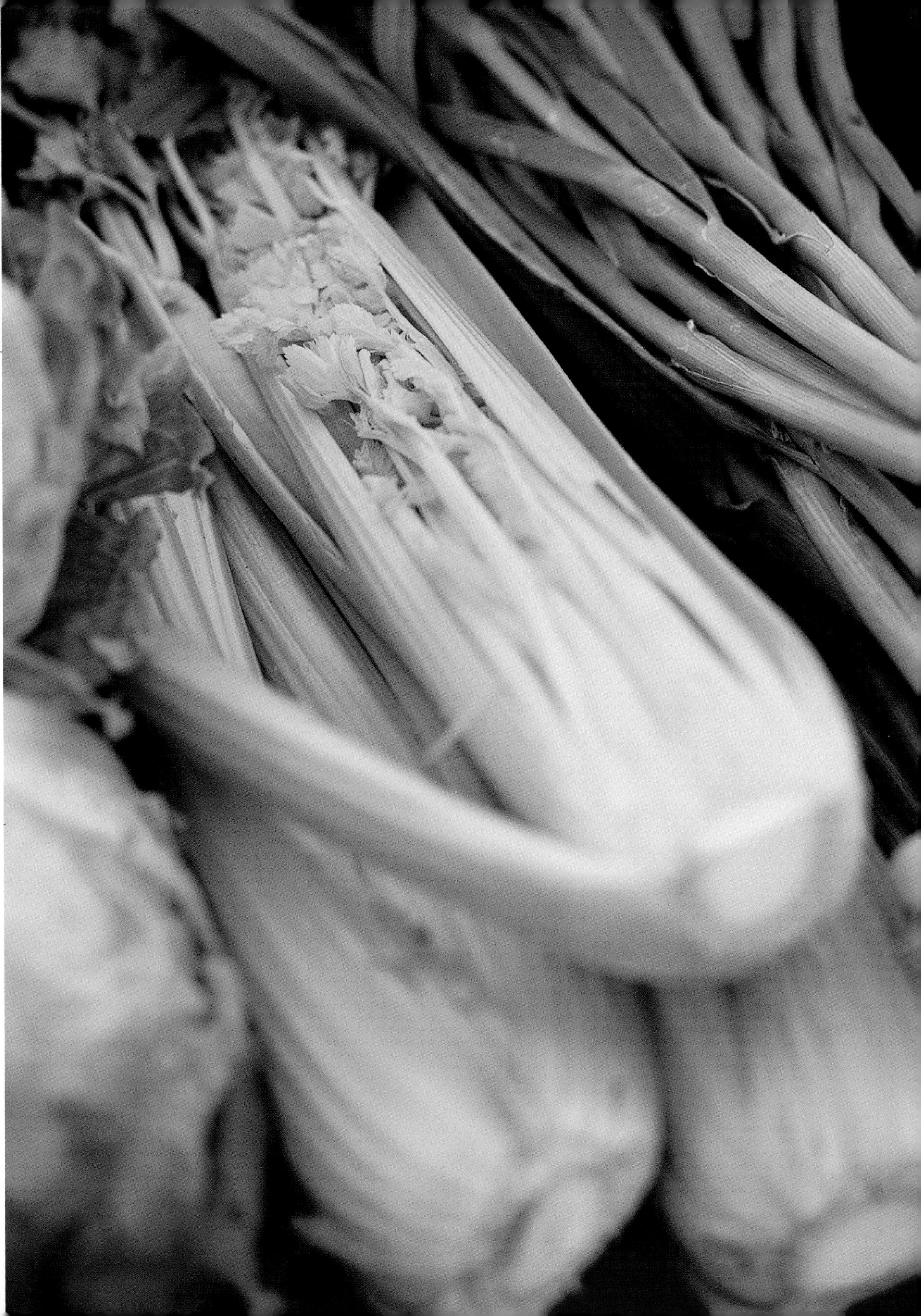

celery

Celery is a somewhat utilitarian, under-appreciated vegetable. It is one of those greens that most cooks have in their refrigerator, ending up chopped into a soup, a sauce or a salad. Mainly providing background flavour and texture in dishes, celery is also considered classic dieters' food and, along with raw sticks of carrot, a predictable component of the pre-dinner crudité platter.

There are two main types of celery grown commercially today—self-blanching celery which is a yellowish colour and is favoured in Europe, and the green-stalked type which is common in Asia, Australia and the United States. Originally, all cultivated celery was 'blanched'—grown in deep troughs with soil packed around the stalks to protect them from the greening effect of the sun. This was to produce less fibrous stalks, but modern breeding has made this growing method unnecessary.

Celery contains pthalides, an active component that relaxes the artery muscles that regulate blood pressure—it also reduces stress hormones which have a constricting effect on blood vessels. Celery has powerful diuretic properties and the volatile oils in celery seeds have been credited with effectiveness against a plethora of complaints: from flu and colds to liver and spleen ailments, poor digestion and arthritis.

In ancient times celery was widely used for a variety of medicinal purposes, never culinary. The Greeks called celery
selinon and as such, it is mentioned in Homer's Odyssey; Pliny, Hippocrates and Theophrastus wrote of it too.
Celery was considered a holy plant in ancient Greece and its leaves were worn by victors in the Nemean Games,
similar to the use of bay laurel at the more famous Olympic Games.

selection and storage

The celery you are most likely to encounter at the markets will be vibrant green, with thick, juicy outer stalks and a profusion of leafy tops. The 'heart' of a bunch of celery, which is much prized for its delicate flavour and texture, will be a tender, yellow colour.

Try to always buy celery with leaves attached, as these are a good indicator of freshness. Take a good look over the outer stalks for signs of browning or limpness and avoid bunches with these. You shouldn't be able to bend the stalks at all (they should be snappingly crisp).

Store celery in the crisper section of the refrigerator in plastic, for up to 1 week—if very fresh, it may keep longer. Take care not to keep it in the coolest part of the refrigerator as, with a 95 per cent water content, it may freeze.

preparation

The tough, outer stalks of celery are best suited for stocks, soups, sauces, braising and baking, although they can, of course, be used in raw dishes such as salads.

Sometimes celery can benefit from peeling to remove the fibrous layer (a regular potato peeler is ideal for this) and discarding the dark green leaves and first few centimetres of the stalks, although when washed, they can be utilized in stock-making.

culinary uses

Tender celery hearts, leaves included, are lovely in salads and other raw preparations such as salsa, for example, or chopped with capers, lemon, onion and parsley and a dash of olive oil and served with fish. Finely chopped and folded through home-made mayonnaise with a few capers and some mustard, they form the basis for an admirable sauce to have with fish or poached chicken.

Celery stands up well to cooking and it is a pity more cooks don't think of solo uses for it. A pureed celery soup (with a potato or two included, for a particularly velvety texture), is delicious, especially if finished with some cream and a crumbling of blue cheese. Continuing on the blue cheese theme, trimmed stalks of celery can be baked into a lush gratin with béchamel sauce and blue or gruyere cheese; they can also be braised in the Italian sweet-and-sour way, with stock, vinegar, tomato, raisins, pine nuts and anchovies.

Waldorf salad is legendary, as is the use of a celery stalk swizzle stick in a vodka-based bloody mary. Ring the changes by making a salad using celery hearts, crisp pears and parmesan and serving with slices of prosciutto, loads of olive oil and some lemon juice, or serve the hearts simply with walnut bread and sweet cultured butter, as a prelude to an informal dinner or lunch.

waldorf salad

Line a serving bowl with lettuce leaves. Cut the apples into 2 cm (3/4 inch) chunks and place in a large mixing bowl with the celery and walnuts.

In a small bowl, combine the mayonnaise and sour cream and mix well. Fold the dressing through the apple, celery and walnut mixture, then transfer to the lettuce-lined serving bowl and serve immediately.

lettuce leaves, to serve
2 red apples, quartered and cored
1 large green apple, quartered and cored
1½ celery sticks, sliced
25 g (1 oz/¼ cup) halved walnuts
2 tablespoons ready-made egg mayonnaise
1 tablespoon sour cream

stems, shoots and bulbs ■ celery

braised celery

serves 4

Preheat the oven to 180°C (350°F/Gas 4). Grease a shallow baking dish.

Melt the butter in a large frying pan. Add the celery, toss to coat evenly in butter. Cover and cook for 2 minutes. Pour the stock, lemon zest and juice into the pan; cover and simmer for a further 10 minutes. Remove the celery with a slotted spoon and place into the prepared dish. Reserve 60 ml (2 fl oz/¼ cup) of cooking liquid.

Blend the cream, egg yolks and cornflour in a separate bowl. Whisk in the reserved cooking liquid. Return to heat and cook until the mixture boils and thickens. Add parsley and mace. Season with sea salt and freshly ground black pepper.

Pour the sauce over the celery in a baking dish. Cook in the oven for 15–20 minutes or until the celery softens. Serve warm with poached chicken breast, chargrilled lamb or slices of corned beef.

1 bunch celery, trimmed and cut into 5 cm (2 inch) lengths
30 g (1 oz) butter
500 ml (17 fl oz/2 cups) ready-made chicken or vegetable stock
2 teaspoons finely grated lemon zest
60 ml (2 fl oz/¼ cup) lemon juice
60 ml (2 fl oz/¼ cup) pouring (whipping) cream
2 egg yolks
1 tablespoon cornflour (cornstarch)
1 small handful chopped parsley
½ teaspoon ground mace

fennel

vegetables ▪ **stems, shoots and bulbs**
season ▪ **autumn, spring–early summer**

In 1824, an American official, posted to the
Italian city of Florence, sent some fennel seeds
to the former US president, Thomas Jefferson, along
with a gushing letter: 'fennel is beyond every other
vegetable, delicious …' The Americans, though,
along with various other nations, were slow to
catch on to what the Italians have known
forever—that fennel is a wonderful, and versatile,
vegetable. Although commonly referred to as a
'bulb', cultivated fennel is not a true bulb at all
but rather has thickened leaf stems; it is this
which distinguishes it from wild fennel which,
in favourable conditions, grows like a weed.

In ancient times, the use of fennel was
believed to improve eyesight and, curiously,
Pliny's contemporaries in 23–79 AD thought
snakes ate fennel to help them shed their skins.
In 1614, author Giacomo Castelvetro wrote that
fennel 'improves the taste of bad wine', claiming
that scurrilous merchants offered fennel to tasting
customers, presumably to mask any vinous
inferiority they might taste.

Fennel has numerous health-giving properties—
it is rich in vitamin C, iron, magnesium, folate
and phosphorus.

preparation

Fennel can be enjoyed raw or cooked. To serve raw, trim tops and base of smaller bulbs with a small, sharp knife, discarding any outer leaves that are tough and fibrous. The stalks can be sliced and the leaves finely chopped for raw use—soak stalks in iced water to make them crisp. Cut the bulb in half lengthways and trim the core. Slice fennel into paper-thin slices for salads or slightly wider strips if serving as crudités. Prepare the fennel just before using, or place in a bowl of acidulated water (water with lemon juice), for once it's cut, fennel discolours.

For braising and roasting, cut halved, trimmed bulbs into wedges, but don't trim the core as this will hold the fennel together. Fennel can also be finely chopped or sliced then sautéed for use in sauces, various vegetable dishes or stews.

roasting To roast fennel, brush wedges with olive oil, arrange in a tight-fitting single layer in an oiled baking dish and season with sea salt and freshly ground black pepper. Cook in a 180°C (350°F/Gas 4) oven for 35–40 minutes (depending on size), turning once, or until tender.

braising To braise fennel, pour hot chicken stock over wedges in a dish to nearly cover, add a generous slug of olive oil, scatter with fresh thyme and season with sea salt and freshly ground black pepper. Cover the dish tightly with foil and cook in a 180°C (350°F/Gas 4) oven for 35–45 minutes, or until tender.

culinary uses

Fennel has many uses. Salads are an obvious one—thin raw slices (or shaved fennel) pair well with any of the following: oranges (especially the voluptuous blood), capers, olives, almonds, watercress, radicchio, parmesan, pecorino and goat's cheese. It is sublime tossed with home-made anchovy or tuna mayonnaise, or dressed with olive oil and lemon juice and served on a platter with prosciutto or smoked salmon.

Lightly cooked and tossed through pasta, fennel begs for cream, lemon and parsley. Braised in stock, fennel wedges complement fish or chicken—although it is important to note that cooking does mute its bright aniseed flavours somewhat. Braised fennel is also good with a cheesy sauce, or serve blanched slices baked in cream with nutmeg, thyme and a sharp cheese.

Finely chopped fennel is excellent cooked in a tomato sauce. Thin slices of fennel, cut lengthways from the bulb, can be dusted in flour or polenta and shallow-fried until golden and tender, making a sensational addition to an antipasti selection.

selection and storage

Never purchase fennel without its tops as these indicate freshness. Tops should be bright green with no signs of wilting; the bulbs should be tight, firm and a creamy green-white colour. Pass over any that look wrinkled, are bruised or whose outside layers are loose and flabby-looking.

The size of bulbs can vary significantly. The smaller ones will be milder and therefore excellent for slicing thinly and serving raw in salads or as crudité—larger ones can also be used this way but are also suitable for cutting into quarters or large wedges and roasting or braising.

Fennel doesn't keep especially well; store it in a plastic bag in the refrigerator for up to 4 days.

stems, shoots and bulbs ■ fennel

serves 6

florentine roast pork

3 large fennel bulbs
½ tablespoon finely chopped
  rosemary
4 garlic cloves, crushed
1.5 kg (3 lb 5 oz) pork loin,
  chined and skinned
3 white onions
90 ml (3 fl oz) olive oil
185 ml (6 fl oz/¾ cup) dry white
  wine
80 ml (2½ fl oz/⅓ cup) extra
  virgin olive oil
250 ml (9 fl oz/1 cup)
  ready-made chicken stock
3–4 tablespoons thick
  (double/heavy) cream

Preheat the oven to 200°C (400°F/Gas 6). Cut the green fronds from the tops of the fennel and chop to give 2 tablespoons fronds. Add these to a small bowl with the rosemary, garlic and plenty of sea salt and freshly ground black pepper. Make deep incisions with a sharp knife all over the pork and rub this mixture into the incisions and the splits in the pork bone. Cut two of the onions in half and place in a roasting tin. Put the pork on top of the onion and drizzle the olive oil over the top.

Roast in the oven for 30 minutes. Baste the pork with the pan juices, then reduce the temperature to 180°C (350°F/Gas 4). Roast for a further 30 minutes. Baste and lightly salt the surface of the pork. Pour in half the white wine. Continue roasting for another 30–45 minutes, basting once or twice.

Meanwhile, remove the tough outer layers of the fennel and discard. Slice the bulbs vertically into 1 cm (½ inch) sections and place in a large saucepan. Thinly slice the remaining onion and add to the saucepan with the extra virgin olive oil and a little salt. Add enough water to cover. Put a lid on the saucepan and bring to the boil. Simmer for about 45 minutes, or until the fennel is creamy and soft and almost all the liquid has evaporated.

Remove the pork from the tin and leave to rest. Spoon off the excess oil from the tin and discard the onion. Place the tin over high heat on the stovetop and stir in the remaining wine to deglaze. Add the stock and boil the sauce until slightly thickened. Remove from the heat, season with sea salt and freshly ground black pepper and stir in the cream. Slice the pork and serve on the fennel, with the sauce passed separately.

fennel crumble

Preheat the oven to 180°C (350°F/Gas 4). Grease a large ovenproof serving dish. Trim fennel and cut into thin slices. Wash and drain well. Bring a large saucepan of water to the boil over high heat. Add the lemon juice and fennel slices. Cook over medium heat for 3 minutes. Drain; rinse under cold water.

Put the fennel in a large bowl. Add the extra lemon juice with the black pepper and honey; toss to combine. Sprinkle with the flour. Spoon into the prepared dish and pour the cream over the top.

To make the topping, combine the oats, flour and breadcrumbs in a bowl. Heat the butter in a small saucepan, add the garlic and cook for 30 seconds. Pour over the dry ingredients and mix well. Sprinkle the crumble over the fennel. Bake for 20–30 minutes or until fennel is tender and crumble is browned.

note   White or wholemeal breadcrumbs can be used in place of rye bread if preferred.

2 fennel bulbs
60 ml (2 fl oz/¼ cup) lemon juice
   plus 2 tablespoons, extra
1 tablespoon honey
1 tablespoon plain (all-purpose)
   flour
310 ml (10¾ fl oz/1¼ cups)
   pouring (whipping) cream

crumble topping
75 g (2½ oz/¾ cup) rolled
   (porridge) oats
60 g (2¼ oz/½ cup) plain
   (all-purpose) flour
110 g (3¾ oz/1 cup) fresh black
   rye breadcrumbs
60 g (2¼ oz) butter
1 garlic clove, crushed

stems, shoots and bulbs ∎ fennel

garlic

vegetables ■ stems, shoots and bulbs
season ■ peak season spring–late autumn

The kitchen would be a lesser place without the sweet pungency of garlic; who could imagine cooking without it? In fact, garlic is the most widely used herb flavouring in the culinary world, with few cuisines not utilizing it.

Garlic, with leeks and onions, is a member of the *Allium*, or lily, family. For a long time it was used only medicinally or was considered a food for the poor—the veritable 'stinking rose'. Mrs Beeton, in her famous *Book of Household Management* (1861), pronounced that the smell of garlic 'is generally considered offensive, and it is the most acrimonious in its taste of the whole alliaceous tribe'.

It is generally accepted that garlic is native to Central Asia, or at least the European sort is— Native Americans were using a form of wild garlic way in advance of European settlers bringing it there. Both good, and good for you, garlic is an essential staple of every good cook's larder.

varieties

There are many, indeed hundreds, of garlic varieties, which all taste essentially the same, they just vary in intensity of flavour. Some have white papery skin around the cloves and bulb while others have reddish, pink or mauve-striated coverings. Some have large, fat, rounded cloves (the best-known of this sort being mild-flavoured elephant garlic, which is technically not a true garlic at all, being closer botanically to the leek), and others have thin, small and long cloves.

Our modern word garlic comes from the old English gar *(spear) and* leac *(leek), in reference to the long, spear-like green shoot the plant sends up as it grows. Whatever its etymology, few other members of the vegetal world have attracted as much lore and legend as garlic. All sorts of powers have been attributed to garlic, from Eleanor Roosevelt, who consumed chocolate-coated garlic pills every morning (to help her memory) to Pliny the Elder, who took garlic, spice and wine-based love potions to improve his manly vigour, to the Central Europeans and Indians who used garlic to ward off demons and vampires.*

selection and storage

When buying garlic, choose bulbs with firm cloves that show no signs of powdery mould or green sprouting. The papery shells should be crisp and crinkly to the touch and the cloves should look as though they are about to burst from tight skins.

It is difficult to tell how large individual cloves are—the size of the bulb is no indication. Store garlic in a dark, well-ventilated place. In general, avoid storing it in plastic or in the refrigerator, although a week or so won't hurt too much.

Well-stored, away from light and moisture, garlic will stay fresh for weeks. Garlic cannot be frozen, as this ruins both flavour and texture, and don't prepare garlic until you absolutely need it—exposure to the air causes bitterness to quickly set in.

preparation

The simplest way to peel garlic is to lay the individual cloves on a board, place the flat side of a large knife-blade over each clove and administer a firm tap with the heel of your hand—the skin will then just pull off.

The most effective way to finely chop quantities of garlic is to do this on a board with a little sea salt—the salt helps to break down and soften the garlic and in a relatively short time, you will have a pile of fine pulp. Purists eschew the garlic crusher claiming it alters the flavour, although it is nonetheless a handy device.

The volatile component in garlic responsible for its haunting smell is an enzyme called allinaise, which only asserts itself when cell walls inside the garlic cloves are cut or crushed. The human nose is said to be so sensitive to this compound that it can detect it in the air in as small a concentration as one part per billion. And the more finely the garlic is cut, the more of this sulphurous compound gets released, which has distinct consequences for cooking with garlic. Thus, in the French classic, chicken with 40 cloves of garlic, for example, the garlic flavour is actually extremely subdued as the garlic is cooked whole, and for quite some time. On the other hand, just one or two garlic cloves, crushed and added fresh to a salad dressing or mixed into butter, will lend quite a jolt.

Heat destroys allinaise so the longer you cook garlic, and the higher the heat it is cooked at, the milder the resulting flavour. If sautéing garlic in oil or butter, take care not to brown or burn it as this will make it bitter and ruin your dish—cook over a low-medium heat.

As noted above, garlic flesh oxidizes very quickly on contact with the air so avoid preparing garlic in advance—although storing crushed or chopped garlic under a layer of olive oil will slow this process down.

aïoli

Put the egg yolks, garlic, salt and half the lemon juice in a mortar or food processor and pound with a pestle or mix until light and creamy. Add the oil, drop by drop from the tip of a teaspoon, whisking constantly until it begins to thicken, then add the oil in a very thin stream. (If you're using a food processor, pour in the oil in a thin stream with the motor running.) Season with sea salt and freshly ground black pepper, add the remaining lemon juice and, if necessary, thin with a little warm water.

Serve the aïoli in a bowl as a dipping sauce. You can keep aïoli sealed in a sterilized jar in the refrigerator for up to 3 weeks. It tastes delicious served with poached fish, chicken or seafood. Try it with a selection of crudités—carrots, celery, blanched asparagus, beans, cauliflower—as an appetizer, or spooned beside barbecued or roast beef fillet or as an accompaniment to whole baked potatoes.

4 egg yolks
8 garlic cloves, crushed
½ teaspoon salt
2 tablespoons lemon juice
500 ml (17 fl oz/2 cups) olive oil

stems, shoots and bulbs ■ garlic

garlic prawns

serves 4

Heat the butter and olive oil together in a large frying pan. When hot, add the garlic and chilli. Cook, stirring continuously, for 30 seconds.

Add the prawns and cook for 3–4 minutes on each side, or until they turn pink. Sprinkle the prawns with the parsley and serve immediately on hot plates, with the lemon wedges.

25 g (1 oz) butter
100 ml (3½ fl oz) olive oil
2 garlic cloves, finely chopped
1 small red chilli, seeded and finely chopped
24 large raw prawns (shrimp), peeled and deveined, tails intact
3 tablespoons chopped flat-leaf (Italian) parsley
lemon wedges, to serve

green onion (scallion)

vegetables ▪ **stems, shoots and bulbs**
season ▪ **available year-round**

This onion has a confusing number of names. It is variously called the green onion, scallion and in some places and quite erroneously, the spring onion (spring onions are similar, but have slightly bulbous white ends). The green onion, with its long, elegant green end atop a bright white stem end is much-used around the world, particularly in Asian climes from where it was thought to have come from. Indeed, this is the only onion commonly used in traditional Japanese cooking. The green part is highly nutritious, being particularly high in vitamins A and C. Generally, the green onion is used finely sliced or cut into thin matchsticks, raw or very lightly cooked only; it is not suited to long cooking.

preparation

The root end needs to be removed, as does the fine, tough membrane that invariably covers the white parts of the onion. Cut off the top 4 cm (1½ inches) or so, then finely slice on the diagonal, widthways or cut into 5 cm (2 inch) long sections and cut these into fine matchsticks.

culinary uses

Use green onions in stir-fries (they are particularly compatible with garlic and ginger), stirred through salads, or sprinkled on soups as a garnish. The finely chopped green tops work well, with their mild-hot flavour, stirred into vegetable fritter mixtures, potato (and other root vegetable) purees and gratins.

selection and storage

Choose bunches of green onions with deep green shoot ends and firm, unblemished white root ends. Avoid any with signs of wilting or yellowing green ends.

Wrap bunches of green onions in plastic wrap and store in the crisper section of the refrigerator—they are fairly perishable so use within 2–3 days.

green onion pancakes

Place the flour and ½ teaspoon salt in a bowl and stir to combine. Add the oil and 220 ml (7¾ fl oz) water and mix into a rough dough using a wooden spoon. Turn the dough out onto a lightly floured surface and knead for 5 minutes, or until smooth and elastic. Cover the dough with a cloth and rest for 20 minutes.

On a lightly floured surface, use your hands to roll the dough into a long roll. Divide the dough into 24 pieces. Working with one portion of dough at a time, place the dough, cut edge down, on the work surface. Using a small rolling pin, roll it out to a 10 cm (4 inch) circle. Brush the surface with sesame oil and sprinkle on some green onion. Starting with the edge closest to you, roll up the dough into a log and pinch the ends to seal. Lightly flatten the roll, then roll it up lengthways to form a snail, pinching the ends to seal. Repeat with the remaining dough, sesame oil and green onion. Let the rolls rest for 20 minutes.

Place each roll flat on the work surface and press down with the palm of your hand. Roll out to a 10 cm (4 inch) circle with a rolling pin. Place on a lightly floured baking tray. Stack the pancakes between lightly floured sheets of baking paper and leave to rest for 20 minutes.

Heat a frying pan over medium heat, brush the surface with oil and add two or three pancakes at a time. Cook for 2–3 minutes on each side, turning once, until the pancakes are light golden and crisp. Remove and drain on paper towels. Serve immediately.

note You can reheat pancakes, wrapped in foil, in a 180°C (350°F/Gas 4) oven for 15 minutes if you want to prepare them in advance.

250 g (9 oz/2 cups) plain (all-purpose) flour
1 tablespoon oil
3 tablespoons roasted sesame oil
2 green onions (scallions), green part only, finely chopped
oil, for frying

stems, shoots and bulbs ■ green onion (scallion)

leek

vegetables ▪ stems, shoots and bulbs
season ▪ peak season late spring–autumn

Leeks with honey and pepper, leeks in raisin sauce;
fish fillets with leek and coriander (cilantro); these
recipes sound as though they come straight from
any modern chef's menu. Yet, they are, in fact,
just a few of the many leek recipes that appear in
the recipe collection of the famous ancient Roman
epicure, Apicius. Which just serves to illustrate
how esteemed this vegetable once was and how
versatile it was thought to be. Indeed, the leek is
still highly valued in many food cultures, while in
others, it gets relegated to the soup or stock pot
and that's about it.

Leeks have thick, long, white cylindrical stalks
of many tightly packed layers that flow into green,
flat and tightly bunched leaves. Probably native to
Central Asia from where they spread throughout
Europe a very long time ago, leeks have come
to be mostly associated with Wales, of which
country it is the national symbol.

Like all the alliums (shallots, onions, garlic),
leeks have great health-promoting properties.
They are attributed with lowering high cholesterol
levels, protecting against high blood pressure and
also against certain cancers—notably prostate
and colon.

preparation

The coarse green leek tops are discarded and the white part only used for cooking although the green part can be utilized, well washed, in stock-making. The trickiest aspect of preparing leeks for cooking is the removal of all the dirt that hides, trapped between the layers. If you plan to use the leeks sliced or cut into matchsticks, this isn't a problem as the prepared leeks can be washed in plenty of water to remove any soil.

If you are planning to serve leeks whole, make a deep, crosswise slit through the leafy end of the leeks then soak them in a bowl of water, shaking them well to dislodge any dirt. Alternatively, you can cut the leeks in half lengthways, right through the root end, thereby holding the leeks together as they cook.

steaming To steam leeks, cut them into 5 cm (2 inch) rounds, place in a steamer basket over boiling water, cover, then cook for 10–15 minutes, or until completely tender. Leeks can also be trimmed and steamed whole—depending on their size, this will take 15–25 minutes.

culinary uses

Leeks suit braising whole, in chicken stock with some aromatic herbs such as thyme. They are also excellent stewed, that is, chopped, cooked in unsalted butter and their own juices and finished with a dash of cream and some grated nutmeg.

They can be steamed too, but never simply boil leeks; the result will be soggy and tasteless. Leeks go very well with fish and seafood, with vinaigrette dressings, anchovies, mustard, cheeses (gruyere and blue cheese, especially), chicken, prosciutto, cream, potatoes (think of Vichyssoise soup), walnuts, hazelnuts (and their oils) and parsley.

selection and storage

Leeks should feel very firm and heavy for their size and be straight, bearing dark green leaves. There should be no yellowing or withering in evidence and it is best to choose leeks that have a diameter of no more than 4 cm (1½ inches)—any larger than this and they tend to be fibrous and less sweet.

Never buy leeks that have been trimmed of their leaves. Inspect very closely before buying leeks at the end of the season, as these can have a woody inner core and are best avoided.

Store leeks with leaves attached, in the refrigerator, in a loosely sealed plastic bag, for up to 7 days.

serves 4

chicken and leek pie

50 g (1¾ oz) butter
2 large leeks, white part only,
 thinly sliced
4 green onions (scallions), sliced
1 garlic clove, crushed
30 g (1 oz/¼ cup) plain
 (all-purpose) flour
375 ml (13 fl oz/1½ cups)
 ready-made chicken stock
125 ml (4 fl oz/½ cup) pouring
 (whipping) cream
1 barbecued chicken, removed
 from bones and chopped
375 g (13 oz) block ready-made
 puff pastry
60 ml (2 fl oz/¼ cup) milk

Preheat the oven to 200°C (400°F/Gas 6). Lightly grease a 20 cm (8 inch) round baking dish.

Melt the butter in a saucepan and add the leek, green onion and garlic. Cook over low heat for 6 minutes, or until the leek is soft but not browned. Sprinkle with the flour and mix well. Gradually pour in the stock and cook, stirring, until the mixture is thick and smooth.

Stir in the cream and add the chicken. Put the mixture in the pie dish and set aside to cool.

Divide the pastry into two pieces and roll each piece between two sheets of baking paper to a thickness of 3 mm (⅛ inch). Cut a circle out of one of the sheets of pastry to cover the top of the pie. Brush the rim of the pie plate with a little milk. Put the pastry on top and press to seal around the edge. Trim off any excess pastry and crimp the edge with the back of a fork. Cut the other sheet into 1 cm (½ inch) strips and roll each strip up loosely like a snail. Arrange on top of the pie, starting from the centre and leaving a gap between each one. The spirals may not cover the whole surface of the pie. Make a few small holes between the spirals to let out any steam, and brush the top of the pie lightly with milk.

Bake for 25–30 minutes, or until the top is brown and crispy. Make sure the spirals look well-cooked and are not raw in the middle.

note Make small pies by dividing the mixture among four greased 1¼ cup (315 ml/10 fl oz) round ovenproof dishes. Cut the pastry into 4 rounds to fit. Bake for 15 minutes, or until the pastry is crisp.

leeks a la grecque

Put the oil, wine, tomato paste, sugar, bay leaf, thyme, garlic, coriander seeds, peppercorns and 250 ml (9 fl oz/1 cup) water in a large frying pan with a lid. Bring to the boil, cover and simmer for 5 minutes.

Add the leeks in a single layer and bring to simmering point. Reduce the heat, cover the pan again and cook for 20–30 minutes, or until the leeks are tender (pierce with a fine skewer to test). Lift out the leeks and put them in a serving dish.

Add the lemon juice to the cooking liquid and boil rapidly until the liquid is slightly syrupy. Remove the bay leaf, thyme and peppercorns. Season with salt and pour over the leeks. Serve the leeks cold, sprinkled with chopped parsley.

60 ml (2 fl oz/¼ cup) extra virgin olive oil
30 ml (1 fl oz) white wine
1 tablespoon tomato paste (concentrated puree)
¼ teaspoon sugar
1 bay leaf
1 thyme sprig
1 garlic clove, crushed
4 coriander seeds, crushed
4 peppercorns
8 small leeks, white part only, trimmed
1 teaspoon lemon juice
1 tablespoon chopped parsley

The leek has historically been associated with a beneficial effect on the throat; the Roman emperor, Nero, allegedly took a daily potion of leeks to improve his singing voice, and Aristotle believed the partridge possessed such a clear voice because of its diet of leeks.

For other leek recipes see:
parsnip and leek puree 210

onion

vegetables ■ stems, shoots and bulbs
season ■ available year-round

The onion is one of those ancient, venerable foods with a fascinating history. People began using onions way before recorded history, making it one of the earliest of all cultivated crops. It is thought the onion originated in Central Asia although it has been dispersed over the world for so long, experts aren't really sure.

Through most of history however, onions were considered fit only for the poor—possibly because their strong smell offended the fine sensibilities of the rich. Onions were cheap, easy to grow and quite frequently eaten raw on bread for breakfast by the less well-off. It wasn't until the Middle Ages, when onions became a hoi-polloi staple, along with cabbage and beans, that the upper classes began to appreciate them. And the rest, as the saying goes, is history.

Aside from a few religious groups who prohibit onion consumption (for example, Jainists and Buddhists both believe certain pungent foods, of which the onion is one, excite the passions), there isn't a culture anywhere that doesn't use onions. American author Maggie Waldron expressed the idea thus: 'It's probably illegal to make soup, stews and casseroles without plenty of onions.' Illegal no, but, religious convictions notwithstanding, it's certainly illogical.

varieties

There are over 300 varieties of onions and very few are sold by named variety. Rather, onions are generally sold by types. Some of the most common onion types are listed below.

baby onions These are very small onions, usually brown-skinned but sometimes white, which are perfect for pickling whole. They can also be roasted, braised or used in stews, such as the French dish *coq au vin*, to great effect. Baby onions are sometimes called pickling or pearl onions.

brown onions About 75 per cent of all onions used are the classic brown or yellow-skinned onion that comes in a variety of sizes and degrees of bulbousness. This is a good all-purpose cooking onion, suitable for stewing, frying, roasting and stuffing. These onions taste quite strong and unless you particularly favour their throat-catching flavour, they are not a good choice to use raw.

red onions A mild, sweet-tasting onion with distinctive red-mauve skin and pink-tinged white flesh. Red onions are wonderful eaten raw—perfect in salads, dressings, salsas and sandwiches. They are also delicious when grilled (broiled) or barbecued but can be disappointing in stews or when long-cooked or roasted.

spanish onions These are a large, round, yellow-skinned variety favoured for use in salads or for eating raw, on account of their juicy, mild-tasting flesh. Confusingly, in Australia, red onions are also called Spanish onions.

sweet onions Sweet onions are popular in the United States. Also referred to as 'short-day' onions because they are grown over winter months then harvested in spring–summer, they are distinct from 'storage' onions (the majority of brown and white onions are classic 'storage' onions) which are harvested in late summer–autumn and, because of their firmer texture and lower moisture content, are suited to curing and storing. Storage onions have a sugar content somewhere around 3–5 per cent, whereas sweet onions hover around 15 per cent. As well as being sweeter, they have a subtle, mild flavour and thin, light-coloured skins, which tend to be quite fragile. Some of the best-known examples of sweet onions are the vidalia, the walla-walla and the maui—they are well-suited to raw use.

white onions As the name suggests, white onions have white skin and white, green-tinged, juicy flesh; their flavour is clean and tangy and tends to be stronger than brown and yellow onions. White onions contain their fair share of pungent sulphur compounds, so beware when peeling. A good choice for sautéing, roasting, baking and for use in casseroles.

selection and storage

Onions should feel firm and heavy. Their skin should be shiny and the skin around the neck should be very tightly closed. There should be no soft or dark spots or sprouting. Onions, even if they taste strong, should smell mild when unpeeled—a strong odour can indicate spoilage. Don't choose onions sporting green areas either as these will taste unpleasant.

Store onions in a cool, dry and well-ventilated place; light can cause bitterness so keep them somewhere dark. They readily absorb moisture so avoid leaving them anywhere damp (in a cupboard under a sink, for example) and also, don't store them near potatoes as these give off moisture and gas and will make onions spoil more rapidly.

stems, shoots and bulbs ■ onion

It's agreed that onions were cultivated as long as 5000 years ago. The Egyptians venerated onions, believing them to be a symbol of eternity, on account of their circle-within-a-circle structure. Pharaohs were buried with onions for this reason although it has been conjectured that the strong antiseptic qualities of the onion could have been another contributing factor in this. The labourers of the pyramids were sustained by onions and other vegetables, and in Greece, athletes would drink onion juice, consume raw onions and rub onions over their bodies to strengthen themselves before competing in the Olympic Games.

nutrition

Onions are something of a wonder food, not so much for their vitamin content (they do contain vitamins C and B6 but not in startling quantities) but for the 150 or so phytochemicals they contain. For example, they contain saponins, which are associated with cholesterol reduction and also inhibiting tumour growth.

Red and yellow onions have been found to contain quercetin, a substance which blocks formation of cancer cells; research has also shown that compounds in onions can prevent certain causes of asthma, kill infectious bacteria and act to dissolve blood clots. Consumption of onions may also be helpful in preventing gastric ulcers and cataracts.

preparation

Onions contain over 100 volatile sulphur compounds in their cells and these are released when the cell walls are chopped or sliced with a knife. The effects of this are legendary—once caught in the eyes, the potent, compound-laden juices of an onion quickly reduce the cook to tears. The older the onion, the stronger these compounds are.

peeling If you need to peel a quantity of onions, especially baby ones which will be used whole, the best way to do this is to pour boiling water over them in a bowl and let them stand for 5 minutes. This loosens the skins considerably. Whether employing this method or not, peel onions from the neck end down, leaving the root intact, which holds the onion effectively together, facilitating easier chopping. Also, when planning to cook onions whole, halved or in wedges, they will break up into layers if the root end has been chopped through.

cutting The cooking fraternity abounds with suggestions for reducing the effects of onion-chopping and these run the gamut from the whimsical to the utterly ludicrous. Possibly the most effective and convenient method is to refrigerate onions for 30 minutes before chopping them, as this seems to subdue their potency. Also, make sure your knife is very sharp as this will slice through cells causing minimal damage, whereas a blunt knife will bruise and batter its way through the cells, releasing far more sulphur compounds into the air.

The best way to chop an onion is to first peel and halve it, then place it, flat side down, on a board before slicing and chopping. Do not prepare onions in advance as they quickly oxidize and can taste extremely unpleasant.

roasting To roast onions, either peel them or leave them unpeeled for different results. When unpeeled, the onion flesh steams to a creamy mass inside the skins, which can then be squeezed or scooped out to eat. Peeled roast onions result in a crusty, crunchy, deeply caramelized exterior and a softish interior.

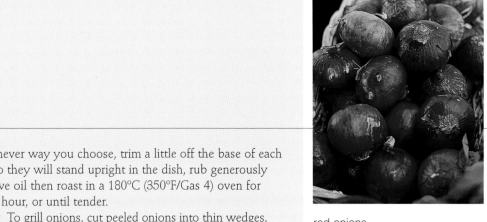

red onions

Whichever way you choose, trim a little off the base of each onion so they will stand upright in the dish, rub generously with olive oil then roast in a 180°C (350°F/Gas 4) oven for about 1 hour, or until tender.

grilling To grill onions, cut peeled onions into thin wedges, brush with oil then cook on a barbecue or chargrill plate for 3 minutes on each side, or until lightly charred and tender.

caremelizing To caramelize onions, finely slice 6–8 onions (they lose much of their 90 per cent water content during this process so it isn't really worth doing with just one or two), then cook in olive oil over medium heat in a large saucepan for 45–60 minutes, stirring often, or until golden and 'melted'. You can add a dash of sugar, some red wine vinegar and red wine near the end of cooking if you like, to reduce this down to a jammy mess to make a savoury 'marmalade'—an excellent accompaniment for roast meats.

culinary uses

Onions are an assumed part of practically all savoury recipes and for this reason risk being overlooked as a vegetable in their own right. They are sublime when baked, grilled (broiled), barbecued or stewed to a caramelized mass—onions contain substances which, when reduced down through long cooking, are many times sweeter than table sugar.

Grilled onions are wonderful doused with good balsamic vinegar, sprinkled with sea salt and scattered with chopped mint and served at room temperature as a side dish. Expand this idea into a salad by adding some rocket leaves, black olives and slices of medium-rare lamb and you have a delicious, light main course meal.

onion and thyme marmalade

2 kg (4 lb 8 oz) onions, cut into rings
750 ml (26 fl oz/3 cups) malt vinegar
6 black peppercorns
2 bay leaves
10 cm (4 inch) square of muslin (cheesecloth)
800 g (1 lb 12 oz/4⅓ cups) soft brown sugar
2 tablespoons fresh thyme leaves
10 sprigs fresh thyme, about 3 cm (1¼ inch) long

Put the onion in a large saucepan with the vinegar. Put the peppercorns and bay leaves in the muslin and tie securely with string. Add to the saucepan. Bring to the boil, then reduce the heat and simmer for 40–45 minutes, or until the onion is very soft.

Add the sugar, thyme leaves and 1 teaspoon salt. Stir for 7–8 minutes, or until all the sugar has dissolved. Bring to the boil, then reduce the heat and simmer for 20–30 minutes, or until thick and syrupy. Remove any scum from the surface with a slotted spoon. Discard the muslin bag and stir in the fresh thyme sprigs.

Transfer to a heatproof jug and immediately pour into hot streilized jars and seal. Allow to cool, then label and date each jar. Store in a cool, dark place for 6–12 months. Refrigerate after opening for up to 6 weeks.

The term 'to know one's onions' developed in the United States in the 1920s—one suggested meaning of this is that, with so many varieties of this easily-hybridized vegetable being developed at the time, to 'know your onions' became synonymous with expertise in a given field.

stifatho (beef and onion stew)

Preheat the oven to 160°C (315°F/Gas 2–3). Cut the beef into 2 cm (¾ inch) thick slices, then into 3 cm (1¼ inch) chunks. Heat half the olive oil in a large frying pan, over high heat. Fry the beef, in batches, for 7–8 minutes, or until browned, then transfer to a bowl.

Add the remaining oil, chopped onion and garlic to the frying pan, reduce the heat to low and fry for 5–6 minutes, or until soft. Add the allspice and cumin and cook for 1 minute. Return the beef to the frying pan, increase the heat and stir well to coat with the spices. Add the tomato paste, wine and vinegar and cook for 1 minute. Add the bay leaf, cinnamon stick, stock and enough hot water to cover the beef. Bring to the boil, then quickly transfer to an ovenproof casserole dish with a lid. Cover and cook in the oven for 1 hour.

Remove the loose outer skin of the baby onions but do not peel them entirely or top and tail them. Cut a cross in the root. Bring a large saucepan of water to the boil and add the onions. Boil for 1 minute, then drain. The inner skins will have been loosened and will peel off easily.

Add the baby onions to the casserole dish, along with the sultanas, and toss lightly. If necessary, top up with hot water to keep the meat and onion just covered. Bake for a further 1 hour, or until the meat and onions are tender but not breaking up. Discard the pieces of bay leaf and cinnamon stick before serving.

1 kg (2 lb 4 oz) blade or chuck steak, trimmed
80 ml (2½ fl oz/⅓ cup) olive oil
1 large brown onion, finely chopped
2 garlic cloves, thinly sliced
¼ teaspoon ground allspice (pimento)
½ teaspoon ground cumin
60 g (2¼ oz/¼ cup) tomato paste (concentrated purée)
170 ml (5½ fl oz/⅔ cup) dry red wine
2 tablespoons red wine vinegar
1 bay leaf, torn in half
1 cinnamon stick, broken in half
250 ml (9 fl oz/1 cup) ready-made beef stock
800 g (1 lb 12 oz) baby onions
2 tablespoons sultanas (golden raisins)

stems, shoots and bulbs ∎ onion

rhubarb

vegetables ■ stems, shoots and bulbs
season ■ available year-round

The use of rhubarb as a food crop is relatively recent. For millennia the root of this cold weather plant was an important medicine crop in China, and from there it was eventually exported to Europe, where it became incredibly popular. In sixteenth century France rhubarb was reputed to be ten times as expensive as cinnamon—in 1650s England it sold for over two and a half times the price of opium! Culinary rhubarb was developed in the pre-Islamic East where it was a much-favoured ingredient for drinks and meat stews—such preparations are still a striking feature of Middle Eastern cuisines.

Technically a vegetable, only the stalks, called 'petioles', are edible—the leaves contain oxalic acid (the stalks do too but, unless great amounts are ingested, in non-harmful quantities). Supposedly this feature is responsible for its slowness to gain popularity in Europe, as early experimenters consumed the leaves with dire results. Not until the nineteenth century, when strains of the plant were developed that had juicy, tender stalks, did cultivation and consumption begin in earnest—particularly in England and North America.

selection and storage

The first rhubarb stalks to appear in early spring are the most tender. Field-grown rhubarb tends to be juicier, sourer, less tender and more deeply red than that grown in greenhouses. Both field-grown and indoor-grown rhubarb have their fans, some preferring the fuller flavour and thicker stems of the former, others prizing the softer texture and gentler flavour of the latter.

Stalks can range in colour from pink and red to green; colour is no indicator of maturity although generally the red stalks are sweeter than the others.

Rhubarb dries out quickly once picked and becomes flaccid, so look for stalks that are firm and upright, avoiding very thick ones as these will be fibrous. Discard the leaves before wrapping the stalks in plastic wrap—they will keep for up to 1 week in the refrigerator.

preparation

Rhubarb is generally cooked, or stewed, with sugar for use in sweet dishes such as fools, jams, compotes and a range of baked desserts, such as cobblers, crumbles and pies.

stewing Simply slice 1 kg (2 lb 4 oz) rhubarb into 2 cm (3/4 inch) pieces—if stalks are fibrous, remove these first (a potato peeler is ideal for this but beware of the fine red juices which are likely to spurt and can stain clothing). Put the chopped stalks in a saucepan with 90 g (3¼ oz/¼ cup) caster (superfine) sugar and 2 tablespoons of water—add the sugar in small amounts to begin with then increase to taste as the rhubarb cooks; rhubarb can vary widely in sourness so no two batches will necessarily need the same amount. Cover the saucepan and simmer, stirring occasionally, for 5–8 minutes, or until the rhubarb is tender. Serve with vanilla or strawberry ice cream, or with whipped cream and a shortbread-style biscuit on the side.

culinary uses

Rhubarb can be flavoured with a little rosewater or cinnamon, sweetened with honey instead of sugar, or cooked with a little orange juice and finely grated orange zest. Stewed rhubarb is equally delicious whether served hot, warm or chilled and needs little more than some cream, custard or ice cream to cut the acid edge. Rhubarb and orange marmalade is lush, as is rhubarb and strawberry jam (or rhubarb and strawberry pie filling or crumble base—the two have a great affinity).

Rhubarb is also used in savoury dishes—notably in the spiced meat koreshes of Iran, lamb stews of Georgia (in the former Soviet Union) and fragrant tagines of North Africa. Lightly sweetened and pureed, rhubarb makes a wonderful sauce for pork and, cooked with apple into a rich chutney, a perfect foil for smoked meats like ham.

rhubarb and ginger jam

Chop the rhubarb into small pieces. Layer the rhubarb, sugar and lemon juice in a large non-metallic bowl. Cover and leave overnight.

Put two small plates in the freezer. Place the rhubarb mixture in a large saucepan. Finely chop the fresh ginger, place in the muslin, tie securely with string and add to the pan. Stir over low heat for 5 minutes, or until all the sugar has dissolved. Bring to the boil and boil rapidly for 20–30 minutes, stirring often. When the jam falls from the back of a tilted wooden spoon in thick sheets without dripping, start testing for setting point. To do this, remove from the heat, put a little jam onto one of the cold plates and place in the freezer for 30 seconds. A skin should form on the surface and the jam should wrinkle when pushed with your finger. If not, continue to reduce the syrup over heat and use the second testing plate to test for setting point. Discard the muslin bag and add the glacé ginger.

Transfer to a heatproof jug and immediately pour into hot sterilized jars and seal. Allow to cool, then label and date each jar. Store in a cool, dark place for 6–12 months. Refrigerate after opening for up to 6 weeks.

note To warm sugar, preheat the oven to 150°C (300°F/Gas 2). Spread the sugar evenly in a baking dish and warm in the oven for about 10–15 minutes, or until warmed through. Do not overheat the sugar or it will start to lump together.

1.5 kg (3 lb 5 oz) rhubarb, trimmed

1.5 kg (3 lb 5 oz/6¾ cups) sugar, warmed (see note)

125 ml (4 fl oz/½ cup) lemon juice

4 cm (1½ inch) piece fresh ginger, bruised and halved

10 cm (4 inch) square of muslin (cheesecloth)

100 g (3½ oz/½ cup) glacé ginger, finely chopped

stems, shoots and bulbs ▪ rhubarb

rhubarb and apple
upside-down cake

Preheat the oven to 180°C (350°F/Gas 4). Lightly grease a deep 20 cm (8 inch) round cake tin and line the base with baking paper.

Put the sugar in a saucepan with 80 ml (2½ fl oz/⅓ cup) water and heat gently, shaking occasionally, until the sugar has dissolved. Increase the heat and cook until it turns a pale caramel colour—it will turn a deeper colour in the oven. Pour into the tin and then press the rhubarb and apple into the caramel.

Beat the eggs, icing sugar and vanilla extract in a small bowl with electric beaters until the mixture is frothy. Fold in the melted butter. Sift the flour over the top and stir (the mixture will be soft). Spoon gently over the fruit, being careful not to dislodge it.

Bake for about 45 minutes, or until set on top. Run a knife around the side of the cake and turn out very carefully onto a wire rack to cool. Be sure to do this straight away, otherwise the caramel will cool and stick to the tin. Serve warm with cream as a dessert, or cool as a teacake.

variation Fresh plums can be substituted for the apple and rhubarb in this recipe. The plums should be halved and cored, then sliced and pressed into the caramel in a decorative spiral pattern, or randomly. Bake the cake as for the original recipe and serve either warm or cold.

250 g (9 oz/1 cup) sugar
250 g (9 oz) rhubarb, chopped into 2 cm (¾ inch) pieces
1 small apple, peeled, cored and chopped
2 eggs
40 g (1¼ oz/⅓ cup) icing (confectioners') sugar
½ teaspoon natural vanilla extract
100 g (3½ oz) unsalted butter, melted and cooled
125 g (4½ oz/1 cup) self-raising flour

stems, shoots and bulbs ■ rhubarb

For other rhubarb recipes see:
papaya lime fool (variation).............117

shallot

vegetables ■ **stems, shoots and bulbs**
season ■ **peak season summer**

Shallots have papery, thin, brittle skins which range in colour from copper and gold to greyish with flesh that can be yellowy, pink-tinged or white. The pink-fleshed sort is held to have the best flavour. Prized for their distinct but polite flavours, shallots never 'take over' a dish in the way onions or garlic can and are valued by good cooks everywhere.

Another member of the allium family, true shallots grow not from seed but from a bulb. A 'mother' bulb is planted and produces endless 'daughters'—in France it is against the law to label anything but bulb-grown shallots as shallots. Seed-propagated shallots look, to many, like 'proper' shallots. They do not, however, possess that singular flavour (elegant, sweet and intense) for which shallots are so valued.

preparation

If using shallots in any quantity, the skins can be tedious to peel. Pour boiling water over shallots in a bowl, weight them with a plate to submerge, then stand for 5 minutes. Drain well, and cool slightly. To peel, slice across the skin from the very top of each bulb then, using a small, sharp knife, pull a section of skin away from flesh, then pull it down to the root end.

Trim the root ends but don't cut them off completely, especially if you want to cook shallots whole, as this will help them stay together. Although shallots are generally used finely sliced, chopped or minced, they can also be cooked whole.

selection and storage

Choose bulbs that feel hard and whose papery skins are shiny and brittle. Be vigilant in not purchasing any that are sprouting, soft (which could indicate a powdery mould) or withered. Shallots will store very well (for several months) if they are fresh when bought.

Keep them in a dark, well-ventilated place at cool room temperature; if you must refrigerate them, do so after you have loosely wrapped them in paper towels to protect them from damp and humidity

shallot, bacon and cheddar breakfast muffin

Preheat the oven to 200°C (400°F/Gas 6). Grease a 6-hole giant muffin tin. Slice 1 of the shallots into rings. Heat 2 teaspoons of oil in a frying pan over low heat. Add the shallot and fry for 3 minutes. Remove and drain on paper towels. Set aside.

Finely chop the remaining 4 shallots. Increase the heat to medium and add these shallots and bacon to the pan. Fry for 5 minutes, or until the shallots are soft. Drain on paper towels.

Sift the flour, baking powder, sugar, mustard and 1/2 teaspoon salt into a bowl. Add 90 g (3 1/4 oz/3/4 cup) of the cheddar cheese. Add the bacon and shallots and stir through. Combine the milk, egg and remaining oil in a jug. Pour into the bowl and fold gently—the batter should be lumpy.

Divide the batter among the muffin holes. Top with the fried shallot and remaining cheddar cheese. Bake for 20–25 minutes, or until the muffins are golden and a skewer inserted into the centre of the muffin comes out clean. Cool in the tin before turning out on a wire rack. Sprinkle paprika on top to serve.

60 ml (2 fl oz/1/4 cup) oil, plus
  2 teaspoons, extra
5 shallots, peeled
2 bacon slices, finely chopped
250 g (9 oz/2 cups) plain
  (all-purpose) flour
1 tablespoon baking powder
1 tablespoon caster (superfine)
  sugar
1 teaspoon dry mustard
140 g (5 oz/scant 1 1/4 cups)
  grated mature cheddar cheese
185 ml (6 fl oz/3/4 cup) milk
1 egg
sweet paprika, to serve

beurre blanc

makes 250 ml
(9 fl oz/1 cup)

Put the white wine vinegar, white wine and shallots into a saucepan and bring to the boil over high heat. Simmer for 6–7 minutes, or until the liquid has reduced to about 60 ml (2 fl oz/1/4 cup). Strain the liquid and return to the saucepan. Discard the shallots.

Whisk in the butter, one cube at a time, over low heat, so the butter melts into the sauce and doesn't split. Season with sea salt and freshly ground black pepper. Serve with fish, chicken, eggs, asparagus or artichoke.

50 ml (1 3/4 fl oz) white wine
  vinegar
125 ml (4 fl oz/1/2 cup) white wine
2 shallots, finely chopped
250 g (9 oz) unsalted butter,
  cubed

stems, shoots and bulbs ▪ shallot

sprouts

vegetables ▪ **stems, shoots and bulbs**
season ▪ **available year-round**

The Chinese have long been sprouting beans and seeds; for millennia Chinese physicians have been prescribing them on account of their health-giving properties and particularly high nutritional value. Their use in Western cuisines is fairly recent—it has only been in the last 30 years or so that they have become widely popular.

Sprouts are seeds that have just started to grow. Loosely, there are those sprouts which come from beans and those which are sprouted from vegetable seeds. The most common bean sprouts are the mung bean and soya bean, while well-known vegetable seed sprouts include radish, cress, alfalfa and mustard. Both types are eaten whole—the only sprout that requires cooking is the soya bean sprout while certain others (notably the mung bean sprout) can be lightly cooked (by steaming, stir-frying, blanching); mostly though, they are used raw.

Seed sprouts are diminutive, with fine, silvery shoots topped with several tiny green leaves. Their soft, delicate texture makes them perfect in sandwich fillings or salads.

Bean sprouts are less starchy than the beans they sprout from as the sprouting process causes starches and sugars to be used up. Sprouts from beans (adzuki, mung and soy) typically have long, translucent ends and tiny, light yellow leaves.

selection and storage

Look for seed sprouts with fresh bright colours that are dry-looking, with no damp or brown patches. Often these types of sprouts are sold ventilated in plastic boxes—keep them in these, in the refrigerator, until ready to use and use quickly (within 2 days) as they are highly perishable.

Bean sprouts should have shoots that are crisp, clear-coloured and with no mushy, brown or soft spots. Bean sprouts should be stored in a roomy, sealed plastic bag in the refrigerator and used within 2 days of purchase, as they are at their nutritional peak and flavour for only a short time.

pear and sprout salad with sesame dressing

Put all the sesame dressing ingredients in a small screw-top jar and shake well to dissolve the sugar. Set aside.

Peel and core the pears, then slice them into thin strips. Put the pear strips in a bowl and cover with water to prevent discoloration.

Drain the pears and put in a large serving bowl with the snow pea sprouts, bean sprouts, chives, snow peas, celery and coriander. Pour the dressing over, toss lightly, sprinkle with sesame seeds and serve.

sesame dressing
1½ tablespoons soy sauce
1 teaspoon sesame oil
3 teaspoons soft brown sugar
1½ tablespoons peanut oil
3 teaspoons rice vinegar

2 small firm, ripe pears
200 g (7 oz) snow pea (mangetout) sprouts
200 g (7 oz) bean sprouts, tails trimmed
1 handful chives, snipped into 4 cm (1½ inch) pieces
65 g (2¼ oz) snow peas (mangetout), cut into matchsticks
1 celery stalk, cut into matchsticks
1 small handful coriander (cilantro) sprigs
1 teaspoon sesame seeds

stems, shoots and bulbs ■ sprouts

tropical sprout salad

serves 4

Peel the papaya, cut in half and scoop out the seeds. Cut the flesh into 1 cm (½ inch) slices and arrange in a single layer. Drizzle with lime juice and allow to sit for 10 minutes.

Arrange half the papaya slices in a serving bowl, then add half the snow pea sprouts, half the kiwi fruit slices and half the alfafa sprouts. Repeat with the remaining ingredients and serve immediately.

1 small papaya
2 tablespoons lime juice
50 g (1¾ oz) snow pea (mangetout) sprouts
2 small kiwi fruit, peeled and thinly sliced
35 g (1¼ oz/½ cup) alfalfa sprouts

artichoke

vegetables ■ **flowers**
season ■ **spring**

storage and selection

Globe artichokes are in peak condition when their leaves are green and tight and they feel heavy for their size. The best test for freshness is to rub the leaves together to check for a characteristic 'squeak'. This is often considered a more reliable indicator than colour alone, as artichokes with some bronzing on the tips of their leaves (called the 'winter kiss' in some countries) have been touched by frost, which actually enhances their flavour and makes them the most highly prized of all.

Artichokes are dry and well past their prime when their leaves appear to be opening. They start deteriorating from the moment they are picked so freshness is of the essence. While best used on the day of purchase, unwashed artichokes can be stored in a sealed plastic bag in the refrigerator for up to 2 days.

Synonymous with spring, globe artichokes are the unopened flowers and stems of an edible thistle. Along with broccoli and cauliflower, they are classified as an inflorescent vegetable, that is, one with an edible flower, which in the case of the artichoke, if allowed to bloom, transforms into a magnificent large purple blossom. They grow on perennial plants that only produce the edible flowers in their second and third years. This, coupled with the fact that they are a low yield per acreage crop, explains their status as a delicacy and their relatively high price tag.

First thought to have been cultivated in Sicily, artichokes appear in ancient Greek and Roman literature and were grown in Granada by the Moors from around 800 AD. Globe artichokes are entirely unrelated to the tuberous Jerusalem (which is not only not an artichoke, it is not even from Jerusalem) and Chinese artichokes, which are thus named as their flavour is said to resemble that of the globe artichoke. The main types of commonly available artichoke are the green globe, purple globe and purple Roman varieties.

Artichokes contain limited levels of vitamin A and potassium, and fair amounts of folate.

preparation

Much of a mature artichoke is inedible. The fleshy base of each leaf is succulent while the prickly tops are cut off and discarded, as is the hairy 'choke' inside each artichoke. The tender 'heart' of the artichoke is the most prized part, although there is a ritualistic element attached to eating the outer leaves—customarily you tear off individual leaves from a boiled artichoke, dip the base into melted butter and then pull the flesh away with your teeth, discarding the leaf, thus working your way toward the heart.

Although home cooks often find the thought of preparing artichokes off-putting, it is really quite a straightforward process requiring no particular skill, just a little time. Working one at a time and using a small, sharp knife, trim the stalks, leaving 4–6 cm (1½–2½ inches) of stalk, then snap off the tough outer leaves until you start to see leaves with a tender, yellowy base. Cut off about 4 cm (1½ inches) across the tops of each artichoke. The stems can then be peeled, and the hairy choke scooped out from the top of the bulb with a teaspoon and discarded.

Alternately, you can trim the artichokes right down to the tender heart, discarding all the outer leaves. As you go, place the artichokes in acidulated water (water with lemon juice) to prevent discolouration until ready to use. They should not be cooked in iron or aluminium pans, as this can cause them to brown.

boiling To boil artichokes, cook them in a saucepan of boiling, salted water for 20–25 minutes or until tender through the thickest part (a skewer is ideal for this)—cover the vegetables with an upturned plate to keep them submerged. Drain, then serve whole with butter or sauce; provide finger bowls and paper towels for dealing with the aftermath.

culinary uses

Luxuriant artichokes are most often served simply boiled or steamed with mayonnaise, hollandaise or vinaigrette for dipping their tender inner leaves, but they can also be stuffed and braised or baked, enjoyed raw, grilled, fried, marinated and preserved in oil or even added to spring stews.

Their brief spring season begs for their use with other quintessentially spring ingredients like asparagus, broad (fava) beans, peas, and lamb, veal and capretto. Herbs such as flat-leaf (Italian) parsley, marjoram, thyme and sage complement artichoke's fine flavour and delicate texture and they pair well with butter, prawns, pancetta, prosciutto, saffron, and cheeses such as parmesan, pecorino and gruyere.

artichokes vinaigrette

To prepare the artichokes, bring a large saucepan of salted water to the boil and add the lemon juice. Break the stalks from the artichokes, pulling out any strings at the same time, and then trim the bases flat. Add the artichokes to the water and put a small plate on top of them to keep them submerged. Cook at a simmer for 20–25 minutes, or until a leaf from the base comes away easily. (The base will be tender when pierced with a skewer.) Cool quickly under cold running water, then drain upside-down on a tray.

To make the vinaigrette, heat 1 tablespoon of the oil in a small saucepan, add the green onion and cook over low heat for 2 minutes. Leave to cool a little, then add the white wine, vinegar, mustard and sugar and gradually whisk in the remaining oil. Season with sea salt and freshly ground black pepper and stir in half the parsley.

Put an artichoke on each plate and gently prise it open a little. Spoon the dressing over the top, allowing it to drizzle into the artichoke and around the plate. Pour the remaining dressing into a small bowl for people to dip the leaves. Sprinkle each artichoke with a little parsley.

Eat the leaves one by one, dipping them in the vinaigrette and scraping the flesh off the leaves between your teeth. When you reach the middle, pull off any really small leaves and then use a teaspoon to remove the furry choke. Once you've got rid of the choke, you can eat the tender base or 'heart' of the artichoke.

juice of 1 lemon
4 artichokes

vinaigrette
5 tablespoons olive oil
2 green onions (scallions), finely chopped
2 tablespoons white wine
2 tablespoons white wine vinegar
¼ teaspoon dijon mustard
pinch of sugar
1 tablespoon finely chopped parsley

flowers ■ artichoke

lamb and artichoke fricassée

To prepare the artichokes, bring a large saucepan of salted water to the boil and add the lemon juice. Trim the stems from the artichokes and remove the tough outer leaves. Cut the hard tips off the remaining leaves using scissors. Cook the artichokes for 5 minutes. Remove and turn upside-down to drain. When cool enough to handle, use a small spoon to remove the choke from the centre of each. Scrape the bases well to remove all the membrane. Cut the artichokes into quarters and set aside.

Score a cross in the top of each tomato, plunge into boiling water for 20 seconds, transfer to a bowl of iced water to cool, and then peel the skin and discard. Cut each tomato in half and scoop out the seeds with a teaspoon. Chop the tomatoes.

Heat half the oil in a deep heatproof casserole dish and fry batches of the lamb until golden. Add the remaining oil and cook the onion for about 8 minutes, or until soft and caramelized. Add the flour and cook for 1 minute. Add the garlic, tomato, wine and chicken stock. Return the lamb to the pan, add the bouquet garni and simmer, covered, for 1 hour.

Put the artichokes in the casserole dish and simmer, uncovered, for a further 15 minutes. Remove the lamb and artichokes with a slotted spoon and place in a serving dish. Keep warm. Discard the bouquet garni. Cook the sauce over high heat until it thickens. Pour the sauce over the lamb and garnish with parsley. Serve with lemon wedges.

6 artichokes
60 ml (2 fl oz/¼ cup) lemon juice
2 large tomatoes
80 ml (2½ fl oz/⅓ cup) olive oil
2 kg (4 lb 8 oz) diced lamb
750 g (1 lb 10 oz) brown onions, thinly sliced
1 tablespoon plain (all-purpose) flour
2 garlic cloves, crushed
185 ml (6 fl oz/¾ cup) white wine
350 ml (12 fl oz/1⅓ cups) ready-made chicken stock
1 bouquet garni (see page 413)
chopped fresh flat-leaf (Italian) parsley, to garnish
lemon wedges, to serve

flowers ▪ artichoke

broccoli

vegetables ▪ **flowers**
season ▪ **peak season autumn–winter**

selection and storage

When buying broccoli, look for heads with tightly closed, compact, deep green florets, with no signs of yellowing. Broccoli with yellow flowers attached is over-mature and should be avoided. The stalks should be firm and not too thick or they will be woody. Any leaves attached to the stalk should be green and sprightly.

A fairly perishable vegetable, broccoli should be stored in a perforated or open plastic bag in the refrigerator crisper and used within 3–4 days. It should not be washed before storing, as water clinging to its surface will cause it to rapidly deteriorate.

Broccolini, which is a recent innovation and an Australian-developed hybrid, should have long, firm, clean stems topped with a smallish, compact head. Florets should be blue-green or green-purple in colour and leaves should be healthy looking (no wilting or browning) and olive green. A few yellow flowers per bunch are acceptable (about six or so) but more than this indicate over-maturity. Store in the same manner as broccoli.

Like others in the brassica family, broccoli began its life in the Mediterranean. It originated as a form of wild cabbage that eventually evolved to develop buds rather than large leaves. The most common sort of broccoli is the familiar emerald green variety with tightly clustered tiny buds sitting atop thick stalks.

The less well-known Calabrese broccoli, named after the southern Italian region of Calabria, is an heirloom variety with a deep bluish-green colour. Prized for its succulence and delicate flavour, it is often compared to asparagus. The Italians also eat broccoli raab (alternately known as rabe or *brocoletti di rape*), which despite its name and appearance is not directly related to broccoli, although it is a member of the cabbage family.

A more recent addition to the broccoli line-up is broccolini, a cross between broccoli and Chinese broccoli (also known as gai larn or Chinese kale), broccolini is gaining in popularity due to its slender, tender long stalks, deliciously subtle flavour and loose, small buds.

Broccoli is one of the healthiest of vegetables, containing excellent doses of folate, phytonutrients including betacarotene and lutein, manganese and potassium. A single cup of broccoli boasts as much calcium as a cup of milk. Broccolini is especially rich in vitamins A and C, folate and potassium.

The purple sprouting variety was the first form of broccoli, featuring tender green stems and edible purple buds. This was the type cultivated and eaten by the ancient Romans, who typically cooked it in wine, added it to a hearty chickpea and lentil soup or dressed it with olive oil and garum, a pungent fermented fish sauce. This primitive variety of broccoli can still occasionally be found today. It turns green when cooked and is especially delicious when picked young, then cooked whole and served with melted butter and a squeeze of lemon juice.

preparation

When preparing broccoli, use a small sharp knife to separate the florets from the stalks, cutting florets into roughly even-sized pieces if large, then soak them in salted water to drive out any caterpillars—broccoli seems very susceptible to these.

It is the habit of many cooks to throw away the thick stalks, however, peeled, sliced and steamed, these are actually delicious and it is a waste to not use them. Stalks take longer to cook than the florets so they need to be cooked separately or put into the steamer about 2–3 minutes before the florets.

boiling To boil broccoli, use plenty of boiling, salted water and boil them uncovered, for 3–4 minutes or until tender but still bright green. Drain well as cooking water can sit, trapped among the tiny buds, causing the eating experience to be a soggy one. Broccolini requires just a wash and the trimming of the very base of the stem. It can be steamed or boiled whole for about 3–4 minutes, or chopped and stir-fried.

culinary uses

Broccoli tends to be treated in a fairly one-dimensional way (boiled, steamed or topped with cheese sauce, perhaps) but one need only look to the Italians for inspiration for how best to cook and consume broccoli—after all, they were the first to cultivate it. In Italy, they might slowly braise chopped broccoli in garlic, lemon juice and loads of olive oil until it collapses into a delicious mass, then serve it at room temperature with rustic bread as an antipasto offering, or tossed warm with pasta and grated pecorino cheese.

The Asian lineage of broccolini makes it a perfect choice for steaming, then drizzling with oyster sauce thinned with chicken stock, as an accompaniment to poached salmon, or teriyaki-glazed ocean trout fillets. Broccolini also makes excellent tempura and it gives a crisp burst of green when added to a gingery beef and sweet soy sauce (or kecap manis) stir-fry.

broccoli and ricotta soufflé

Preheat the oven to 190°C (375°F/Gas 5). Cook the broccoli florets in boiling salted water for 4 minutes, then drain.

Heat the olive oil and butter in a frying pan over medium heat. Fry the onion for 6 minutes, or until soft. Transfer to a large bowl and add the broccoli, ricotta cheese, parmesan cheese, eggs, nutmeg and cayenne pepper. Season with sea salt and freshly ground black pepper. Mix well.

Whisk the egg whites with a pinch of salt and the cream of tartar in a bowl until stiff peaks form. Gently fold one-third of the egg white into the broccoli mixture, then gently incorporate the remainder.

Grease a 1 litre (35 fl oz/4 cup) soufflé dish and sprinkle with the dry breadcrumbs, turn the dish to coat, then shake out the excess. Spoon the broccoli mixture into the dish and bake for 35–40 minutes, or until puffed and golden brown.

- 60 g (2¼ oz/1 cup) small broccoli florets
- 2 tablespoons olive oil
- 40 g (1½ oz) butter
- 1 onion, finely chopped
- 450 g (1 lb/1¾ cups) ricotta cheese
- 55 g (2 oz/½ cup) grated parmesan cheese
- 3 eggs, lightly beaten
- 1 pinch nutmeg
- 1 pinch cayenne pepper
- 4 egg whites
- 1 pinch cream of tartar
- 25 g (1 oz/¼ cup) dry breadcrumbs

broccoli and almond stir-fry

serves 4

Lightly crush the coriander seeds in a mortar, using a pestle. Cut the broccoli into small florets.

Heat the oil in a wok or a large heavy-based frying pan. Add the coriander seeds and almonds. Stir quickly over medium heat for 1 minute, or until the almonds are golden.

Add the garlic, ginger and broccoli to the pan. Stir-fry over high heat for 2 minutes. Remove the pan from the heat. Pour the combined vinegar, sauce and oil into the pan. Toss until the broccoli is well coated. Serve immediately, sprinkled with toasted sesame seeds.

- 1 teaspoon coriander seeds
- 500 g (1 lb 2 oz) broccoli
- 3 tablespoons olive oil
- 2 tablespoons slivered almonds
- 1 garlic clove, crushed
- 1 teaspoon finely shredded fresh ginger
- 2 tablespoons red wine vinegar
- 1 tablespoon soy sauce
- 2 teaspoons sesame oil
- 1 teaspoon sesame seeds, toasted

flowers ■ broccoli

cauliflower

vegetables ▪ **flowers**
season ▪ **peak season winter**

Like its close relation broccoli, the edible part of cauliflower is composed of tightly clustered florets of immature flower buds called the 'curd', which is hugged by tight green leaves. The leaves serve to shield the curd from the sun. Unlike broccoli though, the leaves prevent the development of chlorophyll, which would turn it green, thus explaining the cauliflower's characteristic, milky-white colour.

Like other members of the brassica family, cauliflower is high in vitamin C, folate, potassium and cancer-fighting antioxidants. Take note though, cauliflower also contains naturally occurring compounds called purines, which break down to form uric acid, so people with gout are often advised to avoid eating it in copious quantities.

varieties

Although cauliflowers are now generally quite enormous, the restaurant-driven trend for 'baby' vegetables has seen the cultivation of miniature cauliflowers, which is quite ironic considering that early cauliflowers were no larger than tennis balls, and over time, were bred to be bigger.

Occasionally, lesser known purple and green versions (such as Romanesco cauliflower) can be found, with the purple turning green upon cooking. Broccoflower, as its name suggests, is a cross between broccoli and cauliflower. Originating in the Netherlands, it is light green, with a milder taste than either of its progenitors.

preparation

To prepare cauliflower, first remove the outer leaves and any tough stalk, then, using a small, sharp knife, cut florets from the base. The stems and leaves are completely edible and can be added to vegetable soups and braises if desired. Cauliflower should generally be cooked only until just tender, as it contains phytochemicals which release an unpleasant sulphurous smell when cooked for too long. For the same reason, it is best to cook cauliflower in non-reactive cookware, as the reaction with aluminium and iron can cause it to develop an unsightly brownish hue.

steaming To steam cauliflower, place small florets of the vegetables in a steaming basket over boiling water, cover, then cook for about 10–12 minutes, or until just tender.

roasting While most cooks wouldn't think to roast cauliflower, it tastes wonderful prepared this way, with all of its nutty sweetness concentrated and none of the trademark sulphurous smell. Simply lay cauliflower florets in a single layer in a roasting dish, drizzle generously with olive oil then cook in a 180°C (350°F/Gas 4) oven for about 30 minutes, turning the cauliflower often, or until soft and golden.

culinary uses

Cauliflower is popular in many cuisines. It appears in numerous guises in Indian cooking—cooked with potatoes, mustard seeds, cumin, ginger and fresh coriander to become aloo gobi, a north Indian standard. When cooked with lentils and basmati rice, it transforms into a satisfying pilaf; and coated with turmeric and coriander-spiced chickpea flour batter, then fried, it becomes crisp little fritters called pakoras.

In Sicily, cauliflower finds itself matched with pasta, pine nuts, capers, anchovies and raisins in a dish typical of the sweet-sour flavours the region favours. Braised in a tomato, garlic and flat-leaf (Italian) parsley sauce and finished with lots of grated parmesan cheese, it makes a great accompaniment for the boiled meat dishes of the country's north.

Serve roasted cauliflower with a tasty dip or spread, or combine with rocket, cooked bacon and some crumbled blue cheese and dress with a little balsamic vinegar to make a delicious salad. The English make many variants of cream of cauliflower soup, arguably the best of which includes a decent amount of sharp stilton cheese to add pungency. Cauliflower is also essential to that very English of pickles, piccalilli.

selection and storage

Choose cauliflower with compact, creamy white curds that are surrounded by perky green leaves. Cauliflower will remain fresh for longer if the leaves are intact. Avoid any with black spots as this signifies spoilage or water damage.

Raw cauliflower should be stored, stem side down (to prevent condensation), in a perforated plastic or paper bag in the refrigerator for up to 5 days.

flowers ■ cauliflower

serves 6

cauliflower and pasta bake

150 g (5½ oz/1⅔ cups) short
   pasta (such as penne)
600 g (1 lb 5 oz) cauliflower,
   cut into florets
2 tablespoons olive oil
2 red onions, chopped
2 garlic cloves, finely chopped
80 g (2¾ oz) butter
4 tablespoons plain (all-purpose)
   flour
1 litre (35 fl oz/4 cups) milk
200 g (7 oz/2 cups) freshly
   grated parmesan cheese
3 handfuls fresh basil, torn
5 slices of day-old bread, crusts
   removed
50 g (1¾ oz) butter, melted

Preheat the oven to 180°C (350°F/Gas 4). Cook the pasta in boiling salted water until *al dente*. Drain and set aside. Steam the cauliflower for 10 minutes, or until just tender.

Heat the olive oil in a frying pan. Fry the onions and garlic over medium heat for 5 minutes, or until the onions are soft. Combine in a bowl with the cauliflower.

Melt the butter in a large frying pan. Blend in the flour and cook, stirring constantly, for 1 minute. Gradually whisk in the milk. Stir constantly until the mixture boils and thickens. Remove from the heat and stir through 125 g (4½ oz/1¼ cups) of the grated parmesan cheese and the basil. Add the cauliflower, pasta and onions to the sauce; mix thoroughly.

Spoon the cauliflower and pasta mixture into a large ovenproof dish. Cut the bread into large cubes. Toss the cubes in melted butter and then scatter them over the cauliflower mixture. Sprinkle with the remaining parmesan cheese. Bake for 35–40 minutes until the top is golden.

Originating in Asia Minor, cauliflower traces its antecedents to wild cabbage, and was initially cultivated by the ancient Romans around 600 BC. It remained an almost exclusively Italian vegetable until the 1600s, when it became somewhat fashionable in France for a brief period. From there its use spread to Northern Europe and the United Kingdom, where it flourished.

cauliflower pilaf

Put the rice in a sieve and rinse under cold running water. Set aside to drain. Heat the oil in a saucepan that has a tightly fitting lid. Cook the onion over medium heat, stirring frequently, for 5 minutes, or until soft and lightly golden. Add the spices and cook, stirring, for 1 minute.

Add the rice to the pan and stir to coat in the spices. Add the stock and cauliflower, stirring to combine. Cover with the lid and bring to the boil. Reduce the heat to very low and cook for 15 minutes, or until the rice and cauliflower are tender and all the stock has been absorbed. Fold the coriander through the rice and serve immediately.

200 g (7 oz/2 cups) basmati rice
2 tablespoons olive oil
1 large onion, thinly sliced
¼ teaspoon cardamom seeds
½ teaspoon ground turmeric
1 cinnamon stick
1 teaspoon cumin seeds
¼ teaspoon cayenne pepper
500 ml (17 fl oz/2 cups) ready-made vegetable or chicken stock
800 g (1 lb 12 oz) cauliflower, trimmed and cut into florets
2 large handfuls fresh coriander (cilantro) leaves, chopped

flowers ■ cauliflower

aloo gobi

serves 4

Heat the oil in a large heavy-based frying pan over low heat. Add the mustard seeds, cover the pan and wait for the seeds to pop. Add the onion and potato and fry until lightly browned.

Add the turmeric, cumin, coriander and garam masala to the pan and cook for a couple of seconds. Add the tomato and stir until the spices are well mixed. Add the cauliflower florets and stir until thoroughly coated. Stir in the ginger, sugar and 125 ml (4 fl oz/½ cup) water, increase the heat to medium and bring to the boil. Reduce the heat, cover and simmer for 15 minutes, or until the vegetables are tender. Season with sea salt and freshly ground black pepper.

Uncover the pan and if the sauce is too runny, simmer for a further 1–2 minutes before serving.

3 tablespoons oil
½ teaspoon black mustard seeds
½ onion, finely chopped
200 g (7 oz) potatoes, cut into 2 cm (¾ inch) cubes
¼ teaspoon ground turmeric
1 teaspoon ground cumin
1 teaspoon ground coriander
1½ teaspoons garam masala
4 tomatoes, chopped
1 large cauliflower, cut into florets
2 cm (¾ inch) piece of ginger
1 teaspoon sugar

asian greens

Although Asian greens, in their myriad varieties, are eaten by more than half the world's population up to three times every day, they have only fairly recently become familiar to Western countries. Migration and international travel have inspired an appreciation of Asian cuisines, cooking methods and ingredients, including Asian greens, which now take pride of place alongside broccoli, peas and beans on dining tables the Western world over. Extremely versatile, highly nutritious and easy to cook, Asian greens suit stir-frying, steaming, poaching or adding to braises, curries and soups. All you need for the makings of a satisfyingly quick meal are a bunch of Asian greens, some seafood, meat or tofu and steamed rice or boiled noodles.

Excluding water spinach, Asian greens are cruciferous vegetables that belong to the brassica family. As a group, Asian greens, like other leafy green vegetables, are high in antioxidants, folate and vitamins A and C. Gai larn (Chinese broccoli) boasts the highest concentration of calcium of any green vegetable, with the added plus of also being high in iron and fibre. Baby bok choy and choy sum are ideal vegetables for pregnant women, as they are rich in folate. Water spinach is especially high in iron.

varieties

baby bok choy Also known as Shanghai bok choy or *mei quing choi*, this popular Asian vegetable is a squat, bulbous-based, small variety of bok choy featuring upright spoon-shaped green leaves and crunchy pale green stems. The succulent leaves have a mild, mustard-like flavour.

Baby bok choy are at their peak during autumn and spring—this is the time to steam or braise them whole, then drizzle with oyster sauce and serve as an accompaniment to Asian meals, or halve lengthways and stir-fry with julienned ginger, then finish with a little chicken stock and light soy sauce.

bok choy (pak choy) With a rounded base, lustrous dark green leaves and long ivory-coloured stems, bok choy are the Asian green with the longest cultivation pedigree, appreciated for their crisp thick stems and pleasantly cabbage-flavoured, slightly tangy leaves. Separate the stems and leaves before cooking, as the stems take slightly longer to cook, then cook quickly to retain their green colour and crunchy texture as they quickly become soggy due to their high water content. A biennial plant at its best in early summer and late autumn, bok choy leaves are a fine addition to clear Asian soups or stir-fries.

choy sum (Chinese flowering cabbage) Also called Chinese flowering cabbage, due to the usually yellow (but sometimes purple) flowers attached to pale green, slender stems, choy sum has long oval green leaves. While the leaves have a pleasingly sweet mustard flavour, the stems maintain a crunch when properly (that is, briefly) cooked. They are the Asian green of choice for steaming, stir-frying or poaching.

gai choy Also called mustard cabbage thanks to its distinctly mustardy flavour, gai choy should have thick, bulbous, pale green stems with crinkled, broad light green leaves. Traditionally braised, added to soups or pickled, gai choy can also be stir-fried, although some prefer to blanch it first to temper its strong, tangy flavour.

gai larn (Chinese broccoli) Also called Chinese broccoli, gai larn is one of the most nutritious vegetables available; one cup of cooked gai larn has as much calcium as a glass of milk. This healthy vegetable has dark green leaves, delicate white flowers, and green extended broccoli-like stems that should be peeled and halved lengthways before cooking.

Gai larn best suits parboiling, stir-frying, steaming or adding to soups just before serving; but ensure that it is briefly cooked until just tender.

water spinach A member of the morning glory (*Convolvulaceae*) family, water spinach is an edible aquatic vine that grows rampantly in very moist garden beds or suspended in water.

Alternately called water convolvus, *ong choi*, *kang kung* or *pak bung*, depending on where you are, water spinach has numerous dark green, pointy, elongated, narrow leaves radiating from its succulent, hollow, long stems. To cook water spinach, wash well, cut into 5 cm (2 inch) lengths and add to Thai-style curries, Asian soups or stir-fries.

wom bok (Chinese cabbage) Variously known also as Peking or napa cabbage, wom bok belongs to a different species of brassicas to the European cabbage varieties. Shaped like a cylindrical barrel, wom bok has tightly packed layers of crinkled green and white leaves that are softer and thinner than those of European cabbage, and a thick white midrib. Its delicate flavour is excellent shredded and eaten raw in salads, lightly steamed, stir-fried or added to hotpots and clear Asian soups.

preparation

When cooking varieties of Asian greens with thick stems, it is best to separate the leaves from the stems and cook the stems first, as they take longer to cook. Asian greens should be trimmed before cooking, then soaked in cold water to remove any traces of dirt clinging to their bases.

To stir-fry gai larn, cut trimmed stems into 2 cm (3/4 inch) pieces and cook in a wok over high heat for 1–2 minutes—they should still be crunchy. To steam gai larn, cut wide stems in half lengthways and steam for 5 minutes, or until just tender. More delicate greens, like wombok and bok choy, require just brief stir-frying—sliced leaves will wilt in about 1 minute. Bok choy can be steamed whole, which will take about 6–10 minutes.

culinary uses

Unless braising whole or halved bok choy or gai choy, or steaming or poaching gai larn, Asian greens generally require little cooking—a brief steam or stir-fry is all that is required. Asian greens work best when matched with other defining flavours of Asian cuisines, especially rice, noodles, chilli, garlic, ginger, black bean sauce, hoisin sauce, oyster sauce, soy sauce, pork, chicken, duck, seafood, coconut milk, fish sauce, rice wine, tofu, shiitake mushrooms and sesame oil. They are at their best when simply prepared—sliced bok choy stir-fried with ginger and garlic, for instance, or steamed gai larn dressed with black bean or oyster sauce.

storage and selection

Generally speaking, Asian greens should have dark green leaves with no signs of limpness, wilting, tears or blemishes. Their bases should be dry and firm.

Because of their high water content they generally don't store well, so if possible it is best to use them on the day of purchasing. Otherwise, they can be stored in a perforated plastic bag in the crisper section of the refrigerator for 1–2 days.

leaves ▪ asian greens

serves 4

stir-fried tofu with asian greens

2 tablespoons lime juice
3 tablespoons vegetable oil
1½ tablespoons fish sauce
1 teaspoon sambal oelek
½ teaspoon soft brown sugar
200 g (7 oz) smoked tofu
400 g (14 oz/1 bunch) choy sum
  (Chinese flowering cabbage),
  trimmed
150 g (5½ oz/4 cups) torn
  English spinach leaves
2 teaspoons sesame seeds,
  toasted
1 small handful coriander
  (cilantro) leaves

To make the dressing, put the lime juice and 2 tablespoons of vegetable oil, the fish sauce, sambal oelek and brown sugar in a bowl and whisk well.

Cut the smoked tofu into 2 cm (3/4 inch) cubes. Trim the choy sum and cut into 8 cm (3¼ inch) lengths.

Heat 1 tablespoon oil in a large wok over medium heat and gently stir-fry the tofu for 2–3 minutes, or until golden brown. Add half the dressing and toss to coat. Remove from the wok and set aside.

Add the choy sum to the wok and stir-fry for 1 minute. Add the spinach leaves and stir-fry for 1 minute. Return the tofu to the wok, add the sesame seeds and the remaining dressing and toss lightly. Serve with the coriander (cilantro) leaves piled on top.

Cultivated in China since the fifth century, bok choy and its descendants did not make their way west to Europe until the mid 1700s, where they did not make much of a mark until the twentieth century. The average person in China consumes 500 g (1 lb 2 oz) of Asian greens each day, most of which are cruciferous..

gai larn with ginger, lime and peanuts

Put the tamarind in a bowl and pour in the boiling water. Allow to steep for 5 minutes, then strain. Discard the solids.

Heat a non-stick frying pan over high heat, add the peanut oil and swirl to coat. Add the gai larn and stir-fry for 2–3 minutes, or until wilted. Add the chilli, garlic and ginger and cook for another minute, then add the sugar, lime juice and 1 tablespoon of the tamarind liquid and simmer for 1 minute. Transfer to a plate and drizzle with the sesame oil. Scatter with peanuts to serve.

40 g (1½ oz) tamarind pulp
60 ml (2 fl oz/¼ cup) boiling water
1 tablespoon peanut oil
600 g (1 lb 5 oz/1 large bunch) gai larn (Chinese broccoli), trimmed and halved widthways
1 small red chilli, seeded and finely chopped
2 garlic cloves, finely chopped
3 teaspoons finely grated ginger
1 tablespoon sugar
1 tablespoon lime juice
1 teaspoon sesame oil
1 tablespoon finely chopped roasted unsalted peanuts

leaves ■ asian greens

beef and bok choy

serves 4

Wash the bok choy and drain. Cut the leaves into thin strips. Heat 1 tablespoon of oil in a frying pan or wok; add the garlic and stir-fry for 30 seconds.

Heat the remaining oil; add the meat in small batches and stir-fry for 3 minutes over high heat until the meat has browned but is not cooked through. Remove the meat from the pan.

Stir-fry the bok choy for 30 seconds or until it is just wilted. Add the meat, soy sauce and sherry. Stir-fry for 2–3 minutes or until the meat is tender. Add the basil and sesame oil and toss well. Serve immediately. Garnish with strips of red capsicum, if desired.

600 g (1 lb 5 oz/1 large bunch) bok choy (pak choy)
2 tablespoons oil
2 garlic cloves, crushed
250 g (9 oz) rump steak, thinly sliced
2 tablespoons soy sauce
1 tablespoon sweet sherry
2 tablespoons chopped basil
2 teaspoons sesame oil
¼ red capsicum (pepper), sliced, to serve

brussels sprout

vegetables ▪ **leaves**
season ▪ **winter–spring**

Guaranteed to evoke a passionate response—of either love or loathing—Brussels sprouts are undoubtedly one of the most misunderstood and maligned members of the vegetable kingdom. Over-boiled, sulphurous smelling Brussels sprouts may have prejudiced many from their childhoods; yet like their cabbage cousins, when handled correctly they can be a sweet revelation.

Resembling Lilliputian cabbages, Brussels sprouts are actually compact buds that grow in clusters along the stems of the *Brassica oleracea* plant. Like other brassicas, Brussels sprouts are an excellent source of vitamin C and also contain healthy quantities of fibre, iron, phosphorus, potassium and vitamin A.

selection and storage

Choose firm, verdant green, uniform-sized Brussels sprouts with no splitting, browning or mottling of the outer leaves.

The smaller the Brussels sprout, the sweeter and more tender they will be to eat. To store, loosely wrap them in absorbent paper, then place in a perforated plastic bag and refrigerate in the vegetable crisper for up to 3 days; their flavour intensifies the longer they are kept.

preparation

As well as boiling, steaming is a good way to par-cook Brussels sprouts if you intend to sauté them, bake them in a gratin or want to finish them in a reduced, creamy sauce. Slice them finely to stir-fry or to use raw in salads. Before cooking, wash the sprouts well, and, if they have come directly from the garden, soak them in cold water in case they contain a few worms. Remove any discoloured outer leaves and score a cross into their base to promote even cooking.

boiling To boil sprouts, cook them whole, uncovered, in plenty of boiling salted water for 6–8 minutes or until just tender, then drain well. To steam, cook them halved or whole, for about 8–12 minutes, or until just tender.

brussels sprouts with pancetta

Preheat the grill (broiler) to hot. Spread the pancetta on a baking tray or on a grill rack lined with foil and put the grill tray or rack about 8–10 cm (3 1/3–4 inches) under the heat source. Grill (broil) for 45–60 seconds, or until crisp. Set aside to cool.

Peel the shallots and cut them into thick rings. Heat the butter and oil in a large frying pan over medium heat. Add the shallots and garlic and cook for 3–4 minutes, or until just starting to brown. Add the Brussels sprouts and season with freshly ground black pepper. Cook, stirring often, for about 4–5 minutes, or until partly golden and crisp. Turn off the heat, cover and set aside for 5 minutes.

Break the pancetta into large shards. Add to the Brussels sprouts and toss lightly; some will break up into smaller pieces. Serve immediately.

100 g (3½ oz) pancetta, thinly sliced
4 shallots
20 g (¾ oz) butter
1 tablespoon olive oil
1 garlic clove, crushed
500 g (1 lb 2 oz) Brussels sprouts, trimmed and thickly sliced

leaves ∎ brussels sprout

Although there is not an endless array of Brussels sprouts recipes to try, they match brilliantly with bacon, butter, caraway seeds, chives, cream, garlic, horseradish, mace, mustard, nutmeg, roast pork and shallots. Tiny whole sprouts can be blanched and added to the French classic poached chicken dish, poule au pot, *or stir-fried with garlic, soy sauce and sesame seeds.*

cabbage

vegetables ▪ **leaves**
season ▪ **red**—autumn; **green**—winter; **savoy**—spring

Although cabbage tends to be regarded as a rather dreary, soggy excuse for a vegetable, when treated with restraint (not overcooked, that is), it can be most agreeable to eat. Crisp coleslaw is a case in point (the Dutch, incidentally, invented coleslaw or *koolsla,* which in that language simply means 'cabbage salad'), as is ribollita, the robust Tuscan bean and cavolo nero or black cabbage soup. Wine-braised red cabbage with apples, brown sugar and caraway seeds, savoy cabbage with speck, and potato bubble and squeak are other cabbage-based delicacies—there really is no excuse for badly cooked cabbage.

Along with Brussels sprouts, broccoli and cauliflower, cabbages are members of the extended brassica family. This has long been known for its therapeutic properties; in the Middle Ages, stems of brassicas were applied as a tonic for fractures and wounds, while the seafaring explorers who ate cabbage to guard against scurvy were onto something, as modern science now tells us that it is relatively rich in vitamin C. As a general rule, cabbage also contains potassium, manganese, folate (especially savoy cabbage), vitamins B6 and K and to a lesser degree, iron, thiamine and riboflavin. Savoy cabbage also boasts five times more betacarotene than its green and red counterparts.

The Romans adored cabbage, believing it fended off melancholy, and tradition has it that workers on the Great Wall of China were sustained by preserved cabbage. Apparently it was the Chinese who imported preserved cabbage know-how into Europe, where today it is a mainstay of many countries—witness the popularity of sauerkraut.

varieties

cavolo nero This dark blackish cabbage with thick, long, curly leaves originated in Italy, where it is prized for its slightly bitter, yet rich flavour. The Tuscans in particular favour this handsome vegetable, utilizing it in stews and soups, most notably the aforementioned ribollita and various hearty lentil soups. When sautéed or braised with garlic and chilli and drizzled with peppery olive oil, it is a magnificent accompaniment to poached, grilled (broiled) and roast meat or, along with crumbled gorgonzola cheese, an easy bruschetta topping.

green or white The most common of all the cabbages, the green and white varieties have rounded heads consisting of tightly packed leaves, thick stems and largish cores.

Sometimes called Dutch cabbage, the white cabbage's smooth, crisp and crunchy leaves suit use raw in salads. They are also good cooked in lashings of butter and sprinkled with freshly ground black pepper, or cut into wedges and poached along with corned beef. This type is also the cabbage of choice for making sauerkraut.

The more delicately flavoured baby or dwarf green cabbages that can also occasionally be found require minimal cooking, and are suited to stir-frying, blanching or steaming, while larger green cabbages are also ideal for stuffing.

red With a unique purple hue and mellow taste, red cabbage is a vibrant addition to wintry salads, stir-fries, soups and stews. It is best to cook this cabbage with an acidic ingredient, such as lemons or apples, wine or vinegar, to preserve the distinct colour; otherwise, upon cooking, it turns a curious colour somewhere between grey, blue and purple.

Red cabbage makes a vinegary pickle popularly served with cold meat and game; it is also a commendable accompaniment to pork or beef casseroles when baked in a casserole dish with red wine vinegar, onions and prunes.

savoy The distinctive, dark green, loose heads of savoy cabbage contain large crinkled leaves with tough inner stalks. Savoy cabbage is often regarded as the king of the cabbages due to its milder flavour and attractive leaves; blanched savoy cabbage leaves are the perfect vehicle for a rice, minced pork and veal and dill stuffing. Its Italian origins also make it perfect for sautéing with porcini mushrooms, potatoes and sage, then served with short pasta, or added to a creamy fontina cheese and pancetta risotto.

preparation

A whole cabbage is best dealt with by removing all the tough outer leaves, then cutting the vegetable in half lengthways. Using a large, sharp knife, cut out the hard central core then thinly slice cabbage for use in salads, to braise, steam or stir-fry. Any unused cabbage will store in the refrigerator, in a plastic bag, for 2–3 days.

If you require whole leaves for stuffing, cut these away at the base, easing them off the head with your fingers—tears are inevitable and you will always need more than a recipe requires to compensate for this. To prepare leaves for stuffing, simply cook them a few at a time in a large saucepan of boiling water for 3–5 minutes, or until tender, then drain well and pat dry.

Boiled cabbage exudes an unpleasant, sulphurous smell, which possibly explains the legions of non-cabbage eaters. Cabbages contain sulphur compounds which are released when the vegetable is boiled; in fact, the longer the boiling, the more of these compounds are released into the air. For this reason boiling cabbage, and certainly over-boiling it, is the least preferred method of cooking. It is far more pleasant to eat cabbage which has been thinly sliced and cooked, covered, with butter and its natural juices—it takes about 7 minutes to cook to tenderness this way.

culinary uses

Cabbage leaves wrapped around various permutations of rice, minced meat, herbs and spices are a time-honoured tradition from Eastern Europe to the Middle East, while life minus the fermented cabbage staple, sauerkraut, would be unimaginable for many Central Europeans. Cabbage pairs admirably with anchovies, apples, bacon, butter, caraway seeds, cheese, chestnuts, chicken, cider vinegar, corned beef, cream, duck, mayonnaise, nutmeg, pancetta, pasta, potatoes, pulses, pork, rice, salmon, smoked meat, sour cream, veal and walnuts.

selection and storage

Cabbages should be firm and heavy for their size with no yellow or brown patches. Tight-leaf cabbages such as green and red varieties should have tightly closed outer leaves enclosing the heads. They can be stored in a plastic bag in the crisper section of the refrigerator for up to 1 week.

Their loose-leaf cousins, like savoy cabbage and cavolo nero, should have crisp, strongly coloured leaves that show no signs of wilting or browning. More perishable than the tight-leaved versions, these should only be refrigerated in a plastic bag in the crisper section for 2–3 days.

Any discoloured or wilted external leaves, as well as tough stalks, should be removed and discarded before cooking or eating raw.

pork chops with braised red cabbage

To braise the cabbage, heat the clarified butter in a large saucepan, add the onion and garlic and cook, stirring often, over medium heat for 6 minutes, or until softened but not browned. Add the cabbage, apple, wine, vinegar, cloves and sage and season with salt and pepper. Cover the pan and cook for 30 minutes over very low heat. Uncover the pan and cook, stirring, for a further 5 minutes, increasing heat if necessary, to evaporate any liquid.

Meanwhile, trim the pork chops, heat the clarified butter in a frying pan, season the meat and cook for 4–5 minutes, turning once, over medium-high heat, or until brown on both sides. Add the wine and stock, cover and simmer for 20 minutes, or until the pork is tender.

Remove the meat from the frying pan and strain the liquid. Return the liquid to the pan, bring to the boil and cook until reduced by two-thirds. Add the cream and mustard and stir over very low heat, without boiling, until the sauce has thickened slightly. Pour over the pork chops and garnish with sage. Serve with the red cabbage.

braised red cabbage
30 g (1 oz) clarified butter
1 onion, finely chopped
1 garlic clove, crushed
1 small red cabbage, shredded
1 dessert apple, peeled, cored and finely sliced
80 ml (2½ fl oz/⅓ cup) red wine
1 tablespoon red wine vinegar
¼ teaspoon ground cloves
1 tablespoon chopped sage

15 g (½ oz) clarified butter
four 200 g (7 oz) pork chops
80 ml (2½ fl oz/⅓ cup) white wine
375 ml (13 fl oz/1½ cups) ready-made chicken stock
3 tablespoons thick (double/heavy) cream
1½ tablespoons dijon mustard
4 sage leaves

classic coleslaw

Remove the hard core from the cabbages and shred the leaves with a sharp knife. Toss in a large bowl and add the carrot, radish, capsicum, green onion and parsley. Refrigerate until ready to serve.

Just before serving, add the mayonnaise, season to taste with sea salt and freshly ground black pepper and toss until well combined.

½ small green cabbage
¼ small red cabbage
2 carrots, coarsely grated
4 radishes, coarsely grated
½ red capsicum (pepper), chopped
3 green onions (scallions), sliced
3 tablespoons chopped parsley
175 g (6 oz/⅔ cup) ready-made egg mayonnaise

lettuce

vegetables ▪ **leaves**
season ▪ **spring-summer**

Lettuce is without a doubt one of the world's favourite vegetables, and with good reason. Whether adding crunchy interest to an anchovy-spiked Caesar salad, a spicy Thai beef salad or a simple vinaigrette-dressed garden salad, long summer days are unthinkable without the refreshing presence of lettuce.

Allegedly, lettuces originated in Asia Minor. A member of the sunflower family, lettuce was enjoyed by the ancient Romans and Egyptians, and even graced the tables of Persian kings. The original wild lettuce contained a narcotic similar to opium and the Romans ate lettuce in the evening to induce sleep—however, the ancients also believed lettuce sparked the appetite so, confusingly, also ate it before dining. Although these civilizations declined, the fortunes of lettuce continued to prosper. Some form of lettuce has been known in China since the fifth century. There it is generally eaten cooked, although the Cantonese made a culinary art form out of raw lettuce with their invention of san choy bau (trimmed crisp leaves filled with aromatic pork, water chestnuts and shiitake mushrooms).

Consisting of approximately 95 per cent water, the darker varieties of lettuce are the most nutritious, with the highest concentrations of vitamins A and C, betacarotene, folate and calcium.

leaves ▪ lettuce

selection and storage

When buying lettuce, look for crisp-looking, brightly coloured heads and avoid any that are wilted, blemished or slimy.

Keep lettuces in perforated plastic bags in the refrigerator crisper for up to 2 days. Lettuces need to be washed well before using—they should not be soaked in water as this can make the leaves limp and soggy, particularly the loose-leaved varieties.

A salad spinner is excellent for eliminating excess water from the leaves, which is especially useful if using in a salad, as the drier the leaves, the better the dressing will adhere to them. Remove and discard tough, outer leaves before using.

varieties

With varieties grown around the globe numbering in the hundreds, cultivated lettuces can be divided into four categories.

crisphead Generally rotund and consisting of tightly-packed layers of juicy, crisp leaves, the most famous member of the crisphead clan is the iceberg—so named because it was first developed in the United States before widespread refrigeration, so heads were packed in boxes and covered with ice for transport and said to resemble icebergs. The English favour webb lettuce, while in the US the imperial, western and vanguard lettuce are popular.

butterhead As the name suggests, the butterhead lettuce has a mild buttery flavour, with smaller, looser heads than their crisphead cousins, and leaves with a soft, thin texture, said to resemble a blossoming rose. With soft, pale green leaves, butter lettuce is the definitive example of this variety, which also contains the curly, reddish purple-tinged dark green-leaved mignonette. In the US the bibbs and boston varieties are popular.

cos (romaine) As it is alternately known, the cos or romaine lettuce is so-named because it originated on the Greek island of Cos, where it was discovered by the ancient Romans. Its narrow, upright, elongated, deep green leaves boast a sweet, crisp, almost nutty flavour. Very young, tender-hearted versions, sold as 'baby cos' or 'little gems', are also available.

loose-leaf Distinguished by the fact that they do not form a distinct heart or head, loose-leaf lettuces have soft, eclectically coloured and shaped leaves emanating directly from their core. Main varieties include the earthy, pale green to rose tinted oakleaf (*feuille de chêne*); the tender, frilly, light green or reddish-leaved coral; and the magenta ruffle-tipped and slightly bitter lollo rosso.

culinary uses

Lettuce is undeniably at its best when served as the star ingredient of a simple salad. While we remain hooked on the classics, the diversity and versatility of lettuce provides ample opportunities for thinking beyond the usual lettuce-tomato-cucumber-radish assemblages. For instance, some cuisines cook the leafy green to great effect. The French serve lettuce braised with peas and mint with fish or fowl, while the Greeks use cos lettuce in a summery lemon and dill-infused lamb stew. However you wish to eat lettuce, it works best with avocado, bacon, beef, bread, cheese, chicken, chilli, crème fraîche, cucumber, fish sauce, herbs, lobster, mayonnaise, mustard, noodles, olive oil, peas, pork, prawns, radishes, tomatoes, turkey, vinaigrette and vinegar.

salata baladi

To make the dressing, whisk together the oil and lemon juice in a bowl. Season well with salt and freshly ground black pepper.

Put all the vegetables and herbs in a large serving bowl and toss together well. Add the dressing and toss again. Serve at once, while the salad is crisp.

1½ tablespoons extra virgin olive oil
1½ tablespoons lemon juice
1 baby cos (romaine) lettuce, leaves torn
2 tomatoes, each cut into 8 wedges
1 small green capsicum (pepper), chopped
2 Lebanese (short) cucumbers, seeded and chopped
4 radishes, sliced
1 small red onion, thinly sliced
2 tablespoons chopped flat-leaf (Italian) parsley
1 small handful mint leaves

leaves ▪ lettuce

red leaf salad

serves 4 as a side salad

Wash and dry the lettuce leaves, then tear them into bite-sized pieces.

Finely slice the fennel and onion and toss into a serving bowl with the shredded lettuce. Just before serving, drizzle the oil over the salad, then the vinegar. Toss lightly and serve.

150 g (5½ oz) mixed red lettuce leaves (such as coral lettuce or lollo rosso lettuce)
1 baby fennel bulb
1 small red onion
2 tablespoons olive oil
1 tablespoon balsamic vinegar

radicchio

vegetables ▪ leaves
season ▪ late autumn–winter

The bold magenta colour and distinctive bitter flavour of radicchio add vigour to any dish it adorns; from striking salads to rich risottos, radicchio makes a handsome impression. Along with chicory, curly endive and witlof (Belgian endive), radicchio belongs to the *Cichorium* branch of the daisy (Compositae) family. All radicchio begin their lives green, turning various shades of purple-red as they mature and the weather cools.

Radicchio is associated with the Veneto region of Italy. The ancient Roman author and philosopher, Pliny the Elder, referred to the region's red-flushed lettuces in his authoritative tome of the time, *Naturalis Historia*. Although Pliny credited the Egyptians with cultivating radicchio from wild chicory, it was the Italians who cultivated the numerous modern variants. The original radicchio wasn't red at all—the technique for turning the plants red involves a rather complex process of 'blanching' the plants after premature harvesting, in darkened rooms, with the root ends placed in water—resulting in its deep red-coloured leaves.

The characteristic bitter flavour of radicchio is due to a chemical called intybin, which both stimulates the appetite and digestive system and assists the functioning of the liver and blood.

selection and storage

Choose radicchio that shows no signs of browning, wilting or sliminess, and with unbroken, crisp and brightly coloured leaves. Inspect the stem end to make sure it looks fresh and not slimy or browned. Like lettuces, radicchio is best stored whole in perforated plastic bags in the vegetable crisper section of the refrigerator, and should be used within 1–2 days.

varieties

The four most common varieties of radicchio are the deep garnet-coloured, round-headed radicchio di chioggia; the more elongated and slender headed radicchio di treviso which has thick white ribs and splayed, crisp, maroon leaves; the soft, crumpled and speckle-leaved castelfranco; and America's favourite, the elongated, bright red radicchio di verona.

In homage to their birthplace, all of these are named after towns in the Veneto region of Italy. Treviso radicchio is the variety best suited to cooking. Castelfranco and chioggia radicchio are the types most often found in salads, as their decorative, red-tinged green leaves and pale hearts are milder in flavour.

preparation

As with lettuces, remove tough, outer leaves and discard. Remove inner leaves and carefully wash them to remove all dirt then gently dry—do this in a salad spinner having first shaken off excess water, or pat dry on paper towels.

culinary uses

While most people are familiar with a splash of radicchio in a salad, its bold flavour mellows and sweetens when cooked and it is suited to other uses besides brightening up the salad bowl. Try halving treviso radicchio lengthwise, drizzling with olive oil and grilling (broiling), then serving with barbecued quail, tuna steaks or lamb. Sauté strips of radicchio with butter, garlic and prosciutto and toss through *al dente* spaghettini. Thinly sliced radicchio also makes an invigorating last-minute addition to a hearty barley soup.

Almonds, artichokes, butter, chicken, duck, cheese (especially goat's, gorgonzola and parmesan), duck livers, hazelnut oil, pasta, rice, rocket (arugula), swordfish, tuna or watercress are all good partners to radicchio.

chargrilled radicchio

Trim the radicchio, discarding the outer leaves. Slice into quarters lengthways and rinse well. Drain, then pat dry with paper towels.

Put a frying pan over high heat or preheat a chargrill pan or plate to hot. Lightly sprinkle the radicchio with some of the olive oil and season with sea salt and freshly ground black pepper. Cook for 2–3 minutes, until the under leaves soften and darken, then turn to cook the other side. Transfer to a dish and sprinkle with the remaining oil and vinegar.

Serve hot with grilled (broiled) meats, or cold as part of an antipasti selection.

2 heads radicchio
60 ml (2 fl oz/¼ cup) olive oil
1 teaspoon balsamic vinegar

leaves ▪ radicchio

radicchio with figs and ginger vinaigrette

serves 4

Wash the radicchio and frisée leaves thoroughly and drain well. Tear any large leaves into bite-sized pieces and toss in a salad bowl.

Peel and segment the oranges, discarding all the bitter white pith. Add to the salad leaves with the onion and 8 of the fig quarters, reserving the remaining fig quarters.

Whisk the oil, vinegar, cinnamon, orange juice, ginger and ginger syrup in a small jug. Season with sea salt and freshly ground black pepper. Pour over the salad and toss lightly.

Arrange the reserved figs in pairs over the salad. If you are using the pomegranates, scoop out the seeds, scatter over the salad and serve.

1 head radicchio
1 baby frisée (curly endive)
3 oranges or mandarins
½ small red onion, thinly sliced into rings
8 small green figs, cut into quarters
3 tablespoons extra virgin olive oil
1 teaspoon red wine vinegar
1 pinch ground cinnamon
2 tablespoons orange juice
2 tablespoons very finely chopped glacé ginger, plus 2 teaspoons syrup
2 pomegranates (optional), halved

rocket (arugula)

vegetables ■ **leaves**
season ■ **winter–spring**

Whether called by its Italian tag *rucola*, French name *roquette*, or American label arugula, rocket by any other name is still a peppery, mustard-flavoured leafy green, used to best advantage raw in salads or lightly wilted in pasta dishes or risotto. The Italian fondness for this native vegetable is widely celebrated—one need go no further than the simple combination of rocket and shaved Parmigiano Reggiano cheese, drizzled with fruity extra virgin olive oil, to experience it in all its pungent glory.

The ancient Romans were the first to appreciate the fiery flavour of rocket; they used its seeds to infuse oil, and, along with the ancient Egyptians, considered it to have aphrodisiac qualities. Cultivated rocket has much larger, broader leaves (it is sold as baby rocket in its immature state), while wild rocket has small, thin, serrated leaves. Rocket is rich in vitamins A and C and iron.

culinary uses

In Italy, rocket is not just relegated to the salad bowl, but used to add a fresh, sharp note to endless cooked dishes as well; scattered over a crisp pizza along with prosciutto after it appears bubbling from the oven or included at the last minute in a creamy potato soup, or wilted in pasta sauces. The intense flavour of rocket pairs well with many ingredients, among them avocado, beef, lamb, balsamic vinegar, butter, bresaola, cheese, garlic, lemon juice, olive oil, pasta, pears, pine nuts, potatoes, radicchio, seafood, tomatoes and walnuts.

selection and storage

Choose rocket with deep green, dry, unblemished leaves which are not wilted or torn. The smaller the leaves, the milder the flavour, as rocket has a tendency to go quickly to seed and these larger, rampant leaves can be extremely biting.

Store rocket in a loosely sealed plastic bag in the crisper section of the refrigerator and use within 1–2 days, as it is extremely perishable. Wash thoroughly to remove any grit before using and dry carefully using a salad spinner or by blotting the leaves on absorbent paper towels.

rocket tarts

Preheat the oven to 180°C (350°F/Gas 4). Cut four 15 cm (6 inch) circles from the sheets of puff pastry and use them to line four greased 10 cm (4 inch) loose-based tartlet tins.

Prick the bases with a fork. Line the pastry with baking paper, fill with baking beads or dried beans and cook in the oven for 15 minutes. Remove the weights and paper and bake for a further 5 minutes. Remove from the oven and set aside.

Heat the olive oil in a frying pan over medium heat and gently cook the onion for 5 minutes. Stir in the baby rocket and remove from the heat.

Put the beaten eggs, ricotta cheese and nutmeg into a small bowl. Season with sea salt and freshly ground black pepper. Beat lightly, leaving some of the ricotta in lumps. Stir in the rocket mixture. Spoon into the pastry shells and bake for about 25 minutes, or until set.

2 sheets ready-made puff pastry,
1 tablespoon olive oil
½ small onion, finely diced
1 large handful baby rocket (arugula) leaves
3 eggs, beaten
125 g (4½ oz/ ½ cup) ricotta cheese
1 pinch ground nutmeg

leaves ■ rocket (arugula)

spaghetti with rocket and chilli

Put the pasta into a large saucepan of boiling salted water and cook until *al dente*. Drain the pasta and return it to the pan.

Meanwhile, heat the olive oil in a large heavy-based frying pan. Add the chilli and cook for 1 minute over low heat. Add the rocket and cook, stirring often, for a further 2–3 minutes, or until softened. Add the lemon juice and season with sea salt and freshly ground black pepper. Add the rocket mixture to the pasta and toss until combined. Serve immediately.

500 g (1 lb 2 oz) spaghetti or spaghettini
2 tablespoons olive oil
2 teaspoons finely chopped small red chilli
450 g (1 lb) rocket (arugula) leaves
1 tablespoon lemon juice

silverbeet (swiss chard)

vegetables ▪ **leaves**
season ▪ **spring–autumn**

Although sometimes called Swiss chard, silverbeet, like beetroot and other members of the *Beta vulgaris* family, actually originated in the Mediterranean, not Switzerland, as the name might suggest. A Swiss botanist named Koch gave it its scientific name, hence the 'Swiss' in its common name.

While many people cook just the leaves and the tender white ribs, in many parts of Europe the tougher stalks are actually considered the most prized part of the plant. Unless these are particularly young and tender though, they are best cooked separately, as they take longer to cook. Occasionally, so-called rainbow chard, featuring alternating red, yellow and white stalks and green leaves, can be found.

Thanks to modern science, we now know that silverbeet is one of the healthiest of vegetables, rich in folate, vitamins, A, K and C, magnesium, potassium, iron and fibre. However, it is useful to note that silverbeet also contains decent amounts of oxalates, natural substances which, when excessively ingested, can concentrate in one's body fluids, exacerbating kidney or gallbladder problems. The oxalates can also interfere with the absorption of calcium.

leaves ■ silverbeet (swiss chard)

selection and storage

This hardy perennial vegetable will grow under diverse conditions and even thrive if neglected, but once picked, is not quite so robust. Its vivid, deep green leaves are easily bruised, and it is best not to store it for too long.

Favour silverbeet with shiny, firm leaves that show no signs of wilting, browning or yellowing. The ivory coloured stalks of common silverbeet should be unblemished and crisp-looking, while the ruby version should have firm, slender, deep red stalks and scarlet leaves.

Store silverbeet in a perforated plastic bag in the refrigerator's vegetable crisper for up to 3 days—for ease of storage, you may want to cut off the stalks and store these separately.

preparation

Wash the leaves very well before using as dirt can lurk in their many folds. Lay several leaves on top of each other, roll up tightly then slice. Cook the leaves, covered, in a very small quantity of boiling water for 5 minutes, or until tender, then drain very well. To do this, transfer silverbeet to a colander and press down on it with the back of a large metal spoon to extract as much liquid as possible.

To cook the stalks, trim several centimetres from the root end of stalks and, using a small, sharp knife, remove any tough strings. Steam or simmer stalks for 8–10 minutes or until tender, then drain well and dress with melted butter or olive oil.

culinary uses

Silverbeet can be used to fill myriad dough-based dishes such as ravioli, filo pastry pies such as the *spanakopites* of Greece, and quiche. The Italians make much of it in frittatas, and shredded silverbeet adds vim to the many cumin-spiced, lemony lentil soups and chickpea casseroles of the Middle East.

Blanched, whole leaves can be used to wrap spiced rice and minced meat combinations or even used to enclose salmon fillets before steaming. The stems can also be blanched then baked into a gratin with cream, nutmeg and cheese (parmesan, pecorino, gruyere or a blue, for preference) and they can also be diced, sautéed in oil or butter and included in dishes where the leaves feature, such as risotto, pasta sauces and vegetable tagines—it is such a shame to waste them!

sautéed silverbeet

Trim the leaves from the stalks of the silverbeet and rinse them in cold water. Blanch the leaves in a large saucepan of boiling salted water for 1–2 minutes, or until tender but still firm. Drain well in a colander, lay out on a tea (dish) towel, then, using your hands, gently wring out any excess water.

Heat the oil in a heavy-based frying pan and cook the garlic over low heat until just starting to turn golden. Add the silverbeet, season with sea salt and freshly ground black pepper and cook over medium heat for 3–4 minutes, or until warmed through. Transfer to a serving plate and drizzle with extra virgin olive oil, to serve.

1 kg (2 lb 4 oz) silverbeet (Swiss chard)
2 tablespoons olive oil
3 garlic cloves, finely sliced
extra virgin olive oil, to serve

warm silverbeet and chickpea salad with sumac

serves 4

Put the chickpeas in a large bowl, cover with water and leave to soak overnight. Drain and place in a large saucepan. Cover with water and bring to the boil, then simmer for 1¾ hours, or until tender. Drain and set aside.

Heat the oil in a heavy-based frying pan, add the onion and cook over low heat for 5 minutes, or until softened and just starting to brown. Cut the tomatoes in half, scrape out the seeds with a teaspoon and dice the flesh. Add the tomato flesh to the pan with the sugar, cinnamon and garlic, and cook for 2–3 minutes, or until softened.

Thoroughly wash the silverbeet and pat dry with paper towels. Trim the stems and finely shred the leaves. Add to the tomato mixture with the chickpeas and cook for 3–4 minutes, or until the silverbeet wilts. Add the mint, lemon juice and sumac, season, and cook for 1 minute. Serve immediately.

250 g (9 oz/1 cup) dried chickpeas
125 ml (4 fl oz/½ cup) olive oil
1 onion, cut into thin wedges
2 tomatoes
1 teaspoon sugar
¼ teaspoon ground cinnamon
2 garlic cloves, chopped
1.5 kg (3 lb 5 oz) silverbeet (Swiss chard)
3 tablespoons chopped mint
2–3 tablespoons lemon juice
1½ tablespoons ground sumac

leaves ■ silverbeet (swiss chard)

sorrel

vegetables ■ **leaves**
season ■ **spring**

Of all the different types of sorrel, it is the cultivated French one that is the best for eating. Its lemony flavour extends a tangy note to salads, sauces, soups and vegetable purees, and is a particularly good addition to omelettes.

Belonging to the buckwheat family, sorrel is a hardy perennial that has grown wild across Europe, Asia and the United States for centuries. Similar in shape to spinach, but more elongated and paler green in colour, the young leaves are the most tender and have the finest flavour. Extremely rich in oxalic acid, sorrel should be enjoyed in moderation. Sorrel also contains quantities of vitamin A, and to a lesser extent, vitamin C, calcium, magnesium, phosphorus and potassium.

selection and storage

Sorrel is highly perishable and wilts quickly, so choose bunches with crisp-looking, brightly coloured leaves. Those with yellowing, saggy leaves and woody stems are best avoided as they are well past their prime. Store sorrel in perforated plastic bags in the crisper section of the refrigerator, then use within 3 days.

Utilize young sorrel in salads, and more mature leaves in soups and sauces. When cooking sorrel, be sure to add it to your dish at the very last moment, as overcooking turns it an unappealing shade of khaki.

culinary uses

The sharpness of sorrel acts as a great foil for sweet and delicate and very rich ingredients like chicken, cream, eggs and salmon. In combination with dandelion leaves, young sorrel makes a refreshing salad when dressed with a walnut oil-based vinaigrette. Buttered, just-wilted sorrel is an ideal accompaniment for ocean trout fillets poached in stock, and, when combined with herbs such as thyme, flat-leaf (Italian) parsley, chervil, fresh breadcrumbs and butter to moisten, it makes an intriguing crust for baked chicken breasts. Add sorrel to a potato-based cucumber Vichyssoise then chill and serve as a refreshingly simple first course for an alfresco summer meal; top with a dollop of crème fraîche and salmon roe for a wow-factor finish.

sorrel and asparagus risotto

Combine the stock and wine in a large saucepan and bring to a boil, covered, over high heat. Reduce heat to low and keep at a gentle simmer.

Melt half the butter in a large, heavy-based saucepan, add olive oil, onion and garlic then cook, stirring often, over medium heat for 5 minutes, or until onion is soft. Add rice and cook, stirring, for 2 minutes or until rice is hot and coated in oil. Add 1 cup of stock mixture and stir rice until stock has been absorbed. Add another cup of stock, stirring until liquid has been absorbed, then repeat process using another cup of stock.

Add the asparagus and sorrel then continue adding stock to rice, 1 cup at a time, stirring until completely absorbed before adding more. Stir in any remaining butter and the parmesan cheese. Season with sea salt and freshly ground black pepper and serve immediately.

1 litre (35 fl oz/4 cups) ready-made chicken stock
250 ml (9 fl oz/1 cup) dry white wine
50 g (1¾ oz) unsalted butter, cut into cubes
60 ml (2 fl oz/¼ cup) extra virgin olive oil
1 onion, peeled and finely chopped
2 garlic cloves, peeled and crushed
300 g (10½ oz/1⅓ cups) risotto (arborio) rice
24 asparagus spears, trimmed and cut into 2 cm (¾ inch) pieces
100 g (3½ oz) sorrel, washed, trimmed and finely chopped
60 g (2¼ oz/⅔ cup) grated parmesan cheese

leaves ■ sorrel

Sorrel is a source of oxalic acid, as is rhubarb. Oxalic acid combines in the body with calcium to form oxalate crsystals, which can be a stomach and kidney irritant and can lead to the formation of kidney stones. Sorrel therefore, although high in various nutrients and utterly delicious, should be consumed in moderation.

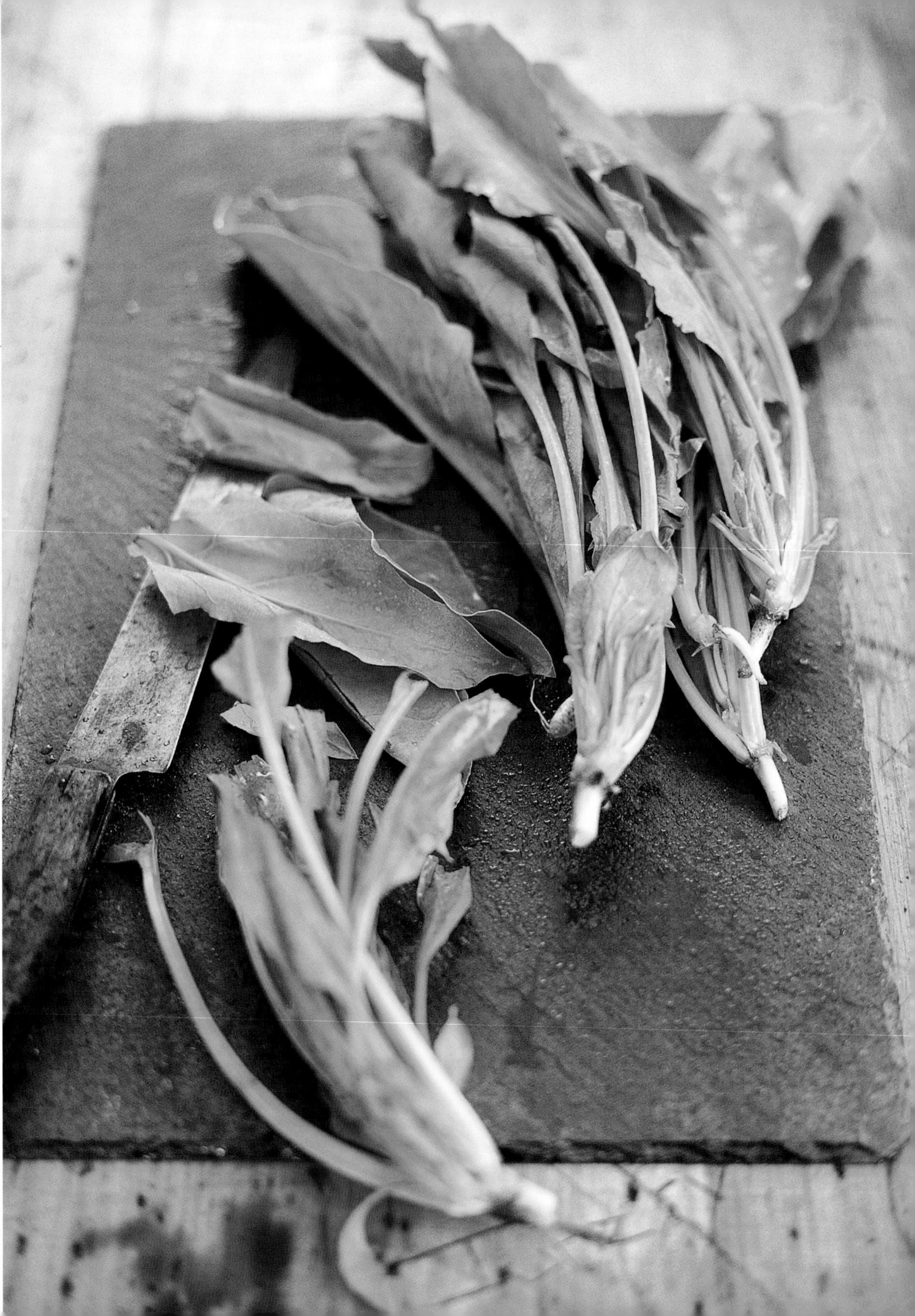

spinach

vegetables ■ **leaves**
season ■ **available year-round but best winter–spring**

Although many childhood memories of spinach revolve around the comic strip character Popeye exhorting us to eat the healthy vegetable, humans can't readily assimilate the high iron content for which it is so fabled. Nonetheless, it is an excellent source of vitamin C, betacarotene, folate and calcium.

Eaten since antiquity, spinach is thought to have originated in the temperate climes of ancient Persia, where it is still eaten in vast quantities as an integral part of the modern-day Iranian diet. In the Arab world, spinach is considered the 'prince of vegetables', featuring in many permutations—combined with eggs and bounteous herbs in thick omelettes, added to lamb stews, consumed in conjunction with pulses or enjoyed as a side dish with pine nuts and raisins.

From Persia, spinach travelled eastwards to China. The Moors took spinach with them to Spain in the twelfth century, but it did not really find favour in Europe until the sixteenth century, when Catherine de Medici brought her favourite vegetables (and Italian chefs to cook them) with her from Florence to France upon her marriage to Henry of Orleans. Since this time, French dishes including a high spinach quotient have come to be known as 'a la Florentine'—this description is most applied to eggs, chicken, sole and quiche.

selection and storage

When buying bunches of spinach, look for those with broad, spade-shaped, jade leaves and undamaged stems. Baby English spinach leaves can also be bought either loose or in pre-packed bags. These are an ideal salad green, but take care to choose small, dry leaves with no bruising, wilting or yellowing as they are extremely perishable.

Spinach needs to be washed carefully in several changes of cold water to eliminate any muddy residue; first remove all the leaves and discard the stalks.

A delicate green, prone to bruising and other leaf damage, spinach shouldn't be stored for longer than 2 days in a plastic bag in the refrigerator.

preparation

Once washed, spinach leaves can be simply cooked, covered, in a saucepan, with the water from washing still clinging to the leaves until just wilted—this will take about 3–4 minutes over medium-high heat. It should then be drained in a colander using a large spoon to press down on the spinach to rid it of as much water as possible. The spinach can be served as is, or returned to a pan with a little butter or cream and perhaps some freshly grated nutmeg, and cooked until the butter melts and the spinach is coated, or the cream is reduced and thickened slightly.

To make spinach puree, simply process the cooked spinach in a food processor and treat it in the same manner as above—serve it as it is, or cook it in a little cream or with some butter.

Whether sautéed, steamed, pureed or added to stuffings, soups, braises, sauces or egg dishes, spinach reduces in volume dramatically when cooked, so be sure to buy plenty. As a general guide, two bunches (about 1 kg/2 lb 4 oz) of spinach will suffice for four to six spinach-loving adults.

culinary uses

Matching well with anchovies, butter, cheese, cream, eggs, ham, mushrooms, olive oil, pasta, pastry, prosciutto, soy sauce, sesame seeds, walnuts and yoghurt, spinach's tender, sweet flavour also has a natural affinity with allspice, black pepper, garlic, ginger, lemon juice, mace, mustard, nutmeg and paprika.

For a Japanese take on spinach, try dressing cooled, wilted baby leaves with soy sauce, rice vinegar and sesame oil, then sprinkling with toasted sesame seeds and serving with yakitori chicken or grilled (broiled) salmon skewers. The classic European preparation of creamed spinach is a sumptuous way to deal with a glut of the leafy green and makes an elegant companion for meatloaf.

spinach and feta triangles

Trim any coarse stems from the spinach. Wash the leaves thoroughly, roughly chop and place in a large frying pan with just a little water clinging to the leaves. Cover and cook gently over low heat for 5 minutes, or until the leaves have wilted. Drain well and allow to cool slightly before squeezing tightly to remove excess water.

Heat the oil in a heavy-based frying pan. Add the onion and cook over low heat for 10 minutes, or until golden. Add the green onion and cook for a further 3 minutes. Remove from the heat. Stir in the drained spinach, parsley, dill, nutmeg, parmesan cheese, feta, ricotta and egg. Season with sea salt and freshly ground black pepper.

Preheat the oven to 180°C (350°F/Gas 4). Grease two baking trays. Combine the melted butter with the extra oil. Work with 3 sheets of pastry at a time, keeping the rest covered with a damp tea (dish) towel. Brush each sheet with the butter mixture and lay them on top of each other, then cut in half lengthways.

Spoon 4 tablespoons of the filling on an angle at the end of each strip. Fold the pastry over to enclose the filling and form a triangle. Continue folding the triangle over until you reach the end of the pastry. Put the triangles on the baking trays and brush with the remaining butter mixture. Bake for 20–25 minutes, or until the pastry is golden brown.

1 kg (2 lb 4 oz) English spinach
60 ml (2 fl oz/¼ cup) olive oil
1 onion, chopped
10 green onions (scallions), sliced
1 handful parsley, chopped
1 tablespoon chopped dill
pinch ground nutmeg
35 g (1¼ oz/⅓ cup) grated parmesan cheese
150 g (5½ oz/1 cup) crumbled feta cheese
90 g (3¼ oz/⅓ cup) ricotta cheese
4 eggs, lightly beaten
40 g (1½ oz) butter, melted
1 tablespoon olive oil, extra
12 sheets ready-made filo pastry

leaves ■ spinach

For other spinach recipes see:
stir-fried tofu with Asian greens 294

makes 2 x 30 cm
(12 inch) pizzas

pizza spinaci

pizza dough

1 tablespoon caster (superfine) sugar
2 teaspoons dried yeast or 15 g (1/2 oz) fresh yeast
215 ml (7 1/2 fl oz) lukewarm water
450 g (1 lb/3 2/3 cups) plain (all-purpose) flour
3 tablespoons olive oil

topping

4 tablespoons olive oil
4 garlic cloves, crushed
4 tablespoons pine nuts
2 kg (4 lb 8 oz) English spinach, trimmed and roughly chopped
cornflour (cornstarch), to dust
2 quantities tomato sauce (see page 360)
440 g (15 1/2 oz/3 cups) grated mozzarella cheese
30 very small black olives
6 tablespoons grated parmesan cheese

To make the pizza dough, put the sugar and yeast in a bowl and stir in 90 ml (3 fl oz) water. Leave in a draught-free spot to activate. If the yeast does not bubble and foam in 5 minutes, throw it away and start again.

Mix the flour and 1/4 teaspoon salt in a bowl or food processor fitted with a plastic blade. Add the olive oil, remaining water and the yeast mixture. Mix until the dough loosely clumps together. Transfer to a lightly floured surface and knead for 8 minutes, adding a little flour or warm water if necessary, until you have a soft dough that is not sticky but is dry to the touch.

Rub the inside of a large bowl with olive oil. Roll the ball of dough around in the bowl to coat it with oil, then cut a shallow cross on the top with a sharp knife. Cover with a tea towel or put in a plastic bag and leave in a draught-free spot for 1–1 1/2 hours, or until doubled in size.

Punch down the dough to its original size, then divide into two portions. Working with one portion at a time, push the dough out to fit a 30 cm (12 inch) lightly oiled circular tray. Preheat the oven to 240°C (475°F/Gas 9).

To make the topping, heat the oil in a frying pan and fry the garlic and pine nuts, stirring often, over low heat for 5–6 minutes, or until golden. Add the spinach, increase the heat and stir until wilted. Season with sea salt and freshly ground black pepper.

Dust each pizza base with cornflour and spoon over half the tomato sauce on each base, spreading to cover. Sprinkle with half the mozzarella cheese. Spread the spinach and olives over the top, followed by the rest of the mozzarella and the parmesan cheese. Bake for 12–15 minutes, or until golden and puffed. Brush the rim with a little extra olive oil before serving.

watercress

selection and storage

Choose vibrant, glossy green watercress, with no wilted, yellowing, brown or slimy leaves or bruised stems. Darker leaves and thicker stems identify older watercress, which has an overly intense flavour.

Store watercress in a plastic bag in the crisper section of the refrigerator for up to 2 days, or refrigerate with the stalks placed in water and the leaves loosely covered by a plastic bag.

vegetables ■ **leaves**
season ■ **available year-round**

The natural habitat of watercress, as its name would suggest, is in countryside streams and brooks. Like other cruciferous vegetables, watercress is characterized by a tangy, mustard-like flavour. Believed to have originated in the Mediterranean and Asia Minor, its small, embossed leaves have a faintly tart, peppery bite (which becomes distinctly pronounced as it matures) that has been appreciated since ancient times.

Brimming with vitamins C, A and K, plus potassium, iron, calcium and copper, watercress was so highly rated by the 'father' of modern medicine, Hippocrates, that he sited his very first hospital by a stream in order to have the vegetable close at hand.

preparation

When ready to use watercress, pick through the bunch, removing sprigs and the single, tender stalks that occur further down the central stems. Discard thick, tough stems, gently wash and pat dry.

culinary uses

Watercress is often relegated to the minor role of garnish, but it is deserving of far more attention than this. It lends itself to various other uses—pureed into a potato-based soup, for example, or tossed into all manner of salads. Use it like wilted spinach in a quiche filling or add chopped handfuls at the last moment to Asian-style noodle broths. Watercress cuts the richness of roast meats and pâtés, and a sprig or two served alongside these is a nice touch.

warm spring lamb, watercress and citrus salad

To make the dressing, put all the ingredients in a small bowl, season with sea salt and freshly ground black pepper and whisk to combine.

Cut the lamb fillets in half and season with freshly ground black pepper. Heat the olive oil in a frying pan over high heat and cook the lamb for 3–4 minutes all over until browned, but still a little pink in the middle, turning once or twice. Season with sea salt and remove from the heat.

Peel the oranges and grapefruit, removing all the white pith. Holding them over a bowl to catch the juice, segment them by using a small, sharp knife to cut between the membranes. Put the segments in the bowl with the juices.

Cut the lamb on the diagonal into 2.5 cm (1 inch) thick slices and add to the bowl, along with the watercress and red onion. Pour the dressing over the salad and lightly toss to coat.

dressing
1 tablespoon red wine vinegar
1 garlic clove, crushed
½ teaspoon honey
2 teaspoons walnut oil
1½ tablespoons olive oil

300 g (10½ oz) lamb fillets
1 tablespoon olive oil
2 oranges
1 small pink grapefruit
3 large handfuls watercress, picked over
½ small red onion, finely sliced

leaves ■ watercress

Watercress became a staple part of the working class English diet in the 1800s, when it was eaten in sandwiches for breakfast. Those too poor to buy bread often ate it on its own; hence it came to be known as 'poor man's bread'. The British still hold watercress sandwiches in high esteem, although they have now entered more illustrious realms, and these days often include boiled eggs, chopped prawns or smoked salmon.

For other watercress recipes see:
orange, hazelnut and goat's cheese
  salad 37
watercress salad 415

witlof (chicory/ belgian endive)

vegetables ■ **leaves**
season ■ **winter–early spring**

selection and storage

Look for crisp, tightly packed heads with pale, yellow-green or pink tips. Witlof is highly perishable and increases in bitterness the longer it is stored, so wrap it in a paper towel, place inside a plastic bag, then keep in the refrigerator vegetable crisper for no more than 1 day.

Noted for its slightly bittersweet flavour and featuring compact, slender, elongated heads consisting of yellow (or pink) tipped, cream leaves, witlof did not really take off until the twentieth century when its cultivation began in earnest.

Expensive and labour-intensive to harvest, witlof is grown in the dark, using a technique called blanching, to prevent sunlight from creating chlorophyll, which would turn its white leaves green. It is then hand-picked and stored carefully, wrapped to prevent exposure to light, which even at this stage would turn it green and make it bitter. While not as nutrient rich as green vegetables, witlof contains vitamin A, potassium, dietary fibre, vitamin C, folate and some iron.

preparation

To prepare witlof, cut away the base, then separate leaves and wash under cold running water; do not soak witlof as this tips the balance of the flavour to the sour side of bittersweet. Do not use cast iron utensils for cooking, as they will turn the leaves an unappealing shade of grey.

braising Cut heads of witlof in half and pack snugly into an ovenproof dish. Add enough hot chicken stock to cover to halfway, cover the dish tightly with foil and cook in a 180°C (350°F/Gas 4) oven for 40 minutes or until tender.

sautéing To sauté witlof, simply cut into chunks and toss in a large pan with plenty of butter over medium-high heat for 5–6 minutes or until softened and golden.

sautéed witlof with olives, anchovies and caperberries

Chop the olives and put them in a small bowl. Finely chop the anchovies and add them to the olives. Chop 2 of the caperberries to the size of baby capers and add to the olives. Add half the olive oil and mix together.

Discard the outer leaves and cut the heads of witlof in half lengthways. Open out the leaves a little and spoon the olive mixture over and between the leaves. Join the 2 halves together again and tie to secure with string.

Heat the remaining oil and the butter in a saucepan over low heat. Add the witlof, garlic and chilli flakes, cover and braise the witlof for 8–10 minutes, turning halfway through. Add a little hot water if necessary to prevent sticking.

To serve, untie the string and arrange four equal portions of witlof, cut side up, on a serving plate. Spoon over any pan juices. Slice the remaining caperberries in half lengthways and scatter them over the witlof. Serve hot.

40 g (1½ oz/¼ cup) pitted kalamata olives
2 anchovy fillets
5 small caperberries
1 tablespoon olive oil
2 heads pale cream or red witlof (chicory/Belgian endive)
20 g (¾ oz) butter
1 garlic clove, crushed
1 pinch chilli flakes, optional

leaves ■ witlof (chicory/belgian endive)

Introduced to Paris to rave reviews in 1872, witlof was so revered that it became known as 'white gold'. There is a restaurant called Traiteur Restaurant Veilinghof, in the Belgian town of Kampenhout, the hometown of witlof, whose menu is entirely devoted to the vegetable. On the menu are 50 witlof dishes, heaven for the true aficionado.

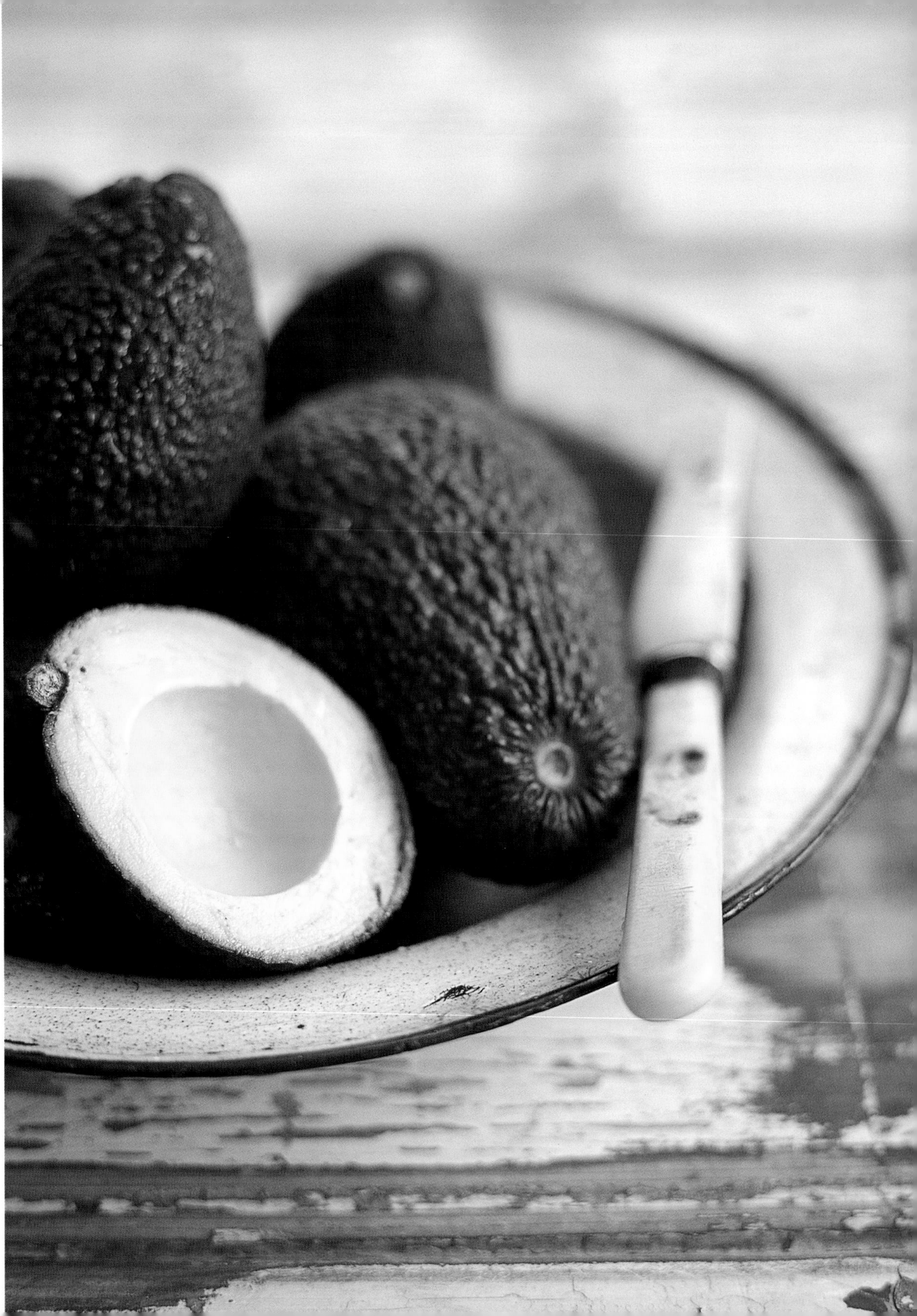

avocado

Indigenous to Mexico and tropical Central America, the avocado is an incredible vegetable—although more correctly it is classified as a fruit. With its unique buttery green flesh, which increases in unsaturated fat content and decreases in sugar content as it ripens, there is nothing else quite like it. The avocado is the only member of the laurel family to bear edible fruit; the fruit is also an oddity as it only ripens, or softens, once it has left the tree. The fruits will keep, mature but hard, on the tree for up to seven months without deteriorating, with a single tree bearing up to 120 fruit in a season.

The name 'avocado' is a derivation of the Spanish word for the fruit, *ahuacate*, which itself comes from the Aztec name, *ahuacatl*; intriguingly, this word is also Aztec for 'testicle'. Perhaps because of this, the avocado has long been considered an aphrodisiac.

Avocados have the decadent richness of a dairy food but their fat is mainly of the 'good' sort, that is, monounsaturated. This type of fat can actually play a part in lowering certain types of cholesterol in the body. The avocado is also particularly rich in vitamin E and other powerful antioxidants, as well as providing good quantities of potassium, betacarotene, B vitamins and calcium.

selection and storage

Avocados should only be used when fully ripe, otherwise they are hard and completely tasteless. To determine ripeness, cradle the fruit in your hands and apply slight pressure—it should 'give' slightly.

Avocados are perishable so, unless you plan to use them straight away, it is best to purchase them a little under-ripe—they will only take 2–3 days to fully soften at room temperature. Once ripe, store them in the refrigerator and plan on using them within 1–2 days.

varieties

Spanish explorers took enthusiastically to the avocado and by the 1650s the three principal strains had been catalogued; these are the Mexican, Guatemalan and West Indian. Some of the most favoured varieties we enjoy today (such as the hass and the feurte) are hybrids of Mexican and Guatemalan types.

The Mexican avocado strain is typified by plum-sized fruits with very dark, smooth skin and particularly aromatic, anise-scented leaves. Guatemalan types are larger, with green or purple skin, while the lesser-known West Indian varieties are very large, producing fruits that weigh in at over 1 kilogram (2 lb 4 oz).

hass This is the only variety that grows year-round. Discovered by chance in the 1920s in California, it has gone on to become one of the world's favourite avocados. The fruit features knobbly green skin which turns inky-purple when fully ripe and has rich green, buttery flesh. The skin can be difficult to remove.

fuerte Fuertes have smooth green skin which remains that colour when ripe. The flesh is a creamy, pale yellow; make sure they are really ripe as their subtle flavour can be lost to blandness if not fully ready for eating.

reed Reeds are large, rounded fruits with thin, shiny green, easy-peeling skin, which appear in the summer months. Inside, their pale yellow flesh is mild flavoured and buttery.

zutano An attractive, pear-shaped fruit with yellow-green skin and rich green flesh; this avocado is particularly easy to peel.

preparation

The easiest way to deal with an avocado is to cut it in half lengthways around the large central stone. Rotate the halves to separate them, then nudge out the stone with the tip of a spoon—this can also be done by striking the stone with a sharp knife while cradling the avocado half in your other hand—care needs to be employed with this method though, as you can cut yourself if the stone is soft (unlikely) or splits.

Once cut, an avocado browns quickly on exposure to the air —brush it with lemon or lime juice to slow the process down. The skin of some avocados can be brittle or reluctant to come off. In this instance you can employ a large metal spoon to scoop the halved avocado out of its shell or, if you wish to slice or dice it first, do this while still in its skin. Then, using the large spoon, scoop the pieces out in one swoop and use immediately.

Avocado varieties can be used interchangeably in recipes. Don't cook avocados as heat brings out bitter tannins.

avocado salsa

Finely chop the onion. Cut the avocados in half; remove the seed and cut into cubes while still in the skin. Use a large spoon to scoop the cubes into a bowl and toss lightly with lime juice.

Cut the tomato in half widthways, squeeze gently to remove seeds and chop finely. Remove the seeds and membrane from the capsicum and finely dice.

Put the ground coriander and cumin in a small pan; stir over medium heat for 1 minute to enhance fragrance and flavour. Allow to cool. Add all the ingredients to a bowl with the avocado and gently combine, so that the avocado retains its shape and is not mashed. Refrigerate until required and serve at room temperature with corn chips.

1 red onion
2 large avocados
1 tablespoon lime juice
1 tomato
1 small red capsicum (pepper)
1 teaspoon ground coriander
1 teaspoon ground cumin
3 tablespoons chopped fresh coriander (cilantro) leaves
2 tablespoons olive oil
4–5 drops Tabasco sauce
corn chips, to serve

avocado, bacon and tomato salad

Preheat the oven to 180°C (350°F/Gas 4). Put the unpeeled garlic cloves on a baking tray and roast for 30 minutes. Remove, allow to cool, then squeeze the flesh out of the skins and mash in a small bowl. Add the oil, vinegar and mustard, then whisk to combine well.

Chop the bacon into bite-sized pieces, then cook under a medium-hot grill (broiler) or dry-fry in a frying pan over medium heat for 3–5 minutes, or until crisp. Gently toss the bacon, salad leaves, onion, avocado and tomato in a bowl. Drizzle the garlic mixture over the salad just before serving.

3 garlic cloves, unpeeled
2 tablespoons olive oil
3 teaspoons balsamic vinegar
1 teaspoon dijon mustard
125 g (4½ oz) bacon slices
50 g (1¾ oz) mixed green salad leaves
½ small red onion, finely sliced
1 avocado, cut into chunks
2 small tomatoes, cut into chunks

capsicum (pepper)

The large, non-pungent members of the capsicum or chilli family are variously called capsicums or, in the United States, 'bell peppers'; perhaps this latter name is in reference to their squat, blocky shape. They contain a recessive gene which means they don't contain any capsaicin, the heat-producing compound common to all other chillies.

Fleshy, crisp and (the non-green ones, at least) sweet, capsicums show up in all sorts of culinary guises. They can be eaten raw (as a crudité or in salads), stir-fried, grilled (broiled), braised, stuffed and baked, or roasted.

A member of the nightshade family, capsicums are native to Central America where they have been cultivated by indigenous populations from around 3500 BC. They were introduced to Spain and Portugal by returning explorers during the thirteenth century and were quickly embraced in Europe.

They are a feature of many of the world's great ethnic cuisines—Italian, Spanish, Chinese and Mexican among them. There are a number of famous sweet capsicum dishes; ratatouille and piperade, both tomato-based vegetable stews from the South of France, are two such examples. Mechouia, a popular salad in Tunisia and Mahamurra, a hauntingly flavoured sauce from Turkey, also use capsicum to great effect.

fruit vegetables ■ capsicum (pepper)

selection and storage

Choose capsicums that are heavy for their size and that have bright, tight, smooth, glossy skin with no watery-looking spots or wrinkled patches.

Capsicums are prone to mould and wrinkling, so store them in a ventilated bag in the crisper section of the refrigerator for up to 1 week.

For other capsicum (pepper) recipes see:

varieties

Sweet capsicums come in a variety of colours—green, red, orange, yellow, purple and brown. Green capsicums are actually mature but not quite ripe yellow or red capsicums, therefore they tend to be less sweet than fully ripe fruits. Green capsicums also contain less vitamin C than their more brightly-coloured counterparts, although they are hardly deficient in this department, containing twice as much vitamin C, by weight, than the equivalent in citrus. Red capsicums contain three times as much vitamin C as green ones and they also contain good quantities of betacarotene.

preparation

peeling Sweet peppers can be used peeled or unpeeled—some find the skin difficult to digest so if in doubt, take it off. If using sweet capsicums raw, or preparing them for a stir-fry, you can take off the skin using a potato peeler (avoid very creviced capsicums for peeling raw). Then slice off the fleshy lobes or sides of the pepper, leaving just the seed-filled core and hard stem end. Discard these then slice, dice or chop the flesh and use as desired. The skin can also be removed by chargrilling or roasting the capsicum, a common way to prepare the vegetable as these cooking methods render it particularly tender and sweet. Thus prepared, the cooked, peeled flesh can be used in salads, sauces, chutneys and stews.

roasting To roast capsicums, brush whole capsicums lightly with oil, place on a single layer in a roasting dish then cook in a 220°C (425°F/Gas 7) oven for 15–20 minutes, turning occasionally, or until flesh has softened and skin is burnt-looking and will pull away from the flesh. Cool capsicums for 10 minutes in a paper bag, or in a large bowl covered with a kitchen towel, after which the skin will be particularly easy to remove. Once peeled, cut away the stem end, pull out seeds and tough inner ribs, then cut or tear flesh into desired size.

chargrilling To chargrill or barbecue capsicums, place them whole on a hot chargrill plate or barbecue and cook, turning frequently, until skin blackens and blisters. This will take about 10 minutes. Cool charred capsicums in the same manner as roasted ones, then pull off all the black skin. Always resist any temptation to wash away skin and seeds under running water as you will greatly dilute the taste of the vegetable—far better to discover an occasional seed or piece of skin in your food than to eat peppers washed of their flavour.

capsicum and bean stew

Put the beans in a large bowl, cover with cold water and soak overnight. Rinse well, then transfer to a saucepan, cover with cold water, bring to the boil and then simmer for 45 minutes, or until just tender. Drain and set aside.

Heat the oil in a large saucepan. Cook the garlic and onion over medium heat for 2–3 minutes, or until the onion is soft. Add the capsicums and cook for a further 5 minutes.

Stir in the tomato, tomato paste, stock and beans. Simmer, covered, for 40 minutes, or until the beans are cooked through. Stir in the basil, olives and sugar. Season with sea salt and freshly ground black pepper. Serve hot with crusty bread.

note   1 cup of dried haricot beans yields about 2½ cups cooked beans. Use 2½ cups of drained tinned haricot or borlotti beans instead if you prefer, but add these at the end with the basil, olives and sugar, and just heat through.

- 200 g (7 oz/1 cup) dried haricot beans (see note)
- 2 tablespoons olive oil
- 2 large garlic cloves, crushed
- 1 red onion, halved and cut into thin wedges
- 1 red capsicum (pepper), cubed
- 1 green capsicum (pepper), cubed
- two 400 g (14 oz) tin chopped tomatoes
- 2 tablespoons tomato paste (concentrated puree)
- 500 ml (17 fl oz/2 cups) ready-made vegetable stock
- 2 tablespoons chopped basil
- 125 g (4½ oz/¾ cup) kalamata olives, pitted
- 1–2 teaspoons soft brown sugar

red capsicum puree

makes 300 ml (10½ fl oz/ 1¼ cups)

Grill (broil) the capsicums under high heat for 10 minutes, turning often, until the skin blisters and blackens all over. Place capsicums in a paper bag or a bowl covered with a tea (dish) towel, cool slightly, then peel, remove seeds and roughly chop.

Put the capsicums in a food processor, add the green onions, garlic and chilli. Process until smooth. Transfer the puree to a saucepan and stir in the fish sauce, lime juice and coriander. Cook over medium heat until slightly thickened. Serve as a dip with an antipasti selection or as a pasta sauce.

- 3 large red capsicums (peppers)
- 4 green onions (scallions), chopped
- 2 garlic cloves, crushed
- 2 small red chillies, finely chopped
- 2 tablespoons fish sauce (optional)
- 2 tablespoons lime juice
- 2 tablespoons chopped coriander (cilantro) leaves

fruit vegetables ▪ capsicum (pepper)

chilli

vegetables ▪ **fruit vegetables**
season ▪ **available year-round**

There are hundreds of varieties of chillies—not all provide a distinctive wallop of heat; some are rather tame—but they are all very nutritious, high in vitamins C and A and betacarotene levels and are also mildly antibacterial. The heat factor comes from the presence of capsaicin, a compound that causes burning sensations in the mouth and throat. Extreme care should be taken when handling chillies, as the volatile juices can be transferred to eyes and other sensitive parts of the body via your hands. In general, red chillies are hotter than green or yellow chillies, and the smaller the chilli, the hotter it will be.

storage and selection

Choose chillies that have tight, glossy skins with no trace of bruising or soft, wet spots.

Store them in a loosely sealed plastic bag in the refrigerator—they will keep for up to 1 week.

varieties

banana A mild-tasting chilli, practically benign when immature and only pleasantly tangy when fully red. They are sold with pale yellow, waxy-looking skin. They are a conical-shaped, tapering chilli, about 18 cm (7 inches) long.

bird's eye These are either green or red and are a very small, bullet-shaped chilli with smooth, glossy skin and are very hot.

habanero An extremely hot, fruity-tasting chilli with a rounded lantern shape, these small chillies have thin, waxy flesh.

jalapeno A famous, moderately hot green chilli with a red blush (later in the season they mature and turn red) and are about 5–7.5 cm (2–3 inches) long.

serrano A small, cylindrical chilli with a blunt end. They are thin-skinned with meaty flesh and are bright green, ripening to red-brown or orange. They are reputed to be five times hotter than the jalapenos.

chilli con queso

Melt the butter in a saucepan over medium heat. Add the onion and green and red chillies and cook for 5 minutes, or until softened. Increase the heat to high, add the garlic and paprika, and cook for 1 minute, or until fragrant.

Add the beer, bring to the boil and cook until almost evaporated. Reduce the heat to low and add the sour cream, stirring until smooth. Add the cheese and stir until the cheese is just melted and the mixture is smooth. Remove from the heat, stir through the coriander and jalapeno, and season to taste. Serve with corn or tortilla chips for dipping.

30 g (1 oz) butter
1/2 red onion
2 large green chillies, seeded and finely chopped
2 small red chillies, seeded and finely chopped
1 garlic clove, crushed
1/2 teaspoon sweet paprika
1 1/2 tablespoons beer
125 ml (4 fl oz/1/2 cup) sour cream
200 g (7 oz/1 2/3 cups) grated cheddar cheese
1 tablespoon chopped coriander (cilantro) leaves
1 tablespoon sliced jalapenos
corn or tortilla chips, to serve

fruit vegetables ■ chilli

sweet chilli sauce

makes 60 ml
(2 fl oz/1/4 cup)

In a mortar using a pestle or in a blender, pound or blend the chillies into a rough paste.

Put the vinegar, sugar and salt in a small saucepan over high heat and bring to boiling heat, stirring constantly. Reduce the heat to medium and simmer for 15–20 minutes, until the mixture forms a thick syrup. Spoon the chilli paste into the syrup and cook for a further 1–2 minutes. Remove from heat and pour into a serving dish to serve as a dipping sauce.

7 long red chillies, seeded and roughly chopped
185 ml (6 fl oz/3/4 cup) white vinegar
8 tablespoons sugar
1/2 teaspoon salt

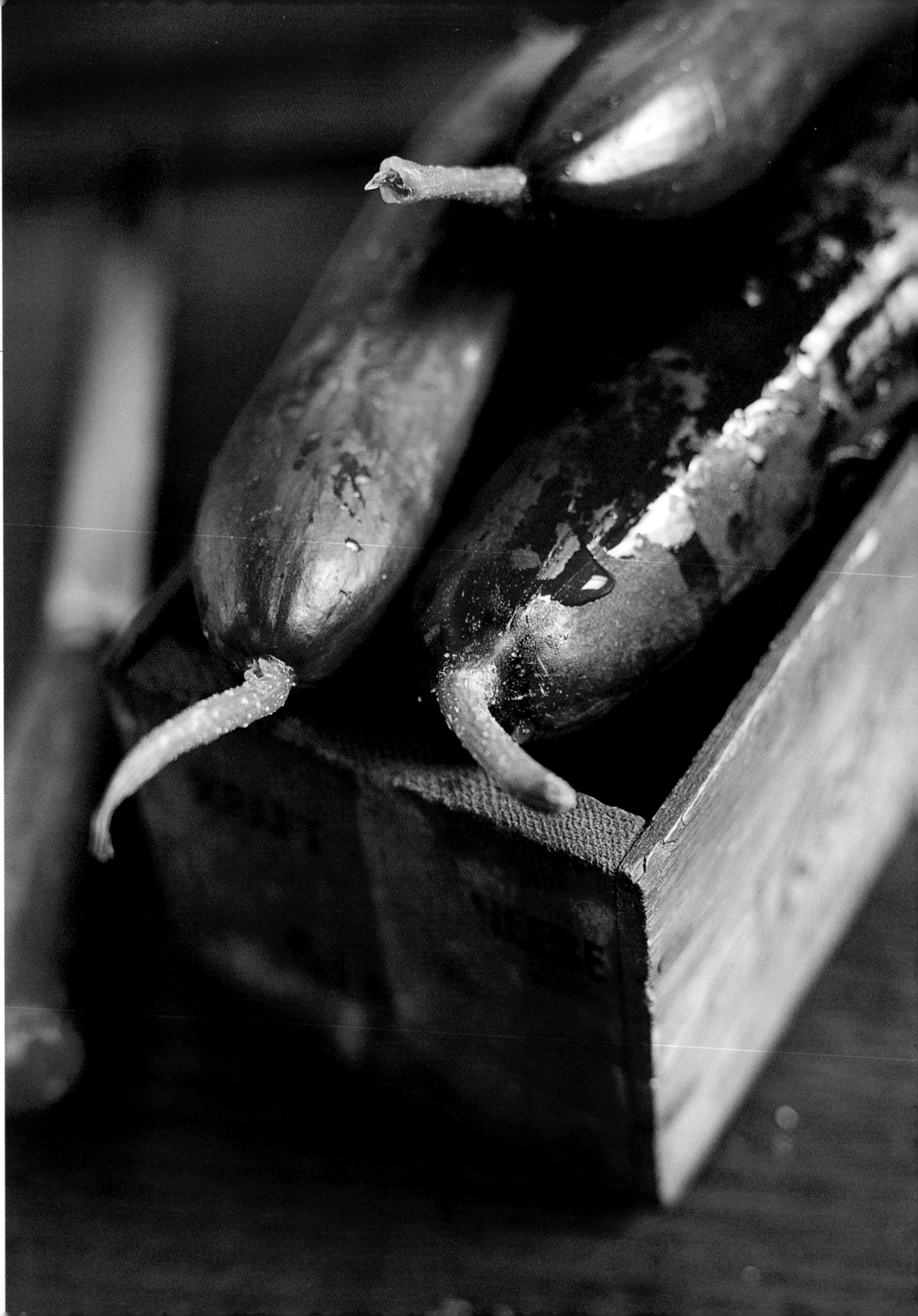

cucumber

vegetables ▪ fruit vegetables
season ▪ peak season summer

Belonging to the same botanical family as melons and gourds, cucumbers have suffered somewhat during modern cultivation processes, in much the same way as has the tomato. Major varieties are grown and packaged for supermarket supply, requiring that cucumbers be uniform in size and are able to transport and store well. With their shiny, shrink-wrapped (or worse, waxed) skins, and bland interiors, they often end up as nothing more than an innocuous, crunchy presence in the salad bowl.

There are boundless cucumber varieties though, coming in round and oval shapes, yellow, pale green and bronze colours and various sizes, from gherkins that are barely over 2 cm (1 inch) long, to mammoth English types which can be over 50 cm (20 inches) long. Do try to search out those produced by a caring grower, and a whole world of herbal, sweet, grassy flavours will be opened up.

Cucumbers contains silica, an essential component of healthy connective tissue and therefore very good for the skin. Over the centuries cucumber has been used topically to treat dermatitis, sunburn and eye-swelling. Containing significant amounts of ascorbic and caffeic acids, the cucumber is also helpful in preventing fluid retention, no mean feat considering it is comprised of 96 per cent water itself.

selection and storage

Select cucumbers that are heavy for their size and that are firm and unblemished. Inspect ends closely to check for softness or wrinkling (a sign of age or poor storage) and go for ones that are small and slender for their type. These will be younger and therefore sweeter than more mature cucumbers. Green varieties should have little, if any, signs of yellowing.

Store unwashed cucumbers in the vegetable crisper section of the refrigerator in a ventilated plastic bag—note that they do not like excessive cold so don't store them in the coldest part of the refrigerator.

varieties

garden Also called the common cucumber, this variety is generally sold waxed, and is a slicing cucumber. It is stumpy and has rounded ends and a thick, slightly bitter skin with large seeds. It is best to peel and seed this cucumber. The chopped or grated flesh is good in soups and dips or tossed at the last moment into a reduced cream and tarragon (or dill) sauce for serving with fish.

gherkin The classic pickling cucumber, these short, slightly warty-skinned specimens have been bred specifically for this purpose. They are pickled whole—no peeling, slicing or seeding is required before use.

lebanese (short) These are smallish, about 10 cm (4 inches) in length and sweetly mild-tasting—they can be eaten out of hand, skin, seeds and all, as a refreshing snack. These are especially juicy and are great in salads or any recipe calling for raw, unpeeled cucumber.

telegraph (long) This is also called the English, continental or 'burpless' cucumber and invariably comes plastic-wrapped (to protect against drying out). It is long and slim with tapered ends and has glossy green, quite thin skin and small seeds. This cucumber can be used without being peeled or seeded and is therefore great in salads and salsas. Check with your supplier though, that the skin is not waxed—if it has been, you will need to peel before using.

preparation

To seed cucumbers, simply slice them in half lengthways then use a teaspoon to scoop out all the seeds. If adding sliced or grated cucumbers to a yoghurt or sour-cream based dip or soup, do so at the last moment as they will release a lot of water upon standing.

culinary uses

Generally speaking, the flavour and texture of cucumber goes very well with mint, parsley, chives and tarragon, vinegar, chilli, ginger, sour cream and cream, butter, yoghurt, lemon and seafood. Also think of putting it with certain cheeses, particularly the likes of feta or sharp, soft-textured goat's cheese, which makes a fine match.

cucumber, feta, mint and dill salad

Put the crumbled feta in a large bowl. Peel and seed the cucumbers and cut into 1 cm (1/2 inch) dice. Add to the bowl along with the onion and dill.

Grind the mint in a mortar using a pestle until powdered. Combine with the oil and juice, then season with sea salt and freshly ground black pepper. Pour over the salad and toss well.

120 g (4¼ oz/¾ cup) roughly crumbled feta cheese
4 Lebanese (short) cucumbers
1 small red onion, thinly sliced
1½ tablespoons finely chopped fresh dill
1 tablespoon dried mint
3 tablespoons olive oil
1½ tablespoons lemon juice

fruit vegetables ■ cucumber

tsatsiki

makes 500 ml
(17 fl oz/2 cups)

Cut the cucumbers in half lengthways, scoop out the seeds with a teaspoon and discard. Leave the skin on and coarsely grate the cucumber into a small colander. Sprinkle with a little salt and leave to stand over a large bowl for 15 minutes to drain off any bitter juices.

Meanwhile, stir together the yoghurt, garlic, mint and lemon juice in a bowl. Rinse the cucumber under cold water then, taking small handfuls, squeeze out any excess moisture. Combine the cucumber with the yoghurt mixture and season to taste. Serve immediately or refrigerate until ready to serve. Garnish with mint. Can be served as a dip with flat bread or as a sauce for seafood and meat dishes.

2 Lebanese (short) cucumbers
400 g (14 oz/1⅔ cups) Greek-style yoghurt
4 garlic cloves, crushed
3 tablespoons finely chopped fresh mint
1 tablespoon lemon juice
chopped fresh mint, extra, to garnish

eggplant (aubergine)

vegetables ■ fruit vegetables
season ■ peak season mid-summer–early autumn

The eggplant is often thought of as a Mediterranean vegetable, and with good reason; some of the world's most iconic eggplant dishes come from that region. There's caponata and eggplant parmigiano from Italy, ratatouille from the south of France and moussaka from Greece. Turkey is thought to have over 1000 recipes for eggplant of which imam bayildi is perhaps the most famous. So it may surprise some to learn that the eggplant is native to Asia, probably originating in India or Burma (experts can't quite agree).

The only member of the deadly nightshade clan to be native to the East, the eggplant was once viewed with enormous suspicion in certain parts of Europe. Arab traders took the vegetable west, first to Spain. The Spanish warmed to it quite readily and called it the 'apple of love' as they believed it to possess aphrodisiac powers. The Italians also, cautiously, developed an appreciation for the culinary possibilities of the eggplant but in northern Europe and England it was used ornamentally only, as superstition held that eating it would induce insanity, which explains why some called it the 'mad apple'. The English gave it the name we have today (the word 'aubergine' is French) as the first eggplants they encountered were smallish, egg-shaped and ivory-white.

varieties

There are many eggplant varieties. They come in more shapes, sizes and skin colours than most of us are likely to encounter—some are yellowish or orange or brown, black, pink-and-white striped, lavender or green. They vary in size from well over 500 g (1 lb) in weight to the diminutive pea eggplants used in Thai cookery. Some of the most commonly-grown varieties are listed below.

japanese These eggplants are long, about 15–20 cm (6–8 inches) and slim, about 3.5 cm (1¼ inches) in diameter. They are usually purple-skinned but can also be light mauve. Their flesh is cream-coloured and mildly sweet-tasting. This eggplant is great for stuffing and baking, pickling, stir-frying, grilling (broiling) and steaming. It doesn't require peeling.

pea These grow in tiny clusters and come in a variety of colours—red, orange, green and purple. They have an assertive, bitter flavour and are used in Asian cuisines, mainly in pickles and curries, although in Thailand they are eaten raw, accompanied by chilli jam.

thai These are small and round (about the size of a ping pong ball), lavender with green striations, or green or cream. They have tough skin, a seedy interior and a strong flavour—they are used, unpeeled and sliced in Thai soups, salads and curries where they add a pleasantly bitter note.

western or globe This is the classic, large, dark purple eggplant and the sort most commonly available. These vary in size from around 350–550 g (12 oz–1 lb 4 oz) and, when in perfect condition, have pale flesh with few visible seeds. When they are past their prime, the flesh becomes darker, the seeds become more numerous and the flavour deteriorates into bitterness. These are the most versatile eggplant and can be sliced for frying or grilling (broiling), or cut into chunks for roasting, stewing or sautéing. They can be peeled or not—many prefer to peel—as the skin can be tough.

preparation

salting Debate rages over the necessity of salting eggplant flesh before cooking it. The reason generally given for salting is that salt extracts bitterness, but generally commercially grown eggplants are not bitter unless they are old and past their best. However, there are other reasons to salt eggplant.

The food scientist Harold McGee believes that salting collapses air pockets in the spongy flesh, resulting in eggplant less prone to soaking up excess oil when cooked. Salting also seems to improve the cooked texture of eggplant, especially when it is to be sliced and grilled (broiled) or barbecued.

To salt, remove the green calyx (which is spiky so be careful) then slice the eggplant into the desired thickness or cut into chunks. Layer these in a colander, scattering with sea salt as you go, then stand the colander over a sink or bowl to collect juices, for about 30–40 minutes. Discard juices and rinse eggplant well in plenty of cold water, drain then pat dry on paper towels. You can then proceed with your recipe. Note that eggplant is one vegetable that should never be undercooked—it needs to be cooked to the point of sweet collapse.

baking To bake eggplant, toss chunks or wedges of eggplant in oil, arrange in a single layer in a baking dish, then cook in a 180°C (350°F/Gas 4) oven for 40–50 minutes (depending on size) or until golden and soft.

chargrilling To chargrill whole eggplant (useful for making dips and spreads) prick a whole, unpeeled eggplant several times with a thin metal skewer, then cook directly over a gas flame, turning often, for 25 minutes or until the skin is completely blackened and the eggplant is soft. When cool enough to handle, remove all of the skin, then drain the flesh well in a colander, squeezing to remove excess moisture. This method results in wonderfully smoky-flavoured eggplant but can be somewhat messy (put foil around the gas element to catch juices).

Chargrilling can also be done less messily in the oven, although the cooked eggplant flesh won't have that smoky flavour. Brush a whole eggplant lightly with oil, prick several times with a thin metal skewer, place in a roasting dish, then cook in a 180°C (350°F/Gas 4) oven for 45 minutes, or until very soft. Allow to cool before peeling.

grilling (broiling) To grill (broil) eggplant, cut it into slices and brush with oil. Cook over medium heat (on a barbecue or a chargrill plate) for about 3 minutes each side or until well-marked and tender.

selection and storage

Eggplants are quite perishable, so it is important to choose them at their peak. They should be firm and heavy for their size and have taut, shiny, smooth skins. When you press the skin of a larger eggplant, a dent should form but should disappear soon after.

The smaller, tender Japanese eggplants may not spring back when pressed. The calyx end should be a little moist and firmly attached. Store eggplants for no more than 2–3 days, and at cool room temperature in preference to refrigerating. Eggplants don't like cold, and can brown and alter in flavour if refrigerated.

fruit vegetables ▪ eggplant (aubergine)

serves 4

moroccan eggplant
with couscous

185 g (6½ oz/1 cup) instant
  couscous
200 ml (7 fl oz) olive oil
1 onion, halved and sliced
1 eggplant (aubergine)
3 teaspoons ground cumin
¼ teaspoon ground cinnamon
1 teaspoon paprika
¼ teaspoon ground cloves
50 g (1¾ oz) butter
1 handful parsley, roughly
  chopped

Put the couscous in a large bowl and add 375 ml
(1½ cups) boiling water. Leave for 10 minutes, then fluff
with a fork.

Add 2 tablespoons of oil to a large frying pan and cook the
onion for 8–10 minutes, or until browned. Remove from the
pan using a slotted spoon, retaining the cooking oil.

Cut the eggplant into 1 cm (½ inch) slices, then into
quarters, and place in a large bowl. Combine the cumin,
cinnamon, paprika, cloves and ½ teaspoon salt, and sprinkle
over the eggplant, tossing until it is well coated. Add the
remaining oil to the pan and reheat over medium heat. Cook
the eggplant, turning once, for 20–25 minutes,
or until browned. Remove from the pan and cool.

Using the same pan, melt the butter, then add the couscous
and cook, stirring, for 2–3 minutes or until warmed through.
Stir in the onion, eggplant and parsley, allow to cool,
then serve.

For other eggplant (aubergine)
recipes see:

eggplant marinated in chermoula

Cut the eggplants into 1 cm (½ inch) thick slices and sprinkle with salt. Set aside for 30 minutes, then rinse and pat dry. Brush the eggplant slices liberally with olive oil and cook under a preheated grill (broiler) until golden brown on both sides. Drain on paper towels.

To make the chermoula, combine all of the ingredients. Add the eggplant and toss. Cover and refrigerate for 1 hour. Serve at room temperature.

note   Chermoula is also used to marinate fish. The fish, either whole fillets or pieces, is left to marinate overnight, then can be fried, grilled or baked.

2 eggplants (aubergines)
olive oil

chermoula
2 garlic cloves, crushed
1 tablespoon ground cumin
1 teaspoon ground cinnamon
¼ teaspoon cayenne pepper
1 teaspoon allspice
60 ml (2 fl oz/¼ cup) lemon juice
3 tablespoons chopped fresh
   coriander (cilantro) leaves
2 tablespoons chopped mint
125 ml (4 fl oz/½ cup) olive oil

eggplant jam

serves 6–8

Cut the eggplants into 1 cm (½ inch) thick slices. Sprinkle with salt and drain in a colander for 30 minutes. Rinse well, squeeze gently and pat dry. Fill a large frying pan with 5 mm (¼ inch) of olive oil. Place over medium heat and fry the eggplant in batches for 4–5 minutes, turning once, or until golden brown on both sides. Drain on paper towels, then chop finely.

Put the eggplant in a colander and leave it until most of the oil has drained off, then transfer it to a bowl and add the garlic, paprika, cumin, coriander and sugar.

Wipe out the pan, add the eggplant mixture and stir constantly over medium heat for 2 minutes. Transfer to a bowl, stir in the lemon juice and season. Serve at room temperature as a dip, or with other salads.

2 eggplants (aubergines)
olive oil, for shallow-frying
2 garlic cloves, crushed
1 teaspoon paprika
1½ teaspoons ground cumin
2 tablespoons chopped
   coriander (cilantro) leaves
½ teaspoon sugar
1 tablespoon lemon juice

pumpkin (winter squash)

vegetables ▪ **fruit vegetables**
season ▪ **peak season autumn–winter**

Pumpkins, also known as winter squash in the United States, must surely be one of the most versatile of all the vegetables. What other vegetable can be baked alongside the Sunday roast, pureed into the silkiest of soups, can take on intense spices to be cooked in a curry or baked into the sweetest of dessert pies? Pumpkin flesh can even be candied and made into jams and other preserves.

The word 'pumpkin' ultimately traces back to the Greek word for 'melon', *pepon*. American settlers are credited with coining the word pumpkin, deriving it from 'pompion', the English name for pumpkin.

In Mexico, the flowers are enjoyed as a delicacy and pumpkin seeds, called pepitas, have long been roasted and used as a snack, or ground for use as a thickener for all sorts of pastes and sauces. The seeds provide oil too and in the pre-Columbian Americas the shells of some varieties of pumpkin were used to make containers and spoons.

One of the few things you wouldn't do with a pumpkin is serve it raw—other than this caveat, the sky is the limit. Whether it appears in a risotto or a gratin, a mash, a warm salad or in a cake, the unmistakably mellow flavour of pumpkin is a sweet treat.

varieties

There are myriad varieties of pumpkin. They come in all shapes, sizes and colours, from hand-small miniatures to 45 kg (100 lb) monsters. Their skin can be smooth, segmented, ridged or warty and in colour they can range from blue to grey to green and yellow striped to creamy tan. Some are squat and round while others are oblong or bell-shaped.

Generally, pumpkins have very similar flavour although sweetness, flavour intensity, water content and colour of the flesh will vary from type to type. Exceptions to this are the very small types, which are ideal for stuffing, baking and serving as an individual portion—their flavour tends to not be very developed. The highly distinctive spaghetti squash, with its bland, watery flesh that cooks magically into long strands resembling spaghetti, is something of a pumpkin-family oddity.

preparation

Thin-skinned varieties don't need peeling—the skin is quite edible although many prefer to remove it before cooking. Thick skin should be peeled away, best done with a large, sharp knife (sometimes brute strength is required to do this). When cutting away the skin, ensure that you have the pumpkin sitting firmly on a cut side so it can't wobble while you peel.

roasting Pumpkin is sublime when roasted as this method of cooking concentrates its sweetness better than any other. For this purpose it should be cut into chunks, about 5 cm (2 inch) cubes, depending on preference—then tossed in olive oil or butter and cooked in a roasting dish at 200°C (400°F/Gas 6) for about 20–30 minutes, or until golden and very soft. Even pumpkin destined for soup benefits from roasting before being pureed with stock and other ingredients—boiling pumpkin in liquid seems to dull its flavour significantly.

steaming Pumpkin is also good when steamed, after which it can be mashed or pureed—steam large chunks for about 15 minutes in a perforated double-boiler arrangement. Any excess moisture in steamed pumpkin (especially if it is to be mashed) can be driven out by heating it in a saucepan over medium-high heat for 3–4 minutes. Make sure you stir it continuously though, as it will easily catch and burn. For pumpkin pie or other recipes where mashed pumpkin is required, do steam it, as boiling will lead to disappointingly tasteless results.

selection and storage

Buy what is locally grown and seasonally available, according to your needs. For example, a hubbard can weigh over 5 kg (11 lb) and once cut, needs to be used within a few days or it will quickly become mouldy—so decide how much you can deal with at a time before you buy. Butternut pumpkins or the so-called jap and kent pumpkins are a more manageable size, if storing leftovers is an issue.

Whole pumpkins are very good keepers if stored in the right conditions. They should be unblemished and have thick skin, with an amount of stalk remaining to protect the interior from damp.

In a cool, well-ventilated place, they will last for several months; cut pumpkin, as previously noted, is very perishable and should be refrigerated then eaten within a few days. If purchasing cut pieces of pumpkin, select those with bright, gleaming flesh and healthy looking, moist interiors.

serves 4

pumpkin, feta and pine nut pastie

800 g (1 lb 12 oz) pumpkin
  (winter squash), skin
  removed and cut into 1 cm
  (½ inch) thick slices
2 tablespoons olive oil
3 garlic cloves, crushed
4 sheets ready-made puff pastry,
  cut into 15 cm (6 inch) squares
100 g (3½ oz) marinated feta
  cheese in oil
3 tablespoons oregano leaves,
  roughly chopped
2 tablespoons pine nuts, toasted
1 egg yolk
1 tablespoon milk
1 tablespoon sesame seeds

Preheat the oven to 220°C (425°F/Gas 7). Put the pumpkin on a baking tray and toss with the olive oil and garlic and season with sea salt and freshly ground black pepper. Roast for 40 minutes, or until tender and golden. Remove from the oven and cool.

Evenly divide the pumpkin among the four pastry squares, placing it in the centre. Divide feta, oregano and pine nuts into four, placing on top of pumpkin. Drizzle with a little of the feta marinating oil. Bring two of the diagonally opposite corners together and pinch in the centre above the filling. Bring the other two diagonally opposite corners together and pinch to seal along the edges. The base will be square, the top will form a pyramid. Twist the top to seal where all four corners meet.

Place the egg yolk and milk in a small bowl and whisk with a fork to make an eggwash for the pastry.

Place the pasties on a greased baking tray and brush with the eggwash mixture. Sprinkle with sesame seeds and sea salt and bake for 15 minutes, or until golden brown.

Native Americans have been growing and using pumpkins for centuries, as have the Mexicans. In Mexico, Columbus collected pumpkin seeds, taking them back to Europe where initially the fruits of the pumpkin plant were used to nourish pigs. The Europeans ultimately did embrace the pumpkin, although not with as much fervour as the American colonists did—witness its association in that country with festivities such as Halloween and Thanksgiving Day.

spiced pumpkin
and lentil tagine

Rinse the lentils in a sieve. Tip into a saucepan and add
1 litre (35 fl oz/4 cups) cold water. Bring to the boil, skim
the surface to remove any scum, then cover and simmer
over low heat for 20 minutes, or until tender.

Meanwhile, halve the tomatoes widthways and squeeze out
the seeds. Coarsely grate the tomatoes into a bowl down to
the skin. Set the tomato aside. Peel and seed the pumpkin
and cut into 3 cm (1¼ inch) cubes. Set aside

Heat the oil in a large saucepan, add the onion and cook
over low heat until softened. Add the garlic, cook for a few
seconds, then stir in the cumin, turmeric and cayenne
pepper. Cook for 30 seconds, then add the grated tomatoes,
paprika, tomato paste, sugar, half the parsley and coriander.
Season with sea salt and freshly ground pepper. Add the
drained lentils and chopped pumpkin, stir well, then cover
and simmer for 20 minutes, or until the pumpkin and lentils
are tender. Adjust the seasoning and sprinkle with the
remaining parsley and coriander. Serve hot or warm
with baguette.

275 g (9¾ oz/1½ cups) brown
  lentils
2 tomatoes
600 g (1 lb 5 oz) firm pumpkin
  (winter squash) or butternut
  (squash)
60 ml (2 fl oz/¼ cup) olive oil
1 onion, finely chopped
3 garlic cloves, finely chopped
½ teaspoon ground cumin
½ teaspoon ground turmeric
⅛ teaspoon cayenne pepper
1 teaspoon paprika
3 teaspoons tomato paste
  (concentrated puree)
½ teaspoon sugar
1 tablespoon finely chopped
  flat-leaf (Italian) parsley
2 tablespoons chopped
  coriander (cilantro) leaves
baguette, to serve

fruit vegetables ■ pumpkin (winter squash)

For other pumpkin (winter squash)
recipes see:
carrot and pumpkin risotto 186

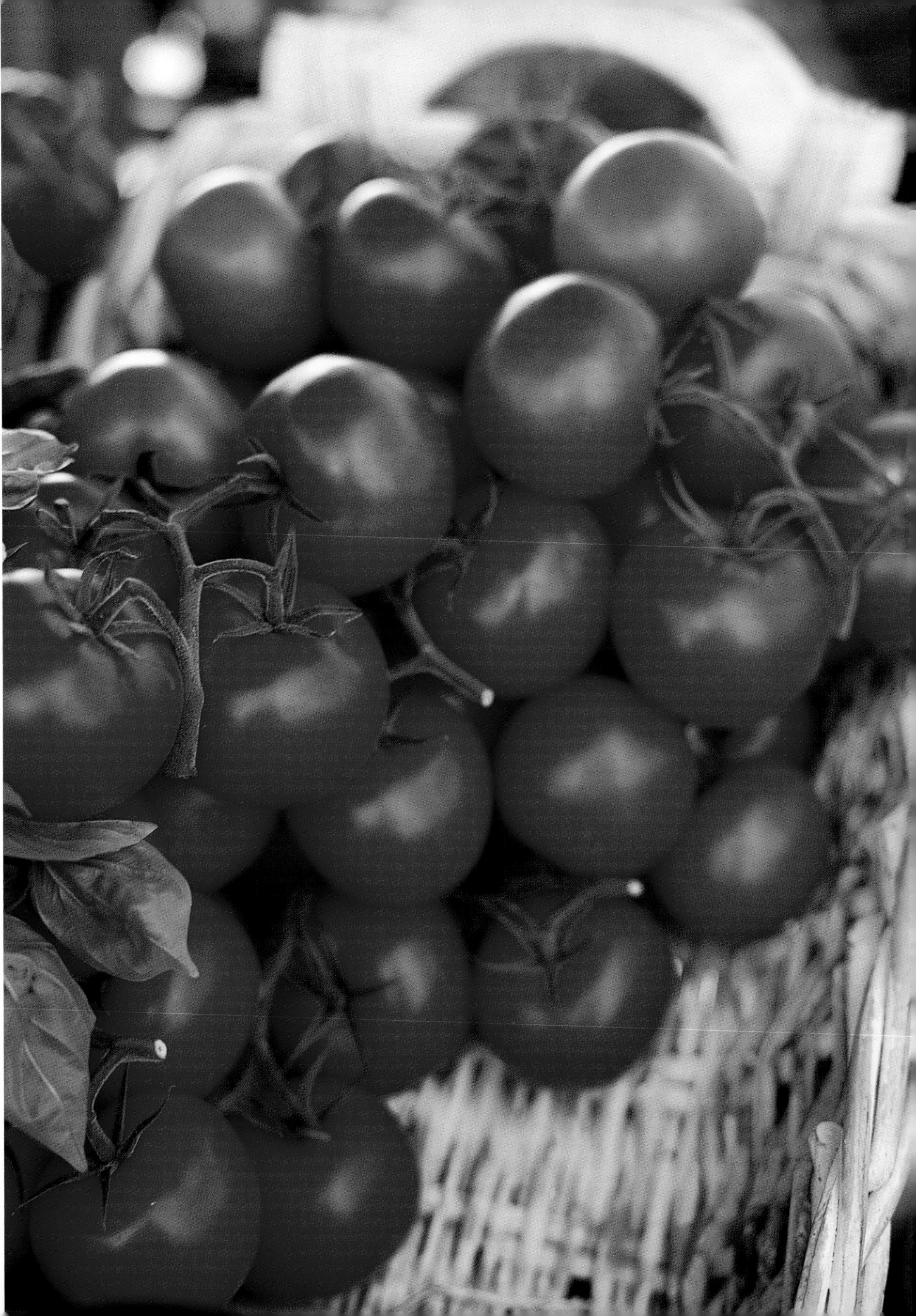

tomato

Thanks (or, more accurately, no thanks) to year-round supply, tomatoes have all but lost their association with the arrival of summer. Not, however, for the legions of home gardeners who lovingly tend their vines and anticipate the summer's crop; in fact, only by growing your own tomatoes, or buying seasonally from a local grower, can you hope to experience that sweet-acid, fragrant, juicy hit of a 'real' tomato. In her worthy *Vegetable Book*, the late Jane Grigson declared the tomato 'needs someone to save it from the dragon of commerce', and it is indisputable that the vast majority of tomatoes that adorn supermarket shelves are pallid, flavourless specimens; one is better off using a good tinned product in cooking instead.

Although the tomato is associated closely with Italy, it is interesting to note that tomato sauce wasn't paired with pasta until the mid-1700s and the tomato didn't become widely popular (and then, only in Italy's south) until the late 1800s. Also of interest is the fact that the Italian name for tomato, *pomodoro*, comes from the earliest name they coined for it, *pomi d'oro* (golden apple), hinting at its original colour. The English name comes ultimately from the Aztec name *tomatl* while the fruit's Latin nomenclature, *Lycopersicon esculentum*, means 'edible wolf's peach'.

nutrition

There's been a lot of press in recent years for the health-promoting properties of tomatoes. This has mainly concerned the lycopene they contain, a substance that gives tomatoes their red colour. Lycopene is a potent antioxidant and is believed to be an effective protector against the development of cancers (particularly prostate cancer in men) and heart disease.

Lycopene is particularly abundant near the skin of the tomato and is said to be more readily absorbed when cooked with certain oils—particularly olive oil.

Tomatoes are also generous providers of vitamins A and C and, in their raw state, vitamin E. They contain a veritable brew of minerals, including potassium, calcium and folic acid.

selection

The best test of a great tomato, even more than its colour, is aroma—smell the stem end and you should be able to inhale strong, sweet-acid tomato wafts. If not, then don't bother buying.

Tomatoes that have been fully ripened on their vines by the sun are terribly perishable, which is exactly the reason that, for supermarket sale, they are picked while green. These tomatoes are then ripened to redness, or sunny yellowness, in controlled environments using ethylene gas and, even though they may look the part, their flavour, aroma and texture never fully develop.

Choose tomatoes that are plump-looking and shiny and that 'give' slightly to pressure when pressed. They should feel heavy for their size and, needless to say, be free of soft spots, blemishes and bruises.

Tomatoes with such skin damage will quickly turn mouldy and spoil.

varieties

It would be near-impossible to comment on every variety of tomato—even to include all those which are commonly available worldwide would require a lengthy discourse. It is perhaps more helpful to talk generally of types of tomatoes. Each tomato variety has unique characteristics. Variables include skin thickness, flesh density, juiciness and the size and quantity of seeds, making some more suitable for certain uses over others.

cherry Cherry tomatoes have the greatest amount of sugar of all the tomato types and their taste is a concentrated burst of tomato sweetness. These are a good choice for eating raw whether tossed through salads, coarsely chopped into a salsa or pureed to form an uncooked sauce or used to flavour vinaigrette. They can, of course, be cooked and are perfect when halved and used to top a home-made pizza or, tossed with a little olive oil, briefly roasted and served as a vegetable side dish with fish, chicken or meat. They can also be cooked in the pan with quick-cooking meat cuts (a lamb loin for example) or fillets of fish.

beefsteak These are the giants of the tomato world, needing hot, late-summer sun to fully ripen. Beefsteaks have a unique ribbed shape and their firm, juicy flesh (of which their name is highly descriptive) is punctuated throughout by little pockets of seeds. Because of their shape and size, they lend themselves to being sliced and slipped into hamburgers or sandwiches. They can be used in salads—cut into pieces or baton shapes—and are also a good choice for cooking.

green Some heirloom varieties are green when ripe but generally, tomatoes sold as 'green' are those at the end of the season, which will fail to fully ripen in the cooling weather. If set on a sunny ledge, though, they may continue to ripen; however green tomatoes have special characteristics and uses of their own. Firm, not as juicy as their ripe counterparts and piquant-tasting, green tomatoes are wonderful when made into relishes and chutneys, and their suitability for frying is legendary.

golden or yellow Most red varieties have a golden equivalent, from cherry tomatoes through to plums and the large beefsteaks. These taste more or less identical to red tomatoes (although some claim that yellow cherry tomatoes are sweeter than red) and can be used in exactly the same ways.

round or salad These rounded, squat, medium-sized tomatoes are the best known and most used, perhaps, of all the tomato types. Generally they have quite juicy interiors with large seed cavities and are a good all-purpose tomato; their shape lends itself to slicing, dicing or cutting into wedges for salads, to hollowing out for stuffing and baking, or to cutting in half (either width or length-wise) or quarters and roasting, grilling (broiling), pan-frying or semi-drying in a coolish oven. They are also suitable for chopping, and using in sauces, stews and soups.

roma (plum) These tomatoes are characterized by their thickish skin, elongated shape and large interior 'core'. They are variously called 'egg', 'Italian' and 'paste' tomatoes and are great for cooking as their flesh is particularly dense and firm—they hold their shape well when cooked. They have fewer seeds than other sorts of tomatoes and have less juicy (but no less flavoursome), meaty flesh. Use these wherever it is necessary to cook tomatoes—in pasta and other sauces, in casseroles, soups and braises. These are also very good for oven- (or sun-) drying and also for preserving for winter use.

preparation

So many recipes tell the cook to peel the tomatoes, but many neglect to explain how. In most dishes that utilize tomatoes, removing the skin is a necessary refinement, as is, on occasion, the removal of the seeds. Author Marcella Hazan puts it thus, 'A tomato's skin is a veil which obscures the wonders of its flesh. If you leave it on, the tomatoes will eventually shed their skin as they cook and later you will either have to spit it out or, since it is not pleasant to chew on, swallow it.'

peeling Using a small, sharp knife, cut a small cross-shaped incision into the base of your tomatoes (some people cut quite large ones; this is unnecessary) then drop them, a few at a time, into a saucepan of boiling water. Leave them for about 20 seconds (the time is variable depending on tomato ripeness and variety) then remove them with a slotted spoon and immediately plunge them into iced water. Pull the skin away, starting from the cross-shaped incision (a small knife can be useful here); it should come off very easily. If not, the tomatoes have not been blanched for long enough. Beware of leaving them in the boiling water for too long as this will cause the flesh to become mushy—it should still be firm and 'suede-like' when the skin is peeled.

seeding To seed tomatoes, cut them into quarters after they have been blanched and the stem end removed. You can use your fingers to nudge the seeds and their flavoursome, jelly-like surrounds out. Collect the seeds and reserve for some other use—in stock-making, soups or pasta sauces for example. To seed a whole tomato for baking, cut the top centimetre or so off an unseeded tomato then use a teaspoon to scoop out the seeds and soft pulp.

storage

Tomatoes should be stored at cool room temperature, out of their packaging and definitely not in the refrigerator—and used within a few days.

The refrigerator diminishes the flavour of tomatoes; as a sub-tropical fruit, they do not like the cold. If you purchase under-ripe tomatoes (those with green 'shoulders' or the occasional green patch, for example) they will ripen fully, given the right conditions. Leave them somewhere warm and in full sunlight if possible.

The best way to store a glut of tomatoes for future use is by freezing. This can most easily be done by simply freezing them whole—once they thaw the skins will slip easily off and you just need to cut away the stem end. Alternatively, they can be frozen peeled and chopped or peeled and pureed.

serves 4

tomato tarte tatin

12 roma (plum) tomatoes
4 tablespoons olive oil
3 red onions, finely sliced
2 garlic cloves, finely sliced
1 tablespoon balsamic vinegar
1 teaspoon soft brown sugar
1 handful basil, finely chopped
60 g (2¼ oz/⅓ cup) crumbled
   goat's cheese
1 sheet ready-made puff pastry

Preheat the oven to 150°C (300°F/Gas 2). Score a cross in the top of each tomato, plunge into boiling water for 20 seconds, transfer to a bowl of iced water to cool, and then peel the skin and discard. Cut tomatoes in half lengthways, and season well. Place the tomatoes, cut side up, on a rack on a baking tray. Cook in the oven for 3 hours.

Heat 2 tablespoons of oil in a heavy-based saucepan, add the onions and cook over very low heat, stirring often, for 1 hour or until caramelized.

When the tomatoes are ready, remove from the oven and increase the oven temperature to 200°C (400°F/Gas 6).

In a 20 cm (8 inch) ovenproof frying pan heat the remaining olive oil over medium heat. Add the garlic, vinegar, sugar and 1 tablespoon of water and cook until the sugar dissolves. Remove from the heat. Arrange the tomatoes in concentric circles inside the pan, cut side up, in one layer. Top with the onions, basil and crumbled goat's cheese. Cover with the puff pastry, trim the edges, and tuck the pastry into the side of the pan around the tomatoes. Bake for 25–30 minutes, or until the pastry is golden. Carefully invert the tart onto a plate, cool to room temperature and serve.

For other tomato recipes see:

spiced baby turnips 236
avocado salsa................................333
avocado and bacon salad 333
nicoise salad with green beans
   and seared tuna 377
greek salad....................................425
tabbouleh 427
thyme-flavoured semi-dried
   tomatoes 435

The tomato is an Andean native. It grew wild in various regions of South America and, although eaten by pre-Colombian peoples, wasn't considered worthy of domestication. These early tomatoes were small (about the size of the cherry tomato we know today) and yellow.

fennel, tomato and garlic gratin

Preheat the oven to 200°C (400°F/Gas 6). Grease a 22 cm (8½ inch) square gratin dish. Cut the fennel in half lengthways, then slice thinly.

Heat the oil in a large frying pan. Cook the onion for 3–4 minutes until softened but not browned. Add the garlic and cook for 2 minutes. Add the fennel and cook, stirring frequently, for 7 minutes, or until softened and golden brown.

Score a cross in the top of each tomato, plunge into boiling water for 20 seconds, transfer to a bowl of iced water to cool, and then peel the skin and discard it. Chop the tomato flesh roughly and add to the fennel. Cook, stirring frequently, for 5 minutes, or until the tomato is softened. Season well and pour into the dish.

To make the gratin topping, mix together all the ingredients, sprinkle over the vegetables and bake for 15 minutes, or until golden brown and crisp. Serve immediately.

900 g (2 lb or about 2) fennel
   bulbs
80 ml (2½ fl oz/⅓ cup) olive oil
1 large red onion, halved and
   thinly sliced
2 garlic cloves, crushed
450 g (1 lb) tomatoes

gratin topping
60 g (2¼ oz/¾ cup) fresh white
   breadcrumbs
65 g (2½ oz/⅔ cup) grated
   parmesan cheese
2 teaspoons grated lemon zest
1 garlic clove, crushed

fruit vegetables ■ tomato

For many centuries it was believed the tomato was poisonous (not an unreasonable assumption given that it is a nightshade family member and its leaves are, in fact, toxic) and an aphrodisiac. The wealthy, in particular, spurned the tomato although they did grow them for ornamental purposes—poorer classes started eating them out of necessity. Eventually, seeds of red tomatoes were taken to Italy from Mexico and then the tomato really started to take off as a culinary item.

slow-roasted balsamic tomatoes

makes 40

10 firm roma (plum) tomatoes
8 garlic cloves, crushed
80 g (2¾ oz/⅓ cup) caster (superfine) sugar
4 tablespoons torn basil leaves
4 teaspoons chopped oregano leaves
few drops good-quality balsamic vinegar

Preheat the oven to 140°C (275°F/Gas 1). Line two baking trays with baking paper. Cut each tomato lengthways into quarters and put the quarters in rows on the trays.

Mix the garlic with the sugar, basil, oregano and balsamic vinegar. Using clean fingers, put a little of the mixture onto the sides of each tomato quarter and season with sea salt and freshly ground black pepper.

Bake in the oven for 2½ hours. The tomatoes are ready when they are slightly shrivelled at the edge and semi-dried (they should still be soft in the middle). Eat warm or cold and store in the refrigerator. Serve with barbecued lamb chops, beef steak or as part of an antipasti selection.

tomato sauce

makes 200 ml (7 fl oz)

125 g (4½ oz) roma (plum) tomatoes
3 basil leaves
2 garlic cloves, crushed
1 tablespoon tomato passata (puree)
2 teaspoons extra virgin olive oil

Core the tomatoes and puree in a food processor with the basil leaves (or chop the tomatoes and basil very finely and stir together).

Stir in the garlic, tomato passata and olive oil and season well. Leave for at least 30 minutes to allow the flavours to blend. Use on pizzas, toss through pasta or serve as a sauce with arancini.

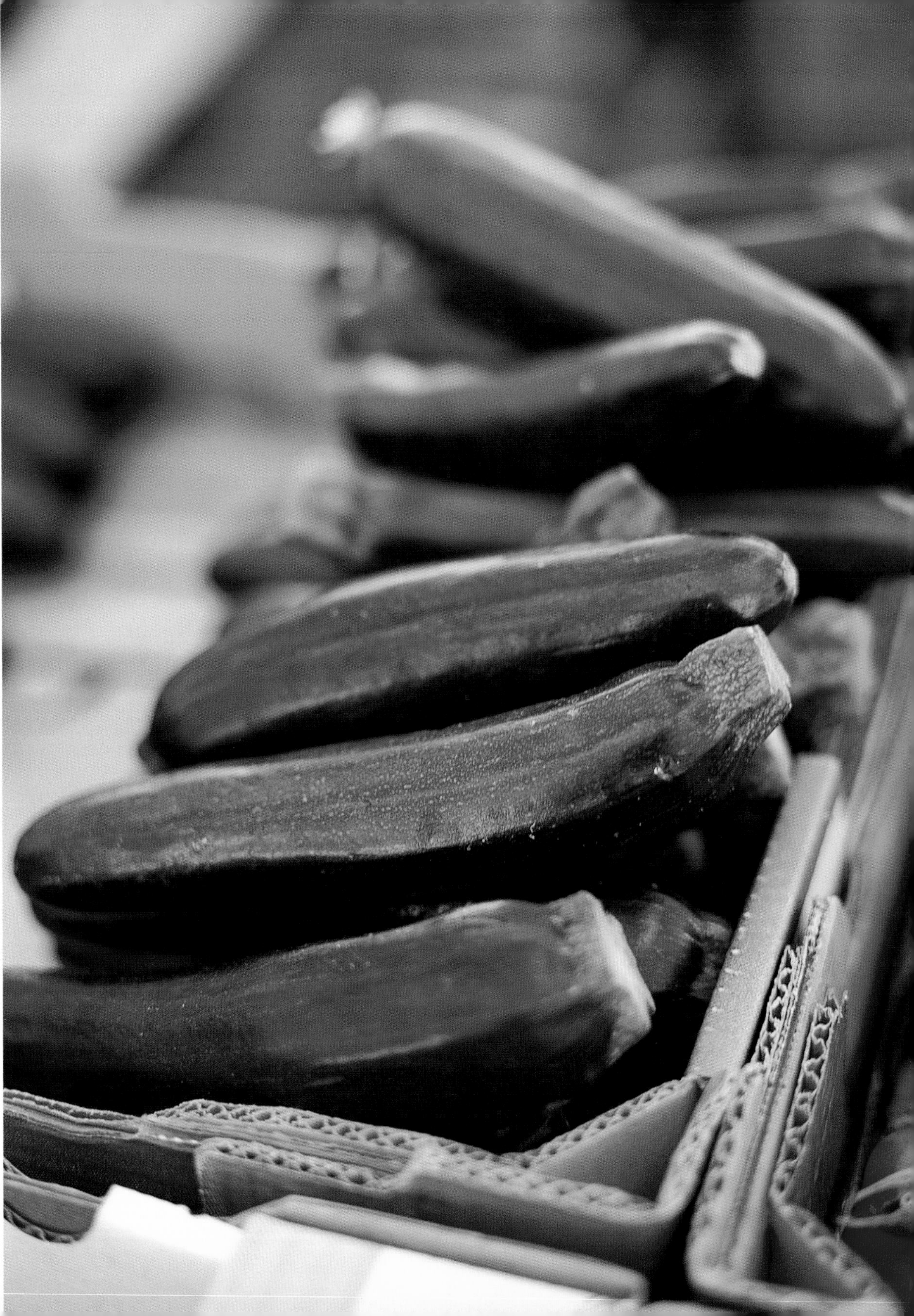

zucchini (courgette)

Despite their distinctly Italian name, these members of the summer squash family are Mexican natives. Since ancient times, squash, beans and maize have been an integral part of the indigenous diet in the Americas, and are a mainstay even today. Squash were one of the many foodstuffs taken back to Europe by Spanish explorers; although embraced in parts of the continent, it has taken a while for them to become mainstream in England and the United States.

Essentially, zucchini are immature vine fruits which, if left to grow, will do so to a prodigious size, very quickly becoming a marrow with tough skin, bland, watery flesh and large, hard seeds. When young and small, they instead have a delicate sweetness and every part is edible—skin, seeds and flesh. They are generally cylindrical, although there are round varieties too, and the pattypan squash, with its flat, round shape and pretty scalloped edge, is a close, and similar-tasting, relative.

Zucchini come in green, yellow and so-called 'white' varieties; this latter is in reality a pale green colour and is slightly bulbous in shape whereas the others are slim and cylindrical. Another newish variety is the round globe which, at about 8 cm (3 inches) in diameter, is perfect for scooping out, stuffing and baking.

squash

zucchini represent just one of the many 'summer' or 'tender' squashes available—there is also the crookneck squash; the round globe squash; the oval squash, like the scallopini; or pattypan squash. Pattypan squash are prized for their flesh which, when young and in prime condition, is buttery and dense. These squash are usually a distinctive yellow colour, but can also be either deep bright or pale green.

Choose small firm squash and steam them whole, for about 8–10 minutes, or until tender. Larger ones can be par-boiled for a few minutes, the insides scooped out, replaced with a stuffing and then baked—a fresh breadcrumb stuffing, with plenty of chopped fresh herbs (basil, parsley, oregano) and parmesan cheese works beautifully.

selection and storage

Zucchinis should be firm and have shiny, tight, unblemished skins with no bruises or brown spots. The skin is very delicate (you should be able to pierce it with your fingernail), so a few scratches from harvesting and transporting are probably inevitable. Inside, the flesh should be creamy and bright and have the tiniest of seeds.

Don't store these vegetables for long as their delicate, sweet flavour is marred by storage—no longer than 2 days in a ventilated bag in the crisper section of the refrigerator. Don't wash zucchini until you are about to cook them or they may start to spoil.

preparation

Zucchinis are a breeze to prepare. They require washing, need their stem-end trimmed, then just have to be sliced, grated, chopped or halved lengthways, depending on the use. They are quickly cooked and the methods they are best suited to are steaming, stir-frying, baking, sautéing, braising or barbecuing.

steaming Steamed zucchini will be tender in about 3 minutes in a double-boiler arrangement. Stir-frying and sautéing are equally quick to accomplish.

chargrilling To chargrill or barbecue zucchini, slice them lengthways into strips about 5 mm (1/4 inch) thick, brush all over with olive oil then cook for about 1 minute on each side on a medium-hot chargrill plate or barbecue.

culinary uses

There are a plethora of fabulous, zucchini-based recipes to cook. And to *not* cook—they can, after all be served raw, as the Italians do, thinly sliced and dressed with oil, lemon juice, mint, and salt and pepper. Grated zucchini can be bound with a little flour and egg and cooked into delicious fritters—there are even recipes for zucchini cakes and sweet zucchini muffins, similar in spirit to the ever-popular carrot cake.

Zucchinis can be employed, along with other summer produce, suh as tomatoes, eggplant (aubergine) and capsicums (peppers), in sunny vegetable salads or soups, but are arguably at their best when simply sliced into thin rounds and quickly sautéed in olive oil with garlic and fresh thyme.

Mild-tasting zucchinis take well to the robust flavours of garlic, ginger, good-quality vinegars (balsamic, red wine and sherry, for example), lemon and anchovies. Classic Mediterranean ingredients like oregano, mint, tomatoes, pine nuts, parmesan and pecorino cheeses, basil and mint also complement zucchini.

zucchini fritters

Put the zucchini and onion in the centre of a clean tea (dish) towel, gather the corners together and twist as tightly as possible to remove all the juices. Combine the zucchini, onion, flour, cheese, mint, parsley, nutmeg, breadcrumbs and egg in a large bowl. Season with sea salt and freshly ground black pepper, then mix with your hands to a stiff mixture that clumps together.

Heat the oil in a large frying pan over medium heat. When hot, drop tablespoons of mixture into the pan and shallow-fry for 2–3 minutes, or until well browned all over. Drain well on crumpled paper towels and serve hot with lemon wedges or tsatsiki.

300 g (10½ oz or about 3) zucchini (courgettes), grated
1 small onion, finely chopped
30 g (1 oz/¼ cup) self-raising flour
35 g (1¼ oz/⅓ cup) grated parmesan cheese
1 tablespoon chopped mint
2 teaspoons chopped flat-leaf (Italian) parsley
1 pinch of ground nutmeg
25 g (1 oz/¼ cup) dry breadcrumbs
1 egg, lightly beaten
olive oil, for shallow-frying
tsatsiki (see page 343), to serve

zucchini, radish and feta salad

serves 4

To make the dressing, combine the white wine vinegar, olive oil and mustard. Season with sea salt and freshly ground black pepper.

Shave the zucchini into strips from top to bottom. Place in a colander, sprinkle with 2 teaspoons of sea salt and set aside to drain in the sink for 30 minutes. Do not rinse. Gently dry with paper towels and put in a large bowl. Finely slice the radishes and onion and add to the bowl. Tear the inner leaves of the lettuce into smaller pieces and add to the bowl with the dressing and toss lightly. Transfer to a serving dish and scatter the crumbled feta cheese over the top before serving.

dressing
1 tablespoon white wine vinegar
2 tablespoons olive oil
2–3 teaspoons wholegrain mustard

5 small zucchini (courgettes)
6 radishes
½ small red onion
1 small cos (romaine) lettuce
100 g (3½ oz/⅔ cup) crumbled feta cheese

serves 8

chargrilled vegetable terrine

8 large slices chargrilled
eggplant (aubergine), drained
(see page 347)
10 slices chargrilled red
capsicum (pepper), drained
(see page 336)
8 slices chargrilled zucchini
(courgette), drained
(see page 364)
350 g (12 oz/1⅓ cups) ricotta
cheese
2 garlic cloves, crushed
2 handfuls rocket (arugula)
3 marinated artichokes, drained
and sliced
85 g (3 oz/½ cup) semi-dried
tomatoes, drained and
chopped
100 g (3½ oz) marinated
mushrooms, drained and
halved

Line a 23.5 x 13 x 6.5 cm (9¼ x 5 x 2½ inch) loaf (bar) tin with plastic wrap, leaving a generous overhang on each side. Line the base with half the eggplant, cutting to fit. Next, layer in half the capsicum, then all of the zucchini.

Beat the ricotta cheese and garlic together until smooth. Season with sea salt and freshly ground black pepper, then spread evenly over the zucchini. Press down firmly and top with the rocket leaves. Arrange the marinated artichoke, tomato and mushrooms in three strips over the rocket. Top with another layer of capsicum and finish with the eggplant.

Cover securely with the overhanging plastic wrap. Top with a piece of cardboard and a weight to weigh down the vegetables (tinned food is good for this). Chill the terrine in the refrigerator overnight.

Peel back the plastic wrap and carefully turn out the terrine onto a plate. Remove the plastic wrap and cut into thick slices to serve.

The word zucchini is from the Italian zuccherino *meaning 'small squash'; the French name* courgette, *which is also used in England, is from* courge, *for marrow. 'Squash' is from the American Indian word* askutasquash, *which means 'green thing eaten green' or 'raw'.*

zucchini flower

vegetables ▪ **fruit vegetables**
season ▪ **summer**

The Italians have known, since they started growing zucchinis (courgettes), that the flowers are an absolute treat—slowly but surely, the rest of the zucchini-loving world is catching on too. They are very perishable (they need to be eaten within a day or two of picking) and actually rather nutritious, containing decent amounts of folic acid.

There are male and female flowers, with females being more robust and requiring a slightly longer cooking time than their more delicate male counterparts. Whichever sex is on offer, only buy zucchini flowers that look firm and fresh, with petals that are only slightly open. Brush them gently to remove their furry down covering and gently rinse the insides to flush out any insect life. Some people detach the pistils, while others don't bother.

The flowers can be put to myriad uses—they can be lightly battered and fried, stuffed and baked, or sautéed with a few aromatics, such as garlic, anchovies and herbs. They can be sliced and stirred through pastas, risottos and soups, or cooked into a frittata. Should you need to store your flowers for a day or so, place them in a damp cloth-lined dish, lay in a single layer then cover and refrigerate.

papardelle with zucchini flowers and goat's cheese

Combine the ricotta, cream, thyme and nutmeg in a bowl and season well with sea salt and white pepper. Set aside in a cool place (do not refrigerate) for 1 hour.

Cook the pasta in a saucepan of boiling salted water until *al dente*. Meanwhile, heat the olive oil in a large frying pan over medium-high heat and cook the zucchini for 4 minutes, or until lightly golden. Remove the zucchini with a slotted spoon and drain on paper towels.

Dust the zucchini flowers with flour, shake off the excess and fry for about 1 minute, or until lightly golden.

Drain the pasta and transfer to a large serving dish. Add the zucchini, zucchini flowers and ricotta mixture and toss lightly. Dot with small pieces of goat's cheese, to serve.

175 g (6 oz/¾ cup) ricotta cheese
125 ml (4 fl oz/½ cup) thick (double/heavy) cream
2 teaspoons fresh thyme
¼ teaspoon ground nutmeg
300 g (10½ oz) dried papardelle pasta or 400 g (14 oz) fresh papardelle or other ribbon pasta
60 ml (2 fl oz/¼ cup) olive oil
4 small zucchini (courgettes), cut into thin batons
16 zucchini (courgette) flowers, no vegetable attached
plain (all-purpose) flour, for dusting
100 g (3½ oz/⅔ cup) crumbled goat's cheese

fruit vegetables ▪ zucchini flower

Any variety of squash, not just the zucchini, provides edible flowers and in many countries (Mexico, Italy and France, for example), these are used as everyday fare, not as a rarified treat, which is often the case. Often, advice is given to remove the pistils and stamens (the upright inner parts of the bloom) but this isn't really necessary—they are perfectly edible, just a little crunchy.

broad (fava) beans

vegetables ▪ **seeds and pods**
season ▪ **early spring–early summer**

selection and storage

Select pods that are smooth and pale green and without blackening on their ends, or any wrinkles. Also avoid any that are bulgy as this indicates large, hard beans within, which will not make for memorable bean feasting. If possible, break a pod open and check that the pillowy white lining is moist and the beans have taut, smooth skins.

Store broad beans, in their pods, in a ventilated plastic bag in the refrigerator for up to 3 days. Podded, the beans can be frozen for up to 3 months— you can cook them while still frozen.

Before green beans and all the other varieties of bean came to Europe out of the New World, broad beans were *the* bean. Broad beans have been around for so long that it isn't known exactly where they came from—they have become very widespread, common to the cuisines of the Mediterranean, the Middle East, China and South America. These are the beans of *Jack and the Beanstalk*, 'spilling the beans' and being 'full of beans'.

Broad beans are enclosed in a soft, downy substance, inside a large, slightly dimpled, green pod. Pods vary in length from 18–23 cm (7–9 inches) and can contain up to eight fleshy seeds. The first broad beans of spring are small and tender; as the season progresses, they become larger and take on starchier, less sweet characteristics. The first fresh broad beans of spring have an almost cult following among chefs and certain ethnic populations; if these are very young and tender, peeling is not necessary. Nothing else comes close to their nutty, vegetal sweetness.

Since ancient times, broad beans, or fava beans as they are also commonly called, have been an invaluable source of non-meat protein, although to provide this they need to be eaten in tandem with grains, such as pearl barley or dried legumes (dried peas and beans) or seeds.

Broad beans have long been associated with the supernatural and were once placed on gravesites in England to repel ghosts. In Scotland, for example, it was believed witches rode not on broomsticks but on bean stalks, and in some cultures it was believed that dead souls could transmigrate into broad beans.

371

preparation

Broad beans require two steps of preparation—first, they must be podded and then you need to peel them. If you intend to serve your beans pretty much straight after cooking, as a simple side dish or in a recipe that requires them to be fully tender (a puree or dip, for example) then simmer the beans until tender (about 10 minutes for young broad beans and 20 minutes for more mature beans). Drain and cool, until they can be handled comfortably, then peel. Reheat them briefly if necessary for a moment or two in a little simmering water or toss in a hot frying pan with some butter or olive oil before serving.

If you intend to add broad beans to a dish such as a risotto or a soup where they will receive additional cooking, just blanch them for 2–3 minutes in boiling water, drain well then cool in a bowl of iced water. Drain again and peel—the skins will slip off quite willingly.

When buying fresh beans it is worth noting that 1 kg (2 lb 4 oz) of broad beans will yield about 300 g (10½ oz/1½ cups) of podded beans.

culinary uses

The first broad beans of the season are sweet and tender and are best treated simply—steam them, drizzle with olive oil and serve with flakes of sea salt as a simple starter—add a few slices of prosciutto or salami and you're practically in Italy. These young tender beans are excellent tossed through fresh pasta with a saffron cream sauce or piled beside a piece of steamed salmon.

Older broad beans have tougher skins, a mealier texture and a less sweet flavour—use these for a puree (with garlic and some olive oil) to spread on crostini, or cook them in a minestrone-style soup or a mixed spring vegetables stew (think artichoke, peas, asparagus and new potatoes).

seeds and pods ■ broad (fava) beans

borlotti beans

Borlotti beans are another type of shell bean—a bean with largish seeds inside a glorious red-speckled pod. It is the seeds that are eaten and, in many cases, these are left to reach full maturity at which point they are dried. When harvested mature, but not yet dried, the beans have a dryish, creamy white flesh inside plump smooth seeds.

Choose borlotti with leathery pods with a lumpy surface. Borlotti should be simmered gently for 15–30 minutes, or until tender. Never boil them, as this will only make them tougher.

serves 4

broad bean rotollo
with salad greens

rotollo

275 g (9¾ oz/1½ cups) shelled
broad (fava) beans
4 eggs
4 egg yolks
2 teaspoons finely chopped mint
2 teaspoons finely chopped basil
20 g (¾ oz) butter
80 g (2¾ oz/1 cup) grated
pecorino cheese

salad

1½ tablespoons pine nuts
1 tablespoon chopped basil
80 ml (2½ fl oz/⅓ cup) olive oil
2 tablespoons lemon juice
2 baby cos (romaine) lettuces,
trimmed
2 witlof (chicory/Belgian endive)
preferably purple, trimmed

To make the rotollo, bring a medium saucepan of water to the boil. Add a large pinch of salt and the broad beans and simmer for 2 minutes. Drain and plunge into iced water. Drain and peel the skins off the beans, discarding the skins.

Preheat the oven to 160°C (315°F/Gas 2–3). Beat the eggs, egg yolks, mint and basil together. Season with sea salt and freshly ground black pepper. Melt half the butter in a non-stick frying pan over medium–high heat. Pour in half the egg mixture and cook until the base has set but the top is still a little runny.

Slide the omelette from the pan onto a sheet of baking paper. Scatter half the pecorino cheese and half the broad beans over the surface. Using the baking paper as a guide, gently roll the omelette into a tight sausage. Roll the baking paper around the omelette and tie both ends with string to prevent it from unrolling. Place on a baking tray. Make another roll with the remaining ingredients and put on the baking tray. Bake for 8 minutes. Remove from the oven, set aside for 2–3 minutes, then unwrap and set aside to cool.

Put the pine nuts in a small dry saucepan over medium heat and toast, stirring and tossing constantly, for 4–5 minutes, or until the nuts are golden-brown and fragrant. Tip the nuts into a bowl so they do not cook further from the residual heat, and allow to cool.

To make the salad, put 1 tablespoon of the pine nuts, the basil, olive oil and lemon juice in a small food processor or blender and process until smooth. Season with sea salt and freshly ground black pepper. Put the cos and witlof leaves in a bowl and dress with 2 tablespoons of the dressing. Serve the rotollo, cut into slices, over the salad.

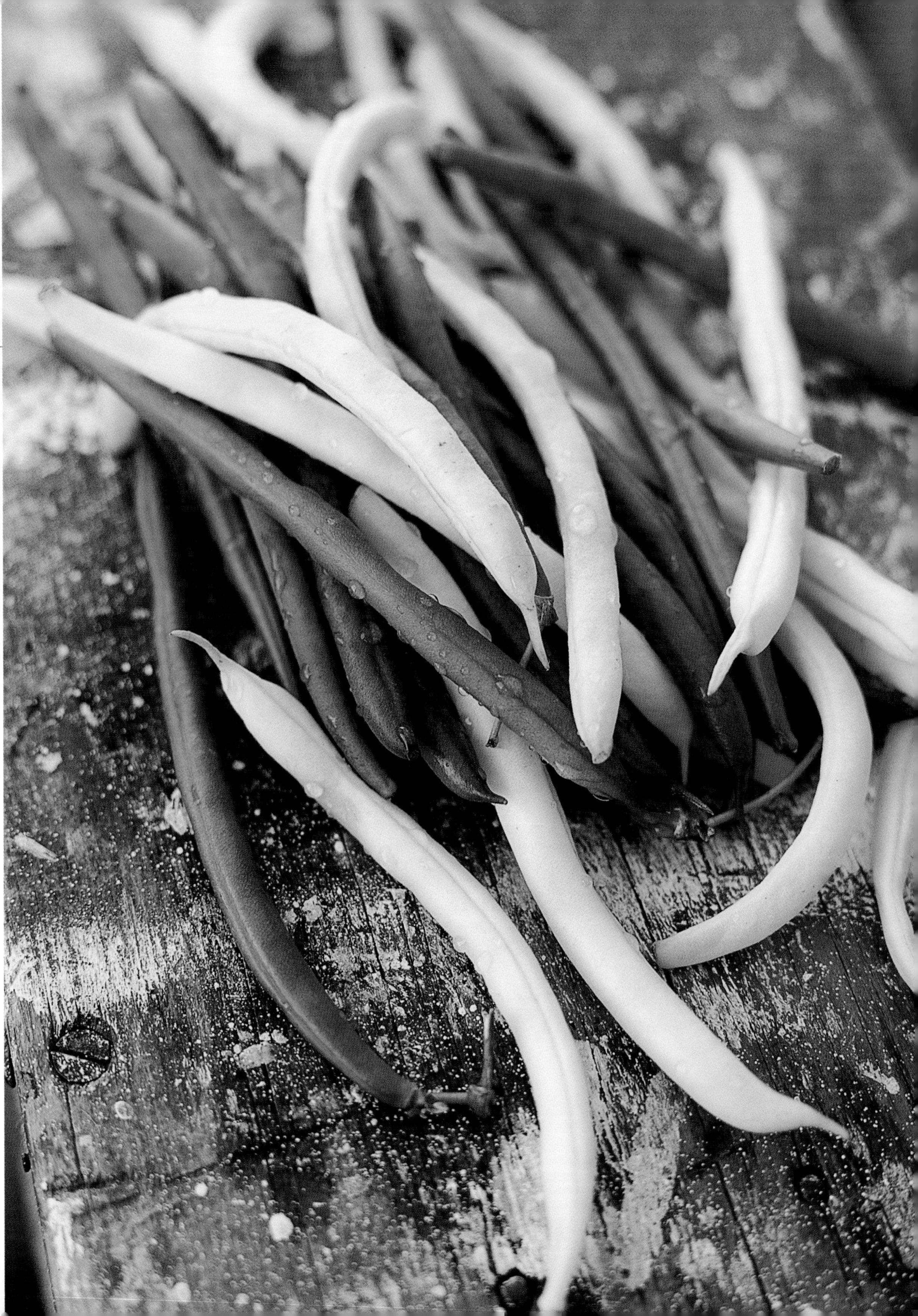

green beans

Green beans are another New World native—most likely from Peru—and are related to kidney beans, pinto beans, black beans, and all those other beans that are only used once reconstituted from a dried state. In fact, the various green beans are amongst the few from the bean family that are consumed fresh, and the only ones used pod and all.

Green beans are actually picked when immature—if allowed to keep growing, their tiny seeds would become large and their pods very tough—the 'green' in their name refers to their immaturity when picked and not their colour. In fact, these beans come in a range of hues, from light to bright to deep green; from yellow to purple to mottled cream and russet. They also vary greatly in pod size and shape, from the tiniest, tenderest *haricots verts* (green string bean), so prized by the French and just a few centimetres long, to the large Italian flat beans which can be up to 25 cm (10 inches) in length. Green beans are also called 'snap' beans (and indeed, a fresh bean should 'snap' when you bend it) and 'string' beans because of the fibrous string that ran down the length of earlier varieties and needed to be removed. Most beans these days are bred to be stringless so this is no longer necessary.

selection and storage

If beans are bendable, leave them behind; they should break crisply. The pods should be smooth and uniformly coloured with almost imperceptible seed bumps underneath; swellings where the seeds are indicate they are over-mature and will not taste great. The pointy ends should be perky and undamaged and there should be no wrinkling, bruises or shrivelled spots.

Store beans in a ventilated plastic bag in the refrigerator for up to 3 days.

varieties

butter (wax) Also known as wax beans, these beans are a pretty yellow colour. Buy butter beans that have a slight green tinge, as these are younger and better tasting than those that are yellow all over. Wax beans have a gentler flavour than green beans so serve them simply; steamed and dressed with butter is perfect.

green Often called French beans, there are many types of green beans—from short and slim to fat and long. Green beans are best boiled in plenty of salted water or steamed; they can also be roasted in olive oil, which concentrates their sweet, grassy flavours.

flat Sometimes called Italian beans, these beans are flat and long, full flavoured and meaty textured. They are suited to long cooking in soups, stews and braises and can even be barbecued until tender.

purple Like green beans only a lovely dark mauve colour, purple beans, unfortunately, don't keep their fabulous colour when cooked, turning green. Use them as you would green beans.

preparation

'If you know how to cook a green bean you know how to cook anything', Australian food personality Joan Campbell once famously declared, possibly in reaction to all those overly crisp, undercooked bright green beans so often served up in fashionable restaurants. In stark contrast, some ethnic cooks aren't afraid to braise green beans for 20 minutes until they are deep olive green and incredibly tender.

boiling The best way to cook beans for most uses is to boil them in plenty of salted water for 4–7 minutes, depending on the size of the bean and whether they are whole, halved or sliced. Before cooking, check there are no strings on your beans—remove these if they are present.

Trim the 'top' end of each bean (where it was attached to the plant). It is not necessary to trim the 'tail' end. To prepare beans for use in salads it is best to sightly undercook them, drain them well then leave to cool. Many sources tell you to plunge the just-cooked beans into iced water to cool—this preserves their bright green colour but compromizes their flavour.

roasting Beans can also be roasted whole. Trim them then toss in generous amounts of olive oil and roast in a 180°C (350°F/Gas 4) oven, in a single layer in a roasting dish. They will take about 20 minutes to cook.

nicoise salad with green beans and seared tuna

Whisk together the olive oil, garlic, dijon mustard and champagne vinegar. Season well. Brush the tuna with olive oil. Fry on a hot barbecue or in a frying pan until browned, about 1½–2 minutes each side. Remove from the heat.

Cook the beans in boiling salted water for 3 minutes, or until just tender. Remove with tongs and drain. Scrub the baby potatoes, cut in half and add to the saucepan. Boil for 12 minutes, or until tender. Drain and put in a shallow salad bowl with the lettuce leaves. Add 2 tablespoons of the dressing and toss gently to coat. Scatter the cherry tomatoes on top.

Slice the tuna diagonally into 5 mm (¼ inch) slices and arrange on the tomatoes. Add the cooked beans and 12 black olives. Cut the hard-boiled eggs into wedges and add to the salad. Arrange the anchovy fillets in a cross on top. Top with salted capers and drizzle with the remaining dressing.

80 ml (2½ fl oz/⅓ cup) olive oil
2 garlic cloves, crushed
1 teaspoon dijon mustard
1 tablespoon champagne vinegar
two 150 g (5½ oz) tuna fillets
225 g (8 oz) green beans, trimmed
450 g (1 lb) baby potatoes
2 large handfuls torn green lettuce leaves
8 cherry tomatoes, halved
12 black olives
2 eggs, hard-boiled
4 anchovies, halved
1 tablespoon salted capers, drained and rinsed

seeds and pods ▪ green beans

butter beans with sun-dried tomatoes and capers

serves 4

Slice the sun-dried tomatoes into long, thin strips. Heat the oil from the sun-dried tomatoes in a small frying pan over medium heat and fry the capers, stirring often, for about 1 minute, or until darkened and crisp. Drain on paper towels.

Bring a saucepan of salted water to the boil. Add the beans and simmer for 3–4 minutes, or until just tender. Drain, season with freshly ground black pepper and toss with the sun-dried tomatoes, capers, olive oil and lemon zest. Serve hot or at room temperature.

2 sun-dried tomatoes in oil, plus 1 teaspoon of oil, extra
2 teaspoons capers, drained and rinsed
250 g (9 oz) young butter beans (wax beans), trimmed
1 teaspoon light olive oil
zest of 1 lemon, cut into thin strips

okra

vegetables ■ seeds and pods
season ■ summer–autumn

The world is divided firmly into two types of people—the okra lovers and the okra haters. Few other vegetables seem to spark such polarization and the number one reason for it is, in a word, ooze. Okra contains mucilaginous juices that give it its renowned texture and although there are claims that okra can be purged of its sliminess, really, it can't. One has to either embrace the gummy characteristics of okra, along with its utterly delicious flavour (which is faintly sweet and reminiscent of both eggplant and asparagus), or avoid it altogether.

Okra is the immature seed pod of an annual, tropical herb which is a member of the mallow family. Okra is related to the hibiscus, the hollyhock and cotton and indeed, it produces a hibiscus-like flower—it is believed to be native to Ethiopia and parts of the Sudan

There are two types of okra; one with green skin and one with red. The latter tends to be larger than the former but no different in flavour but its gorgeous maroon colour, unfortunately, disappears when cooked (it becomes green).

You are most likely to encounter the green sort, which can have ridged or smooth skin. Pods can vary from 8–25 cm (3–10 inches) in length.

It is surmised that the conquering Moors took okra to Spain and North Africa. Somehow it also ended up in India (perhaps the Moguls were responsible), where it is immensely popular today. African slaves almost certainly conveyed it to the Caribbean and the southern states of America where it is a much-loved feature of the culinary landscape today, as it is in Greece and Turkey, Middle Eastern countries and South America.

selection and storage

Only buy okra which are super-fresh, as they do not store particularly well. A good test of this is whether they snap cleanly and crisply in half.

Avoid any that are dull-looking or are limp or dry. Mature okra pods are used to make paper and rope in some parts of the world so you don't wish to be eating these—try to get young ones and if in doubt, choose the smallest on offer.

Okra doesn't like very cold temperatures, so store pods in the crisper section of the refrigerator in a paper bag and try to use them within 1–2 days.

preparation

Perfectly fresh okra requires nothing more than washing—it can then be steamed or braised whole (which has the advantage of containing the juices), but by all means snip off the stem end if preferred. It is possible to remove the 'cap' at the stem end without exposing the interior and thus encouraging the juices to escape, although many recipes require sliced okra.

Okra cooks quickly, reaching tenderness when steamed, in about 3 minutes, although it can also be braised for much longer—witness the classic gumbo of the southern United States, in which it is simmered for a couple of hours. Whole, small okra can also be deep-fried, coated lightly first in cornflour (cornstarch).

culinary uses

There are a number of iconic okra dishes from various parts of the world apart from those mentioned above. In the Middle East, where it is called bamia, okra is stewed to luscious effect with lamb, tomatoes and coriander, or with dried limes, tomato, lemon, garlic and parsley. In India, they stuff okra pods with spices then slowly fry them. They also stir-fry them with mustard seeds and green chilli and add them sliced and cooked, with ginger, curry leaves and an assortment of spices, to yoghurt. On the Bahia coast of Brazil, okra is used in a rich dish called carurú, a complex brew of fresh and dried prawns, coconut milk, tomatoes, peanuts, lime juice and okra, while in Senegal it is used in a substantial fish stew called soupokandia.

okra and chicken curry

Grind the chilli flakes, turmeric, cumin, peppercorns and coconut in a spice mill or in a mortar using a pestle until uniform. Trim the okra by cutting off the tip and tough stem end, being careful not to cut into the body.

Heat the oil in a deep frying pan over medium heat. Fry the onion and garlic for about 5 minutes, or until light brown. Stir in the spice mixture and fry for 1 minute. Add the okra, chicken, tomato, sugar, coconut milk and chicken stock and bring to the boil.

Reduce the heat and simmer gently for 20 minutes. Add the vinegar and 1 teaspoon sea salt and simmer for a further 5 minutes. Check the seasoning. Serve with steamed rice or flat bread.

1 teaspoon chilli flakes
1/2 teaspoon turmeric
1/2 teaspoon cumin seeds
4 white peppercorns
30 g (1 oz/1/3 cup) desiccated coconut
500 g (1 lb 2 oz) okra
2 tablespoons oil
2 onions, sliced
3 garlic cloves, crushed
400 g (14 oz) chicken thigh fillets, trimmed and cut into quarters
1 large tomato, chopped
1 teaspoon sugar
250 ml (9 fl oz/1 cup) coconut milk
375 ml (13 fl oz/1 1/2 cups) ready-made chicken stock
1 tablespoon malt vinegar
steamed rice or flat bread, to serve

seeds and pods ▪ okra

okra with tomato sauce

serves 4–6 as a side dish

Trim the okra by cutting off the tip and tough stem end. Heat the olive oil in a large frying pan over medium heat. Add the onion and cook for 5 minutes, or until golden. Add the garlic and cook for a further 1 minute.

Add the okra and cook, stirring, for 4–5 minutes. Add the tomatoes, sugar and lemon juice and simmer, stirring occasionally, for 3–4 minutes. Stir in the coriander leaves. Remove from the heat and serve immediately as a side dish.

500 g (1 lb 2 oz) okra
60 ml (2 fl oz/1/4 cup) olive oil
1 onion, chopped
2 garlic cloves, crushed
400 g (14 oz) tin chopped tomatoes
2 teaspoons sugar
60 ml (2 fl oz/1/4 cup) lemon juice
60 g (2 1/4 oz/1 1/2 cups) finely chopped coriander (cilantro) leaves

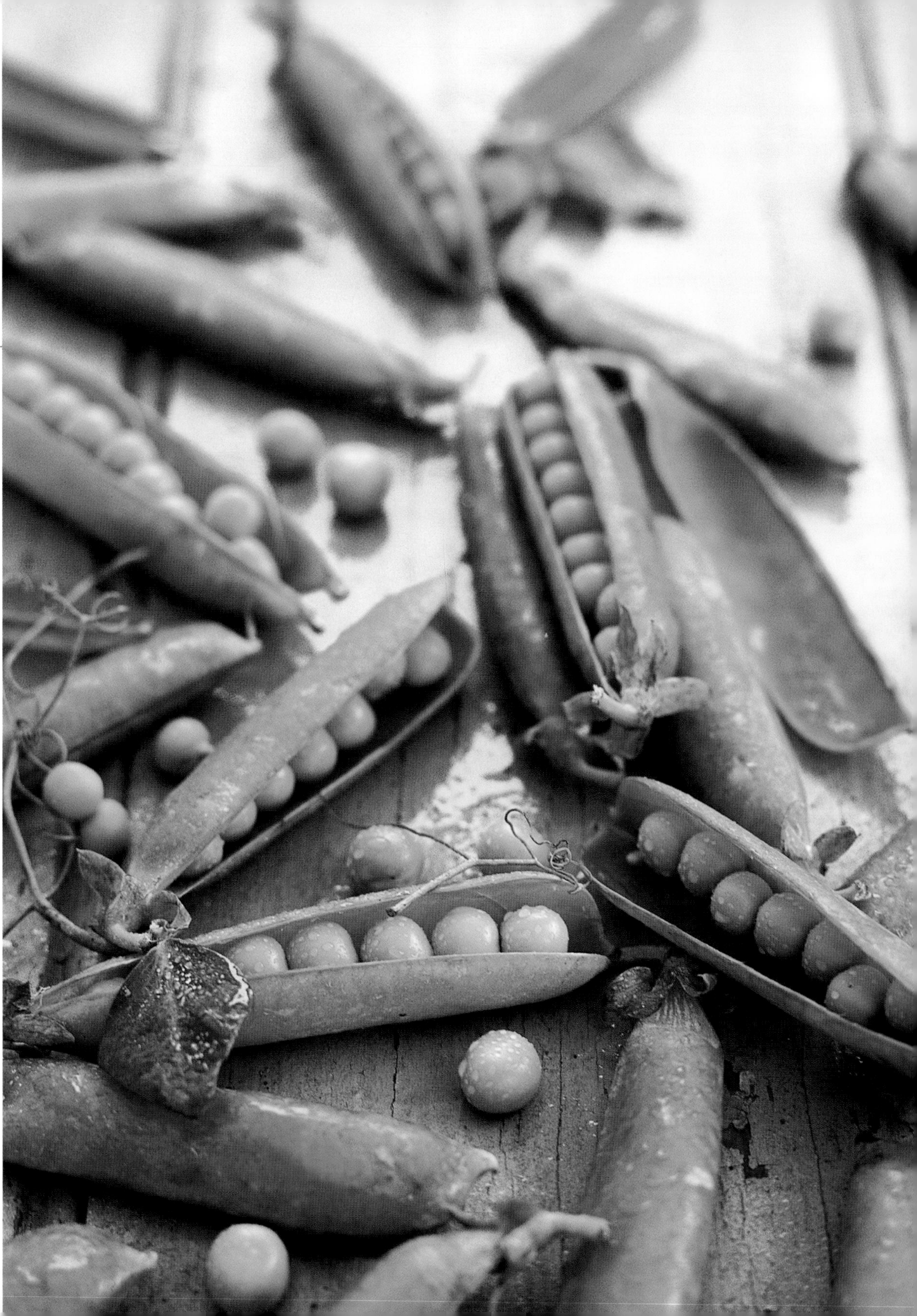

peas

Frozen peas, an innovation in food preservation that dates back to the 1920s, are a blessing and a curse. A blessing because they are generally the closest thing most pea-eaters ever get to the freshest of newly harvested peas and a curse because, thanks to their ubiquity, peas have all but lost the 'special' status they fully deserve. Within hours of harvesting, the succulent sugars in peas start turning to starch and unless you purchase straight from a grower it's likely most 'fresh' peas are quite past their prime by the time of purchase. Frozen peas, processed just after harvesting, most closely mimic the fresh pea, in colour, flavour and nutritional value.

Debate rages as to exactly where the pea originated but what is agreed is that the pea, along with wheat and barley, is one of the oldest cultivated crops. The pea is a legume, that is, a plant whose fruit is in the form of a seed-bearing pod, and is one of the few that are eaten this way. But it wasn't until around the sixteenth century, when breeding know-how enabled tender varieties to be developed, that peas were eaten fresh. By the late seventeenth century peas had become so trendy that a noblewoman in the court of King Louis XIV was moved to write to a friend, 'there are some ladies who, having supped well, take peas at home before going to bed … it is a fashion, a craze!'

For other pea recipes see:
minted peas 423

Catherine de Medici took her beloved piselli novella *(sweet, tiny peas) with her to France, where they became a popular novelty and quite the rage. King Louis XIV made* petit pois *fashionable by featuring them on royal dinner party menus.*

selection and storage

Ripe pea pods are vibrant green, fat and anywhere from 3.5–10 cm (1½–4 inches) long. They contain up to ten round greyish green seeds. Pods are considered ripe when the seam on the side of the pod has gone from being convex to concave. The pods should be shiny, velvety and plump—avoid ones which are dull-looking as these are old and will have lost moisture. Also, avoid any that are yellowish or have grey speckles.

Purchase pods that don't rattle when shaken—the peas inside should fill the pods quite tightly but should not cause the unopened pods to bulge (these peas will be too mature).

Peas deteriorate rapidly once picked, quickly turning starchy and dull-flavoured. Therefore, store them for as little time as possible—2 days maximum and then in the refrigerator, sealed in a plastic bag. Podded, blanched peas can be frozen for up to 2 months.

Note when purchasing fresh peas that 1.25 kg (2 lb 12 oz) of unpodded peas will yield sufficient for four people, as a side dish.

preparation

Shelling peas is surely one of the most therapeutic of all kitchen chores. To do this, split the pods open along their seam then run your thumb under the peas to dislodge them into a bowl.

In *The Garrulous Gourmet,* William Wallace Irwin wrote 'there is nothing so innocent, so confiding as the small green face of the freshly shelled spring pea … [it is] so helpless and friendly that it makes really sensitive stomachs suffer to see the way it is treated in the average home. Fling him into water and let him boil—and that's that.' It's true that mostly we tend to boil peas and, if you do, at least do this in a minimum of water and simmer them for no more than 3 minutes. Over-boiled peas are not pleasant. Peas benefit from a slick of melted butter or really good olive oil.

culinary uses

Some 95 per cent of the world's pea crop is either frozen or tinned so fresh peas really are a seasonal treat. The most common pea is the garden pea, also called the English pea. Very fresh, tiny peas are sublime raw, tossed into salads. At the other end of the cooking spectrum, the French braise peas in stock with lettuce, drastically altering their character but only in the most delicious of ways. Peas are also the star in the classic Venetian dish risi e bisi, little more than a very wet risotto containing the simplest of ingredients (rice, peas, stock, butter) but far more delicious than this description might suggest.

Peas make admirable mash, either on their own or in tandem with some potatoes, and the addition of mint is also favoured by many. Otherwise, add peas to soups such as minestrone, pasta dishes, stir-fries, omelettes and frittatas.

dry potato and pea curry

Dry-roast the mustard seeds in a frying pan over medium heat for 2–3 minutes, or until they start to pop. Add the ghee or oil, onion, garlic and ginger and cook, stirring, until the onion is soft.

Add the spices and potato to the pan and season with sea salt and freshly ground black pepper. Stir until the potato is coated with the spice mixture. Add 125 ml (4 fl oz/½ cup) water and simmer, covered, for 15–20 minutes, or until the potato is just tender. Stir occasionally to stop the curry sticking to the bottom of the pan.

Add the peas and stir until well combined. Simmer, covered, for 3–5 minutes, or until the potato is cooked and all the liquid is absorbed. Stir in the mint and season again before serving.

2 teaspoons brown mustard seeds
2 tablespoons ghee or oil
2 onions, sliced
2 garlic cloves, crushed
2 teaspoons grated fresh ginger
1 teaspoon ground turmeric
½ teaspoon chilli powder
1 teaspoon ground cumin
1 teaspoon garam masala
750 g (1 lb 10 oz) potatoes, cubed
100 g (3½ oz/⅔ cup) peas
2 tablespoons chopped mint

seeds and pods ∎ peas

risi e bisi

serves 4

Put the stock in a saucepan, bring to the boil and then maintain a low simmer. Heat the oil and half the butter in a large wide, heavy-based saucepan and cook the onion and pancetta over low heat for 5 minutes until softened. Stir in the parsley and peas and add 2 ladlefuls of the stock. Simmer for 6–8 minutes.

Add the rice and the remaining stock to the pan. Simmer for 12–15 minutes, or until the rice is *al dente* and most of the stock has been absorbed. Stir in the remaining butter and parmesan cheese, season with sea salt and freshly ground black pepper, to serve.

1.5 litres (52 fl oz/6 cups) ready-made chicken or vegetable stock
2 teaspoons olive oil
40 g (1½ oz) butter
1 small onion, finely chopped
80 g (2¾ oz) pancetta, cut into small pieces
2 tablespoons chopped parsley
375 g (13 oz/2½ cups) shelled young peas
200 g (7 oz/1 scant cup) risotto (arborio) rice
50 g (1¾ oz/½ cup) parmesan cheese, grated

soya beans

vegetables ▪ **seeds and pods**
season ▪ **summer–early autumn**

Soya beans, an East Asian native, have been a vital source of protein in that part of the world for over 5000 years. Also known as edamame, which means 'branched bean' in Japanese, soya beans present as bright apple-green pods, covered with a slight white or brown hairy fuzz. Inside the pods are anywhere from two to eight pea-like seeds, which have a sweet, nutty and delicate flavour and buttery texture. They are of the same species as field or grain soy crops (grown for various uses such as miso, tofu and soy milk).

The soya bean is the only vegetable to contain all nine essential amino acids, making it a source of complete protein; soya beans also contain a veritable cocktail of other nutrients including antioxidants, phytochemicals, essential fatty acids, calcium and B vitamins.

selection and storage

Fresh green soya beans are not widely available, although they can, with increasing ease, be purchased whole and frozen. Fresh soya beans should have bright green pods with healthy-looking whitish or brown furry down—avoid any that look dried, withered or whose seeds rattle when you shake the pods. They should be consumed within 2 days—refrigerate them in a ventilated plastic bag for no longer than this.

preparation

boiling Soya beans are easier to pod after cooking. To boil them, cook them in their pods for 5 minutes or until beans inside are tender—you may need to test one to determine if they are tender. Drain well, cool slightly then serve with salt as a snack or refresh in iced water, pod and use in stir-fries, soups or salads.
roasting Soya beans can also be roasted. Simply toss whole, unpodded beans with some olive oil and garlic, season them well then roast in a 180°C (350°F/Gas 4) oven for 15 minutes or until tender.

soya beans, snow peas and prawn noodle stir-fry

To make the dressing, combine the red wine vinegar, kecap manis, soy sauce, sesame oil, ginger, sweet chilli sauce and garlic and set aside.

Cook the egg noodles in boiling water for 2 minutes, then drain and set aside.

Peel and devein the prawns, leaving some with their tails on, if desired. Heat the oil in a large wok over high heat and add the prawns, snow peas, capsicum, soya beans and green onion. Stir-fry for 1 minute, or until the prawns are just opaque. Add the noodles and cook for 20–30 seconds. Add the dressing and coriander and mix through.
Serve immediately.

dressing
80 ml (2½ fl oz/⅓ cup) red wine vinegar
80 ml (2½ fl oz/⅓ cup) kecap manis
2 tablespoons soy sauce
2 tablespoons sesame oil
2 tablespoons grated ginger
1 tablespoon sweet chilli sauce
1 garlic clove, crushed

250 g (9 oz) egg noodles
140 g (5 oz) raw prawns (shrimp)
1 tablespoon oil
200 g (7 oz/2 cups) small snow peas (mangetout)
1 red capsicum (pepper), seeded and thinly sliced
80 g (1⅓ cups) soya beans
6 green onions (scallions), sliced
2 large handfuls coriander (cilantro) leaves

A couple of hundred years BC, the Chinese started using the mature but still-green pods of soya beans as a fresh vegetable, while the Japanese learnt the technology 400 years ago. Although little-known in the West (but with interest in fresh, green soya beans growing by the moment), soya beans have reached enormous popularity in Taiwan, Japan, Korea and China.

sugarsnap and snow peas (mangetout)

vegetables ■ seeds and pods
season ■ peak season summer

selection and storage

Buy snow peas with bright, light green skin. The ideal length is about 8 cm (3 inches)—avoid any really large ones as these tend to be tough. Also spurn those with largish seeds inside, as the seeds should make a minimal impression on the pod.

Try to buy snow peas that still have vestiges of petals at the stem end, which are a good indicator, depending on their condition, of super-freshness. Don't store snow peas for too long—2 days in a ventilated plastic bag in the refrigerator at most. They don't like humid conditions so the ventilation factor is important.

Sugarsnap peas should have taut, bright green, bulging pods and give out a distinct 'snap' when broken in two. Avoid any that are even a little flaccid or damp-looking as these have been too long off the vine. Their flavour diminishes quickly so they need to be stored in the same way as snow peas.

Also called mangetout, snow peas are widely associated with China and many assume they come from there. But their Chinese name, *hoh laan dau* (Holland pea) holds the clue to their provenance. The Dutch grew snow peas as early as 1536 and somehow (possibly via the English) the snow pea arrived in the Orient—snow peas are the main type of garden pea eaten in China and Japan today. It is believed the name 'snow pea' came from Cantonese farmers in the San Francisco area who called them *shii dau*, meaning snow pea, and somehow, the name has stuck.

The sugar snap, also classified as a 'shell' pea (denoting an edible pod and seeds) is even newer on the scene; a cross between the snow pea and the regular English podding pea, it was not perfected until 1979 (it was mentioned in seventeenth century gardening journals but never completely took off).

Both types of pea are characterized by a sweet tenderness and a bright green colour, although sugarsnaps are darker in hue than snow peas. Sugarsnaps are around 6–8 cm (2½–3 inches) in length and have a plump, firm pod holding pea-like seeds while snow peas are somewhat flat, showing the slight bulge of small seeds within.

seeds and pods ■ sugarsnap and snow peas (mangetout)

preparation

Snow peas require very little preparation. Snip off the stem end and pull away the string that runs down the side of the pod then cook briefly (1–2 minutes), either by steaming, stir-frying or simmering

The succulent, sweet juiciness of the sugarsnap is best preserved by minimal (and simple) cooking; steam them for about 4 minutes or boil for just 2 minutes. Blanch them briefly before stir-frying or using in salads—although, like snow peas, they can be served raw, a quick cooking brings out their flavour. Some varieties of sugarsnaps require stringing—to do this just break off the stem end and pull off the strings which run down the side of the pod.

culinary uses

The sweet, snappy qualities of both snow peas and sugarsnaps shouldn't be masked by heavy flavours or long cooking. Hence, steaming, stir-frying and quick blanching are appropriate treatments—serve either as a simple side dish for meats or fish or in salads.

They are brilliant with all the classic Asian flavours of ginger, garlic, chilli, fish and soy sauce, and absolutely shine in light oriental-style soups and wok-tossed dishes. Toss blanched snow peas and sugarsnaps in a salad bowl with other sweet seasonal greens (peas, beans, asparagus) for a sensational hot-weather dish (chopped mint and slices of bocconcini would be perfect additions). You can also make classic beurre blanc (see page 273) or orange-flavoured hollandaise (see page 36) and spoon these over warm, just-cooked peas.

sugarsnap peas and carrots in lime butter

Peel the carrots and cut into thin diagonal slices. Wash and string the sugarsnap peas. Heat the butter in a large heavy-based frying pan. Add the garlic, then cook over low heat for 1 minute. Add the lime juice and sugar and cook until sugar has completely dissolved. Add the carrots and peas and cook over medium heat for 2–3 minutes, or until just cooked. Serve hot with lime zest as a garnish.

variation If limes are unavailable, substitute lemon juice and zest. This dish can be adapted to make a light salad—replace the butter with 2 tablespoons of olive oil and cook according to the recipe. Cool to room temperature and sprinkle with finely chopped cashews or toasted pine nuts.

125 g (4½ oz) carrots
125 g (4½ oz/1¼ cups) sugarsnap peas or snow peas (mangetout)
60 g (2¼ oz) butter
2 garlic cloves, crushed
1 tablespoon lime juice
½ teaspoon soft brown sugar
zest of 1 lime, peeled and cut into thin strips

steamed snow peas with blood orange mayonnaise

serves 4

To make the blood orange mayonnaise, whisk together the egg yolk, white wine vinegar and dijon mustard. Whisking constantly, gradually drizzle in the olive oil until you have a thick emulsion. Mix through the blood orange juice, to taste. Season with sea salt and freshly ground black pepper.

Trim the snow peas and put them in a steamer. Add 3–4 very thin strips of fresh ginger. Cover and steam over a rolling boil for 2–5 minutes, or until tender. Transfer to a bowl and combine the snow peas with the celery, green onions and orange segments. Serve with the mayonnaise.

blood orange mayonnaise
1 egg yolk
1 teaspoon white wine vinegar
½ teaspoon dijon mustard
125 ml (4 fl oz/½ cup) olive oil
2 tablespoons blood orange juice

150 g (5½ oz/1½ cups) snow peas (mangetout)
2 cm (¾ inch) piece ginger, cut into thin strips
½ celery stick, sliced
4 green onions (scallions), sliced
1 orange, broken into segments

seeds and pods ■ sugarsnap and snow peas (mangetout)

sweet corn

vegetables ■ **seeds and pods**
season ■ **summer**

Few other foods epitomize North America in the way that corn, or maize, does. Called *mahiz* by the indigenous peoples, meaning 'that which sustains us', corn was considered one of the vital 'three sisters' of their food supply, the other two being pumpkin (winter squash) and beans. The Native Americans venerated corn, believing it to be a food-gift from their gods; their name for it is the source of the English word 'maize'.

An exceedingly ancient crop, fossilized remains of corn have been found in Mexico that are around 80,000 years old. By the time Columbus arrived in the Americas, large fields of corn were growing throughout America—corn is credited with the native Americans' evolvement from a nomadic to an agrarian society. It is also thought that the early settlers of America may have been saved from starvation by corn; the Native Americans taught them how to make it into flour, cakes and soups.

Corn is the most widely-grown crop in the world, second only to rice. There are five main types of corn grown around the world, of which sweet corn is the most familiar. This is the classic 'corn on the cob' corn. Over recent decades, varieties high in sugar content have been developed. The kernels are most popularly yellow or white or a mixture of these two colours.

Mark Twain proclaimed that the only way to eat corn is to take your own kettle of water into a corn field, set it over a fire and plop the just-picked, freshly-shucked corn straight into the boiling pot. Sweet corn kernels contain a greater proportion of sugar to starch than any other vegetable, but as soon as it is picked, the sugars in corn begin converting to starch, reducing sweetness. Corn loses 25 per cent of its sugars within around 24 hours of harvest; thus Twain was dead right in insisting corn be cooked as soon after harvesting as possible, for the sweetest, most flavoursome results.

preparation

When ready to prepare corn, simply strip away the layers of husk and the silk, rinsing to remove the last of the latter as the fine strands are persistent in sticking to the kernels. An ear or cob of corn contains about 800 kernels, arranged in neat rows; one ear of corn will yield about 100 g (3½ oz/½ cup) of kernels. If you wish to remove the kernels for cooking, simply hold each ear upright on a board then run a sharp knife down the ear, as close to the core as possible—the kernels will come away neatly. Thus prepared, the kernels can be cooked in boiling water for several minutes until tender then served immediately, tossed with butter.

boiling Corn kernels can be used in any number of ways—in fritters, to make creamed corn, or in soups, risottos or salads. The classic way to enjoy corn is 'on the cob'. This involves simmering the whole cobs in lightly salted water (salt toughens the kernels so just use a little) for 5 minutes until tender, drain well, then serve slathered with butter and sprinklings of sea salt and pepper.

chargrilling Corn can be wrapped in foil with some butter and cooked on the barbecue or chargrill plate (turn it often, over medium heat, for about 20 minutes) or wrapped in foil and baked in a 180°C (350°F/Gas 4) oven for 25 minutes until deliciously tender.

culinary uses

Simmer plenty of corn kernels in pouring (whipping) cream until the cream has reduced and thickened and spoon over grilled red meats or even poached chicken. Pre-cooked corn kernels are legendarily good in fritters, chowders and baked into savoury cornbread, lovely to eat with sausages and golden fried onion.

On the cob, corn is very good when cut into thick rings and cooked on the barbecue—serve with a flavoured butter (garlic, parsley or cumin-flavoured) and a steak. Baby corn is a specially bred type of corn and is good utilized in Asian stir-fries and soups.

selection and storage

You can tell by the freshness of the cuts to their stems how long ago corn was harvested—the fresher the cuts, the fresher the corn. The cobs should feel and look moist and plump, with the kernels inside fat and shiny; press against the husk and you should be able to feel the kernels within. The silk of the corn should also be a little sticky and should look glossy, stiff and moist. Store corn, in its husks, in the refrigerator for 2–3 days only.

corn chowder

serves 8

90 g (3¼ oz) butter
2 large onions, finely chopped
1 garlic clove, crushed
2 teaspoons cumin seeds
1 litre (35 fl oz/4 cups)
   ready-made vegetable stock
2 potatoes, peeled and chopped
250 g (9 oz/1 cup) tin creamed corn
400 g (14 oz/2 cups) fresh corn
   kernels (about 4 cobs)
3 tablespoons chopped parsley
125 g (4½ oz/1 cup) grated
   cheddar cheese
3 tablespoons pouring (whipping)
   cream, optional
2 tablespoons snipped chives

Heat the butter in a large heavy-based saucepan. Add the onions and cook over medium-high heat for 5 minutes, or until golden. Add garlic and cumin seeds, cook for 1 minute, stirring constantly. Add the vegetable stock and bring to boil. Add the potatoes and reduce heat. Simmer, uncovered, for 10 minutes.

Add the creamed corn, corn kernels and parsley. Bring to the boil, reduce heat, simmer for 10 minutes. Stir through the cheese. Season with sea salt and freshly ground black pepper. Add the cream. Heat gently until the cheese melts. Serve immediately, sprinkled with snipped chives.

corn and polenta pancakes with bacon and maple syrup

serves 4

90 g (3¼ oz/¾ cup) self-raising
   flour
110 g (3¾ oz/¾ cup) fine polenta
250 ml (9 fl oz/1 cup) milk
310 g (11 oz/1½ cups) sweet
   corn kernels (about 3 cobs)
olive oil, for frying
8 bacon slices
175 g (6 oz/½ cup) maple syrup
   or golden syrup

Sift the flour into a bowl and stir in the polenta. Add the milk and corn and stir until just combined, adding more milk if the batter is too dry. Season with sea salt and black pepper.

Heat the oil in a large frying pan and spoon half the batter into the pan in batches, making four 9 cm (3½ inch) pancakes. Cook for 2 minutes each side, or until golden. Repeat with the remaining batter. Keep warm on a plate in a 120°C (235°F/Gas ½) oven while cooking the bacon.

Add the bacon to the pan and cook for 5 minutes. Put two pancakes and two bacon slices on each plate and drizzle with maple syrup, to serve.

mushrooms

field mushrooms

fungi ▪ cultivated and wild mushrooms
season ▪ cultivated mushrooms available year-round;
wild mushrooms autumn–winter

Not technically a vegetable, mushrooms are the fruit-body of a form of fungus, which thrives on dead trees or the roots of living trees. Although there are thousands of fungus varieties around the world, only a tiny fraction of these are edible. Since ancient times, the precious few that are edible have developed and sustained a devoted following. The Egyptian pharaohs forbade commoners from eating them, declaring them an exclusively royal food. Other ancient cultures ascribed all manner of magical properties to mushrooms—some believed they imparted super-human powers while others thought they could aid in the recovery of lost objects.

An intriguing and diverse ingredient, mushrooms range in size, shape, flavour and texture from the smallest button mushrooms to enormous puffballs, which can grow up to 1 metre (40 inches) in diameter. While some mushrooms, such as field mushrooms and portobellos, taste almost meaty, others like chanterelles have a mild, delicate flavour.

Mushrooms are rich in proteins, fibre and B group vitamins including folate, niacin and riboflavin. Consisting of approximately nine per cent water, mushrooms contain enough nutrients to form the main component of a meal. It is worth noting that cultivated mushrooms contain lower levels of vitamins C and K than their wild counterparts.

cultivated mushrooms

Edible fungi can be broadly divided into two categories: cultivated and wild. Cultivated mushrooms are available year-round, are grown in compost in temperature- and moisture-controlled environments and are often hand-harvested in the dead of night.

Although the ancient Egyptians ate mushrooms, and the Romans spread them throughout their empire, mushroom cultivation was initially revolutionized in France in the 1600s, where they were grown in designated caves located close to Paris. All modern-day cultivated mushrooms belong to the *Agaricus bisporus* family and are harvested at different stages of maturity.

button (*A. bisporus*) The most commonly available mushroom, button mushrooms derive from swiss browns and were bred to be whiter, with closed veils, that is, their caps sit snugly against their stems. Their mild flavour intensifies when cooked, but they are also delicious eaten raw in salads. Whole, they are excellent sautéed then marinated in olive oil, used as the basis for cream of mushroom soup or added to casseroles, or sliced then used in sauces and pies.

chestnut (*A. bisporus*) Featuring a meaty, firm texture and strong, nutty flavour, chestnut mushrooms look similar to button mushrooms, but are darker in colour, with open caps and pink to dark brown gills. They are ideally eaten raw or lightly cooked and suit using in pastry fillings, pâtés and breads.

portabello/portabella (*A. bisporus*) Growing up to 10 cm (4 inches) in diameter, these are the largest of the cultivated mushrooms and are in fact swiss brown mushrooms that have been allowed to continue growing before harvesting. Mushrooms double in size every 24 hours, so they are essentially more mature swiss browns, whose caps have opened. Boasting a meaty texture and rich flavour, portabello mushrooms are ideal for stuffing and baking, grilling (broiling), barbecuing or pan-frying whole and using as a sandwich filling.

swiss brown (*A. bisporus*) Also known as 'criminis' in the United States, swiss browns are actually the original form of the common button mushroom, not a distinct variety in their own right. Their caps range in colour from light tan to deep brown, and their flavour is more intense than that of buttons. Use swiss browns in meat or game dishes and pasta sauces.

button mushrooms

The odd word 'mushroom' is thought to have developed from the French word mousserons, *which was used to describe all mushrooms, poisonous and edible. Nowadays, 'mushroom' is used to denote edible fungi and generally just those with a stem and a cap—other sorts are known by their specific names, for example, morels, ceps and truffles. In these days of widespread mushroom (and other produce) cultivation, their wild equivalents are one of the last remaining, truly seasonal ingredients. Mushroom devotees worship the unique, deep earthy flavours and spongy texture of wild mushrooms.*

pine mushrooms

wild mushrooms

Wild mushrooms are truly seasonal produce, and rely upon the weather conditions of the cooler months to flourish. Both excessive and insufficient rain impedes their growth, so there are some years, such as during droughts, when they are scarce. Autumn heralds the start of wild mushroom season (including saffron milk caps and slippery jacks) and extends into late winter, when morels are at their peak. During this eagerly-anticipated time, mushroom foragers dot the countryside where the fungi grow wild. Clutching baskets as they embark in a cloak-and-dagger flurry worthy of any detective, most keen mushroom hunters have their own special spot, the secret location of which some even take to the grave.

It is crucial to always forage for mushrooms with an experienced mushroom hunter or have the edibility of mushrooms validated by a fungus expert, as there are many more poisonous varieties than edible ones and mistakes can be fatal. Although cultivation guarantees a constant, ready supply of common varieties, it has lead to some compromise in flavour, so it is good to take advantage of wild mushrooms when they are in season.

chanterelles (*Cantharellus cibarius*) Also called 'girolles', these frilly golden-hued wild mushrooms are prized for their subtle, fruity flavour and firm, rubbery texture. Delicate by nature, they are best added to the cooking process at the last minute to prevent them from toughening and are excellent in pasta dishes, risotto, sauces for meat, paired with chicken and pheasant, or sautéed in foaming unsalted butter and served with scrambled eggs and warm brioche.

field (*Agaricus campestris*) Characterized by an aniseed-accented flavour, field mushrooms are large, open and flat capped wild mushrooms with exposed pinkish brown gills and thick, white flesh. They grow in grassy meadows and cow pastures from late winter to early spring and are the United Kingdom's most popular wild mushroom.

Enjoy this substantial specimen pan-fried, crumbed and deep-fried, roasted, grilled (broiled), stuffed, barbecued, pickled and served as antipasto or added to braised meat dishes. If used in braised poultry recipes, they can turn the dish an unappetizing grey, although this of course does not affect their flavour.

morel (*Morchella vulgaris* and *M. esculenta*) Closely related to the truffle, the most luxurious of all the fungi, morels are one of the few specifically spring mushrooms. Relatively scarce, they come with commensurately steep price tags and are highly prized by mushroom hunters for their earthy, smoky, nut-like flavour.

Their conical, tan to deep brown-black coloured, perforated, spongy caps must be cleaned well to remove any bugs lurking in their hollow centre. The darker the morel, the more intensely flavoured it is. They add a depth of flavour to game, veal and chicken dishes and are commonly cooked with cream. Morels are also available dried.

pine (*Suillus luteus* and *Lactarius deliciosa*) As the name suggests, pine mushrooms grow wild at the roots of pine trees. This category includes slippery jacks, which have a delicate flavour, moist slippery caps and spongy flesh; and saffron milk caps, so-named due to their lurid saffron tone and the milky liquid they emit. They have a nutty flavour and firm texture and are excellent when combined with other mushrooms and used in sauces, soups and stews.

porcini/ceps (*Boletus edulis*) Indigenous to France and Italy's alpine regions, porcinis are adored by fungus fans for their distinctly sweet, strong mushroom flavour. Available fresh (although only during late summer and autumn), dried or frozen, their pungent aroma invigorates any dish they are added to.

Pale brown in colour, porcinis are distinguished by their fleshy dome-shaped caps and thick, bulbous stems. Very young fresh porcini are a delicacy and can be shaved and eaten raw in salads, while older specimens make the best risottos, omelettes, pasta sauces, soups and stews.

storage and selection

When buying mushrooms, look for unblemished specimens, with no signs of bruising, tearing or soft spots. The stems should still be intact and the caps firm, not shrivelled, dry or 'tacky', which indicates spoilage.

Store mushrooms in a paper bag (this prevents dehydration and allows them to 'breathe') in the refrigerator for up to 3 days. Mushrooms absorb other flavours, so it is best not to store them near strong-smelling foods.

Mushrooms are porous and readily absorb water—they should not be washed before storing or using. Rather, trim stems, then lightly dust with a pastry brush or carefully wipe with a damp cloth to remove any dirt clinging to their surface. As with all rules, there is of course an exception—morels need to be thoroughly washed as bugs can hide in their hollow centres.

If planning to cook mushrooms whole then choose uniform-sized specimens so that they cook in approximately the same amount of time.

fungi ■ cultivated and wild mushrooms

preparation

After wiping mushrooms clean, trim the stalks (you can reserve these for use in stocks). If you are intending to stuff mushrooms you will need to remove the stalks completely.

roasting A good method for roasting larger-capped roast mushrooms is to place them in a single layer in a large roasting dish, skin side down, drizzle with oil and scatter over some herbs—fresh thyme, marjoram or rosemary are good. Season with sea salt and freshly ground black pepper and cook, turning once, in a 200°C (400°F/Gas 6) oven for 12–15 minutes.

sautéing To sauté mushrooms, slice or chop them and cook in oil in a large frying pan over medium-high heat for 5–7 minutes, or until soft and golden. Make sure the oil is quite hot before adding the mushrooms and be aware that they will absorb the oil so don't be tempted to keep adding more; they will release juices and the soaked-up oil as they soften.

grilling To grill (broil) or barbecue mushrooms, brush liberally with oil and place under a medium-high grill (broiler) for 7–10 minutes, turning once—the cooking time may vary depending on size.

culinary uses

Mushrooms may well be the ultimate autumn food. A plate laden with garlic and thyme-scented wild mushrooms, with thick slices of buttery, sourdough toast is simplicity personified, but a memorable way to start, or end, a chilly day. Sliced swiss browns cooked slowly with olive oil and garlic and finished with lots of chopped flat-leaf (Italian) parsley make a terrific crostini topping or frittata filling. Portobello or field mushroom caps topped with a stuffing of breadcrumbs, sage, pancetta and grated parmesan cheese, then baked, are the perfect partner for barbecued sirloin steaks. For a sophisticated dinner party, sauté saffron milk caps and slippery jacks in anchovy and chive butter, then serve with wilted spinach as an accompaniment for pan-fried trout, crisp skinned salmon fillets, or roasted blue eye trevally.

Mushrooms go particularly well with bacon, barley, bread, beef, butter, cheese (for instance parmesan, asiago, cheddar, fontina, boursin, stilton, gruyere), chestnuts, chicken, cream, dill, duck, eggs, parsley, garlic, lemon, lentils, Madeira, marjoram, noodles, olive oil, polenta, thyme, pasta, pastry, pork, potatoes, quail, rabbit, rice, rosemary, sage, sherry, speck, spinach, turkey, venison and white and red wine, and seafood such as bugs (lobster), kingfish, rainbow trout and tuna.

mushroom pâté on mini toasts

Heat the butter in a large frying pan. Cook the onion and garlic over medium heat for 2 minutes, or until soft. Increase the heat, add the mushrooms and cook for 5 minutes, or until the mushrooms are soft and most of the liquid has evaporated. Leave to cool for 10 minutes.

Roughly chop the almonds in a food processor. Add the mushroom mixture and process until smooth. With the motor running, gradually pour in the cream. Stir in the herbs and season with sea salt and freshly ground black pepper. Spoon into two 250 ml (9 fl oz/1 cup) ramekins and smooth the surface. Cover and refrigerate for 4–5 hours to let the flavours develop.

To make the toasts, preheat the oven to 180°C (350°F/Gas 4). Toast one side of the bread under a hot grill (broiler) until golden. Remove the crusts and cut each slice into four triangles. Place on a large baking tray in a single layer, toasted side down, and cook for 5–10 minutes, or until crisp. Serve immediately with the pâté.

60 g (2¼ oz) butter
1 small onion, chopped
3 garlic cloves, crushed
375 g (13 oz) button mushrooms, quartered
125 g (4½ oz/1 cup) slivered almonds, toasted
2 tablespoons pouring (whipping) cream
2 tablespoons finely chopped thyme
3 tablespoons finely chopped flat-leaf (Italian) parsley
6 thick slices wholemeal (whole-wheat) bread

fungi ■ cultivated and wild mushrooms

Mycophobia is a condition where the sufferer has an extreme fear of, or aversion to, mushrooms. Such fears have their genesis in history—because the mushroom magically appears, from seemingly nowhere, favours damp and dark conditions and loves to grow near decaying matter, it was regarded with deep suspicion in times past. That it has no leaves, seeds, obvious root structure or way of gaining nutrients only added to its mysterious aura.

serves 4

open lasagne of mushrooms, pine nuts and thyme

200 g (7 oz or 2 medium) fresh
   pasta sheets
80 g (2¾ oz/⅓ cup) butter
1 tablespoon olive oil
300 g (10½ oz/3⅓ cups)
   assorted mushrooms, sliced
2 bacon slices, cut into pieces
   of similar size to the mushroom
   slices
2 garlic cloves, finely sliced
1 tablespoon fresh thyme
1 tablespoon pine nuts, toasted
3 tablespoons thick
   (double/heavy) cream
3 tablespoons extra virgin olive
   oil
35 g (1¼ oz/⅓ cup) pecorino
   cheese, coarsely shredded

Bring a large saucepan of salted water to the boil. Cut the lasagne sheets into sixteen 8 cm (3¼ inch) squares. Boil half of the squares for 4 minutes, or until *al dente*. Using a slotted spoon, transfer to a bowl of cold water, leave for about 15–20 seconds, then drain. Lay flat on a dry tea (dish) towel and cover with another tea towel; it doesn't matter that the squares may have cooked to uneven sizes. Repeat this process with the remaining pasta squares.

Heat the butter and olive oil in a large frying pan. Add the mushrooms and bacon and cook over high heat, stirring often, for 3–4 minutes, or until golden brown. Add the garlic and thyme and cook for a further 1 minute. Add the pine nuts, cream and 2 tablespoons of extra virgin olive oil and stir until combined. Remove from the heat and season to taste.

Preheat the griller (broiler) to medium–high. Put a pasta square in each of four shallow heat-proof pasta bowls. Cover with a heaped tablespoon of mushroom mixture. Repeat twice more, then top with the last four pasta squares; the pasta doesn't have to be in uniform stacks, nor the piles neat.

Drizzle the remaining extra virgin olive oil over the top and scatter with the cheese. Place the bowls under the heat for 1–2 minutes, or until cheese has melted. Serve hot or warm.

note Use your favourite type of cap mushroom, such as chestnut, swiss brown, portobello or even shiitake, as long as they are no bigger than 4 cm (1½ inches) across. To prepare, cut off the dirty end of the stalks, shake off excess soil and leaves and wipe the caps with a damp cloth.

exotic mushrooms

fungi ▪ **exotic mushrooms**
season ▪ **available year-round**

Once exclusive to Japan, China and Korea, where they originate and have been cultivated for centuries, so-called 'exotic' mushrooms are now increasingly available fresh almost everywhere, as demand for their unique flavour spreads.

While edible fungi have been integral to the cuisines of Asian countries for thousands of years, they are also eaten for medicinal purposes. In China, mushrooms are regarded as a symbol of longevity and used to boost immunity. Shiitakes in particular are high in amino acids, thiamine, riboflavin, niacin and dietary fibre, and contain nutrients not usually found in non-animal matter, like vitamins B2, B12 and D. In general, like other mushrooms, these exotic varieties contain varying levels of niacin, selenium, riboflavin and potassium.

culinary uses

With their unique textures, flavours and character, Asian mushrooms add an interesting note and appealing look to many dishes. Shiitakes contribute a smoky undertone when slowly cooked in a star anise-infused Chinese master stock with pork, chicken or beef. Braise a mixture of exotic mushrooms in dashi stock, mirin and soy sauce or brush oyster mushrooms with tamari and sake and briefly barbecue as an accompaniment for teriyaki beef. Exotic mushrooms work best with flavours favoured in the countries they are indigenous to; consider rice, soy sauce, tofu, fish, duck, prawns, ginger, garlic, coriander (cilantro), green onions (scallions), Asian greens, soba noodles and miso.

varieties

enoki (*Flammulina velutipes*) Growing in clusters linked by a communal base, with tiny caps and slender long stems, enokis are named after the hackberry tree of the same name that is their natural habitat. Cultivated enokis are creamy coloured, with an almost fruity, sweet flavour and crunchy texture. Extremely delicate, they require only minimal cooking, so should be added at the last minute to Japanese soups and hotpots, or used raw in salads.

king trumpet (*Pleurotus eryngii*) Also called eryngiis or king oysters, these intriguing mushrooms grow in pairs and have small thick caps. Their long, stout stems contain most of their flavour, which is often compared to almonds and abalone and is best when cooked with seafood and meat or used in clear soups.

nameko (*Pholiota nameko*) Indigenous to Japan, these mushrooms are prized for their aromatic flavour. They have a brief shelf life and while they can occasionally be found fresh, they are also sold tinned and dried. With slippery, honey-hued rounded caps and gills and paler, thick curved stems, namekos are traditionally added to sushi, used in miso soup and braises.

oyster (*Pleurotus ostreatus*) With pale beige to grey, fluted fan-shaped caps, oyster mushrooms can be enjoyed raw, but gentle cooking elicits their juicy texture and almost peppery, delicate flavour. They are a treat when fried in butter and garlic, grilled whole, used in Japanese-style seafood and chicken braises, added to casseroles or clear soups. They are best matched with clean, unassertive flavours that won't overwhelm their delightful delicacy.

shiitake (*Lentinus edodes*) Indigenous to Japan, shiitakes are now the most widely cultivated of all the Asian mushrooms and are increasingly available fresh as well as dried. In their natural habitat their spores grow on oak trees. With broad, plump and firm tan to dark brown caps and creamy gills, shiitakes are intensely flavoured with a woodsy aroma. Their assertive flavour best suits braising, sautéing, stir-frying, roasting and adding to soups, or finely chopping and included in fillings for dumplings and stuffed vegetables or fish.

shimeji (*Tricholoma conglobatum*) Confusingly, 'shimeji' refers to around 20 mushroom species. The hon-shimeji is regarded as the 'true' shimeji and, as its name suggests, it was first cultivated in Japan. The flavour of the hon-shimeji is nutty and a little sweet and is suited to a wide range of dishes, from soups to stir-fries and sauces. Light grey to taupe in colour, it is often sold in the dense cluster in which it grows. The base needs to be cut off and the mushrooms only require wiping—do not wet them or they will become soggy. Shimeji mushrooms aren't suitable for eating raw, but can be cooked whole, sliced or chopped.

selection and storage

Generally sold on plastic wrapped trays or in disposable conatiners, choose exotic mushrooms that look plump and firm, not dry or shrivelled, then transfer to perforated plastic or paper bags and refrigerate on a shelf, not the crisper, for up to 3 days.

fungi ■ exotic mushrooms

shiitake wontons with chilli-ginger dipping sauce

makes 24

dipping sauce
2 teaspoons grated fresh ginger
1½ teaspoons sweet chilli sauce
100 ml (3½ fl oz) light soy sauce
2 tablespoons rice wine
½ teaspoon finely chopped
   coriander (cilantro) stems

80 g (2¾ oz) finely diced fresh
   shiitake mushrooms
1 teaspoon grated fresh ginger
6 water chestnuts, finely chopped
1 teaspoon chopped coriander
   (cilantro) leaves
1 teaspoon soy sauce
1 teaspoon rice wine
1 teaspoon sesame oil
3 teaspoons cornflour (cornstarch)
24 wonton wrappers
vegetable oil, for deep-frying

To make the dipping sauce, combine the ginger, sweet chilli sauce, light soy sauce, rice wine and coriander stems. Mix thoroughly and set aside.

To make the filling, combine the shiitake mushrooms, ginger, water chestnuts and coriander leaves. Stir in the soy sauce, rice wine, sesame oil and cornflour. Put a heaped teaspoon of filling in the centre of a wonton wrapper. Moisten the edges with water and gather up the four corners to a peak, encasing the filling. Twist the peak tightly.

In a wok or deep-fryer, heat plenty of vegetable oil to 180°C (350°F/Gas 4), or until a cube of bread dropped into the oil browns in 15 seconds. Deep-fry the wontons, in batches, for about 1 minute, or until golden brown. Drain on paper towels and serve with the dipping sauce.

Since ancient times, traditional physicians throughout Asia have prescribed shiitake mushrooms for a whole gamut of complaints— from sinus ailments to liver disease, from bad eyesight to gastrointestinal conditions. Modern science has identified a phytochemical in shiitake called lentinan, which is believed to assist in the treatment of cancer, coronary disease and high blood pressure. Little wonder then, that in the East they have long considered it to promote long life and wellbeing.

exotic mushrooms with dashi

In a small bowl or jug, combine the dashi granules with 125 ml (4 fl oz/½ cup) boiling water, then stir in the shoyu and mirin. Set aside.

Heat a wok or frying pan over high heat, add 1 tablespoon oil and swirl to coat. Add the oyster, shiitake and enoki mushrooms in batches and stir-fry for 1–2 minutes, or until wilted and softened.

Heat the remaining oil in the wok, add the ginger and white part of the green onions and stir-fry for 30 seconds, or until fragrant. Return all the cooked mushrooms to the wok along with the dashi mixture and bring to the boil. Stir-fry for an additional minute or until the mushrooms are heated through. Remove from the heat, add the shimeji mushrooms and toss through to wilt with the heat from the other mushrooms. Garnish with the green onions to serve.

1 teaspoon dashi granules
1 tablespoon shoyu
1 tablespoon mirin
1½ tablespoons vegetable oil
150 g (5½ oz) oyster mushrooms, cut into halves if large
300 g (10½ oz) fresh shiitake mushrooms, sliced
300 g (10½ oz) enoki mushrooms, separated into small bunches
1 teaspoon finely grated ginger
1 green onion (scallion), white part finely chopped, green part shredded
300 g (10½ oz) shimeji mushrooms, separated

tofu and mushroom stir-fry

Heat a wok or heavy-based frying pan over high heat. Add 2 teaspoons of peanut oil and swirl to coat the sides of the wok. Add the tofu in two batches and stir-fry for 2–3 minutes, or until golden on all sides, then transfer to a plate.

Heat the remaining oil in the wok, add the sambal oelek, garlic, snow peas, mushrooms and 1 tablespoon water and stir-fry for 1–2 minutes, or until vegetables are cooked but still crunchy.

Return the tofu to the wok, add the kecap manis and stir-fry for 1 minute, or until heated through. Serve with steamed rice.

60 ml (2 fl oz/¼ cup) peanut oil
600 g (1 lb 5 oz) firm tofu, drained and cut into cubes
2 teaspoons sambal oelek
2 garlic cloves, finely chopped
300 g (10½ oz) snow peas (mangetout), trimmed
400 g (14 oz) mixed Asian mushrooms, sliced
60 ml (2 fl oz/¼ cup) kecap manis
steamed rice, to serve

herbs

basil

Basil belongs to the mint family and probably originated in India, from where it was dispersed throughout Mediterranean regions via the ancient spice routes. One of its first important uses was as an embalming agent; basil has been found inside Egyptian mummies and, incredibly, modern research confirms that basil does act as a powerful antibacterial medium. Basil has many other properties too, with high vitamin A and magnesium levels among them. Much legend and lore has sprung up around basil—from Salome hiding John the Baptist's severed head in a pot of basil, to the ancient Greeks and Romans believing that the only way to make it grow was to shout belligerent curses as one planted the seeds.

There are over 60 varieties of basil, each with distinct characteristics, from lemon basil and cinnamon basil to Thai holy basil and the ruffly-edged purple basil, but the most common is the verdant-green sweet basil.

selection and storage

Basil tastes its best when harvested before the plant flowers, so when purchasing, avoid any with flowers in evidence. Leaves should be verdantly green, slightly glossy and devoid of holes or signs of decay.

A bunch of basil should keep for 1 week in the refrigerator—trim the ends of the stalks then place in a glass of water. Place the whole bunch in a plastic bag and seal. The leaves bruise very easily so don't wash or chop them until just before you need them.

If you grow basil and have more than you can use, excess leaves can easily be frozen. Blanch them briefly in boiling water and drain. Plunge into iced water and drain again, then pat dry and freeze in airtight bags. There is no need to defrost before using.

culinary uses

Widely used in many cuisines, basil's flavours go well with summer vegetables like eggplant, tomatoes, zucchini (courgettes); cheeses like parmesan, feta and mozzarella; with chicken, lamb, pasta, rice and eggs. It can even be used to great effect in desserts, subtly flavouring custards, creams, ice creams and syrups, particularly those made with red wine, cinnamon, cloves or allspice.

pesto

Put the garlic in a large mortar or food processor, add a pinch of salt and the pine nuts. Pound to a paste using a pestle, or process. Gradually add the basil leaves and pound the leaves against the side of the bowl, or continue to process. Stir in the grated parmesan cheese, then gradually add the olive oil. Use immediately or store covered in the fridge for 1 week. If storing, cover the pesto surface with a thin layer of olive oil.

2 garlic cloves, crushed
50 g (1¾ oz/⅓ cup) pine nuts
2½ large handfuls basil leaves
75 g (2½ oz/¾ cup) grated
   parmesan cheese
100 ml (3½ fl oz) olive oil

herbs ■ basil

spaghetti puttanesca

serves 4

Cook the spaghetti in a large saucepan of boiling salted water until *al dente*.

Meanwhile, heat the olive oil in a large frying pan and add the onion, garlic and chilli. Gently fry for about 8 minutes, or until the onion is soft. Add the anchovies and cook for a further 1 minute. Add the tomato, oregano, olive halves and capers, and bring to the boil. Reduce the heat and simmer for 3 minutes. Season with sea salt and freshly ground black pepper.

Drain the spaghetti and add it to the sauce. Toss together well so that the pasta is coated in the sauce. Scatter the basil over the top and serve immediately.

400 g (14 oz) spaghetti
2 tablespoons olive oil
1 onion, finely chopped
2 garlic cloves, finely sliced
1 small red chilli, seeded and
   sliced
6 anchovy fillets, finely chopped
400 g (14 oz/1⅔ cups) tin
   chopped tomatoes
1 tablespoon fresh oregano,
   finely chopped
16 black olives, halved and pitted
2 tablespoons baby capers,
   rinsed and drained
1 large handful basil leaves,
   to serve

bay leaf

selection and storage

Fresh leaves will keep, stored in a loosely sealed plastic bag, in the refrigerator for at least 1 week.

Bay leaves are harvested from the handsome bay laurel tree, which can grow to 55 metres (60 feet) tall. The bay thrives in Mediterranean regions, where the culinary and curative properties of the glossy, deep green leaves have long been appreciated, although it is actually an Asian native.

Bay leaves are common to many food cultures, used in stocks, soups, sauces, stews, marinades and casseroles. Generally, they are used as a background flavour, lending a warm, woodsy complexity to dishes—there are very few occasions when the flavour of bay would be the predominant one.

preparation

The leaves are large, glossy green and leathery and their flavour is very strong; a single, fresh leaf can go a long way. Drying, the form in which most cooks use them, greatly mellows their flavour. If you have a supply of fresh leaves, it is a simple matter to dry your own. Simply tie small bunches of leaves with string and hang them in a well-ventilated place for several days or until completely dry, then store them in an airtight container and use within a few months.

When using fresh leaves, add them whole and bruised to a dish, or torn into a few large pieces so they can be retrieved before serving—when chopped into small pieces they can cause choking, if eaten.

french onion soup

Melt the butter in a heavy-based saucepan over low heat and add the onions. Cook, stirring occasionally for 25 minutes, or until the onions are a deep golden brown and begin to caramelize.

Add the garlic and flour and stir continuously for 2 minutes. Gradually blend in the stock and the wine, stirring all the time, and bring to a boil. Add the bay leaf and thyme and season with sea salt and freshly ground black pepper. Cover the saucepan and simmer for 25 minutes. Remove the bay leaf and thyme and check the seasoning.

Preheat the grill (broiler) to high. Toast the baguette slices on a tray, then divide among six warmed soup bowls and ladle the soup over the top. Sprinkle with the grated cheese and grill (broil) until the cheese melts and turns a light golden brown. Serve immediately.

60 g (2¼ oz) butter
680 g (1 lb 8 oz) onion, finely sliced
2 garlic cloves, finely chopped
40 g (1½ oz/⅓ cup) plain (all-purpose) flour
2 litres (70 fl oz/8 cups) ready-made beef or chicken stock
250 ml (9 fl oz/1 cup) white wine
1 bay leaf
2 thyme sprigs
12 slices day-old baguette
115 g (4 oz/¾ cup) grated gruyere cheese

herbs ■ bay leaf

bouquet garni

makes 1

To make a bouquet garni, wrap the green part of a leek around the bay leaf, sprig of thyme, sprig of parsley and celery leaves. Tie the bundle with string, leaving it long at one end for easy removal. Use as directed in recipes.

1 green strip from a leek
1 bay leaf
1 thyme sprig
1 parsley sprig
1 celery top with leaves

chives

A member of the lily (allium) family along with leeks, onions and garlic, the botanical name *Allium schoenoprasum* is Greek for 'reed-like leek' whereas the English 'chive' is from the Latin for onion, *cepa*.

Chives, which grow in grassy clumps, are graceful and slender, with hollow leaves that grow to about 30 cm (12 inches) in length. They have mauve, puff-ball shaped flowers which are also edible (these look lovely strewn over a green salad) although the leaves themselves taste coarse and strong after the plant has flowered. Another variety of chives is the garlic chive, which, as the name suggests, has a pleasant, mild garlic flavour. It has narrow, flat leaves and white flowers and is most used in and best suited to oriental-style dishes.

culinary uses

Chives are best used raw or just warmed through as strong heat kills both their pleasant, mild-onion flavour as well as their vibrant green colour; to preserve colour and flavour, they should always be cut and added to dishes at the very last moment. They need to be cut with a very sharp knife or snipped with kitchen scissors otherwise they bruise.

Regular chives (sometimes called 'onion' chives to distinguish them from their garlic cousins) have a great affinity with potatoes, eggs and fish (including smoked salmon), they can be used to excellent effect in savoury breads, scones and muffins, vegetable cakes and fritters and creamy sauces for chicken, veal and lamb.

selection and storage

Chives are delicate and do not last long once picked. Choose bunches with leaves that show no signs of yellowing, wilting or decay (water will cause them to start rotting). Store chives, wrapped in damp paper towels then placed in a loosely sealed plastic bag, in the refrigerator for up to 3–4 days.

cheese and chive scones

Preheat the oven to 210°C (415°F/Gas 6–7). Grease a baking tray. Sift the flour and a pinch of salt into a bowl. Rub in the butter using your fingertips. Stir in the cheeses and the chives. Make a well in the centre, add the milk and 125 ml (4 fl oz/½ cup) water. Mix lightly with a flat-bladed knife to form a soft dough, adding more liquid if necessary.

Knead the dough briefly on a lightly floured surface until smooth. Press out the dough to 2 cm (¾ inch) thickness. Using a floured 5 cm (2 inch) plain round cutter, cut rounds from the dough. Place rounds on prepared tray and sprinkle with the extra cheese. Bake for 12 minutes, or until cheese is golden and scones have risen. Serve with butter.

250 g (9 oz/2 cups) self-raising flour
30 g (1 oz) butter
60 g (2¼ oz/½ cup) grated cheddar cheese
25 g (1 oz/¼ cup) grated parmesan cheese
2 tablespoons snipped chives
125 ml (4 fl oz/½ cup) milk
25 g (1 oz/¼ cup) grated cheddar cheese, extra
butter, to serve

herbs ■ chives

watercress salad

serves 4–6

To make the salad, wash and drain all the vegetables. Break the watercress into small sprigs, discarding the coarser stems. Cut the celery into thin 5 cm (2 inch) long sticks. Peel, halve and seed the cucumber and cut into thin slices. Peel the oranges, remove all the white pith and cut the oranges into segments between the membrane. Refrigerate until needed.

To make the dressing, combine the oil, juice, zest, mustard, pepper and honey in a screw-top jar. Shake vigorously to combine well.

Combine all the salad ingredients except nuts in a serving bowl. Pour dressing over and toss. Sprinkle with the pecan nuts or walnuts, to serve.

500 g (1 lb 2 oz) watercress
3 celery sticks
1 cucumber
3 oranges
1 red onion, thinly sliced and separated into rings
35 g (1¼ oz/¾ cup) snipped chives
60 g (2¼ oz/½ cup) chopped pecan nuts or walnuts

dressing
60 ml (2 fl oz/¼ cup) olive oil
60 ml (2 fl oz/¼ cup) lemon juice
2 teaspoons grated orange zest
1 teaspoon seeded mustard
1 tablespoon honey

coriander (cilantro)

herbs ■ coriander (cilantro)
season ■ available year-round

selection and storage

Coriander does not store well, so should be used within 1–2 days or so of purchase and refrigerated in an airtight container until needed.

When purchasing, look for bunches with bright green, unblemished leaves; avoid overly limp bunches and do not purchase any that are bruised or showing signs of sliminess or yellowing.

Coriander is one of the world's oldest herbs. It dates back some 5000 years BC and is actually one of the 'bitter herbs' of the traditional Jewish Passover feast. The entire plant can be used—the seeds are dried and used as a spice, the fresh stems and leaves are used in salads, curries and soups, and in Southeast Asian cooking the roots are incorporated into wet spice pastes.

Coriander is often called cilantro, after the Spanish name, but also goes by the common names of Chinese parsley and Mexican parsley. Not surprisingly then, coriander is related to parsley and carrots and is much used in cookery all over the globe—it is one of the very few fresh herbs Chinese cooks sanction in their cuisine.

Heat quickly destroys the flavour of coriander, so when using the chopped leaves in hot dishes, add coriander at the last moment.

culinary uses

Cooks in western Europe tend not to use coriander and many people find its smell and taste to be objectionably 'soapy'. For lovers of the herb though, there is nothing quite like the distinctive, yet mellow, herbaceousness of fresh coriander. It is used to delicious effect in Mexican dishes such as ceviche and guacamole and in curries, tagines, salads and vegetable dishes from the Indian, Middle Eastern and Asian culinary lexicons.

coriander beef

Combine the garlic, ginger, coriander, oil and beef in a large non-metallic bowl. Cover and refrigerate for 1–2 hours.

Heat a large heavy-based frying pan or wok over high heat, add the meat in three batches and stir-fry each batch for 2–3 minutes, or until the meat is just cooked. Remove meat from the frying pan and keep warm.

Heat 1 tablespoon oil in the pan, add the onion and cook over medium-high heat for 3–4 minutes, or until slightly softened. Add the red and green capsicum, and cook, tossing constantly, for 3–4 minutes, or until the capsicum has softened slightly.

Return the meat to the pan with the lime juice and extra coriander. Toss well, then remove from the heat and season with sea salt and freshly ground black pepper. Serve immediately.

4 garlic cloves, finely chopped
1 tablespoon finely chopped ginger
2 large handfuls fresh coriander (cilantro) stems, roots and leaves, finely chopped
60 ml (2 fl oz/¼ cup) vegetable oil
500 g (1 lb 2 oz) lean beef fillet, thinly sliced across the grain
oil, extra, for cooking
2 red onions, thinly sliced
½ red capsicum (pepper), sliced
½ green capsicum (pepper), sliced
1 tablespoon lime juice
2 large handfuls fresh coriander (cilantro) leaves, extra

herbs ■ coriander (cilantro)

mango salsa

serves 4 as a side dish

Peel the mango and finely dice the flesh. De-seed the chilli and finely chop.

Combine all the ingredients in a small bowl. Season with sea salt and freshly ground black pepper and serve as an accompaniment to macadamia-crusted chicken (page 167) or lemon grass chicken skewers (page 421).

1 small mango
1 green chilli
2 tablespoons finely diced red onion
2 tablespoons roughly chopped coriander (cilantro) leaves
1 tablespoon lime juice

dill

selection and storage

Dill is quite fragile and wilts very quickly after it is picked. To store it, spray with a fine mist of water, wrap carefully in damp paper towels then seal in a plastic bag and keep in the crisper section of the refrigerator for up to 5 days. You can also freeze dill for up to 8 weeks—it will turn an unattractive dark green colour and the flavour won't be as strong as the fresh herb, but is still preferable to using dried dill.

The word 'dill' derives from the Norse word *dilla* which means 'to lull or soothe', and indeed the Greeks placed sprigs of dill over their eyes to induce sleep. Also much used by European herbalists to cure digestive ailments, dill was a common cure for colic during the Middle Ages.

Native to the Mediterranean region, Southern Russia, Central and Southern Asia, dill is a popular culinary herb with diverse uses. It is a vital pickling ingredient in many cuisines (especially with cucumbers; an interesting pairing given that cucumbers have a reputation for being hard to digest and dill can assist with this), and it goes especially well with seafood, chicken, sour cream and yoghurt, eggs, potatoes, leeks, cabbage, carrots and, as noted, cucumbers.

Cooking quickly diminishes the fresh anise flavour of this herb so for the best results, chop and add dill to dishes at the final possible moment.

culinary uses

One of the best possible uses for dill is stirred in generous amounts through thick home-made mayonnaise. Serve this with cold steamed prawns or poached fish or spread on cucumber sandwiches. Finish a creamy fish chowder with a handful of dill or stir it into softened butter, along with some finely chopped sundried tomatoes, and serve this over chicken, lamb or beef steak.

sugar-cured salmon

Place the salmon on a board and check for bones. If there are any bones in the salmon it will be impossible to slice the fish thinly as they will catch on the knife. Any small stubborn bones can be removed using tweezers. Mix the sugar and salt together and spoon half of the mixture into a shallow, rectangular, non-metallic dish large enough to hold the salmon. Place the fish on the mixture. Sprinkle the peppercorns, dill, tarragon and basil over the fish. Cover with the remaining sugar and salt. Cover loosely with plastic wrap and place a tray, small board or plate on top of the fish weighed down with a couple of tins. Refrigerate for 2 days, turning the fish over in the mixture every 12 hours.

To make the mustard sauce, place the egg yolks in a medium-sized bowl with a generous pinch of salt and freshly ground black pepper, and gently whisk together. Mix the oils together in a jug. Slowly add the oil to the egg yolks, drop by drop, whisking all the time. Increase to a slow trickle as the sauce thickens. Fold in the lemon zest and juice, dill and mustard. Whisk the cream to the floppy stage and fold that in too. Taste and season if desired.

To make the cucumber salad, combine the cucumber, dill, olive oil and white wine vinegar in a bowl and toss lightly to coat.

Remove the fish from the dish and brush off the sugar and salt. Discard any brine. Using a sharp knife and cutting along the length of the salmon, slice into paper-thin pieces and serve with mustard sauce and cucumber salad. The sugar-cured salmon will keep in the refrigerator for 2 days.

variation You can use ocean trout as a substitute for salmon if you prefer.

---

450 g (1 lb) middle salmon fillet, skinned
250 g (9 oz/1⅓ cups) soft brown sugar
250 g (9 oz/¾ cup) coarse sea salt
8 black peppercorns, lightly crushed
1 tablespoon chopped dill
1 tablespoon chopped tarragon
1 tablespoon shredded basil

mustard sauce
3 egg yolks, at room temperature
150 ml (5 fl oz) light olive oil
150 ml (5 fl oz) peanut oil
finely grated zest of 1 lemon
1 tablespoon lemon juice
3 tablespoons chopped dill
2 teaspoons wholegrain mustard
80 ml (2½ fl oz/⅓ cup) thick (double/heavy) cream

cucumber salad
1 Lebanese (short) cucumber, finely sliced
1 tablespoon finely chopped dill
2 teaspoons extra virgin olive oil
1 teaspoon white wine vinegar

herbs ■ dill

lemon grass

selection and storage

Although you can purchase dried and powdered lemon grass, these are but pale imitations of the real thing— there really is no comparison.

Choose lemon grass stalks that are plump and firm, with no signs of drying or brittleness. They will keep, stored in a tightly sealed plastic bag in the refrigerator, for 2–3 weeks.

Lemon grass can be successfully frozen. Cut off the tough green ends and wrap stalks tightly in foil and then plastic wrap. Cut from the stalk as you require lemon grass— it will lose a little of its potency but this is a preferable trade-off if the choices are between using frozen or dried alternatives.

Lemon grass is closely associated with the cooking of Southeast Asian countries like Thailand and Vietnam and is thought to be native to Malaysia (although some think India). It is a member of the grass (Poaceae) family and presents as 60 cm (2 foot) long, very stiff, fibrous green stalks, the outer layers of which are cut off when harvested, to reveal the tender, creamy-coloured interior core. Culinarily speaking, this is the most usable part of the lemon grass.

Anyone who knows its distinctively haunting, sweet, lemony-lime aroma will be unsurprised to learn that lemon grass is much used in the manufacture of fragrance, soap and scented candles, and is a close relative of citronella, used widely as an insect repellent. It is widely used for various medicinal purposes; possessing antiviral, antiseptic and antibacterial properties, it is used for everything from a headache, rheumatism and malaria cure, to aiding in recovery after childbirth.

preparation

Strip away the inedibly tough outer layers of each stalk to reveal the smooth, pale, round core and cut off and discard the green tops and 2–3 cm (3/4–1 1/4 inches) from the root end. These off-cuts can be used, whole and bruised, to flavour Asian-style soups, steamed rice or in chicken stock or, chopped finely and steeped, to make a delicious tea.

lemon grass chicken skewers

Discard any excess fat from the chicken fillets and cut them in half lengthways. Combine the brown sugar, lime juice, curry paste and 2 of the lime leaves, shredded, in a bowl. Add the chicken and mix well. Cover and refrigerate for several hours, or overnight.

Trim the lemon grass to measure about 20 cm (8 inches), leaving the root end intact. Cut each lengthways into four pieces. Cut a slit in each of the remaining lime leaves and thread one onto each skewer. Cut two slits in the chicken and thread onto the lemon grass, followed by another lime leaf. Repeat with the remaining lime leaves, chicken and lemon grass. Pan-fry or barbecue until cooked through. Serve with the mango salsa passed separately.

4 chicken thigh fillets
1½ tablespoons soft brown sugar
1½ tablespoons lime juice
2 teaspoons ready-made green curry paste
18 makrut (kaffir) lime leaves
2 lemon grass stems, white part only
mango salsa (see page 417), to serve

herbs ■ lemon grass

lemon grass ice tea

serves 2

Prepare the lemon grass by removing the first two tough outer layers. Slice thinly into rings. Put the lemon grass in a jug and cover with the boiling water. Add the lemon slices and cover. Allow to infuse and cool. When cooled to room temperature, strain. Add the honey, to taste. Place the tea in the refrigerator to chill.

To serve, pour the tea into two glasses with extra slices of lemon. Add ice, if desired.

3 lemon grass stems, white part only
625 ml (21½ fl oz/2½ cups) boiling water
2 lemon slices
3 teaspoons honey, to taste
lemon slices, extra, to serve
ice, to serve

mint

There are over 600 varieties of mint and, as the plant readily hybridizes, even experts have trouble separating the many different types. However, the most common sorts are spearmint and peppermint, the latter having squat, rounded leaves with sharp-toothed edges and an intense, clear flavour, while the former is less strong and a more versatile culinary herb. The leaves of spearmint are longish, spear-like and attractively crinkled.

Mint has been much favoured since ancient times for its aromatic, medicinal and culinary uses. It is thought the Romans were the first to seriously utilize mint in cookery (it was they who introduced mint sauce to Britain) and they also used it to freshen rooms by strewing the leaves over the floor to repel mice and other pests.

culinary uses

The uses of mint are endless, from the simplicity of throwing a handful of leaves into a pot of boiling potatoes, to adding torn leaves at the last minute to salads. It is indispensable in Asian cooking, complementing brilliantly the flavours of chilli, fish sauce, palm sugar (jaggery), limes, coconut and rice noodles. It is also much used in Middle Eastern cuisine, where it works perfectly with the flavours of burghul, yoghurt, lamb, cucumber and sweet spices that so typify that style of cooking.

Mint owes its clean, cool flavour to the presence of the volatile oil menthol which quickly dissipates so, as is the case with most fresh herbs, avoid cutting or tearing the leaves until just before you use them.

selection and storage

When buying mint, choose bunches that are sprightly, with bright green leaves that show no signs of drooping or yellowing.

Fresh mint will store for 3–4 days when wrapped carefully in damp paper and loosely sealed in a plastic bag in the refrigerator.

mint sauce

In a small dish, mix together the mint and sugar. Add the boiling water: this sets the colour. Then, add the sugar and wine vinegar, a pinch of salt and mix together. Leave to stand for about 1 hour to allow the flavours to develop. Serve with a traditional lamb roast.

4 tablespoons finely chopped
   mint leaves
1 teaspoon sugar
2 tablespoons boiling water
2 teaspoons sugar
3 tablespoons wine vinegar

herbs ■ mint

minted peas

serves 4 as a side dish

Place the peas in a saucepan and pour in water to just cover the peas. Add the mint sprigs.

Bring to the boil and simmer for 5 minutes, or until the peas are just tender. Drain and discard the mint. Return to the saucepan, add the butter and shredded mint and stir over low heat until the butter has melted. Season with sea salt and freshly ground black pepper.

625 g (1 lb 6 oz/4 cups) peas
4 mint sprigs
30 g (1 oz) butter
2 tablespoon shredded mint
   leaves

oregano and marjoram

selection and storage

As with all fresh herbs, choose oregano and marjoram that shows no signs of drooping, yellowing or drying; stems of these herbs will store well in the refrigerator (up to 1 week) if wrapped in slightly damp paper towels then loosely sealed in a plastic bag.

When it comes to discussions about these two herbs, confusion often reigns. Marjoram used to have its own genus but has now been subsumed back into that of oregano to become one of the 50-odd varieties of the parent herb. Oregano itself is often referred to as 'wild marjoram' and it is believed that much of the marjoram referred to by the ancients, who used the herb regularly, was actually oregano. Although undoubtedly similar, there are also marked differences.

Marjoram tends to have smaller, softer, more compact leaves than oregano, that are grey-green and ovoid in shape. It bears knotty green buds that open into (edible) white flowers. It has a sweetly pungent flavour. Oregano is considered more 'aggressively' flavoured (indeed, some varieties are so strong their effect is almost numbing) and has larger leaves (these can be either smooth or slightly furry) and purple blossoms. However, the strength of the flavour is very dependent upon where and how the herb has been grown. All varieties of oregano are members of the mint family, with square stems and opposing pairs of leaves.

Both herbs can be used whole or chopped—it is an easy matter to strip them off their stems for preparation. Long cooking subdues their flavour so, as a general rule, add them near the end of cooking.

greek salad

Chop the tomato and cut the cucumber into rounds. Thinly slice the radishes and onion, and cut the feta cheese into small cubes.

Combine the prepared tomato, cucumber, radishes, onion, feta and olives in a serving bowl. Drizzle with the combined lemon juice, olive oil and oregano. Serve on a bed of coral lettuce, if you like.

1 large tomato
1 Lebanese (short) cucumber
2 radishes
1 small onion
100 g (3½ oz) feta cheese
45 g (1½ oz/⅓ cup) pitted black olives
2 tablespoons lemon juice
3 tablespoons olive oil
½ teaspoon fresh oregano leaves

herbs ■ oregano and marjoram

marjoram salmoriglio (dressing)

serves 4

In a mortar use a pestle to pound the fresh marjoram. Transfer to a bowl and gradually add the extra virgin olive oil and lemon juice. Season with sea salt and freshly ground black pepper

note Thyme or oregano can be used instead of marjoram. This simple dressing is used widely in Italy to accompany grilled fish or other seafood.

2 tablespoons fresh marjoram
125 ml (4 fl oz/½ cup) extra virgin olive oil
1 tablespoon lemon juice

parsley

selection and storage

When selecting parsley to buy, try to ensure it is young—this is a little easier to do with the flat-leaf (Italian) variety for as it ages the leaves become large, leathery and resemble celery leaves; their flavour is coarse.

Store parsley with its stalks in a container of water in the refrigerator and with a plastic bag sealing the cup and leaves—flat-leaf parsley can be stored wrapped in damp paper towels then loosely sealed in a plastic bag. Thus stored, parsley will keep for about 4 days.

Parsley, which is native to the Mediterranean, must surely be one of the world's most versatile and well-used herbs—there are few savoury dishes that do not benefit from its clean, grassy flavour and vivid-green appearance. There are two main culinary varieties of this herb; curly-leafed parsley and flat-leaf (Italian) parsley—the latter has a stronger flavour as it contains higher levels of essential oils in its leaves.

Parsley is one of the most nutritious herbs, containing power-pack quantities of vitamins A and C as well as significant amounts of potassium, calcium, phosphorus, magnesium and iron. Parsley has a very high chlorophyll content which accounts for its bright green colour and the way it can 'bleed' into white sauces and such—for this reason, and also because prolonged heating kills its flavour, parsley is mostly added to dishes near the end of cooking.

Curly-leafed parsley, which should feel a little soft to touch, not hard and papery, needs thorough washing to remove any trapped dirt and can be washed and then dried in a salad spinner. In the main, though, and with a few notable examples where recipes will specify a particular sort, the two types of parsley are interchangeable, so long as the leaves are young and tender.

tabbouleh

Put the burghul in a bowl, cover with 500 ml (17 fl oz/ 2 cups) water and leave for 1½ hours.

Cut the tomatoes in half, scoop out the seeds with a teaspoon and cut into 1 cm (½ inch) cubes. Cut the cucumber in half lengthways, remove the seeds with a teaspoon and cut the flesh into 1 cm (½ inch) cubes.

To make the dressing, place the lemon juice and 1½ teaspoons salt in a bowl and whisk until well combined. Season well with freshly ground black pepper and slowly whisk in the olive oil and extra virgin olive oil.

Drain the burghul and squeeze out any excess water. Spread the burghul out on a clean tea (dish) towel or paper towels and leave to dry for about 30 minutes. Put the burghul in a large salad bowl, add the tomato, cucumber, green onion, parsley and mint, and toss well to combine. Pour the dressing over the salad and toss until evenly coated.

130 g (4½ oz/¾ cup) burghul (bulgur)
3 tomatoes
1 telegraph (long) cucumber
4 green onions (scallions), sliced
120 g (4¼ oz/4 cups) chopped flat-leaf (Italian) parsley
2 large handfuls mint leaves, chopped

dressing
80 ml (2½ fl oz/⅓ cup) lemon juice
60 ml (2 fl oz/¼ cup) olive oil
1 tablespoon extra virgin olive oil, extra

herbs ■ parsley

The health benefits of parsley have long been documented—Hippocrates prescribed parsley to improve general health. The Romans, who ate quantities of parsley, knew it was very good for them; they also believed it relieved drunkenness, placing bouquets of the herb on the banqueting table to absorb 'wine vapours'.

rosemary

selection and storage

Rosemary is fairly robust, and not subject to the bruising or wilting of other more fragile herbs. When buying rosemary, look for sprightly, green-leafed sprigs with fresh, resinous aromas when a few are rubbed between your fingers. Elderly rosemary looks dried out and somewhat faded and its smell is similarly diminished.

Store fresh rosemary in an airtight container or sealed plastic bag in the refrigerator for up to 1 week.

Rosemary is a venerable plant. It has a fascinating history and, with its unmistakable piney aroma, many uses in the kitchen. Rosemary is native to Mediterranean coastal areas, its Latin name, *Rosmarinus*, means 'dew of the sea', possibly in reference to its natural habitat.

When utilized in cooking, rosemary is surprisingly versatile; it can be used in myriad dishes—even certain sweet ones. Its pungent flavour should be unleashed in moderation as it can take over a dish and, as the 'needles', or short, spiky leaves of the plant do not soften on cooking, entire sprigs are best used as these can be retrieved and discarded before serving.

Rosemary is used traditionally with meats such as roast pork, lamb and game—its digestive properties help diners deal with rich flavours. Rosemary is also delicious in soups and braises, particularly those involving dried beans and pulses and with cuts of stewing meat like shanks, tails and shins.

Rosemary goes particularly well with potatoes and mushrooms. A sprig of rosemary will perfume a custard or creamy rice pudding wonderfully and the flavour enhances pears, peaches and apricots— add a sprig to fruit poaching liquid, preferably one based on red wine.

roasted rosemary chicken

Preheat the oven to 220°C (425°F/Gas 7). Wipe the chicken inside and out and pat dry with paper towels. Season the chicken cavity and place 4 rosemary sprigs and the garlic cloves inside. Rub the outside of the chicken with 1 tablespoon of oil, season and put on its side in a roasting tin. Put the remaining rosemary sprigs in the tin and drizzle with oil.

Put the tin on the middle shelf of the oven. After 20 minutes, turn the chicken onto the other side, baste with the juices and cook for 20 minutes. Turn the chicken, breast side up, baste again and cook for a further 15 minutes, or until the juices between the body and thigh run clear when pierced with a knife. Transfer the chicken to a warm serving dish and set aside for at least 10 minutes before carving.

Pour most of the fat from the roasting tin and return the tin to the stovetop over high heat. Add 2 tablespoons water and scrape the base of the tin to loosen the residue. Pour over the chicken to serve.

1.5 kg (3 lb 5 oz) whole chicken
6 large sprigs rosemary
4 garlic cloves
3 tablespoons olive oil

herbs ■ rosemary

bean and rosemary dip

serves 4–6

Rinse and drain the beans and set aside. Heat the olive oil in a saucepan and cook the garlic and rosemary for 1 minute, or until the garlic is softened. Add the beans and stock and bring to the boil. Reduce the heat and simmer for 3–4 minutes. Allow to cool.

In a food processor, blend the mixture in batches until smooth. Add the lemon juice and season, to taste. Serve with baguette or crackers. This dip can be kept in the refrigerator in an airtight container for several days.

620 g (1 lb 6 oz/3 cups) tin butter (lima) or cannellini beans
3 tablespoons olive oil
2 garlic cloves, crushed
1 tablespoon finely chopped rosemary leaves
250 ml (9 fl oz/1 cup) ready-made chicken or vegetable stock
2 teaspoons lemon juice

sage

Sage grows the world over and there are literally hundreds of varieties, but it is common sage (*Salvia officinalis*) with its tapered, silver-green, rough-textured leaves and pretty blue flowers that is most often used for culinary purposes. The genus name *Salvia* comes from the Latin word for 'to cure', while the modern French name, *tout bonne*, means 'all is well'.

Thought to be a Syrian native, sage has, for most of history, been used medicinally; the ancients revered it as a healing herb and used it to treat everything from epilepsy, to drunkenness, worms, memory loss and eye problems. Arab physicians in the tenth century believed sage could extend one's life to immortality.

selection and storage

Sage can be purchased in bunches—the leaves should be fresh-looking with no signs of wilting, brown spots or bruising. Stored in the refrigerator in a sealed plastic bag, sage will keep for 5–6 days.

culinary uses

Culinarily, its strong, woodsy aroma is most appreciated in Italy, where sage is often paired with veal, chicken and pork and is also fried until crisp in butter then spooned over pasta.

Traditionally, sage has been paired with rich meats—with goose in England, eel in Germany, sausages and pâté in France. Since ancient times it has been known to be an effective meat preserver, which could account for the French use of it in their charcuterie. Outside Europe, sage is well known as a flavouring in poultry stuffings and is also used to flavour savoury muffins, breads, sauces and marinades.

Because it is so very strong, sage should always be used judiciously in cooking as its flavour can completely overpower a dish.

pork with sage and capers

Preheat the oven to 170°C (325°F/Gas 3). Heat 1 tablespoon oil and the butter in a frying pan. Add the onion and cook for 5 minutes, or until lightly golden.

Put the breadcrumbs, chopped sage, parsley, lemon zest, 1/2 tablespoon capers and the cooked onion in a bowl. Add the egg and season with sea salt and freshly ground black pepper. Split each pork fillet in half lengthways and open out. Spread the sage stuffing mixture down the length of one fillet and cover with the other.

Stretch the bacon or prosciutto with the back of a knife and wrap each piece (slightly overlapping) around the pork to form a neat rolled parcel. Tie with string at intervals.

Put the pork in a baking dish and drizzle with 1 tablespoon oil. Bake for 1 hour. To test if the meat is cooked, insert a skewer into the thickest part of the meat—the juices should run clear. Remove from the tin, cover with foil and rest.

To make the jus, return the juices in the baking dish to the stovetop, add the flour and stir in well. Add the vermouth and allow to bubble for 1 minute. Add the stock and stir while cooking to remove any lumps. Simmer for 5 minutes. Add the remaining capers to the sauce.

In a small saucepan, heat the remaining oil, and when very hot, fry the whole sage leaves until crisp. Drain on paper towels.

Slice the pork into 1 cm (1/2 inch) slices. Spoon a little sauce over the pork and serve each portion with fried sage leaves on top.

60 ml (2 fl oz/1/4 cup) extra virgin olive oil
25 g (1 oz) unsalted butter
1 onion, finely chopped
100 g (3 1/2 oz/1 1/4 cups) fresh white breadcrumbs
2 teaspoons chopped fresh sage
1 tablespoon chopped flat-leaf (Italian) parsley
2 teaspoons grated lemon zest
2 1/2 tablespoons salted baby capers, rinsed and drained
1 egg
two 500 g (1 lb 2 oz) pork fillets
8 bacon or prosciutto slices
2 teaspoons plain (all-purpose) flour
100 ml (3 1/2 fl oz) dry vermouth
310 ml (10 3/4 fl oz/1 1/4 cups) ready-made chicken or vegetable stock
8 whole sage leaves, extra, to garnish

herbs ■ sage

tarragon

herbs ▪ tarragon
season ▪ **peak season spring–autumn**

selection and storage

Choose tarragon with fresh-looking, unbruised leaves that show no signs of wilting. Store tarragon, wrapped in damp paper towels, then loosely sealed in a plastic bag, in the refrigerator for up to 4 days.

Tarragon, unlike most of the better known herbs, does not have a long history of culinary use. Many sources claim tarragon came late to European cookery because, as a native of isolated Siberia and Central Asia, it took some time to find its way westward. Whatever the reason, it didn't find common usage in England and France until around the sixteenth century. The French have embraced tarragon like no other culture has—perhaps its most famous uses are in sauce béarnaise and sauce tartare. It is also much used to flavour vinegar and as a vital component in the ubiquitous *fines herbes* mixture, with chervil, chives and parsley.

There are two types of tarragon commonly available and it is vital to know the difference as their flavour is very different. French tarragon has delicate, flat, spear-shaped green leaves, which exude a distinctively sweet anise flavour when bruised—this is the tarragon you should choose. Russian tarragon (unfortunately often passed off as French as it is much easier to grow) has narrower, spikier leaves than French, lacks its sweetness and has an unappealing, harsh, grassy flavour and smell.

Tarragon leaves (strip them off their woody stem just before you plan to use them) are generally chopped and added to a dish near the end of cooking, otherwise the bright flavours will be lost.

For other tarragon recipes see:

sugar-cured salmon 419

asparagus with tarragon vinaigrette

Preheat the oven to 180°C (350°F/Gas 4). Spread the walnuts on a baking tray and place in the oven for 5 minutes. Remove from the oven and cool. Chop walnuts finely.

Cut any thick, woody ends from the asparagus and discard; trim asparagus with a vegetable peeler. Place in a bowl, cover with boiling water and set aside for 2 minutes. Drain, plunge into iced water then drain again; pat dry with paper towels. Wash and dry the curly endive and tear into separate leaves.

To make the vinaigrette, combine the green onion, vinegar, tarragon and mustard in a small bowl and gradually whisk in the walnut oil. Season with sea salt and freshly ground black pepper.

Arrange the endive leaves in a serving dish. Top the leaves with asparagus spears. Drizzle with dressing and sprinkle with chopped walnuts, to serve.

25 g (1 oz/¼ cup) walnuts
24 fresh asparagus spears
100 g (3½ oz) curly endive (frisée)
1 green onion (scallion), finely chopped

tarragon vinaigrette
2 tablespoons white wine vinegar
1 tablespoon chopped fresh tarragon
1 teaspoon dijon mustard
60 ml (2 fl oz/¼ cup) walnut oil

herbs ■ tarragon

béarnaise sauce

serves 4

Put the vinegar, green onion and tarragon in a small saucepan. Bring to the boil, then reduce the heat slightly and simmer until the mixture has reduced by a third. Set aside to cool completely.

Strain the vinegar into a heatproof bowl and add the egg yolks. Place the bowl over a saucepan of barely simmering water and whisk until the mixture is thick and pale.

Add the butter, one cube at a time, and whisk after each addition until the mixture is thick and smooth. Season to taste and serve immediately. Serve with roast beef or lamb, or pan-fried steaks of poached salmon.

80 ml (2½ fl oz/⅓ cup) white wine vinegar
2 green onions (scallions), roughly chopped
2 teaspoons chopped tarragon
2 egg yolks
125 g (4½ oz) butter, cut into cubes

thyme

selection and storage

When buying thyme, select bunches with a profusion of compact, green leaves with no signs of dropping or drying out. Wrap the bunch in damp paper towels and place in a loosely sealed plastic bag—it will keep for up to 1 week in the refrigerator.

Thyme is, unlike most herbs, at home in nearly any dish, except perhaps those of Asian origin, where it is not used. Native to the Mediterranean and North Africa, fresh thyme, with its peppery, piney aroma is one of the most used of all herbs, lifting the flavour of stocks, soups, casseroles, stuffings for meats and vegetables, sauces, pickles, baked goods, sweet custards and certain fruit dishes. Wild thyme, which grows profusely around the southern Mediterranean region, is the source of the famous thyme honey, which is highly prized in Greece.

Common thyme (*Thymus vulgaris*) has tiny ovoid, tough, deep green leaves which are generally used whole, still attached to a branch as a sprig. Unlike most other herbs, common thyme is best added to dishes at the beginning of cooking and discarded before serving—the flavour subtly perfumes the dish whereas freshly chopped leaves tend to overpower and taste too 'green'.

Another popular type of thyme is lemon thyme, which has fleshier leaves and a pronounced citrus tang. The two types of thyme are not interchangeable; use lemon thyme in salads and with chicken, veal and fish, which pair best with its lemony zing.

thyme-flavoured semi-dried tomatoes

Preheat the oven to 160°C (315°F/Gas 2–3). Quarter the tomatoes lengthways and lay, skin side down, in a baking tray.

Sprinkle the tomatoes with 1 teaspoon each of sea salt and freshly ground black pepper and thyme and bake for 2½ hours. Check occasionally to make sure the tomatoes don't burn. Toss in the oil and cool before packing into hot sterilized jars and sealing. Refrigerate for 24 hours before serving.

16 roma (plum) tomatoes
3 tablespoons thyme, chopped
2 tablespoons olive oil

herbs ■ thyme

lemon, lime and thyme vinegar

makes 1 litre (35 fl oz/4 cups)

Finely grate the zest of the limes and lemons. Squeeze the juice from the lime and 2 lemons.

Put the vinegar, lime juice, lemon juice, lime zest, half the lemon zest and half the thyme sprigs in a saucepan. Bring to the boil, then reduce the heat and simmer for 5 minutes. Remove from the heat and set aside to cool completely.

Meanwhile, put the remaining lemon zest into a hot sterilized jar and add the remaining thyme sprigs. Strain the vinegar and pour it into the jar. Seal and store in a cool place for 1 week.

Line a funnel with muslin (cheesecloth) and strain the vinegar into warm sterilized bottles. Seal, label and date each jar. Store for up to 1 year. Use in place of white wine vinegar for a flavoured vinaigrette.

2 limes
4 lemons
1 litre (35 fl oz/4 cups) white wine vinegar
20 thyme sprigs

index of topics

441

index of recipes

443